A Celebration of Poets

Appalachia
Grades 4-12
Fall 2010

A Celebration of Poets
Appalachia
Grades 4-12
Fall 2010

An anthology compiled by Creative Communication, Inc.

Published by:

Printed in the United States of America

ISBN: 978-1-60050-410-5

Foreword

As we start our nineteenth year of working with student writers across the US and Canada, I think back on the positive effects created by our contests and anthologies. Each year I receive hundreds of letters from students who state that being accepted to be published created a spark that brightened their educational experience. Years later, after these students have graduated, I have other letters that report back on successes after high school. These letters are from students who credited Creative Communication as the start of their writing career and have now published their first book of poems or a novel.

These letters help us to know the importance of what we do. I always tell our judges that behind the entries are students whose lives can be changed. I tell them that Creative Communication doesn't publish poems and essays, we publish hopes and dreams.

So here we are, another contest completed and more "hopes and dreams" being published. We hope that these entries fulfill their purpose of entertaining you and helping these student authors know that they have met a milestone in their lives. The poems in this book represent the best and brightest of today's student writers. Enjoy, and realize that the Hemmingways, Plaths or Frosts of tomorrow may be published today, between these pages.

Sincerely,

Thomas Worthen, Ph.D.
Editor
Creative Communication

WRITING CONTESTS!

Enter our next POETRY contest!

Enter our next ESSAY contest!

Why should I enter?
Win prizes and get published! Each year thousands of dollars in prizes are awarded throughout North America. The top writers in each division receive a monetary award and a free book that includes their published poem or essay. Entries of merit are also selected to be published in our anthology.

Who may enter?
There are four divisions in the poetry contest. The poetry divisions are grades K-3, 4-6, 7-9, and 10-12. There are three divisions in the essay contest. The essay divisions are grades 3-6, 7-9, and 10-12.

What is needed to enter the contest?
To enter the poetry contest send in one original poem, 21 lines or less. To enter the essay contest send in one original non-fiction essay, 250 words or less, on any topic. Please submit each poem and essay with a title, and the following information clearly printed: the writer's name, current grade, home address (optional), school name, school address, teacher's name and teacher's email address (optional). Contact information will only be used to provide information about the contest. For complete contest information go to www.poeticpower.com.

How do I enter?
Enter a poem online at:
www.poeticpower.com
or
Mail your poem to:
Poetry Contest
1488 North 200 West
Logan, UT 84341

Enter an essay online at:
www.poeticpower.com
or
Mail your essay to:
Essay Contest
1488 North 200 West
Logan, UT 84341

When is the deadline?
Poetry contest deadlines are August 16th, December 6th, and April 5th. Essay contest deadlines are July 19th, October 18th and February 15th. Students can enter one poem and one essay for each spring, summer, and fall contest deadline.

Are there benefits for my school?
Yes. We award $12,500 each year in grants to help with Language Arts programs. Schools qualify to apply for a grant by having 15 or more accepted entries.

Are there benefits for my teacher?
Yes. Teachers with five or more students published receive a free anthology that includes their students' writing.

For more information please go to our website at **www.poeticpower.com**, email us at editor@poeticpower.com or call 435-713-4411.

Table of Contents

States included in this edition:

Kentucky
North Carolina
Tennessee
West Virginia

Fall 2010 Poetic Achievement Honor Schools

**Teachers who had fifteen or more poets accepted to be published*

The following schools are recognized as receiving a "Poetic Achievement Award." This award is given to schools who have a large number of entries of which over fifty percent are accepted for publication. With hundreds of schools entering our contest, only a small percent of these schools are honored with this award. The purpose of this award is to recognize schools with excellent Language Arts programs. This award qualifies these schools to receive a complimentary copy of this anthology. In addition, these schools are eligible to apply for a Creative Communication Language Arts Grant. Grants of two hundred and fifty dollars each are awarded to further develop writing in our schools.

Bailey Elementary School
Bailey, NC
Frances Anderson*

Baylor School
Chattanooga, TN
Fontaine Alison
Amy Cohen*
John Bart Loftin
Sally Naylor*
Kendra Wilsher

Bearden High School
Knoxville, TN
Virginia Thurston*
Tim Vacek

Berkeley Springs High School
Berkeley Springs, WV
Heather Lorigan*

Bernheim Middle School
Shepherdsville, KY
Jimmy Carnes*

Bondurant Middle School
Frankfort, KY
P. Boucher
Kelly Neal*

Boyle County Middle School
Danville, KY
Gail Wilson*

Centennial Elementary School
Dickson, TN
Kim Phillips*

Coffee County Central High School
Manchester, TN
Joyce McCullough*

College View Middle School
Owensboro, KY
Tina Hare*
Debbie Hendrix*

Cool Spring Elementary School
Cleveland, NC
Aimee Adkins
Stephanie Flammang

Cool Spring Elementary School (cont.)
Cleveland, NC
Marcia Ireland

Duke Middle School
Durham, NC
Tamara Swartz*

East Millbrook Magnet Middle School
Raleigh, NC
Kathryn Lapinski*

East Mooresville Intermediate School
Mooresville, NC
Amy Smith*

Elkton School
Elkton, TN
Teri Mize*

Evangelical Christian School Ridgelake Campus
Memphis, TN
Vita Swindell*

First Flight High School
Kill Devil Hills, NC
Kimberly Leatherwood*

Freedom Middle School
Franklin, TN
Elisa Baughman*

Germantown High School
Germantown, TN
Billy M. Pullen*

Grey Culbreth Middle School
Chapel Hill, NC
Meghan Thornton*

Heritage Middle School
Maryville, TN
Marie Richardson*
Sharon Trahan

Hunter GT Magnet Elementary School
Raleigh, NC
Angie Parham*

J Graham Brown School
Louisville, KY
Bryan Crandall
Carrie Klingenfus
Allana Thompkins*

JJ Jones Intermediate School
Mount Airy, NC
Kathy Ratcliffe*

Johnson Traditional Middle School
Louisville, KY
Brooke Baker
Erin Singleton
Mr. Wolff

Leesville Road Middle School
Raleigh, NC
Vicki Newland*

Loretto High School
Loretto, TN
Trish Moore*

Love Memorial Elementary School
Lincolnton, NC
Daisy Kemper*

Lynn Camp High School
Corbin, KY
Donna Davis*

Mineral Wells Elementary School
Mineral Wells, WV
Marsha Brady*

Montgomery Central Middle School
Cunningham, TN
DeAnne Murphy*

Mount Washington Middle School
Mount Washington, KY
Michelle Chitwood*

Moyock Elementary School
Moyock, NC
Virginia Gioia
Denise Jewell
Kathy Maxwell
Mary Pepe

Paint Lick Elementary School
Paint Lick, KY
Pam Canter*

Providence Academy
Johnson City, TN
Janet Branstrator*
Cathy Graham
Pam Holben

Ramsey Middle School
Louisville, KY
Kerri Medley*
Mrs. Smith

Robert C Byrd High School
Clarksburg, WV
Rachel Skubis*

Saint Pauls Middle School
Saint Pauls, NC
Donald Weller*

Sissonville Middle School
Charleston, WV
Diane Ferguson*
Susan James
Debbie Walker

Spring Valley High School
Huntington, WV
Patricia Adkins*
Peggy Dingess

St Agnes School
Fort Wright, KY
Nancy Dwyer*

St Joseph School
Cold Spring, KY
Nicole Guidugli*

Tates Creek Elementary School
Lexington, KY
Brenda Jackson*

Tazewell-New Tazewell Primary School
New Tazewell, TN
Jody Kennedy*

Union County High School
Maynardville, TN
Sherrie Collins*

Walker Intermediate School
Fort Knox, KY
Josephine Graven
Vicki Pitcher*

Walton-Verona Middle School
Walton, KY
Deborah C. McNeil*

Weddington Middle School
Matthews, NC
Susan Williams*

White Station Middle School
Memphis, TN
Jennifer Brenneman
Helen C. Erskine*
Ruby Hubbard*
Christy Peterson*

William G Enloe High School
Raleigh, NC
Rita Achenbach*
Priscilla Chappell

Woodland Presbyterian School
Memphis, TN
Carol Percival*

Language Arts Grant Recipients 2010-2011

After receiving a "Poetic Achievement Award" schools are encouraged to apply for a Creative Communication Language Arts Grant. The following is a list of schools who received a two hundred and fifty dollar grant for the 2010-2011 school year.

Adolph Schreiber Hebrew Academy, Monsey, NY
August Boeger Middle School, San Jose, CA
Bedford Road School, Pleasantville, NY
Benton Central Jr/Sr High School, Oxford, IN
Birchwood School, Cleveland, OH
Blue Ball Elementary School, Blue Ball, PA
Bonneville High School, Idaho Falls, ID
Cedar Ridge High School, Newark, AR
Corpus Christi School, San Francisco, CA
Crestwood Elementary School, Rockford, MI
Dodson Elementary School, Canton, MI
Dr Howard K Conley Elementary School, Chandler, AZ
Eastport Elementary School, Eastport, ME
Emmanuel-St Michael Lutheran School, Fort Wayne, IN
Fannin County Middle School, Blue Ridge, GA
Fort Recovery Elementary School, Fort Recovery, OH
Frank Ohl Intermediate School, Youngstown, OH
Frenship Middle School, Wolfforth, TX
Gateway Pointe Elementary School, Gilbert, AZ
Greencastle-Antrim Middle School, Greencastle, PA
Greenville High School, Greenville, AL
Hancock County High School, Sneedville, TN
Holy Child Academy, Drexel Hill, PA
Holy Cross High School, Delran, NJ
Holy Family Catholic School, Granite City, IL
Interboro GATE Program, Prospect Park, PA
John E Riley Elementary School, South Plainfield, NJ
Joseph M Simas Elementary School, Hanford, CA
Lee A Tolbert Community Academy, Kansas City, MO
Malvern Middle School, Malvern, OH
Merritt Central Elementary School, Merritt, BC
Metcalf School, Exeter, RI
Norfolk Christian Middle School, Norfolk, VA

Language Arts Grant Winners cont.

Pioneer Career & Technology Center, Shelby, OH
Providence Hall, Herriman, UT
Ramsay School, Ramsay, MT
Reuben Johnson Elementary School, McKinney, TX
Round Lake High School, Round Lake, MN
Sacred Heart School, Oxford, PA
Selwyn College Preparatory School, Denton, TX
Shadowlawn Elementary School, Green Cove Springs, FL
St Elizabeth Catholic School, Rockville, MD
St Lorenz Lutheran School, Frankenmuth, MI
The Oakridge School, Arlington, TX
Tomlin Middle School, Plant City, FL
Vista Fundamental School, Simi Valley, CA
Walsh Elementary School, Walsh, CO
Washington County Union School, Roper, NC
Woodland Intermediate School, Gurnee, IL
Woodward Granger High School, Woodward, IA

Grades 10-11-12 Top Ten Winners

List of Top Ten Winners for Grades 10-12; listed alphabetically

Emily Alexander, Grade 11
Moscow Sr High School, ID

Yuliya Astapova, Grade 10
Paul D. Schreiber High School, NY

Lauren Bigelow, Grade 12
Marymount Academy, ON

Madison Corbett, Grade 11
Roswell High School, GA

Melissa Crow, Grade 11
Rifle High School, CO

Michaela Cunningham, Grade 10
Hilliard Davidson High School, OH

Beth Mader, Grade 11
Montgomery-Lonsdale High School, MN

Ferin Neff, Grade 11
St Joseph Central Catholic High School, WV

Jake Schwartz, Grade 12
William Mason High School, OH

Courtney Thompson, Grade 12
Lake Braddock Secondary School, VA

All Top Ten Poems can be read at www.poeticpower.com

Note: The Top Ten poems were finalized through an online voting system. Creative Communication's judges first picked out the top poems. These poems were then posted online. The final step involved thousands of students and teachers who registered as the online judges and voted for the Top Ten poems. We hope you enjoy these selections.

The Green Eyed Boy

The beautiful baby boy, perched so happily on the black photographer's stool.
His green eyes sparkle, like wet dew beads on healthy summer grass.
His red hair lays flat, amazingly. He bobs up and down on the stool playfully,
His tiny bib on his jumper bouncing with him. The charming little toddler amuses himself
With the intricate stitching of the red train, the magnificent airplane,
And the little blue car on his chest. Disgruntled, suddenly, he bursts into tears.
No warning, no time for his mother to prevent the display of emotion.

An abrupt change, almost as abrupt as the unstoppable transition from an adolescent boy
To a mad, uncontrollable addict. The toddler's green eyes still remain in the man.
The sparkling emeralds are no longer outlined by endless white pools.
Instead, the beads of dew from the morning grass are stitched with coarse, red, bloodshot lines.
The toddler fat is long gone. the man now towers, as thin as a skeleton.
He could be mistaken for a trauma victim, but his thin frame only causes pain for others.
When the modern poison courses through the emerald-eyed man, he forgets.
His father and sisters are gone from his diseased and polluted mind. His mother?
Only a memory when he soars so viciously. A memory to her, too,
As she weeps over the loss of her beautiful baby boy.

Abigail Hicks, Grade 11
Germantown High School, TN

Josie Who

I approach her doors for the first time in a while.
She looks at me, grins then lowers her head.
She worries that she looks raunchy, she's always an angel in my eyes.
Her hair falls perfectly with every sway of her head.
An infant being chanted a lullaby I am.
She gleams deeply with blue eyes, and illuminates my day like her favorite colors yellow and red.
My pockets are barren, nothing left to give her but my gratitude and rapture.
I tell her I love her, I am now a butterfly freed from my shell.
Her scent races through my nose like the smell of fresh cookies.
As I leave her arms I feel displaced.
A teenage dream I am living.
I kiss her goodbye only until next time.
Like a scar she is always upon me.

Ryan George, Grade 10
Spring Valley High School, WV

This Storm

The rain pounds on my window
Racing like a waterfall
With such an unsteady rhythm

Relentless thunder shatters my thoughts
Vivid flashes illuminate my surroundings
Electricity is racing through the sky

I look out my window to observe
It's shocking how the world can transform so quickly
From a peaceful calm to a staggering energy

The trees whip wildly
Everything seems to lose control
Leaving me with nothing but a lingering uneasiness.

Nicole Baez, Grade 11
Middle Creek High School, NC

Katie Lynn

She stood looking at the rings,
A future maid of honor at her friend's wedding,
Helping the bridegroom finish some things.

She was absorbed in examining the stones,
She didn't notice the man behind her,
His voice sent a chill through her bones.

"Remember me," he said as he slipped a wedding band,
Onto the third finger,
Of Katie Lynn's left hand.

Her sight of him began to fade away,
That morning had marked one year,
She had placed a rose on his headstone earlier that day.

Ethan Willis, Grade 10
Coffee County Central High School, TN

Where I'm From

I am from homemade butter biscuits being cooked every Saturday morning for breakfast,
From Sunny D and Welch's grape jelly I spread on my biscuit.
I am from the well kept house of my mom.
Perfect and cozy whenever I need to be felt loved and secure.
I am from the sunflower, standing tall towards the sun,
The rose, a symbol of love where ever I may go
Always growing tall and strong and never looking back.
I'm from family reunions every year for Labor Day and eating lots of food
From Thelma Sturdevant and Grandma Chillis.
I'm from the late nights when we have lots of fun and dance till the sun comes up.
From "always keep your head up and never look back" and "sit down and be quiet children!"
From the time my cousin Damian Sturdevant was shot and killed, it was late one night, and we still have many memories of him and how happy he was. He was the most appreciative person I knew and didn't take anything for granted.
The many dances of my aunt Pam. She danced like there was no tomorrow and did not care who saw her make a complete fool of herself.
I am from the many photo albums and digital cameras that keep our memories together. Many are under the table in a special place where no one can touch them.
I am from memories that keep the love and the bond strong between us.
I am from happiness.

Shakaria Wilson, Grade 11
Germantown High School, TN

Stuart

My dear pal,
how I love to wrap my arms around you and sniff your earthly scent.
Tired and drained I come home, yet you welcome me with eagerness and happiness.

My silly boy,
how I crack up when you waddle out of the bathroom cabinet and frighten the guest.
Your coat fades and white stripes atop your head appear as an old man's eyebrows,
yet you still hold fire and zeal in that Lab-body-on-Corgi-legs.

My baby doll,
how I adore when you brush against my legs under the table and beg for my attention.
Mom says I shouldn't feed you unhealthy food, but I know you would even snack on lettuce.

My odd pet,
how it confuses me that thunder should startle you and yet I am fascinated by the complexity of lightning.
You burrow yourself in my covers and slobber over my sheets but I'm happy to snuggle with you.

My best friend,
how I want you to always be there when I'm down and lick my cheek and wag your tail.
I know you have to say goodbye sometime, but I hope all dogs go to heaven.

Joanna Bernardini, Grade 11
Germantown High School, TN

Self-Inspiration

I'm supposed to be strong.
Even with the weight of the world on my shoulder.
Mama said, "stay strong," strong like a boulder.
Be a helping hand and a glass that won't shatter.
Turn your life around.
Try not to be lost, but instead be successfully found.

Margaret Henry, Grade 11
Challenger High School, NC

Bubblegum

Sometimes the taste may fade
After the tough situations we wade.
Few just toss it away.
Others may even stray.
But you are my Stride© with never ending taste.
I promise not to let this go to waste.

Christian Hinson, Grade 10
Loretto High School, TN

I Dream

I dream of sunshine, bright in the sky
I dream of lightning, and I cry
I dream of horses, I feel such delight
I dream of mules, and I scream with fright
I dream of turtles, swimming in the sea
I dream of sharks, coming after me
I dream of rabbits, hopping around
I dream of wolves, hunting, no sound
I dream of flowers, I feel peace
I dream of fall leaves, crunching under my feet
I dream of floating, away on a cloud
I dream of kids, screaming so loud
I dream of floating, on a ship at sea
I dream of whales, chasing me
I dream of stars, so shiny and bright
I dream of fear, of the things of the night
I dream of laying, in a field of wheat
I dream of creepy bugs, biting at my feet
Dream awhile with me, and together we'll see
Not all dreams are bad, so dream along with me

Nikki Vaughn, Grade 10
Coffee County Central High School, TN

Pickwick Lake

We pack the night before,
Towels, swimwear, and all the food imaginable.
The morning comes early, but the early rise is well worth it
Once we reach the lake.
With glowing blue-green water,
It's easy to get lost in the appearance.
But there's much more to do than just look.
Tubing, skiing, and boating are among the many
Activities that can be enjoyed.
Dreaded most is the approach to the dock
And back to that boring place called home.
Wiped out form the day's events,
I sleep most of the way home.
As we arrive at the house and settle in,
I discover a horrible sunburn.

Nick Menning, Grade 11
Germantown High School, TN

Untitled

This deep confusion
Is from my seclusion
And the illusion that it's all okay
The inclusion of this intrusion is sending my mind into preclusion
You've led me to this disillusion
Because of the exclusion from your heart
You give me this prelusion of your allusion
Because of the collusion,
The collusion of yourself
I can no longer take this elusion
It hurts me to say that we've come to the conclusion

Tasheena Mabry, Grade 11
Overton High School, TN

My Happy Ending

Why does it have to be me,
left alone like the loneliest sea
Surrounded by the unknown things
flying around with blue and black wings
Why can't anybody see
all the things I hate about me
I'm lost inside my head
I'm say how dreams are soon to be dead
I really don't know why I guess that's what I do
The nice things about me are really coming from you
I put myself down and I don't know why
Just wanna open my wings and take to the sky
My life is like a river it twists, turns, and bends
but you know it's kinda awesome to have such loving friends
I'm now flying in circles round and round I go
Getting dizzy, I'm falling now about to hit the ground below
He is down there waiting on his knee
He has something to tell me
When I get down there he tells me he loves me with all his heart
And I said I'll love him till death do us part.

Natasia Kelley, Grade 10
Havelock High School, NC

Hooked

At the end of the street, there exists
A place which had set its hooks into me.
At her side I sat, waiting patiently in the weather.
With streams of adrenaline constantly rushing
I coil as tightly as a water snake readying to pounce.

There I am, patiently crouching
Relegating my full attention
In the event that the thin rod sleeping in my hands
Might wake up and jump.

I remained in a single place without movement
Slowly dying form the lack of heat because
I had bit the pond's line and I wanted
The pond to bit mine in return.

Jonathan Lin, Grade 11
Germantown High School, TN

Camden Park

Camden Park on a dark, cold Friday night
Pushing kids around the handcar track with a dirty stick
Get so tired have to sit down
See mean little kids running around
Parents screaming get over here now or we're going home
Cars parking, alarms going off in ears
Little kids running, holding cotton candy smiling ear to ear
Getting dead stuff out of 100 year old water
On my break eating famous corn dogs
Park goes dark like you turn out your light
Clocking out, running home

Billy Heaberlin, Grade 10
Spring Valley High School, WV

The Brown Eyed Woman

I sit and stare in her brown eyes recognizing the pain
The hurt that she's has been through all the rainy days she's seen.
Denied by her mom as a child feeling unloved, not understanding where her father was
While she grew up in foster care. Only to have one of her many siblings by her side.
Seeing the pride in her beautiful brown eyes the courage she has, the obstacles she overcame,
The odds that she was up against and she never gave up she kept striving
Doing her best, promising herself she'd never leave her kids
Like her mom did her and her siblings.
Promising to never let her kids feel that pain she felt.
As I stare in her amazing brown eyes I realize she loves me for me,
And that she is the only woman that's always going to love me
For me even through my mistakes.
As I continue to stare in courageous brown eyes they suddenly
Look back at my light brown eyes. Feeling the unconditional love just
Looking in my mother's eyes. As I continue to look at the sweet brown eyes
Of my mother I realize she loves me and would do any thing
In the world for me. Realizing that she gave me the life that she
Wished she had as a child/teen.

Jody Scales, Grade 10
Lee County High School, NC

Cruel and Unusual Punishment

How can it be that time has a mind of its own?
How can it be that it speeds up and slows down of its freewill?
In the most inconceivable way, hours turn to minutes or seconds.
What should be an eternity of smiling is gone in the blink of an eye.
I reach to hold and it melts from my hands.
Yet just when things are speeding, slipping, spiraling away, time decides to halt at the worst moment.
My mind is pleading with time to make the hours turn to minutes once again.
But, as if committing some cruel joke, the hours turn to days and the days into years.
How can it be that time has not been convicted of these crimes?
These of cruel and unusual punishment.
Time is the enemy, the silent killer,
Pushing the moments we want and dragging the moments we dread.
Let us escape to our dreams where time is confused.
Let us dream of times without time.

Desiree Pinol, Grade 12
William G Enloe High School, NC

The Man I Married

It feels my pain, it understands how I feel, the fact that it knows what I'm saying next, is so unreal.
A tear falls and I start to cry, it just slows down as if it was gently wiping my eyes.
As anger feels within my heart, it gets hard like a bench at the park.
When I'm calm and there's barely an emotion left in me, it becomes inanimate, detached and heavenly.
During the speedy hyper times, it picks up the pace from slow motion and pumps me up and gets me going.
Happy as can be it creates a brisk blissful beat, like it is smiling right along with me.
Lying down on the ground confused, it gives me advice I could really use picking me back up for one more round.
It knows me inside and out. I doubt if it will ever leave my side.
I took my vows to it. Together forever we are husband and wife. Together forever until the end of time.
Till death do us part, it is all I need. When I'm cold and lonely music will be there for me.
Singing my song, having my back with its background, holding my head up with its beats, it's the only song I'll ever sing.
Together as one in harmony, helping me become a sweet melody, when my life is high or when it's low, I will always hit my musical note. Never will it betray me or forget who I am; music is my one and only man.

Mikella Fields, Grade 11
Central High School, KY

Lost Continents

You are oceanic, the seaside
that sometimes moves me
to unreasoned tears.
The words faint, and crystallize on my lips.

Forgive me.
I do not blame your hands for accidentally crafting a galaxy;
do not begrudge me for having been born there.

The zealot who is penitent
for praying with inordinate avidity,
for all their piety,
Doesn't cloak fate in mystery.

None of it is fortuitous, after all.
It came to be.
What is more inevitable than that?
Desertification.

Sarah-Kathryn Bryan, Grade 12
William G Enloe High School, NC

Answers?

Why do we still sit at home while the
Earth's forests are burning to black plains?
Why is there still blood flowing in our veins?

Why do we think that they don't matter,
When you stand there not drenched in pain?
When there's no one left to love,
Will you still be full of hope?

Why do chemicals still flood the seas,
And yet you swim and still don't see?
Why have the buckets of trash piled up;
Into a disgusting potpourri?

Singing songs of grief and hate,
Knowing there won't be a bait.
If you think and contemplate,
The answer will keep you awake.

Yuyi Li, Grade 10
East Chapel Hill High School, NC

Together We Can

Together, we must unite
Join together and fight for the right
We need to be seen
We deserve to be heard
Forces combined to spread the word
One man alone,
Abandoned, in the dark
Standing, emotionless, completely stark
The hand of a friend
Offers salvation

Ian Moseley, Grade 11
Germantown High School, TN

Yellow Daffodils

yellow daffodils, smeared along blue chalk
a makeshift carnival
  built on gen-u-ine concrete
  come and look see
  ladies and gentlemen — this you don't want to miss
  now welcome the ferocious, the man-eating 200 pound
  and watch in wonder as
  Slugger the Wonderslug
  tames this beast
the sun sets
voices call
in we go to
warm meals and warm beds
and the carnival morphs
magic lost
back into
  yellow daffodils, smeared along blue chalk
  on gen-u-ine concrete

Angie Wan, Grade 11
Germantown High School, TN

Humble Beginnings

From the small farm house,
On the meandering country road,
Near the small town,
At the county limits,
In a forgotten part of Kentucky.
She learned life.
Milking cows and taming horses,
Raising chickens as well as herself,
She learned life the hard way.
From dawn to dusk,
The workload never waning.
She did it all, never stopping, never quitting.
Her endurance grew and grew,
She became unconquerable on the farm.
From there, she'd grow.
She'd grow up to do great things.
But she still started in Kentucky,
With humble beginnings.

Andrew Flanigan, Grade 11
Germantown High School, TN

Pastries

Warmth radiating off their misshapen tops
Glaze glistening on their succulent forms
Oven sizzling from the overzealous ones
Mother's scolding voice in my head
Their antagonizing aroma
Fear in their little blueberry specs
Their sweetness on my lips
Pure joy
More amazing than ever
Muffins

Nettie Ruppert-Tilton, Grade 11
Berkeley Springs High School, WV

Why Judge Others?

You walk down the road
You see black clothes
You can't help but think
That they're emos

They have no chance
To be expressed
For all you know
They may be depressed

Whether an emo
Jock or prep
We are quick
Not to accept

What's it matter
How they dress
Or the people
They try to impress

There it is
So now you choose
It's up to you
Win or lose

Austin James Ledford, Grade 10
Coffee County Central High School, TN

Spring Joys

The soft rays were shining
Against the Earth's sweet face.
The birds were swiftly floating
In the sky's blue lace.

The wind was blowing softly
Among the young buds opening,
The tree bows hanging loftily
Calling out to the animals sleeping.

Soon the Earth was lively
In its warmth unforgotten,
Animals wander sprightly
In the Spring begotten

Spring is here and life is glory clad.
This is the day the Lord has made,
Let us rejoice and be glad.

Catherine Heuser, Grade 10
Holy Angels Academy, KY

My Little Wish

The darkness is gone
The light has come
I finally understand
The meaning of the word good
Its when I look at you into the eyes
Or when I feel you passing by
Its when I hear your laugh
Or when I smell your rose perfume

When I feel something it reminds me of you
Even if it is hunger or a pencil in my hand
And I just want to hug you
And kiss you, of course

I just want your essence all around my lips
Incredible what you have done
you don't even know me
you have changed my life
like the fall changes every tree

David Camargo, Grade 10
Greenwood High School, KY

Wonder

I see my reflection
then I see your face
I feel your presence
and turn to you
I stare into your eyes
and a smile crosses my face
a faint thought
comes into my head
then I start to wonder
about you and me
were we ever meant to be?
at any time
the future
or the past?
all I can do
is stare at you
and wonder

Emily Pfeifer, Grade 10
Eastern High School, KY

A Wall Once Stood

A wall once stood between us;
Created by stereotypes
Always adding on,
Never demolishing.

We met as strangers
And left as family.
Friendships that will last forever
And never break apart.

We came for a cause;
We came form everywhere.
To share this dream
And to make a change in this world.

Instead of building a wall,
Our plan was to tear down the wall
And build a bridge
connecting all of the people

It could not have been completed alone,
So together we merged.
This bridge we created.
This bridge we now walk upon.

Amber Lee, Grade 11
Germantown High School, TN

Celebrity Zoo

Welcome, young heart,
To the Celebrity Zoo,
Where we stock up on people
That you want to view.

We've got Sir Ian McKellan,
Brad Pitt and Tom Cruise,
But if you wanted musicians,
Who are we to refuse?

We've got Gaga and Lambert
Who compete for attention
With Madonna and Aiken,
Who just want a mention!

Our celebrities are fragile;
They can't handle that much.
Take what pictures you want
And look, but don't touch!

Roxanne Spana, Grade 12
William G Enloe High School, NC

The Best Time of the Year

Christmas! The best time of the year.
The food.
The presents.
But most of all, being around family.
Christmas food!
It's the best of the year.
The Christmas cookies.
The ham and the rolls.
Eating until you feel stuffed.
Christmas presents!
Waking up early on Christmas morning.
Eagerly waiting for Santa's arrival.
Toys, clothes, money, and gift cards galore.
All a person could ever want and much more!
The most important thing about Christmas — family.
Seeing cousins that you have not seen in months.
Spending quality time with your family.
Making new memories.
Cherishing the time with your family.

Laura Irons, Grade 10
Notre Dame Academy, KY

My Last Love

You are the air that I breathe,
You are the smile on face,
You are the one who makes me happy and never sad,
You are the sand and I am the sea,
You are the day and I am the sun,
You are then the night and I am moon,
You are the book and I am the paper,
You the toothbrush and I am the toothpaste,
You are the months and I am the days,
You are my tennis and I am your sport,
You are the ball and I am your bounce,
You are the door and I am the knob,
You are everything to me,
You are my love and I hope it always will be.

Brithany Phelps, Grade 11
Lynn Camp High School, KY

Indescribable Love*

The way I see you it's indescribable.
I love you with passion it's so undeniable.
When I'm with you I get this feeling,
I don't know what it is all I know is it has a meaning.
You make my heart race like you're an addicting drug,
I want you 24/7 just someone to cuddle with and hug.
You make the hairs on my neck stand up,
I promise if I ever lost you I would never give up.
I really want to be with you forever,
There is no other guy that compares to what we have never.
Please just believe me and give me one chance,
I promise I won't hurt you because I know this is the last chance.

Edwin Ramirez, Grade 10
North Mecklenburg High School, NC
**Dedicated to Erika Diaz*

A
Merry
Christmas

Such a beautiful time
Nothing else can rhyme
With the delightful pastries
And all the joy and pleasantries
A sweet, warm aroma filling the air
Toboggans and caps covering your hair
Children peeking at presents beneath a tree
Wondering all the while what it could possibly be
Bundled up carolers sing to all those who need a smile,
And listeners standing around them grinning all the while
Everyone shares in the loving Christmas cheer
It is such a fabulous time of the year
Joyously give,
Graciously get,
Happily live,
Never forget!

Michaela Gregory, Grade 10
Coffee County Central High School, TN

The Lost Lives

Throughout the night they were taken away,
But are not forgotten to this day.
Their fears and screams were silenced by
The deathly flames that caused millions to cry.
Numbers that were tattooed upon their arm,
Remind them of the years of harm.
The yellow stars which made them stand out,
Had people wondering how this all came about.
They've been through so much, had their pride stripped away,
And now their hearts are heavy and full of dismay.
Though the memories are too painful to recall,
Their stories must still be heard by all.
The tragedy that caused so much misery and sorrow
Ensured for many that there would be no tomorrow.

Ashley Campbell, Grade 10
Coffee County Central High School, TN

Band-aids

You thought he meant it when he said forever
You still think every day about when you were together
The memory of him still keeps you feeling down
You haven't moved on you don't even know how
Why did he say he loved you when it was just a lie?
Why does it feel like inside your heart has died?

Does it feel like he took your heart away from you?
Does it feel like he smashed it into hundreds of pieces?
Well then I'll find some band-aids and see what I can do
I'll put your heart together and even smooth out the creases
And if it feels like he killed you and you're dead inside
With one kiss or a thousand I will bring you back to life

Jacob Galloway, Grade 12
McMinn County High School, TN

The One Thing I Know for Sure

The one thing I know for sure is,
That I hate taking the trash out.
My mom says "Alexis take the out the trash,"
"But I'm too sick today,
My head is booming, my nose is on fire,
I swear my eyes just rolled in the back of my head.
Oh please don't make me take that trash out.
My hands will fall off,
If they touch the bag.
What if I fell into that big green bin?
Buried in all that waste,
With maggots crawling all over me.
I'll be dead for sure.
It's too cold outside.
I will freeze out there,
My fingers will go raw.
The bag would collapse,
And I would go crazy.
Do you want a crazy daughter?
I don't think so,
That's why I can't take out the trash today mom."

Alexis Ford, Grade 10
Broughton High School, NC

Shall I Compare Thee to a Piece of Cake?

Shall I compare thee to a piece of cake?
So tempting, so sweet
This piece of cake, I will not take
This piece of cake, I will not eat

You're so good
Yet you are no good for me
I know I shouldn't, but yet I can't help to think I would
You are not what I want you to be

Us, we're no good for each other
This piece of cake will just weigh me down
But yet, I don't want another
All you do is make me frown

Cake is good, cake is great
Full of sweetness, but not worth the extra weight

Genna Willenborg, Grade 10
Loretto High School, TN

Everything

I love you in the morning and I love you in the night.
I love the way you kiss me and the way you hold me tight.
I love you for all the good things you often say and do,
And I love you most of all, just for being you.
I love you for the way you act when things get out of hand.
I love it when you try so hard just to understand.
I love you for who you are and all you try to be,
But most of all I love you, because you are everything to me.

Rachel Kintner, Grade 12
Campbell County High School, KY

I Remember...

I remember...
walking side by side with him through the woods.
I remember...
him teaching me about all of his tools, though I
still have no idea how to use them!
I remember...
how he could fix anything and everyone would call
him when something broke.
I remember...
his shiny bald head
I remember...
him on his riding lawnmower, smiling with his
straw hat on.
I remember...
his white T-shirt and blue shorts he wore so often.
I remember...
his smile, his kindness, his sweet laughter
I remember...
my Papaw Gary

Savannah Stiles, Grade 11
Cherokee High School, NC

Babysitting

There was always a sound of yelling for their mom
And that was because of "Mommy" going to dinner
Hush, she will be home soon enough, I say to tie ends
Maybe, it was the loud scream of the youngest, Tom
Perhaps it was the screaming of "Winner!"
That there was extra chaos and yelling
Then everything became silent, no thud of toys
This was no dream; this was silence that God had to send
This said nothing good, rather a bad tumbling,
Anything but what happened would have been cake
Not without fear did I approach the three young boys
And afraid to see what I saw, I ran to call
They got to the house in time, for him to awake
And once again, there was screaming from down the hall

Adelaide Frey, Grade 10
Notre Dame Academy, KY

The Soccer Field

I step onto the field,
the freshly cut grass supporting my cleats
The white lights turn on,
indicating the time has come.
A nervous rush takes over my body.
Suddenly, the whistle is blown.
The butterflies are released,
as my mind can only think of winning.
I am quickly grasping for air,
but the cheers of the crowd keep me running.
The ref calls the end of the game.
Relieved, I step off the field,
only to return the next day.

Sara Parker, Grade 11
Germantown High School, TN

Fog

The memory grips me, pulling me close to its thin membrane.
I gasp as I slip through the veil and tumble into oblivion.

I blink and open my eyes to a gray cold world.
Cars whizz past me as I stand in front of the bone white ruin,
Shards of alabaster marble floated up from the thick, onyx mud, glittering in the gray air.

A midnight iron fence blocks my entrance, I step closer and wrap an ungloved hand on a gritty post.
Cold snaps at my soft flesh.
I shudder and gray fog slips past my lips into the November night air.

I watched my stream of unfulfilled wishes twist as it floats into the gray twilight clouds.
I wish I could have followed it, floating
Up into the bitter winds as I dissolved into a billion minuscule dots.
My heart skips a beat as the sky roars and flashes, cold rain falls from the heavens a second later.

Each drop chills me slowly to the bone, my teeth begin to chatter
Like a pair of skeleton dice in the hands of Death.
My eyesight begins to blur as the memory ends.
I soar from my seven year old body and watch the child-me huddle close to the cold metal fence,
Alone on the empty sidewalk, as the winter rain continues to fall in the city.

Bettie Yeboah, Grade 11
Northern Guilford High School, NC

Why?

Why keep walking on broken glass, when you could pick up the pieces and mend them back together?
Why wait around in your misery for things to get better?
Why put others down, when you could save or change a life?
Why continue to be around the very things that cause you strife?
Why lie?
You'll be faced with the truth someday.
Why cry?
Life's too short for you not to be okay.
Why take part in gossip, what if it was you?
Why spread about words that aren't even true?
Why give in to addiction, that just shows weakness, right?
Why live in darkness, when you yourself could be the light?
Why give up on love?
Life's too short to hate.
Why blame life for your issues?
When you are the master of your fate.

Bethany Wiles, Grade 11
Preston High School, WV

Me.

A skinny jean wearing, Italian nosed, six month vegetarian, so much like Uncle Joe, water color painting, sixties enthusiastic, thrift store finding, high-school going, Mumford and Sons obsessed, costume winning, leopard print loving, dreaming, sunflower growing, cold weather adoring, horrible singing, shyly outgoing, idealist thinking, positive living, city belonging, obnoxious laughing, little and short, future nurse, notebooking, Christmas music playing, advice giving, TOMS wearing, huge smiling, freckled, memoir reading, bamboo plant owning, not so thorough thinking, nineties, cough drop and sloth scared, shark amazed, big family, too many clothes owning, volunteering, agnostic, organization discovering, animal saving, tattoo getting, tired, helping, Beatles influenced, cupcake baking, special needs working, listening, Black Friday shopping, loving and accepting, freak.

Tara LaMendola, Grade 12
Campbell County High School, KY

Puzzle Buddies

We're puzzle buddies, yes it's true
Finding the right color is a clue,
That left us jumping me and you.
100 and 500 we could do.

Solving puzzles fingers blue,
We were together me and you.
Solving not only outside,
But inside too,
You help me, I help you.
That's what puzzle buddies do.

Each puzzle in life,
Was another piece to find a home,
And another piece not alone.
You finished your puzzle first,
My puzzle buddy.
Now I'm alone to finish mine
On my own.

We're puzzle buddies,
Yes it's true.
Save me a puzzle in eternity,
For you and me,
Me and you.

Resi Ridner, Grade 10
Coffee County Central High School, TN

The Wrong Melody

It just crashed
The life I thought I had
I should have known it would never last
But a blanket over my eyes was cast

Oh how I want this to be a lie
So that way my eyes wouldn't cry
But truth it be
So I must hold my head high
I can't alter or falter
Lest someone figure it out
The sky isn't so blue in my neighborhood
The smile is permanent
To protect the others

Oh how I wish to break this promise
I hope for the music to stop
On this infuriating song

Najja Gay, Grade 12
StudentFirst Academy, NC

Nature

It never ceases breathing
Like a circle, it keeps on living
A passive aggressivist
Never taking sides of this or that
A peaceful slumber in its arms
Until every aspect clashes
Ferocity seems unending
Stopping only to welcome
The yawn of daylight breaking
It's a mother
It's a caregiver
It's a siren
It's a nymph
It's an abuser
It's a murderer
It's every line in between
And it walks outside your window
Every second of your skin and of your ashes

Kysaundra Phillips, Grade 12
Madison High School, NC

The Monster from Within

Jealously, rancid and raw.
It's the evil, green-eyed monster.
Disastrous, it lies in wait;
Ready to snatch in all that come near.

Jealousy, it's ready to destroy,
— A friendship, a love, a lifetime,
It manipulates the mind
It makes you blind.

It seethes under our skin.
It wiggles through your day.
Pathetic, foolish; such a waste.
You no longer see the truth.

You open the door;
Allow it into your soul.
You tear yourself to shambles.
Jealousy smiles, pleased.

It's the evil, green-eyed monster
Rancid and raw.
Disastrous, it lies in wait.
Ready to devour all that come near.

Whytley Driver, Grade 10
Coffee County Central High School, TN

Storm

Thunder claps and
showers barrage the bare ground.
Light flashes in the sky,
illuminating it briefly.

Water runs downhill across my ankles
as rain softly pelts my skin.
The cloudburst rolls across my integument
and drips from my hair.

I stare at the sky
and open my mouth.
The torrent flows in quickly;
many drops miss their mark
and splatter across my face.
A slight stinging sensation surfaces
in my eyes.

The sound of the deluge engulfs me.
Nothing can be heard over the melodious
pitter patter.
The gray skies continue to cry
and bellow at the Earth
from far above

Rishi Malhotra, Grade 12
Germantown High School, TN

Peace in the Storm

The rain
Falling from the sky
As a waterfall
Beating heavily on my roof
Trickling from the gutters

The thunder
Crashing sounds throughout
the air
With it the sharp light of day

Sleep I must
But the wind is strong
Water falls heavier
Trickling faster
Crashing stronger

Should I close my eyes?
Trust I will
Hope I have

As I pray — I close my eyes
But for a brief moment

Awake to the beauty of the day

Damon Owens, Grade 11
Lynn Camp High School, KY

Goodbye to the Pain

Standing there, I'm not getting it, asking why.
Tears run down my face, I'm full of despair, I feel like I could die.

A soft hand comes to rest on my shoulder, I turn to see my mom's face.
She looks upon me with her soft gaze, then said, "Come on, let's get away from this place."

The hammering of the gavel set the ruling in stone. I took the hand of my mom and she led me away,
And I wondered if there was anything I could have done to keep my dad at home for another day.

The ride home takes forever, the cars rush by fast.
I think about my life before; never will things be the same as in the past.

The next day, I hear the phone ring, I slowly trudge over to answer it and put it to my ear.
And the voice I heard was the weirdest thing, my dad's filling me with cheer.

The void in my heart faded away when I heard the sound of my father's voice,
But when the call was done that day, the pain flooded back, not my choice.

My mom comforted me often and she told me everything would be all right.
My sadness went away and the pain did soften; my heart was lifted with delight.

I wondered a lot then how I would live without my dad,
But my family helped me again and again, now I'm no longer sad.

Years have flown by, full of fun and laughter.
I enjoyed life when I said goodbye to the pain, forever after.

Corey Smith, Grade 12
Providence Academy, TN

Where I'm From

I am from unground beans, from Starbucks and Ugly Mug.
I am from the 100 year old bungalow on La-fay-ette
with the wise old willow tree and the pies made of mud and water on the gravel driveway.
I am from Magnolias touching the ground,
the reaching branches and smiling petals welcoming adventurous kid tree-climbers.
I'm from "sing or play a song before you open your gift" and playing with your own hair,
from Angerman and Chamberlain, Schwartz and Jahnke.

I'm from stepping on each other's shoes and "big breakfast Saturday."
From "Komm, Herr Jesu; sei du unser Gast" (Come Lord Jesus, be our guest) before meals.

I am from James traveling by bus adult-less across the country at 7 with his 4 year old sister,
leaving his evil step-dad to find his father.
From Jonathan David, graduating summa cum laude at 16
From Cynthia Louise with a DASD, Ph.D., M.Div, MD, and BAPSY
From my Memaw who died despite the best efforts of her surgeons,
and from my Poppop who died because of the lack of effort by his.

I am from the chestnut armoire with a drawer for each family member.
I am from drawer number 5, the one at the bottom stuffed with hand turkey and diva tween photos.

I am from my mommy and my daddy, my older sister and my oldest sister.
I am from my "Father who Art in Heaven."
I am from laughter and smiles, tears and hugs, love and life through God.

Anya Schwartz, Grade 11
Germantown High School, TN

A Moment in Time

I wish I could freeze this moment, right here, right now and live in it forever.
To be safe from the rest of the world, and wrap you in the comfort of my arms
Away from all the danger. Away from all the madness.
The things that will always haunt us and the memories that have since been taken from us

I wish I could grasp this moment and stay in it forever.
If only it could be that simple — sitting around, quietly, watching the time pass by
Taking with it the fear; the memories of the past
The ones that remind us of the things we will never get back
Life as we once knew it.

I wish I could keep a moment of happiness.
And never again experience the pain and suffering which has taken over my thoughts
To be able to regain a sense of the things that can never be replaced
Our hope...our trust...our hearts...our sanity.

I wish I could take a watch, and prevent the hands from moving.
From ticking into the next hour...down to next minute
So that I can hold on to this very moment in time
And leave it that way forever...Frozen.
So the bitter pain that comes with it can be subsided and happiness reclaimed as we once knew it
Before this fight for power...before this suffering...before all this hurt

But what can we do?
We can't stop time.

Marisa Lorch, Grade 10
Notre Dame Academy, KY

Afterlife

His eye-shore lowers like the sun's horizon setting at dawn.
Darkness has emerged.
Motionless — no spectacle, no sound, no sensibility, no thoughts, no utterance —
A muzzle of silence is over buried with the moon mist thrusting upon death.
Not near breathing, not near a heart beat, not near gesturing —
Massive, similar to a one ton freight — stiff, not so much precise —
Cool mints scent the air.
Parsley pervades the land, but still no fragrance, no pulse no emotions, no sense.

What lies among us...
Alive, yet death is still surrounding, and against the livestock,
Leaving and blood-shedding them until they are destroyed
And can't be grown for next seasons' rebirth.
A shadow projected on a wall panel is seen in the fog.
Roaring vociferously, but some how not a tone being heard.

Furiously, in outrage with exasperation possessing his complete body, he's trapped.
All because of no serenity — outside the Cathedral, he lies seventy-two inches downward.

BOOM! Something wrapped up in a comfort of ambiguity drizzles and sprinkles an ounce of hope.
Fertilizing his seed making him no more a phantom — a shadow is not in vision.
With a thump of a whistle, a flimsy white line soars in the air
Above, the kingdom of paradise is no longer ambushed;
His spirit has risen.

Beaonka Williams, Grade 12
Germantown High School, TN

Eclipse…*

In the dead silence, all the details
Suddenly…
Fall into place, for Bella…
With a burst of intuition.
something Edward didn't want Bella to know.
Something that Jacob wouldn't have kept form Bella…
As Seattle is ravaged by
A string of mysterious killings and a malicious vampire
Continues her quest for REVENGE,
Bella, once again, finds herself surrounded
By danger.
In the midst of it all, she is forced
To choose between her love for Edward
And her friendship with Jacob…
Knowing that her decision has potential to ignite
The ageless struggle between vampire and werewolf.
With her graduation quickly approaching,
Bella has one decision to make: life or death.
But which is which?

Tosha Maney, Grade 10
Cherokee High School, NC
**Based on "Eclipse" from the "Twilight" series*

Test

Asleep on my desk
I'm sure my math is imprinted on my face
I'm supposed to be taking a test
But that's not exactly the case
The bell wakes me up with a jerk
As I frantically realize
I didn't do any work
Because I decided to close my eyes
I write faster than ever before
Guessing at every solution
Then I run to my teacher (pushing classmates to the floor)
And rush out in a state of confusion
I finished the test in about sixty seconds
But I'd hate to see my grade
It's not very high, I reckon
Want to trade?

Jennifer Armstrong, Grade 10
Preston High School, WV

Calculus

Numbers spinning in my head
Make me toss and turn in bed
Limits, derivatives, and quotients, oh my.
I'd much rather lie and stare at the sky
Each night I work for hours on end
For this curse of calculus I cannot mend
If I do not escape from its torturous grasp
My sanity will soon become a thing of the past
Now this poem must end for I have homework to finish
If it is not completed my grade will surely diminish

Loren Grossnickle, Grade 12
Heide Trask High School, NC

Our Story

For every person,
there is a story.
Part already written,
part being written,
and a part still waiting to be written.
Every book cover with scars,
pages torn and wrinkled,
and words slashed through and cut out.
Story of our lives,
bound together to be read.
To be looked at and judged;
Open for the world to tear apart.

The chapters begin,
and the chapters end;
Just as there are new beginnings
and abrupt endings in our lives.
What we have to realize though is that we write our own tale.
We have to be open to being read,
but strong enough not to be written in.
We decide our own stories.

Brittany Nunn, Grade 11
Middle Creek High School, NC

Moon

I stare at the moon for it helps me dream
Dream of knights, fairytales and mysteries
Pondering
Wondering
Pleading for love
I sit
I stare at the moon for it helps me dream
Dream of Shakespeare and his tales of forbidden love
Pondering
Wondering
Wishing for that love
I sit
When the moon fades with the sun rise
Every giggle
Every smile
Every piano note played
I find love

Mandy Wagner, Grade 12
Campbell County High School, KY

Music Is Me

Music is the way I dress, the way I talk.
Music is the way I think, the way I walk.
My personalities even my swag.
I can't be without my iPod in my book bag.
Music is a way for life, the way we think.
Music is food we eat, the juice we drink.
Music to me is real the pleasure feels right.
Music pumps my blood so I know it gives life.

Krysta Johnson, Grade 10
Lee County High School, NC

Let Love Be the Reason

Let love be the reason
Stars shine each night
Let love be the reason
In darkness, there's light
Let love be the reason
For the shine in her eye
Let love be the reason
No more tears must she cry
Let love be the reason
Gray skies turn to blue
Let love be the reason
She clings tight to you
Let love be the reason
Hope's not all gone
Let love be the reason
Forever is so long
Let love be the reason
That two become one
Let love be the reason
For the blessings to come

Kimberly Shaw, Grade 11
Henry County High School, TN

Never Get My Fill

I've been walking streets without names
I've been flying uncharted skies
Ungrounded, without sorrow
Unfazed and blinded
The future is calling my name in whispers
And my mind stumbles over rolling hills
The world is moving but I'm standing still
My mind is changing but my body is still
The world is blazing
My heart is on fire
Changing passions every seconds
New victims of desire
The world is moving but I'm standing still
My mind is changing but my body is still
Sucking the marrow
But I'll never get my fill

Bonnie Scott, Grade 10
Harpeth Hall School, TN

Carpe Diem

Tomorrow is not guaranteed
Today could be your last
Take chances
Have no regrets
Thank your loved ones every day
And love the ones around you every day
Leave your heart on the stage
Push yourself to the max
Don't forget to laugh and smile
Carpe Diem

Korinne Cowles, Grade 12
Berkeley Springs High School, WV

One Last Shot

The stage has been set and the tension has built.
It's the championship game and we won't leave with guilt.

The game has come down to the wire and we've used all our might.
We're down by two but we won't go down without a fight.

There are 3 seconds left and we call a timeout.
We are going to come up with a genius play so the ball will go in...no doubt.

As I look up, I see my team's tired and red faces.
I also see parents and their nervous paces.

The buzzer goes off and the play is set.
I will receive the ball and make it go through the net.

We throw the ball in and it ends up with me.
With a second left, I throw it up with one last plea.

As the ball is in the air, my stomach is doing a flip.
What if I don't make it? Will my team give me lip?

Suddenly, I see the ball go through the net.
The team rushed towards me and rejoices the goal that we met.

Ginny Clayborne, Grade 10
Coffee County Central High School, TN

Perfected Reflections

Love is like the sand.
Present in abundance, enticing, yet destructive,
Moving, powerful.
Many a man walks through it, and holds it dearly in his hands.
Seas and rushing waters approach, but it never ceases.
Lightning strikes it, and still something more beautiful forms,
Perfected reflections.
You can grasp it, but many a crystal only for a moment until it gently slips away.
It is stepped upon: soft, warm, but full of thorns and devastation.
Many, still, are held near the heart,
Having been hit by the waters, formed and faultless.
Held forever and not a day less.
But the true, the stunning, found with careful, quiet eyes,
Hidden by the sun and brought to life in the light of the moon.
Magical, beautiful.
Imperfections, protected by the night, yet faultless in the presence of the stars.
Unexplained, pathway to the sea, the unknown.
Misleading, becoming.
Chosen through the eyes of its beholder.
To each his own, to each, the sand.
Love, endless.

Nichole Lusby, Grade 11
Berean Christian School, TN

When Friendship Ends*

You have been my friend through the years,
I love you with all my heart.
I think about our shared tears,
And hate we had to part.

As I sit here and wonder why,
It had to end this way.
I wonder why you had to die,
Especially today.

As I stumble upon your grave,
I see a lady bug.
I try my hardest to be brave,
As I see the grave dug.

I will never forget your face,
All the memories made.
I have to leave your burial place,
Our love will never fade.

Ally McDow, Grade 10
Loretto High School, TN
**In Loving Memory of Orry Carter*

Cliché

Falling,
And no chance at escaping.
Head over heels and
Can't see my next step.
Blindsided by unexpected charm;
Witty comments and stolen glances.
Butterflies make me feel sick —
I hate to love it.

Closed off.
Unintentionally.
"He loves me, he loves me not."
I'm out of petals,
And low on composure.
Submissive at this point.

Resisting his hell-bent coolness:
Weak in the knees.
I am the love travesty
Your mother warned you about.

Kimberly Bast, Grade 12
Germantown High School, TN

Who's to Judge

Who are we to judge
When we make the same mistakes
We notice others

Sara Starkey, Grade 10
Spring Valley High School, WV

Shattered

I am a broken mirror slowly piecing my way back together.
So many things in my past breaking me, shattering me, crack by crack,
But those things don't matter anymore.

I've been hit in many ways,
And been looked at with strange faces,
As the broken mirror that will never piece its way back together.

I'm gradually assembling my fragile pieces
Back together again,
Because those things don't matter anymore.

I can put myself back together,
But you can still see my cracks
Because I'll always be a broken mirror.

I am forgetting them one by one,
The ones who broke me
Because those people don't matter.

As I mend myself one piece at a time,
I remember that…
I may be a broken mirror, but I am piecing my way back together,
Because none of those things, none of those people, matter anymore.

Brooke Journeaux, Grade 12
Oak Ridge High School, TN

Sister

She helps me: pick out clothes, straighten my hair, stay outta trouble.
She helps me with just about anything we need.
She yells at me: get out, leave me alone, Caitlin quit!
She yells at me, but only every now and then.

She asks me: where's mom, do I look stupid in this,
Does my Myspace look cute, will you paint my toes?
She asks me the same question, a THOUSAND times.

She nags me: did you take my shirt, why do you do that,
have you seen my purse, why do you hang out with them?
She nags me,
But not too much.

She makes me: Straighten her hair, help her with things she could do herself,
come with her, do this, do that.
She makes me:
But I really don't mind.

She can be: the grouchiest, the funniest, the laziest, the
cheesiest, the most annoyingest person EVER.
But she ALWAYS is:
My best friend, my hero, and MOST of all,
MY SISTER.

Caitlin Davis, Grade 11
Lynn Camp High School, KY

There Is a Place Nearby

There is a place nearby
where strong men die
and women cry
where tempus fugit does
not apply
and libertine men
are in no short supply
There is a place nearby
where the old and weak
are burned
and where the young and
strong become concerned
There is a place nearby
where many names apply
where dementia becomes
normal and sanity becomes
irrelevant
There is a place nearby
where many names apply
let's just call it
Auschwitz

Kiley Curtis, Grade 10
Coffee County Central High School, TN

Armistice Love

I'm there for her all the time
When she's down
When she's up
She says my words make her feel the best
That no one speaks to her so kindly
I put myself out there just for her
We hug every day
She smiles at me
Such a good friend, she says
That's what I am
No more than a friend
A friend like no other…
I take interest in what she does
She appreciates it
You're so nice all the time.
I respect you so much.
You're such a good friend, she says
I'm just a friend —
Is that all I am?
Why is it so?
Why don't you see?

Philipp Lindemann, Grade 11
Middle Creek High School, NC

Mountains

Mountains of fury
Standing tall before my eyes
Reaching so far high

Darian Singleton, Grade 10
Union County High School, TN

The Masking of Pain

Deep wishes of being able to seep into the cracks in the wall
A small way of escaping the worries and troubles that plague her
Every day, it's always the same, happy and cheerful
A face made of plaster, molded into a confident smile, it's all a lie

The lie is benign to those who do not know her
But to those who do, the ones who can see the pain, the sadness
They know of the front that she puts on for everyone else, as a way to hide
A front to fool others, her way of putting up walls

When she sits all alone, no one to comfort her
She cries softly, in utter shambles inside
No one has ever felt such a heart-wrenching pain she experiences daily
Can't catch her breath, can't seem to get the weight off of her shoulders

How much longer can this continue, before she is a total wreck
She's so close, a scared little girl, facing her self-inflicted monster
She won't wear her heart out on her sleeve, sharing emotions screams danger
She will forever seem to be a stranger, the black sheep of her own family

Breanna Acton, Grade 12
Heide Trask High School, NC

My Bed

I am hidden from the world, almost like a scared little girl.
It is where I feel safe; my own personal private get away.
Many try and touch me, but sadly they cannot reach thee.
I am in a place that many of us wish to go. Just like we all wish to grow.

I am hidden from the world, almost like a scared little girl.
Oh, how I love being in this place. Where no one can see my face,
Or hear my beautiful voice; keeping me away from all noises
Curled up here like a ball; where I just get away from it all.

I am hidden from the world, almost like a scared little girl.
With my eyes tightly closed and my wandering mind froze.
I am in a peaceful state and it feels so great.
On a pillow, lays my head. Me sound asleep in my bed…

Alexandria Thompson, Grade 11
Germantown High School, TN

Success!

As I chill and observe the structure of the city I'm in,
Acknowledging the children's smiles remind me of the child within.
Searching for sunshine praying to God I don't sin,
Trying to be opposite of what I am from a child to a man,
I love when people think wrong of me and act like they don't care.
Because it just wants me to make them wrong and play the game all fair,
Can't hold back feelings no more because my heart is as fragile as air.
I want to make it when no one else thought I could and watch the whole world stare.
I want to be the garden that grew from a paved street,
Strong and stand tall that makes it so unique.
I want my name to be carried on even if I'm deceased,
Even if it didn't work it was worth a try and it's still my belief.
I will be successful!!

Samuel E., Grade 10
Audubon Youth Development Center, KY

Gone

She twists the sparkling diamond ring
around her finger,
sending showers of
rainbow prisms of light
across her pain-stricken face.

She slowly exhales a breath,
knowing what has to be done.
She forces herself to remember
all the bruises on her arms
and the scars in her heart,
before she changes her mind
and chickens out.

She pulls the band off her finger
and rests it on the damaged
countertop to be surprisingly found.
She walks out the door,
this time
without a glance back.

Emily Arrington, Grade 10
Germantown High School, TN

Jaded

We are consumed with the idea
that we need the truth
of all things.
So raw and uncensored,
that it dulls the mind's fervor
for anything exceptional
or for anything horrendous.
The value of life trampled
by the indifferent expressions
of those who recite:
It happens all the time.
It's not that shocking.
I've seen it before.
Ethics so blurred,
morality obscured,
by the shadow of reason
and logical process.
The rise of mankind
only leads
to the fall of humanity.

Evan Bolano, Grade 11
St Joseph Central Catholic High School, WV

Rust

My body is broke
My mind is not in control
I can feel the rust

Steven Dean Krick, Grade 10
Loretto High School, TN

These Paths (For Those Brokenhearted)

Oh places. Oh these journeys walked by life.
So common — yet so individual that those who traverse these paths feel
so alone, so distant, so isolated, and aloof.
Yet, in isolation — there is a connection.
A connection conceived through distress,
born by faces who stare at the depths of their own despair.

And, in this bond, there is unknown solidarity
joined by one purpose, one bond, one brokenness
between those with minds where thoughts race,
Where the ominous lingering devours souls.
Where outward beauty hides the battlefield within,
and a smile shields the war with whom it resides.

But each path to its observer seems so unique.
When, in reality, how different are they?
In this path of life, it is this longing to laugh, to live, to love
which bears down so heavily because it is so innate, yet so hard to obtain.

But in these moments of struggle,
it is to not seek the path in which one has gone,
but to seek the path in which one will go.
To join as one force, one brokenness — tied by thin, dim threads
to seek, to forgive, to hope, to walk — this path.

Daniel Medina, Grade 12
Northwest Cabarrus High School, NC

My Time Will Come

Wanting more than a town in the South
A plain third child of five and the twin of one
Scarcely five feet tall and none to bright
A feeling I feel wild like my raven mane, fighting of the teeth of combs
My almond eyes burn with a constant hunger
Impatient I am to purge such small and naive life

In the mirror I see, marked and yellow skin
An upturned nose in ceaseless scorning
Eyebrows deep in furrowed thought
But clear to see a solid mind
That mind is who I am

I want to see enamored moons!
I want to live among foreign tongue,
I want to climb and fly away!
Unable, I am stuck like a fly to a web
Too soon is it to disallow the tendrils of youthful susceptibly

Still I smile knowing,
My time is slow approaching
My life is self determined by me alone
Just now I wait in the roaring dreams of dreams
My head bowed low, I pretend to study.

Sarah Hong, Grade 10
Harpeth Hall School, TN

Dream Big

Live life to the fullest
without any regrets follow your heart and do what's best
be persistent in everything you do
never give up for someone is counting on you

Look to the future and don't look back
God gave you a gift and let it attack
Keep your hopes alive and achieve your dream
Never live in agony no matter how hard it may seem

Later you will celebrate and happy you will be
Just dream big and keep your head to the sky
No matter what someone may tell you
Your dream will never die

In the future you will cherish your new beginning
Cherish the fortune and cherish the fame
Be proud of yourself and how far you came

Kyle Cheek, Grade 10
Lee County High School, NC

Pink Magic

To that desperate student
Scribbling life away
A mark not meant
probably a ruined essay
But wait! The student takes up his greatest tool
With the strongest soap he furiously scrubs
Churning up gummy pink bubbles in pools
Falling into the tub
Bit by bit, sud by sud
The soap squelches up the muck
Leaving no trace of the dud
Frantic fingers whisk away the yuck
Fresh, clean, bright, new after the sprinkle
Only now a little bit wrinkled

Vivian Hu, Grade 11
Germantown High School, TN

Music

Music brings happiness
Music is universal
Music brings life into every home
Music gives hope
Music brings families together
Music can create emotions
Music represents the soul of man
Music can unite lovers
Music can create movements
Music can move mountains
Music can bring life into the darkest places
Music can humble the most conceited people
Music can tear down walls
Music is what we make it

Brandon Wayne Taylor, Grade 10
Coffee County Central High School, TN

Olive

Dear Olive, thank you.
When I journey into far off recollections,
It is vague and clouded in a fog.
But still I know it is you;
Thank you for being my first memory.
And thank you for the thousands that followed.
I'll remember those nights,
When you listened to my voice tread on
Even while you fought to stay awake.
And the endless hours we spent in the sun
As children who held on to no fears or worries.
My definition depends upon your existence.
So thank you for who I've become.
You loved me even through the grim part of our story.
And you never tried to wage war.
And I know it was not easy standing in shadows,
Yet you endured and endured.
So, dear Olive, thank you.

Sophia Frantz, Grade 11
Germantown High School, TN

My Beliefs

What is this sacred truth of fear and fright?
When one fears the maggot and a rain of blood;
How inane to fear something so unreal.
The imagination is a fickled soul,
Depraved of a true meaning of reality,
A sickened figment of the mind and thought,
Is all that is needed to rid of truth.
Tell me, if truth of a fairy and elf exist,
Then what of bloodshed and war and death,
What of the impoverished souls of fire,
Lost in time and the end of the string.
The belief in hope is agony, torturous.
Guide me a path, shave me a path of light;
Then, and then only will I believe.

Madhuri Prasad, Grade 11
Germantown High School, TN

Home Sweet Home

It's warm and cozy
You're surrounded by the best people to know
We're all surrounded around Scrabble
Sipping hot cocoa with marshmallow
Occasionally, looking out to the falling snow
The TV's on, a man is talking
But no one really knew
Because spending this time
With these wonderful people
Was the best thing we could do
Of all the days of the entire year
This is the best season to "'tis"
But most important than any other place
Home is where the heart is

Patricia Smith, Grade 12
Oak Ridge High School, TN

What You Are to Me

You are the apple of my eye,
You are sweeter than the sweetest pie.
Your words are like a soothing ocean,
You make my heart swell with emotion.

You are so good to me,
With you my heart feels free.
With you I could climb any wall.
I'll come to you whenever you call.

Now you make my heart feel dead,
You betrayed me, I feel so misled.
You used me and threw me away.
Now without you, my life feels gray.

You're like a rotten apple on the ground.
Your words make me feel like I'm drowned.
You were sweet to me, but now you're not.
My heart is now cold when it used to be hot.

Evan Harmon, Grade 11
Providence Academy, TN

Wasting Time

I sit
Looking outside
The city awakens

Blink
A red light
The heartbeat

Zoom
Cars drive by
Circulating on streets

Windows
Shining in buildings
Offices where progress is made

I sit wondering
Who is more alive
The city or I?

Jennifer Winbigler, Grade 12
Campbell County High School, KY

A Configuring Identity

As I bridge this gap, this defining line,
I find the littlest hope in the footsteps beneath me.
Maybe, this absurdity, this "unrealistic state of mind"
Is exactly where life is supposed to be ventured.
Maybe, this life isn't supposed to be taken so seriously.
This configuring identity in me travels on as if my life were never ending.
Maybe, there's more to life than I think.
Maybe, there's another dimension or a whole other unknown world.
Maybe, there's a hidden identity hidden within me.
Do I configure the only identity that I have fended-for for years or
Do I dig down deep to uncover an unrevealed identity?

Nicole Johnson, Grade 12
Cooper High School, KY

My Soul to Fly

I must go back
To where it all began
When the stars shone bright
Amid the deep blue sky

Against all odds
It faded way
Slowly unveiling
Its treasure of old

A spark of light
So clear and strong
Growing in number
Commanding the sky

A splendor of color
To greet the day
A dawning of light
For my soul to fly

Nicole Seider, Grade 12
William G Enloe High School, NC

Friendship

One cup of kindness
One cup of understanding
Pinch of sorrow
A few bad times
One cup of dependability
Two scoops of laughter
Lots of good times
One cup of prayer
Blend together kindness
Dependability
Understanding and prayer
Add laughter and sorrow
Fold in good times
Store tightly in your heart
Serve generous portions daily
Garnish with a smile

Meagan McPeak, Grade 10
Coffee County Central High School, TN

I Am a Trapshooter

As I walk out on that line
I know I will achieve
The greatest accomplishment
I will ever receive

As I load my shotgun
Gripping it to my face
Looking down the barrel
I seek to the highest place

As I say "pull"
The target releases
Following it with the barrel
I burst it to pieces

As I unload my shotgun
I am relieved with joy
That I can achieve at a sport
That was made for a boy

Shelby Felty, Grade 12
Campbell County High School, KY

Feeling Heart

Violent shivers in the dark
why I'm so cold is unclear
the thrashing memories
cut like a knife
puncturing my healing wounds
once again
without warning
they seep in my skin
trying to get past my armor
which crumbles down
from one touch
just one
is all it takes
to tear open
my feeling heart.

Olivia Hughes, Grade 12
Spring Valley High School, WV

A Place to Live

You can't keep living in the past,
Or else you will get left behind.
That's what she always says.
You can't live in the future,
Or else you will never get there.
She says that too.
You can't live in the present,
Or else you will miss your chance.
She even goes that far.
I ask myself, where am I suppose to live,
If I can't live in the past, present or future?
What else is left?
She has an answer for that too.
Live with the people you care about,
Live as yourself, and don't change.
The places that matter are always with you.
If you can do that then you will live in happiness,
So the places I'm from are the people I care for.
Let us hope they never change,
Because that's where I want to be.

Sheldon McCallum, Grade 11
Germantown High School, TN

Change

At first we were just standing there
an icy breeze blowing around my hair
with a deep voice the announcer spoke
realizing it was too late too choke
then with a quick gesture this dance had begun
only able to stop when the music was finally done
moving fast, thinking quick
hoping no one gets sick
the end finally came and went
rushing to gather the equipment so it would not be bent.
While waiting for awards the nerves came
disappearing when they called our name
A trophy for first place
and the envious look from our rivals face
only to remember that next week it could rearrange
because things change.

Lauren Workman, Grade 10
Spring Valley High School, WV

Zombies

Slow moving but oh so dangerous.
Don't get caught sleeping or it will cost you.
Go for the head, it's the quickest way to guarantee they're dead.
Guns are loud and alerting.
Safety in numbers no longer applies.
What you've heard is most likely lies.
Laws and rules should not be followed.
Get surrounded, and you are dead.
All in all, don't worry no one makes it out of life alive,
So have some fun with the walking dead.

Timmy Fults, Grade 10
Coffee County Central High School, TN

What Do I Do?

What do I do?
I can't see you.
I can't feel you.
I can't even hear you.
But I need you!
I don't know how I am going to live without you.
I feel so blue.
I mean, one day you're here.
The next you're there?
This I can't even bear!
How was I going to know
You were going to end up there?
How am I going to get there?
But now you're high in the sky,
As I watch you fly.
So what do I do?
I mean we all feel so blue.
I go to sleep and all I think about is you!
I mean we all need you!
We all want you!
We all miss you!

Jesse Carpenter, Grade 10
Anson New Technology High School, NC

Wishes of a Black Boy

I wish I didn't see what I saw but wishes don't come true.
I wish I didn't have to pick two colors red or blue.
I wish my stepmother never got into that wreck
I wish my mother had heat while we lived in the projects
I wish she had the money so we lived where you live
I wish all those victims I affected please forgive
See there are a lot of things about me you don't know
There are a lot of things about me I don't show
I wish we had money power respect at least
I wish we can walk in the hood in peace
I wish Obama gave faith to the black residents
Wow it's shocking a black man for president
I wish my cousin would have hidden the evidence
Now he's serving 30 with no jail experience
I wish we weren't left in this world alone
I wish my wish list wasn't so long.

Phillip Wallace, Grade 10
Lee County High School, NC

Computer

Does a computer get mad when you turn it on?
Does a computer get mad when you don't clean it?
Does a computer get lonely when it doesn't have any one to talk to?
Does a computer get sad when you throw it away?
How do you think a computer feels when you give it away?
How do you think a computer feels when you move the mouse?
Does a computer feel sad when you take it apart and fix it back?
Does a computer feel frightened when someone else plays with it?
How do you think a computer feels when you unplug it?

Charlotte McKinney, Grade 12
Lynn Camp High School, KY

Shattered Forgiveness

I see you.
There you are clear as day.
But what's not clear is me and you
The interactions
The ones between me and you,
They're well in the past now
Yet they continue to haunt me in the present.
When I look back
At the blood stained past
All I see is anger, loneliness, anguish, and lust
Not to mention frustration, pain, and regret.
Don't get me wrong
There were some good times filled with laughter and smiles
But alas
All the good doesn't heal my suffering wounds.
Now God tells me to forgive myself
And others that have wronged me.
He also says to bless them;
That's the hardest part.
As much as you don't deserve it
I continue to do so.

Amari Stokes, Grade 11
Germantown High School, TN

Mountain Dream

Light was shining through the trees
Up in the mountains, leaves falling with ease
The hills were like giants, you could feel the breeze
And climbing those mountains was a child
Rugged and dirty, he lived in the wild
Everything was calm, the weather was mild
No one knew who he was or from where he came
He didn't say much, he had no name
Kept to himself, he was never to blame
But they knew this mountain was his home
Where his mind was free, free to roam
Not bothered by anyone, he survived on his own
Too bad this child was stuck in class
Had to follow the rules, was told how to act
Wanted to be free, there was no chance for that
He just wished that he could go back

Kris Adkins, Grade 10
Spring Valley High School, WV

Your Memory

Some people are notorious,
Some are better off gone,
but you are my hero,
You should have never been taken away,
I'll be hating the time you're gone,
but I never weep too hard,
Cause I always know I'm going to see you again,
Through all the confusion, I keep the faith,
and cherish every moment I had with you.

Hailey Chapman, Grade 10
Lee County High School, NC

Ella

She tosses her Barbies about like confetti.
She flings her clothes across the way;
They spill into the hall, like mounds of cotton.
Her small hand darts beneath a pair of overalls
And recovers a limp, stuffed bear.

When I enter the dark cave she calls a bedroom,
I trip over Winnie the Pooh and
Wade through puddles of Osh Kosh B'Gosh.
I just thank God she doesn't know how to
Rollerskate.

I flip the light switch quickly and dodge
The airborne shoe that hurtles from
Behind the twin size bed.

She peers at me mischievously,
Like a meerkat.
I love my sister,
But sometimes she has a savage streak.

Taylor Stevens, Grade 11
Germantown High School, TN

Holocaust

During 1942,
The skies weren't so blue,
Actually a more kind of gray,
Which many Jewish lives were to pay,
As the years changed from season to season,
The world realized that Hitler had no reason,
To this man, they were all just pigeons,
That he and his troops killed only because of religion,
Many looked on,
As Jewish families diminished one by one,
Mothers, daughters, fathers, sons,
The quantity of lives were taken in tons,
See, Hitler didn't care who was killed,
As long as his wishes were fulfilled,
Don't take advantage of what's wonderful,
And always remember life is beautiful.

Dallon Lush, Grade 10
Coffee County Central High School, TN

Dr. Seuss

He brought us the Grinch
And Cindy Lou
The Cat in the Hat,
Thing One and Thing Two
The Sneetches taught us to treat all the same
Oh, The Places You'll Go said life's not a game
Green Eggs and Ham taught about an open mind
The Foot Book says take one step at a time
Who could forget *Fox in Socks*?
One thing's for sure, Dr. Seuss rocks

Zach Winton, Grade 10
Coffee County Central High School, TN

Friday Night Lights

Friday Night Lights, for the glory
As the opponent started stretching I
Stood from the locker room looking
Upon them, we came down the hill
Looking at our counter partners hoping
The next time we walk off of the
Field, hoping we have a victory
And all the glory for tonight's game
In the middle of the game, I
Stood on the field, with sweat
Running down my face and cheeks
While taking a deep breath,
I could smell popcorn
And corn dogs from, the
concession stand. The announcer
Talking rapidly play-by-play
As I heard the final whistle
Wail we had the victory
And the glory for
This game.

Alex Brooks, Grade 10
Spring Valley High School, WV

The Goddess of Love

There once was a goddess
who fell in love.
Except it was forbidden;
nevertheless, she kept it strong.
The goddess was so beautiful;
young men could not resist.
Only one of every thousand
never ended up on her list.
Every young maiden asked for her help;
love was the goddess's trick.
Instead she gave them poison,
no woman would get her wish.
Evil as that was,
someone does still sing,
Of this goddess love,
who herself ended up very lonely.

Courtney Youngbar, Grade 11
Ravenscroft School, NC

Last Forever

His eyes shine like the stars above
when I see him I'm filled with love
With out his love I feel so sad
when we're apart I feel so bad

I wish this love could last forever
through all the trials we endeavor
Although right now we are apart
his love will forever be in my heart

Samantha Ross, Grade 10
Spring Valley High School, WV

I Will

When the moon rises and the sun fades
I will be there in the garden of many thorns and roses
Of love and hate
Of happiness and sorrow
When the dawn breaks the black sky with light
I will fade from all memories
I will leave on a happy note
When the flowers open their petals, and the fireflies turn out their lights
I will fade into the light.
I will show no life
I will be watching over you like an angel
But when the sky turns shades of purple and black
I will arise from my deep slumber
I will once again return to the garden
Where even the most beautiful roses hide the cruelest thorns.
I dance and sing
I will show life and all of it's emotions.
I will not be the angel watching you, but the angel holding your hand
I will be full of rage and joy
Of happiness and sorrow
And until I must leave I will hold your dearest hand.

Megan Ulrick, Grade 10
West Creek High School, TN

Where I'm From

I am from the country
From farming and home-cooked meals.
I am from the oven out back
(Ancient, dusty,
Yet still works like a charm.)
I am from the fig tree
In the front yard
Whose massive limbs I'm sure I could still climb
As if no time has passed at all.
I'm from yogurt and needlework
From a family line too far to trace.
I'm from the talk-a-lots and eat-a-tons
From relax and work hard.
I'm from always do what you believe is right
And family before all else.
I'm from both sides of my family, who are more alike than they know.
From too many sweets and Turkish coffee,
On the top shelf in my cramped closet is an old cardboard box
Packed with memories.
From pictures to trinkets to even my first loose tooth,
Somehow it's never full.

Iman Abutineh, Grade 11
Germantown High School, TN

Scrubbing: A Sponge's Report

There was never a dream inside the house but one
And that was of a clean and tidy floor.
Footprints are tracked through the kitchen. O, this will be fun.
Perhaps no one appreciates my chore.

Body sopping across an unending surface,
Fibrous skeleton being wrung daily,
The clogging of my pores, What's the purpose?
I have been taken for granted lately.

Falling into suds helps repress my fury,
Daydreaming like a schoolboy clears my mind
Scanning my problem I begin to worry
Upon seeing my request, I wish I was blind.

Hair on the table; footprints line the floor.
I regain strength to fight this cleaning war.

Bethany Tabeling, Grade 10
Notre Dame Academy, KY

A Good Friend

What is a good friend?
A good friend is honest.
A good friend would care about you.
A good friend would make you laugh.
A good friend would never make fun of how you look.

A good friend wouldn't make you feel stupid.
A good friend would try to help you with your problems.
A good friend would be there for you if someone made you cry.
A good friend would be sad if you moved.
A good friend will be there with you on your wedding day.

A good friend would go shopping with you.
A good friend would take crazy pictures with you.
A good friend is someone you could tell your deepest secrets to.
A good friend is someone you can have fun with.
A good friend will always be by your side.

Monica Dozier, Grade 11
Lynn Camp High School, KY

Oblivion

In a graveyard, things are quiet.
Bodies resting, beneath my feet.
People piled, six feet deep.
When wandering in this holy place,
Silence is key, walk slowly, have no face.
I stumble upon a cross that's blank.
Looking down, I feel no pain.
I walk through this hallow place, dead but living.
In a graveyard, I will someday lie, cold and shivering.
Following the ghosts of life's past.
I will not last.
Death.

Zack Appel, Grade 12
Berkeley Springs High School, WV

This Is My Place

I am from many places,
From oil and vinegar.
I am from neglect and attentive.
Jagged, smooth, bitterness.
I am from the periwinkles,
The hydrangea,
Those that look sweet, but can kill.
I'm from no family traditions and no family traits,
From my parents Kirk and Veronica.
I'm from true dysfunction and bad habits.
From never get married,
And good luck next time, kid.
From the aunt that gets drunk at Christmas parties,
And the uncle that lives in back allies.
I am from no specific location,
Because I have multiple homes,
Memories fade in the carpets.
I once was told I was from torture,
But I am truly from life.

Cameron Clayborn, Grade 11
Germantown High School, TN

Girls Associated

Associated with daises are blue eyed, long legged,
Wide mind, open mouth,
Barely dressed, soft hearted girls.

They waltz with nature's serenity.
Swaying, balancing on still waters.
These are not just girls
Associated with daisies.

These are tongue tied, kissed goodbye,
Memory faded, yellow ribbon oak trees,
No smile, wishes to become young again

Women
Remembering youth with nature.

Holly Ward, Grade 11
Lafayette High School, KY

You Must Wait the Night

Standing at a window all alone
Not a sound except a joyless moan
A cold winter's night with snow, what a sight!
An eager young girl who can't wait the night
She watches with amazement as the snowflakes play
Grinding her teeth out of spite
But none the less she can't wait the night
So she gets ready to go strapping her boots on tight
She's ready to go but before she knows
Her mother tells her you must wait the night

Austin Mason, Grade 11
Lynn Camp High School, KY

I Have Done Creative?

I am [what is creative] in this world.
When I express myself [it is profound, nothing] hinders my ingenuity.
As my mind spills over the piano keys when I create something [new, nothing] but raw expression fills the room.
There was a kid who [plagiarized everything] I created in Art Class.
But my power is for me, [it isn't like] I can share my abilities with him!
Because [expression is what] releases your own inner world;
Very few [people can achieve] my depth of utter emotional release.
I didn't earn this, it's [only God's] gift to me, the only thing I can really depend on in life.
Others are awestruck by my [expression] because it is always completely new —
My keyboard, my snowboard, my sketchbook, my writing, [answers original] questions posed by my conscience.
And these questions [are what] drive me to be so unique, so different.
As innovative human beings, [we do] things differently than the other animals
That put up instinctually, brutishly, soullessly, [only fronts], to combat their pressing problems.

But... [what is creative? It is profound nothing. New nothing. Plagiarized everything. It isn't like expression is what people can achieve. Only God's expression answers original. Are what we do only fronts?]

Mirrors...?

Well I know animals put up... [fronts only. Do we? What are original answers? Expression gods only achieve. Can people? What is expression? Like, isn't it everything plagiarized, nothing new, nothing profound. Is it creative? Is what]

'I Have Done Creative?'

Bradley Allf, Grade 12
Forestview High School, NC

I Am From...

I am from music that has been played in the halls of the kinds since the Renaissance,
from scrumptious Milano cookies and veggie straws every day before dinner.
I am from the bright sunshine yellow house with caramel brown fences.
Happy, jovial and filled the house with the smell of fresh made dumplings.
I am from giant ancient trees, pleasing smelling roses, and foul smelling mulch from the garden,
the Japanese maple, the colossal yellow sunflowers, and sweet sugary nectar feeding the pink-spotted
swallowtail caterpillars, fat and happy with the satisfying refreshment.
I'm from crowded Chinese New Year gatherings and shiny charcoal black hair, from Wang Jian and Confucius.
I'm from waking up late in the mornings and scrambling for school and sitting before the TV watching CSI during dinner,
From "He who wakes up early, gets to eat breakfast early" and "Grandpa is always right! So don't argue!"
Form the first ballet recital where my six year old cousin almost fainted due to stage fright.
The ancient wise grandpa who always had an answer to everything.
From the old photo albums containing the first birthday parties, flute recitals, and random family gatherings
In the dusty upstairs attic,
Telling the adventures of a cheery, loud, large and loving Chinese family.
I am from good-humored family memories, adorable baby albums, and school photos hanging around the house.
I am form happiness.

Shan Jiang, Grade 11
Germantown High School, TN

What Happened

You told me you would never leave me alone. I was so young when you let me. You promised me you would come back. I was alone and wanting to know when you would come home. I never gave up even as the days, months, even years passed by. You broke your promise. I found out years ago that you will not come back. I don't ask questions knowing that they will not be answered. The only question I have is one that only you could answer. What happened to make you leave me alone? I won't let them lie and say it wasn't, that it was stress. I know better than that now. I know that it was your time to leave me and watch over me every day. I no longer ask what happened. I no longer care what happened. I know the truth even though they don't.

Jasmine Contreras, Grade 10
Loretto High School, TN

Colorado

Cool breeze is blowing through the mountains
Snow is falling all throughout the year
Colorado is one of the most amazing places
The sun isn't too hot
The humidity is nowhere to be found
The trees stay green all year long
Never is there a sad day
The atmosphere simply fills you with joy
Nature is thriving
Moose, deer, bears, and all other kinds of animals
Live in the forests of Colorado
Sitting outside is so peaceful
Listening to the sounds of the world
Seeing all of God's glory
In all of His creations around you
No big city hustle and bustle
No running from place to place
Nowhere to go
Just relaxing.

Hunter Key, Grade 11
Germantown High School, TN

The Dark Fairy Tale

I have lived to watch the misery,
The despair that ran through their lives,
The darkness took over,
And slowly the light dimmed away,
And the happiness went with it.
No smile was ever seen,
The darkness in their hearts;
The sorrow in their eyes,
Hatred, grief, and sadness,
The dull life they longed to live,
In the world I lived,
In a place of no happiness,
In a place of darkness,
There is no such thing as a fairy tale moment,
I am a witness of this misery.

Eliana Figueredo-Zamora, Grade 10
duPont Manual High School, KY

My Reflection

I look in the mirror and wonder "who am I?"
These lips, these eyes, this face.
Who does it all belong to?

In the mirror my reflection is a hollow
representation of someone who I used to know.
But now this person is a stranger to me.
I would find myself again someday if I could.
But since I've changed I've been drowning on
My own.
Left here alone in the dark.
No one's here just me.

Macie McGlone, Grade 11
Lynn Camp High School, KY

The Bacchant

The denizen reaches for the sun
Large long branches; powerful mirth
Warm shining liquid surrounds.

Leaves crumpled about
Branches wavering, dancing.
Crying an umbrageous song with his limbs still reaching.

Another drink of sunshine.
Unaware, forfeited, credulous, but focused.

Here comes the Sun; here comes the fire.
His empire of leaves,
Burns into inconsequence.

Gone with the sun; one by one,
Burnt crisp to dust
Petrified, alone, the sun turns dark.

Intoxicating fumes in deserted ruins
With glasses emptied, remains a ghostly shell

Domain blurring;
His surreal dreams continue.
The bacchant weeps, as his branches fall.

Radiance, indulgence, consumed, gone.
With no drink to imbibe, the night falls forever.

Meng Jiang, Grade 11
Dupont Manual High School, KY

We Stand on the Shoulders of Giants

We stand on the shoulders of giants
Up above the rest of the world
Forgotten, silent, watching…

Upon the shoulders of giants
The sky is at my fingertips,
Everything is what I see —
The goings on of the world
The imperfection.

I see how people frantically search for the meaning of life
Without really caring for life itself,
How people see only their need,
Forgetting others in their quest of self fulfillment,
The narrow focus of selfishness.

People live and thrive
While others struggle and pray for help that never comes.
The loss of faith, the dependence that never truly satisfies
And the power a single person has, but never truly realizes,
Never tries, simply skates along
Content to watch silently, forgotten in the rush of life.

Emily Bowman, Grade 11
Lynn Camp High School, KY

The Feeling of Despondency

The sense of brokenness
It overcomes the barriers of her heart,
Mind and soul

The sense of brokenness
Has made her numb,
Except to the brutal memories and thoughts

The sense of brokenness
She longs for someone to understand
She aches for the embrace of another

The sense of brokenness
It offers no comfort
No longer can she endure it
Sanity has evacuated her body

The sense of brokenness…
Is no longer there…
Neither is she.

Alexis Davis, Grade 10
Pleasure Ridge Park High School, KY

The One I Love

You are the one I love,
And it's because of God above.
He heard my prayers and answered them for me.
So you can see, forever you'll be the one I love.

I want you to know
I'll never let go
Because you are my life.
For you, I'll fight.
So you can see, forever you'll be the one I love.

You are who I miss.
I need your kiss
To get me through the day
Without a trouble in the way.
So I hope you see, forever you'll be the one I love.

Keawanna Greene, Grade 10
David Crockett High School, TN

True Love

Why do I love you?
I'm clueless.
But I guess it can't be answered
By the questions: why? Or how?
Love can be really strange.
I know that now.
But you see I do love you,
And that's true love.
When you don't know why you love someone,
You just do!

Samantha Hunnell, Grade 10
Mount View High School, WV

My Old Man

My old man was the best,
And very unlike the rest.
He'd say a curse word or two,
Well, actually, he'd say a few.
My old man liked to hunt,
And his dogs could sniff out the smallest runt.
There were three with whom he spent most of his time,
And every minute was worth much more than a dime.
My old man loved his grand kids most,
You could tell because about them he'd boast.
Most called him Red,
He'd call them anything but their name, even Fred.
My old man like to sell cars,
He could even sell one to an alien on Mars.
He like to watch TV Land,
He even liked the Nitty Gritty Dirt Band.
My old man died one cold, January day,
Many people came and had words to say.
He is now in a better place,
And I can't wait for the day I see his face.

Amanda Crouch, Grade 10
Coffee County Central High School, TN

I Wear the Mask…

I wear the mask that is hurt and used.
It hides what happened to me.
So many lies, always going to be insecure.
Trusting will always be a big issue.
I should have just listened.
Why do guys have to be that way?
Taking something that meant the most.
Now I'm nothing to him, like it never happened.
Never again will I let my walls down that fast.
I wear the mask.
Now that I have a guy that saved me, he understands.
No matter what I will always be insecure
I'll always be broken in a way
And nobody can fix that feeling.
I'm just happy I'm finally with a guy, that loves me for me
I wear the mask

Raven Evans, Grade 12
Berkeley Springs High School, WV

The Color of the Streets

We classify them as hoodlums
When they pacify the news;
We see them every day living life the fast way
Hearts filled with anger minds filled with hatred
Known to be fatherless and sometimes homeless
But committed they stay to the flag of whichever color
Addicted to the easy money thinking they die with respect
And they were so clever; where in reality they had none and
They deserved much better but instead to a cell block they rest
With a letter to the chest saying "you ended up just like your father."

Ashli Morales, Grade 12
William G Enloe High School, NC

How Do You

How do you verbalize
What you feel inside
When you don't know
How to put into words
What they do when to you
When they say good-bye?
It's so easy for them,
Though they can't feel
The pain you go through
As you watch them walk away.
You try to be strong and not to cry
But it seems so hard when
All you can do is think of
The good times the two of you have shared.
You try to force a smile on your
Face but it soon turns into a frown
Once they walk past you.
And all you want to do is say
"I love you, Come back."

Jessica Bickle, Grade 11
Lynn Camp High School, KY

Mixed Emotions

Shall I compare thee to the dead of winter?
Because you make me feel alone and cold,
You break my heart like a splinter,
And I cannot break free from your hold.

My heart and mind are intertwined,
You make it so hard to choose.
I love you, I hate you, I can't decide,
You leave me beaten and bruised.

Your harsh words ring in my ear,
My feelings mean nothing to you.
Coming alive is my worst fear,
Nothing you've told me is true.

Alone and cold, I look around.
Lost in your love, I can't be found.

Katie Powell, Grade 10
Loretto High School, TN

Change

When life brings no adventure
and the days feel all the same,
When each day holds no surprises
except fear, despair, and shame,
When lastly hopelessness washes over
and the last drops of joy it drains,
Is when a stubborn mind admits…

It's time to make a change.

Ginny Niver, Grade 12
Broughton High School, NC

Never Ending Massacre

The young, so corrupted by mothers and fathers
Who see it as their moral duty to stamp their child's forehead as better?
Than this one and that one

Outside of the preparation is war
To prove who's dominate
The winners stomp the losers down at an attempt to hold their position
Instead of controlling,
Chaos, rage, and death are unleashed

The best turn into homicides
While they push their muses to be suicidal
Cavemen we all are
Darwin was honest, the fittest survive
Off of the most lied to by their parents

A graveyard of slaughtered cows lie beneath our homes and world
How sad, even the dead still get stepped on
And walked over and picked on by us crows
Who feed off of them in any ounce of power we may gain.

Rachel Welborn, Grade 12
Northern Guilford High School, NC

One in a Million

A seed out of many bloomed, I was the one.
A petal out of every one off the flower I was picked, I was the yes.
A flower out of the patch, I was chosen.
I was the one harvested, the one chosen to model. I don't deserve it.
The cloud of all that the kid imagines as a dog, I am the one.
The fish out of hundreds in the river, I am the one caught.
The ant of the whole army, I am the one chased.
I was the one harvested, the one chosen to model. Why am I called?
Out of every crayon in the box, I am fought over.
Out of every gum ball in the machine, I am dispensed.
Out of every house on the street, they wanted me.
I was the one harvested, the one chosen to model. Is it me you're looking for?
Through the entire storm, I am the branch unscathed.
Through the night, I am the one that can see in the darkness.
Through the school day, I am the one with persistence to go on.
I was the one harvested, the one chosen to model. What is the reason behind this?
With every balloon let go, I am the one still drifting.
With every thread sown, I become unraveled.
With every leaf of the tree, I am the one holding on through winter.
I was the one harvested, the one chose to model. I am being called forth.

Lindsey Holthaus, Grade 10
Notre Dame Academy, KY

Sunsets

Something so bright
and beautiful
but after always comes darkness

Slipping down
below the horizon
on a warm Savannah night

Beauty beheld
out of oceans reach
as the stars take their place

The array of colors across the sky
delicately chosen
from the Painters palette

Falling off the face of the earth
where night and day meet
in a beautiful exchange

Matt Pierce, Grade 11
Middle Creek High School, NC

My Faith

We beg for forgiveness
That's never really there;
We just hope our wrongs
Leave our lives to spare.

What else could we do
In a time of need?
To get a flower of faith,
You must first plant a seed.

I don't know about yours,
But my flower died.
There are too many times
I have broken down and cried.

Lost I seem to be,
In an ocean of confusion.
Somehow the big picture
Was just an illusion.

Andrea Brent, Grade 10
North Brunswick High School, NC

Thanksgiving Feast

I can't wait for Thanksgiving feast,
I will eat like no other beast!

Potatoes, carrots, gravy, and meat,
And other delectable things to eat!

Gobble, gobble turkeys galore,
I can't wait to get up and get some more!

Bernadette Kenney, Grade 10
Holy Angels Academy, KY

Future

With her hands curled around a blue pen,
She remembers to perfect the art of penmanship.
A satisfied smile slithers across her face as she looks at her peers smugly.
Failure is not an option.
What's the point?

Mom weeps during an embrace, and even
Daddy tears up when it is his turn to say
goodbye. Proudly, the parents watch their
daughter desiccate out of their reach and
onto a beautiful, lush campus.
What's the point?

Ten years, five nannies, four children, three pets,
and one marriage later, she will find herself
adorned in Chanel and perpetually
affluent. Nevertheless, she will come
home one day to realize that she
never got the opportunity to be a
genuine mother.
What was the point?

Katie Raves, Grade 12
Germantown High School, TN

Understand?

Do you think you could understand? Or will you just sit back and pretend
to tell me what I want to hear? Instead of what I need to hear.
Would you judge like all the rest? Or say life is simply just a mess.
I maybe young you can say. But I know what love is.

I once had a close friend, who I hung around.
'Til school separated us, and good-bye was said.
For awhile I was alone, 'til a man came to town.

I fell in love with him. We were happy together.
He had to leave and then we were crushed.
We fell apart. More alone I became.

Now with my old friend but what about the other.
The man I love still wants me.
Stuck between two who love me.
Who do I pick?
Both love me and care for me.
Only one can have me.
Who do I pick?
How do I decided?

Christine Schuchter, Grade 12
Campbell County High School, KY

You
When I looked into your eyes
I knew it was true
That I had fell in love with you
I thought you loved me too

Day after day,
I wished you would hold me tight
Kiss me with your gentle lips and come to my sight
As you whisper in my ear that you loved me
Even if it was a lie
It means more to me than the truth

But to you my heart was a game
You cracked it in two
One for hate and one for you

Only sometimes you have to move on
And let what you had be gone
Even though you feel so broken
You must leave your words unspoken
Ashley Miller, Grade 11
Lynn Camp High School, KY

Numb
The snowstorm freezes all
Cold icicles cut through cold trees
Like knives put into wrong hands: reckless
The ice shows no mercy as the car veers left, then right
Trapped in a claustrophobic world with no route of escape

Your only hope is to wait it out

I'm trapped inside a frigid hospital
I slip on linoleum ice, sliced by doctors' icicles
They try to shovel a path for my escape, but I have no choice
I have to wait out my eternal snowstorm
There is no sun to melt this snow
The blizzard freezes my soul

Numb, I feel no pain
Frostbit nerves save me the trouble
I go out with the wind that slowly
Taps my tiny window
Alysse Riggs, Grade 12
Oak Ridge High School, TN

Winter
Leaves fall everywhere
The wind stirring within the street
Frosty winter has now come

The winter is now here
Snow falling down little by little
Concealing roof and tree
Yena Ji, Grade 12
William G Enloe High School, NC

Your Tears in God's Hands
So tired of crying,
and of mourning this loss,
going crazy, I don't have what I need,
inside of me, I hurt.
I know how you feel all alone at night,
and the emptiness in your soul,
but I know the One who can heal you,
and make you whole.
Reaching up, crying out,
you'll find someone who really understands.
You won't forget, but when you cry,
you'll realize, you don't cry alone.
All the pain you feel, He feels,
all the tears you've cried, He's cried too.
He loves you, and He loves me.
He is EVERYTHING we need!
Take my advice and offer up your life,
He'll take it in His hand, and you'll know
you never cry alone.
JoAnn Jolin, Grade 10
Coffee County Central High School, TN

Moon Under Water
We make our paradigms in paragons,
An unattainable shift toward the beautiful.
Thoughts of a godlike stature
Flowing like the sea in the direction of Olympus.

Sky thicker than water:
Celestial objects of desire.
A lifetime becomes a journey,
The journey becomes a labyrinth.

Glassed over dreamscapes
Pass through tinted eyes.
The portrait sucks out the life.
The spyglass sees a barren wasteland.

We should consider ourselves fortunate
The notes of true perfection stray from our ears,
For in the endless quest we may fall prey to madness.
Better to let the moon set beneath the waves.
Will Mygatt, Grade 12
William G Enloe High School, NC

Having a Blast
I think
to be
a girl is
to be
ever on the
edge
of
implosion.
Emily Canaday, Grade 12
Heide Trask High School, NC

My World Away

Miles from here in another land
Is my world far away.
A place I love with all my heart
And I will return someday.
Tiny homes with cracks in the floors
Where children live and grow.
No beds for sleep and little food
Is all the life they know.
Lunch is just a "biscuit"
With no money for treats.
They reached out their hands
Begging me for "sweets."
I looked into the smiling faces
And held little hands in mine,
Wishing I could be there
To love them all the time.
I have never met anyone
More precious to me than these.
I gave all of my heart away
To my little Guyanese.

Starr Craigue, Grade 10
Coffee County Central High School, TN

A Girl Like Me*

A girl like me —
So curious,
and brave…
Willing to do anything.

A girl like me —
Afraid to cry,
Afraid to die,
Doesn't want to stick out…
Like a star in the sky.

A girl like me —
Quiet and happy,
Polite and sweet,
Full of joy.

A girl like me —
So in love, afraid to lose her love…
But willing to fight for it.

Elizabeth Maney, Grade 10
Cherokee High School, NC
**Based on the book Twilight*

Flowers

A flower is born
In the brand new springtime sun
I love the colors

Kayla Conner, Grade 10
Union County High School, TN

Richmond, 82 Miles

Half of what I need
Half of what kills me.

I let off after the sign,
Knowing he won't ever be mine.
But I still slow, people fly around gawking at my 45 pace, maybe this is my only chance...
Face to Face.

I go crazy; hit the wheel letting everything go quietly,
Still.
My strong walls come up and I start to pump
The gas pedal
My sobs
And the speed, thankfully, graduates up.

I endure all the signs, the possible exits and
Move on;
On without him.

Catherine Durbin, Grade 10
Currituck County High School, NC

The Eden of Antiquity

Slouched in a frail, old, plastic chair,
Barely ascending the weathered back mesh,
IN total content, I am awake, living in the conversations of the past,
Aunt Marian's voice, distinct among the chattering,
Not loud, but stuttered with a homely tone,
Grandma's porch is Sunday's conglomeration of Pennsylvania folk
Resulting from eventful sermons,
I'm stranded on a boat,
Drifting across the open water of controversy
Where the ocean crest goes I go,
Clashing waves of ideas
Creaks of old wood below our feet,
Floral perfumes permeate from the necks of women splash mist upon the deck,
Warped doldrums ideas envelop me,
"When I saw…" and "this is how…" make my ears seem to be running a record,
I watch, I learn, I listen:
What not to think.

Brett Wagner, Grade 11
Germantown High School, TN

I Remember

I remember saying you always got my back
I remember you saying you would tell me if you decided to leave
I remember you saying you would be back
I remember our friends asking me what happened to you
Then again I remember all the times we had running from the police
I remember you teaching me everything I know now
I remember how you wrecked us in your car
I remember having the feeling when you didn't come out of the car right away
I remember you forgetting us and going to PA with that girl
I remember I lost my best friend
But then again I remember all the good memories we shared

Shane Holliday, Grade 10
Berkeley Springs High School, WV

Daddy's Girl

Pretty little face
Deep green eyes
She can do no wrong,
Only in his eyes.

Clinging to his leg
Everywhere he goes
She loves him so much
That she never lets go.

Waiting by the door
When he comes in
She only prays
That he doesn't leave again.

Although she's older and
He thinks she doesn't care
She thanks God every day
That her daddy is still there.

Kaylyn Stewart, Grade 11
Lynn Camp High School, KY

Happiness

Not always what is expected.
Sometimes exactly as you planned.
Occurring from nothing,
Or being built from the bottom up.

Losing can happen as easy as gaining.
Destroyed as easily as created,
Blooming faster than it takes a fall.
Your outlook on life determines all.

Happiness is a joy to the heart;
A solace to the mind.
It is a healthy state of well-being.
It takes fighting to get it,
But the fight gives everyone
Their fairy-tale ending.

Sam Crossland, Grade 10
Coffee County Central High School, TN

Band Camp

Freshmen out of step
Too bright sun
Loud drum clicks
Obvious wrong notes
A drum major's frustration
Sweat in the air
Ice cold water
Seemingly too short lunch
Blistering heat
Immediate exhaustion
Can't wait for next year

Elizabeth Miller, Grade 10
Berkeley Springs High School, WV

Deception

Screaming for attention never knowing who would hear me
You were there for me but you were wrong for me
You told me stories of love Stories of lies
I never knew how to tell the truth
I believed you and loving you was like loving death I hurt so much
Your web of lies broken
You said things were different with me that I was different
That I was not like the other girls you were with I was the one that made you feel something
I loved him, but there was something like chemistry that made me want you too
I am tired of deception tired of lies
I am tired of you in my head feeding off the one good thing I have
My heart hurts
You let me down you pulled me into a world where I don't wanna be
I feel so hollow inside
My titanium cage does not have a door but you found a way in
Climbed over the wall ripped at my heart you broke me down
Your rein is over I'm kicking you out
It is not your heart to mess up
Its mine you're done
I love you, you know I do but I'm finished
Finished being your little marionette!

Natasha Pearce, Grade 12
Havelock High School, NC

Where I'm From

I'm from playing in the creek
Catching minners, skipping rocks
I'm from Nana's house on Friday nights
Disney movies, and big bowls of ice cream
I'm from my sissy teaching me to be a big girl
I'm from Toy Story, Rugrats, and Scooby Doo

I'm from Mamaw Sue's Sunday dinners
From Papaw Earl buying my first car
I'm from walking on the rail road tracks
Picking blackberries, and being proud of how many I had in my bucket
I'm from my daddy catching lightning bugs
And sleeping in my mommy's bed 'til I was twelve

I'm from Wayne, and Amy, and Tamara
Completing my family, and making me whole
I'm from Carley, watching her take her first steps into life
I'm from God, and forgiveness
Friendship, and falling in love
Family, and learning to grow up.

Ashley Combs, Grade 12
Perry County Central High School, KY

Surreality

My heads high in the blue skies
Watching my life
Through those rays of sunshine
But this isn't reality
Although it's close in my dreams
Down here it's so cloudy
So unhappy
And in more ways than one
I'm bound by a gravity of subtle tragedy
Waiting for new perspectives
Not easy for a young kid
Convince me to search for silver linings
To stargaze when there are no stars
And to go far
Without airplanes or cars
To dance through the night
With my shadow
In a friendly tango
Don't tell me to get real
To forget about the surreal

Michelle Ma, Grade 10
Morgantown High School, WV

The World

The world is not a nice place,
offering you cookies on a silver platter.
The world can be a friendly place,
full of loving family and friends.
The world can be a dark place,
full of hatred and nasty people.
The world can be a fun place,
with time spent with family and friends.
The world can be an evil place,
full of violence, blood, and war.
But the world can be a peaceful place
if people would try harder.
Some say the struggle for world peace
is just some false dream,
but they forget,
that dreams are but another reality.

Michael Brown, Grade 10
Holy Angels Academy, KY

My Only Regret

My only regret
Something that I cannot take back
It all happened so quickly
Something that never should have been
Tears still fill my eyes
Each time it comes to mind
I wish I could forget it happened
Pretend it was all a dream
My only regret
Something that I cannot take back

Jacqueline Allen, Grade 10
Coffee County Central High School, TN

Hate

I hate the way you always leave, the way you're never here.
I hate how when I see you, all I feel is joy.
I hate the way I love you, when the feeling isn't returned.
I hate they way your pants never fit just right,
And the color of your eyes.
I hate the way you style your hair.
I hate how your smile brings me hope, even when it's not meant for me.
I hate how our bond was broken,
Special memories never to be held again.
I hate how when I think about us,
And the promises we made,
I think 'bout the times you said you'd be mine forever.
I hate the way our forever ended.
The one thing I hate the most
The thing I can't forget
I hate the way you never loved me,
The way you never cared.

Cassie Hullett, Grade 10
Coffee County Central High School, TN

Diverse Fall

You're the red sun on the horizon, the yellow smile from the stars
You're the beauty in the rain and clouds above
You're shades of my nightmares, the beauty of my dreams
You're my world below and above

I'm the night chasing you away
I'm the sun clearing your storm, peering past your clouds for something blue
I'm waking up to live my dream with you today
I'm climbing your horizon, exploring each and every shade of you

We're the universe
We're the simplicity, the complexity around
We're the night to day, the world so diverse
We're solving our hearts, falling for a picture we're finding that had never been found.

Jacob Heller, Grade 11
St Patrick School, KY

The Odds

The night I almost died.
I thought I wanted to cry.
They said we should have died.
But really we should have died.
Mom is home crying its actually really funny because no one was hurt at all.
But we totaled our car.
Without a scratch on anybody every one was ok but my brother in law had to get checked out
You know the just in case kind of thing.
Even though we didn't get home until around 1:30 in the morning.
We later found out that for sure that our car was totaled yesterday.
But you can't complain. I thank god that everyone is ok and that's what matters.

Jamel Harris, Grade 10
Lee County High School, NC

Almost Perfect Smile

I haven't written in a while,
But that's because I get so distracted by your almost perfect smile.
But behind it withholds a person much deeper.
Every word spoken leads me astray,
Then again, you always had an act for taking my breath away.
Your light ocean blue eyes hold sorrow and hope for happiness in the forever days of tomorrow.
Your past hurt makes for a heart unsteady,
You've claimed many times that you're not ready.
I understand and am willing to wait,
Because I can't let go of all the moments where I feel like this is fate.
You don't understand what it is in you I see,
Why I stick around instead of just leave.
That choice would seem logical,
But hard to complete,
Because the sight of walking away from you would stay on repeat.
The way you shine, the way you laugh, the way you fill my day with joy,
The times you frustrate me, upset me, and the words you say just to annoy,
I still turn around every day to witness that almost perfect smile,
Long enough to realize, it's what makes this all worthwhile.

Amber Harris, Grade 11
Berkeley Springs High School, WV

The Red Coat

The little girl in her red coat walking into the streets with her mom
With all of the German soldiers shouting and pointing guns at them.
The little girl cries telling her mom that she doesn't want to leave their cozy home.
Her mom holds the little girl tight and says, "Everything is going to be all right."
The little girl believes her as they step into a train going to wherever it leads.
"Mom," says the little girl, "Where are we?"
Her mom can't bear to tell her the truth, but she simply says, "Somewhere we shouldn't be."
As the weeks go by, the little girl sees her friends and others being shot by Germans.
She cries silently at night weeping for those who are gone, but very happy she still has her mom.
Going into about three months at the camp, the little girl's mom becomes suddenly ill and very weak.
Unable to do her work, she is shot. The little girl revolts against the horrible people who killed her mom.
As she was being hung, her last breath was taken to say,
"We are all individuals. We shouldn't be treated exactly the same. We should be treated as humans, not as animals."
Then the chair was kicked out from underneath her.
There hung that one individual that spoke up, the little girl in the red coat.

Alexandria Sartain, Grade 10
Coffee County Central High School, TN

I Miss When…

I miss the days when we walked to church barefoot, and ran to school not caring how we looked.
I miss nap time in kindergarten and running around the playground with no worries.
I miss when drama wasn't in our vocabulary, and when every girl wanted to be a pretty pink princess.
I miss when a secret was when you told someone who you crushed on; not that you're pregnant and then the whole school knows the next day.
I miss when we cried at monstrous storms; not when our best friend got sent to rehab.
I miss when the only thing we snorted was Smarties.
When there were no cliques, no drugs, no nothing.
Just a kid — waiting for the newest action figure to come out.
I miss when divorce was seldom, and instead of aborting children, women actually carried them.
I want things the way they used to be.
No one is trying, and that is what I see.

Breanna Smith, Grade 10
White County High School, TN

Juice*

What is juice?
It's when you're never afraid to do what you really want to do.
The truth
Is that I stand up for things that I really don't believe in.
Remember that Tupac movie called *Juice*?
The one where he killed his friends,
and turned his back on the ones that loved him
That took juice, but not the type of juice I have.
Juice can come in many different appearances.
I lost 3 friends in the past fifteen days,
I spent more than a year locked up and I'll never get that time back.
I have 2 brothers and 3 cousins doing 8 years or more in prison.
And when life seems okay, it just gets harder.
I feel like I'm dying sometimes,
I'm a flower with no water that has never seen sunshine.
I give up on everything, everybody, and every dream.
The juice that I have makes me the man that I am today.
The juice that I have is mine and nobody can take it away.
All the friends and family I lost this year are never coming back.
I got juice, but all I want is my friends and family back.

Dalton D., Grade 12
Audubon Youth Development Center, KY
**In memory of Adrian Hightower*

Love Lost

Never take what you have for granted,
because in the slightest second it could be gone.
The look on your face
The hurt in your eyes
The distraught in your voice
I'll never forget,
the pain I caused. I take the blame,
but it's a shame.
What seemed forever, ended too soon
And now I'm left with an empty wound.
Something that can't be healed
I want every bit of your heart back
I know you feel the pain
That empty expression
Where you thought love stood
I'd give anything just to be called yours again
"It's not going to be easy,
it's going to be really hard,
but that's what I want,
you and me,
every day, forever"

TaKirra Thompson, Grade 10
Southern Nash Sr High School, NC

Slam

Greg "Slam" was good at basketball.
He was 6'4" —
Slam also had...the moves, the eyes, the heart...

But, he didn't have the grades.
He may not get to play.

Slam was very scared.
He could not sleep at night.
So, he better get his grades up soon...

He did not have the best temper.

Slam could go really far in basketball...
But he needed to get his grades up...
So Greg was *going one on one to win his future.*

It was the championship game...
they were filming it for colleges to see.
Slam was nervous about the game.
They won!

Alexis Maney, Grade 10
Cherokee High School, NC

Legends Remembered and Unforgotten

Under the lights,
every Friday.
The burning in my stomach,
the bond of our brotherhood.
The high spike in our emotion, opponents coming to kill our buzz.
Our resistance as a stubborn team,
willing to fight back till the clock hits 0:00 of the 4th.
The sureness of having the next person,
beside you ready to fight so that we will be victorious.
The crowd screaming and dancing,
waiting on the W.
We take care of business as a team,
then we receive congratulations,
and go home.
Why we play this dangerous game,
we do because of the love.
Our love for the game,
having fun,
and people that support us,
keep us out there every Friday night,
looking for a win.

Christian Kelly, Grade 11
Germantown High School, TN

Fall

The many colorful leaves fall to the ground
The ground is covered in many colors
Peacefully they keep falling as fall arrives
This is the sign, the sign of a peaceful fall.

Malia Morris, Grade 10
Union County High School, TN

Night Fall

When I fell into dismay through the night,
When everything left in the dark in June,
I lost all sight in one month so he came
When I fell into dismay through the night.

Samantha Brown, Grade 10
Union County High School, TN

A Lesson Learned

Somewhere between the stars twinkling brightly
And the morning chirping of a bird
Is a story spoken softly
And a moral not well heard

The truest tragedy that comes to last
Is hearing tomorrow's treacherous word
Or the indulgent recording of the past
Before today's wisdom is referred

Hiding behind all the pettiness,
A cloak that keeps it well concealed,
It remains there none the less
Just waiting to be revealed

But for those who are closely listening
The cloak is no obstruction
They can see it clearly glistening
They give the present moment no reduction

Visible to blindness, audible to deafness
Hidden only when the true moment is not discerned
It leads to a transcendent egress
That lesson, there, to be learned

Soorya Kumar, Grade 12
William G Enloe High School, NC

Vuvuzela

Vuvuzela,
I appreciate your support.
Your ceaseless hum never leaves me without encouragement,
a constant reminder of your persistent support.
Your color, design, shape, and sound,
all an excellent expression of your culture and succor.
Love, a fellow fan.

Vuvuzela,
Sorry to admit,
but I'm starting to wonder why you won't stop.
I understand you want your team to win,
believe me, I do too, sometimes enough is enough.
Sincerely, a fellow fan.

Vuvuzela,
This can't work out.
I appreciate your loyalty so far, but this is *too* much.
Your ever-present hum hasn't gone away,
my ears are begging for a break,
I am on the verge of tears.
I believe it's time for us to go separate ways.
Signed, a former fan.

Jeremy Griffin, Grade 10
Germantown High School, TN

A BBQ Story Medium-Rare

It was a few nights into the month of July
And I bid my mother a short goodbye
I went out to the porch
With matches and a torch
To barbecue chicken under the night sky

As I set up my sister stopped to ask
If she could go light the natural gas
I refused her seeking
But methane was leaking
Ignition burned me and my poor lass

I returned to the porch, my arm in ice to heal
A first degree burn wasn't too big of a deal
But another painful burn I got
Seeing if the meat was too hot
And, all of a sudden, charring my finger on scalding steel

Soon my barbecue chicken was adorning
Yet a buzzing sound came as a warning
From above I did see
A new, big hive of bees
Would I live to wake up the next morning?

Tahsin Zaman, Grade 12
William G Enloe High School, NC

Seasons Changing

Here she is sitting by the water in spring
The birds up above her chirp and sing
She looks at the trees that just got back their leaves
Flowers come up from the winter thieves

Now on the dock the sun scorches her cheeks
Nimble creatures running about, she seeks
The fish are out, swimming with grace and agility
New animals are born, without any stability

While leaning over the water, sitting on the wood
She wants to stop time, if only she could
The colorful leaves float off down the stream
To her, this all feels like a dream

Huddle by the ice, snow is falling
She wants to leave, she hears them calling
White collects on her shoulders, chilling her skin
Everything has taken shelter, asleep in their den

The seasons keep on moving no matter what
This is why you must not give in
Everything happens for a reason

Kara Giltner, Grade 10
Coffee County Central High School, TN

The Word

Uttered with such great difficulty, wondering why you must.
Like a child who won't share, they simply won't adjust.
So many feelings, bursting from inside you.
Hello? Can you help me? NO. That I cannot do.
For some this one word, beckons no trouble.
A basic formality. No need to worry double.
But for many others, the pain is unbearable.
Like needles pricking your insides, sometimes not repairable.
My lips refuse to open. They do not wish to part.
I know I'm wasting time. My poor breaking heart.
So much left to say. No idea what to do.
The word is getting nearer. Do you feel it too?
I gape in utter disbelief as I realize what's coming.
It's like a lion chasing after me, and I cannot stop running.
Wondering why this troublesome word, this one word I cannot try.
Too quick the time has come.
Goodbye.

Giannina Rokvic, Grade 10
Notre Dame Academy, KY

A Little Faith

It's like that butterfly, that someone has touched its wing,
like a game of baseball, where you strike out with every swing,
like when you try so hard, and nothing turns out right,
like when you try to conquer your battle, but still lose the fight,
like having that "best friend," trusting them with your all,
but them turning around, and just watching you fall,
like the little kid on the playground, who never gets to play,
sometimes you just wish, superman would come and save the day,
but maybe one day, the butterflies wing will mend,
and the strikeout streak, will finally end,
your trying one day, will lead you to succeed,
when in reality, confidence is all you need,
you got a better strategy, and won your fight,
and your real best friend, was in plain sight,
the little boy grew up big and strong,
and you realize you just needed a little faith,
and not superman all along.

Britiney Storms, Grade 11
Preston High School, WV

Midday Rainbow

A lucent palate of hues strokes the sky with a smile.
The effortless arc of color caresses with mysterious guile.
It romances with a countless beauty in endless shades.
The arch embraces with fluid tinges yet to fade.
Swords of green frolic below in tugs of exhale
An ocean of tears trickles down its vertical trail.
Beaming amidst the suspended sea is the sun.
His glimmers tackling through, not to be outdone.
Soon, the mist of crystals ceases.
The luminary's glare decreases.
The grin of inks evaporates.
It'll reply when sphere and sprinkles accommodate.

Hayley Farless, Grade 10
Coffee County Central High School, TN

Nana Who

Nana who's smile lights up the world
is the color yellow
who is a manicure and a flower dress
who calls me beautiful
and thinks I'm sweet
who's voice is so soft and peaceful
is as loving as a heart
Smells like baby lotion
who is a shopping mall and a bottle of perfume
who sings like a bird
And is my angel necklace
who has hair as soft as a feather
who talks so calm and gentle
who is never hardly here
that I wish I could see more
than three times a year
oh how I miss and love
My nana, dear

Alesia Dingess, Grade 10
Spring Valley High School, WV

My Hero

When I look at what means the most to me,
I don't have to look very far to see
That my dearest treasure by far
Is someone who lives right here where we are.

She always makes sure that I have what I need,
She teachers me kindness through word and deed,
She makes sure that I never have to worry,
And when I need her she comes in a hurry.

She knows how to be my coach and my friend,
And I know she is with me to the very end.
I know she's not perfect, but that's her greatest feature,
She's my hero, my friend, my guide and my teacher.

Courtney Eaton, Grade 10
Coffee County Central High School, TN

Blinding Lies

Your radiant light traps the innocent.
Your searing warmth burns those you're closest to.
You blind me to all else and won't relent.
Sun block can't cloak my eyes from all you do.
You are a star, however malignant.
Your false love instilled addiction in me,
My ray of hope, I was so ignorant.
When you flung me aside, I could then see.
You forever tanned my once white-skinned mind.
Your worthless intrigue I tried not to crave.
Engrossed with your light, I mistook your kind.
Disguised as the Sun, you seemed to be brave.
Weak moon! You are no prince, you are just night.
How could you be the sun, you reflect light.

Morgan Dobbins, Grade 11
Germantown High School, TN

For the Soldiers

Is it sad what we write in poems and books
I wrote this one for those at war
Respecting their honor and nothing more

Aren't they something
Masking their face with paint and coal
Hiding their honor,
hiding their soul

Take a good look at what honors the pledge
the great, the brave, the "I want you!"

Shifting focus from family to armor,
Saving their love for nothing but a charmer

It's hard to fight and think of home
Shooting down memories that stick inside em'

Is it sad what we read in poems and books
In blogs and memoirs. . . just take a look at those in war
What about memories. . . this is nothing more.

Tommy Lofgren, Grade 10
Wilkes Early College High School, NC

The Lasting Breeze

The wind, so certain and with no shame
So confident that it will remain
It is like a two-faced monster
One moment a gentle breeze
The next, a furious storm
But then it leaves as quickly as it came

Without warning, it will suddenly gust
Blowing away the debris and dust
Fluid, untouched and free
Unseen, but felt
Continuing to blow it must

Against the enemy, it inflicts pain
So confident it will remain
Because it made a promise
To save all that it loves
Through all of the toil and blame

And so the wind blows, on and on and on
Blowing, revealing your path, and suddenly it's gone.

Elizabeth Sakowski, Grade 12
William G Enloe High School, NC

Intimidator

It is a hot and glorious Sunday,
A black Chevy flies almost like a dart.
He makes all of the other drivers pay,
Intimidator: thy name is Earnhardt!

Mark Terrones, Grade 10
Union County High School, TN

Transformation

Once locked in a steel cage box
Separated from the world
Was a girl
Now a woman
Able to retrogress and remember her past
Of pain, anger and defeat
That girl averse to accepting her past
Or changing her future
That girl willing to alienate the present
Excepting the world as her adversary
That girl too ignorant to realize
That her stay in that hell hole was momentary
That girl once nonchalant and invulnerable
Now felt expunged
With her agony perpetuated
Searching for redress
Praying from sun down, to sun set
That one day she'd be set free
That girl
Now a woman
I can today say was me

Crystal Hart-Williams, Grade 12
Wakefield High School, NC

Where I'm From

I'm from Nowhere,
From "Nowhere" as in Somewhere,
Somewhere full of clothes lining my bed.
Plates, bowls, and bottles, food long since gone.
I'm from my room — my sanctuary.
I'm from the place that's mine alone,
Where I close out the world,
I close out problems,
And I close out "them."
Where I'm from I can lay and be still
To call upon the thoughts, those thoughts,
The thoughts covered in the motions,
The motions of everyday activity.
The simple wooden walls hold secrets.
They try to sneak through the door,
But are stopped dead in their tracks.
The room aches of smoke, and my attempt to cover it up.
One day my room will move.
My sanctuary will be established far away
But will it be far enough?
Far enough for the secrets not to follow?

Drew Dacus, Grade 11
Germantown High School, TN

Free at Last

People worry about heaven and hell.
If you find Jesus, then the worries pass.
When the time comes to go, no one can tell,
But I know we will all be free at last.

Seth Norris, Grade 10
Union County High School, TN

Glimpsing Neverland

Fairy lights floating
in the fog
dancing
laughing
all night long.

While I sit here
dazed
stuck on the ground
able to hear that sweet melodious sound

Dawn's approaching
back to the hollow hills they go
leaving the faintest trace of a glow

Awestruck and tearful
I made my way home
having glimpsed the place
where I truly belong.

Tyler Sell, Grade 12
Preston High School, WV

Cramming

You sit
cross-legged
on the square brick floor.
Your hair is awry,
your shoes, untied.
Your face contorts
with concentration.
You whip the pages
of your overweight textbook,
246, 328, 417.
What's up?
I ask.
Your answer —
History exam,
next period.

Emily Assaley, Grade 11
St Joseph Central Catholic High School, WV

Tides

I belong to the constant ocean.
Coastal storms
shaping coastlines.
Crashing waves
making driftwood.
Lighthouse beacons
guiding sailors home.
Smooth sands
polishing stones.
Salty wind
moving seawater.
I belong to the constant ocean.

Chynna Bradford, Grade 10
Coffee County Central High School, TN

Fall

The walls around his heart grew year after year
He was locked away, untouchable. No one could reach his fragile heart,
Because this boy felt no more; What's the point of letting someone in?
When they abuse the trust you give.
Why should he open up?
This world doesn't deserve his love.
He had reasons to close his feelings off
After the world dealt him a crappy hand,
This boy had reasons to be an angry kid.
Yes I've tried to find my way to your heart,
But you shut me out when I get too close.
You open up for a second, showing only a glimpse of you;
Then you close up, afraid to show the truth.
I see your pain, won't you let me in?
I won't abuse the love you give, and I won't take for granted your trust.
Oh, I will save you now. I'll hold you when you're broken.
And I'll love you every day, 'til forever.
But he won't let me in because he's scared.
Walls, his walls can't be broken down; Walls too strong to get through.
The walls, your walls, block me from you.
But I'll wait for the day when your walls fall like Jericho.

Terrean Hudson, Grade 12
Providence Academy, TN

Social Acceptance

Is the homeless man unaware of his ascetic ways?
Does he not realize that not possessing worldly things,
Will in fact make him a better person?
Better than most of us any ways.
And that lonely war veteran,
With post traumatic stress syndrome.
Wandering on the side of the highway
With a sign reading "God Bless America."
Doesn't realize that America made him lonely and mentally ill.
And the people driving by mention how he's a trooper.
And say how sorry they feel for him and the homeless man on the next street.
But they never stop to give them praise.
They're too afraid.
They lock their doors and watch with apathy.
So is the homeless man really unaware?
Or does he just choose to not be "socially accepted?"

Madison Saunders, Grade 12
William G Enloe High School, NC

Nana

Reminiscing in her rocking chair,
What once was golden is now snow white hair.
Her countenance reveals the wisdom of her many years;
The wrinkles on her face long ago began to appear.
Her scent a sweet blend of lavender and mint,
For her grandchildren, a perfume that sparks memories of days spent.
She fondly recalls the many days of her past.
No regrets, no misgivings,
Simply cherishing in her heart the imprint she has made for generations to last.

Emily Grace Simmons, Grade 10
Coffee County Central High School, TN

Bunny Funny

There once was a big fat bunny,
Who had lots and lots of money,
We stole his cash,
And made the dash,
He did not find this too funny.

But then out popped a bear,
Who gave us quite a scare,
He robbed our loot,
Chased us off to boot,
Then returned back to his lair.

The lesson here remains,
Stealing yields no gains,
The bear returned the dosh,
With the bunny he did josh,
"I sure caused them some pains."

Jeremy He, Grade 12
Enloe High School, NC

Our Departure

His eyes glow like the midnight moon...
His smile is as wide as the ocean,
While his boots are the beat of my heart.
I wonder...
And think to myself,
Is he thinking of me too?
I count his eyelashes as we sit in class...
His voice is a lullaby in my heart and mind.
They call him "Johnny Cash"
I kiss him as we come to our departure...
He whispers in my ear, "I love you."
I whisper in his ear...
I wanna love like Johnny and June.
...And we come to our departure.

Ricki Medford, Grade 11
Cherokee High School, NC

I Am

worn toms
leather jacket
dark coffee

a liar
an artist
an agnostic

strange
fine
nocturnal

a teenager
who recently found out everything
and wants to get away from it all

Tori LaMendola, Grade 12
Campbell County High School, KY

A Different Kind of Fairy Tale

This is the kind of fairy tale where the dragon is the hero,
and "Prince Charming" is the antagonist;
the kind of story where the princess is just a normal girl,
and doesn't live happily ever after.
She dies just like every other human,
but the dragon continues to live —
long after the princess has breathed her last,
to leave the dragon forever sad and lonely,
and no woman can ever come close to the sweet, kindhearted princess,
to whom he left his heart long ago.
There's always another girl,
another "knight in shining armor"
come to "slay the dragon" and to "rescue his damsel in distress,"
but the knight always dies,
and the princess always dies or leaves eventually, too,
and he always wonders why he falls for another girl
and another storybook routine.
Is it because he's too nice?
Is it because he misses his beautiful lady?
Or is it because he thinks that if he lives a good life
he will see her again, and finally, actually live happily ever after?

Rachel Lewis, Grade 11
Centennial High School, TN

Bright Spots

It was an eerie sight —
Just one yellow spot.
Then it was a red blot,
Then there was a bluish dot.
Wherever I gazed
Or wherever I gandered
The little bright spot would not vanish.
When I looked to the left it slivered to the left corner of my peripheral vision.
Then to the right I glanced but it was too quick.
Even when I closed my eyes completely it went in my head.
It simply would not go away; it filled me with dread.
Then it multiplied into another shiny eye shiner.
When I tried to slay the beast my sight was gone completely.
Finally I had it figured out the beast had tried to cheat me.
Now that it was over, now that it was done
The colorful creature had stalked into my other eye,
Ready for some fun.

Austin Claxton, Grade 11
Lynn Camp High School, KY

Poems

They are: unique butterflies, little girls, teenagers kneeling in prayer, peace and harmony,
waves at night, feeling loved yet alone, effortless dancing,
good music, and driving rain.
They are desperate and futile attempts to:
preserve the astounding beauty of a simple moment,
be creative,
and belong to the filthy and gorgeous world of: rock stars, hikers, hippies, and children
who see the world through the eyes of a poem.

Raegan Johnson, Grade 10
Girls Preparatory School, TN

Truthful Sayings

People say they know me,
People say lies.
People say to trust them,
People say what they don't mean.
People say I can't think,
People say hurtful things.
People say what's on their mind,
People say what they think.
People don't monitor,
People don't think before they speak.

But what do I say?

I say the truth,
I say what you need to hear.
I say I'll never hurt you,
I say what I mean.
Live life as if you'll die tomorrow,
Treat others as if you'll live forever.
That is what I'll always say,
That is what I'll always do.

Kimberly Watson, Grade 10
Westchester Country Day School, NC

Untitled

I feel lost and confused
Why do I feel this way?
I want to stop hurting
But I feel as if this pain is forever
I can't stop, I want to stop
I'm screaming inside
But on the outside all you
See is a girl
Who hardly does anything
Who's been through so much hurt
But how do I make sense of it all?
It's too much to think about
I want to crawl into a ball and cry
But I want
I want to laugh and smile
Just I can't
It's like I'm stuck in reverse
Living the past over and over again
Trying to move forward
I believe that all I can do is try
'Cause trying is believing

Jordan Toineeta, Grade 11
Cherokee High School, NC

Clouds

Clouds high in the sky;
While, high, passing by the sun.
Where are they going?

Sarah Atkins, Grade 10
Union County High School, TN

Who Am I?

Why don't they understand? Why can't they see what they could have?
Do they not know what He'll say when before Him they stand?
Why don't they grasp what the cost will be?

I fear those I love will forever be blind;
The fear that they are not part of the elect who will live with Christ forever,
And I'll be in Paradise without them.

How can you do this Almighty God?
How can you leave those You claim to love, to burn forever without You?
You say You love them, but how can You?

I can't even fathom eternity without them;
Those who I would die for, alone in damnation; I pray and I pray, for them to see,
But am I hindering them by my own impure prayers?

God, I pray, save their souls; is there anything I can do?
I know I could love You more wholly and purely,
Please help me to let You shine through.

I know Your love is so pure and lovely; but how, oh Creator, can you do this to me?
Sometimes my intentions are selfish,
But my heart aches for their dark souls.

Still I question Your love, how can this be?
Rebuke me, my Lord, to forever ask,
"Who are you, oh man, to question God?"

Emily Tumlin, Grade 11
Providence Academy, TN

Four the Trees

From branches naked and forlorn, perfumes diffuse and stars are born.
In them stands a painting, complex, yet simple be.
The stars then wink a fading light, and o'er the canvas make their flight,
Gently brush the cheek, and through the wind they flee;
Bloom in short, and then they leave.

Color flies away from sight, a monochrome bows polite,
A song it sings, a silent movement for the sweltering rays.
Full arms stretched out proud, for the earth a cool light cloud,
Through shriveling winds and drought it stays;
Full of life, but now ablaze.

An artist's palette lit on fire, alit with life, love and desire,
The tragedy begins warm, but ends in cold death's sleep.
Stings so crisp it does surprise, sleeping beauty's sneaky guise,
Into a desert the stage scene does creep;
Arms once full, none it can keep.

For now, now the slate is clean, one so new, clear, and sheen
Choreographed inside the heart, alive it will remain.
Through a hard time it must survive, but soon the dance will be alive,
For only so long it can keep this silent reign;
A measure of rest, to bloom again.

Jasmin Huang, Grade 12
William G Enloe High School, NC

Stormy Night

Pillow under my head,
Darkness surrounds my bed.
Lightning as my light,
Thunder as my lullaby,
It all seems so much greater than you or I.

Tonight is my night to fly.
Tonight is the night of my very last goodbye.
As the thunder roars and the lightning strikes,
With the angels I'll fly high.

But even in the night sky,
They will see these broken wings of mine.
Then down I will fly.

So here in my bed I lie,
Until the next storm passes me by.

Michaela Wilson, Grade 10
David Crockett High School, TN

Color Guard

A symphony of colors spinning through the air,
glitter sparkling in my hair.
The slap of the rifle strap the snap of a flag,
stepping fast no time to lag.

Dancing to the music with confidence and grace,
an excited smile is on my face.
I feel the energy of the crowd,
I hear the band playing loud!

The applause is a welcome sound,
as I float back to the ground.
My life is the guard it's where I belong,
from the first toss to the last note of the song.

Savanna Starnes, Grade 10
East Rowan High School, NC

PM AM

i have been running since the A.M.
i want my rest, i need my rest
i am being consumed by the darkness that chases me
i've got to keep moving
to escape a fate i am not yet ready to face
throat burning
legs are screaming out in anguish
i want my rest, i need my rest
i am not where i am supposed to be
i think of my mother, in all her kindness
to escape a fate i am not yet ready to face
i miss you so much it hurts
i miss me so much it hurts
i want my rest, i need my rest

Shania Conner, Grade 11
Cooper High School, KY

You're a Puppet

What is it that claims you,
Is it the tight grip of that few.
Sometimes I swear you're controlled like a puppet,
Every movement by a string of another who loves it.

Always tamed by the hands of another,
Because you can't keep calm so why bother.
Your emotions are fake and never-ending,
Seem like a total different person my darling.

It sucks because I really did care,
But now I'm just thinking that it's not fair.
I thought you were a great person,
Till you showed the strings which always worsened.

Always wondered why you changed your feelings,
Left me somewhere because you said you had a meeting.
Now I know it was a time to control yourself,
Never should you fall in love for myself.

There was no wonder why you were so perfect,
You were fake and smartly picked.
Oh what a fool I was in all of it,
But you had me tricked a tad bit.

Hannah Gresham, Grade 10
Halls High School, TN

Free

My soul is not for sale,
it's yearning to be free.
It does not like your
style, or ideology.

Our life to live for Capitol's sake,
has robbed us of our zeal.
We sneak to live, our lives, at stake,
we beg, we borrow, we steal.

The games we play are for keeps,
and full of consequence.
Some live, some die, some horribly,
without fanfare or significance.

Our movements, our thoughts, and our words,
the Capitol sought to seize.
With the use of jabber jay,
to destroy us if they please.

Enslave me, control me,
if that's my destiny.
But my soul is not for sale,
it's yearning to be free.

Maddie Seiter, Grade 10
Notre Dame Academy, KY

Where I'm From

I am from smudgy, petroleum-infused plastic,
from Shock chlorine tablets in domestic pools and ancient Simpson Papers
I am from the blurry memory of a six-year-old's home, short and stout, the house in the center of Centerville, with its white, odoriferous carpet leaving its heavy scent clinging to anything and everything.
I am from the spiders and the nightmares they leave,
the algae in all water, from its spotty, green outside, to its soft, living inside.

I'm from Turkey Day in Wisconsin and the "Are you Canadian?" accent,
from Gaydoses and Brian.
I'm from the opinionated and strong-willed,
from "Because I said so" and "Don't butt in."

From when "Captain Morgan paid Aunt Terry another visit tonight," she never could hold her liquor.
From the four severed finger stumps my ex-electrician grandfather won't be using again.

I am from the fresh, crisp scrapbooks constructed in excess time by Aunt Barb and Aunt Jay,
the pictures of cousins with majors inscribed beneath, photos of grandparents, and graduation pictures of my parents. Time and money wasted some would say. But I disagree, for family memories should be savored.

I am from preserved family memories.

Bennett Chappell, Grade 11
Germantown High School, TN

Genius Trapped

Words, feelings, visions, dreams
All trapped in the mind of a young poet
Perceptions too great for an adolescent to handle
Emotions expressed in a way not initially intended
Actions comprehended as evil but meant to be helpful
A wisdom no youth can bear
Usually resulting in furious attacks and continuous tears
Pressure builds with no hope for relief
Destruction is inevitable. The future is uncertain. Fate is inescapable.
A message designed to catalyze the view of the nations
A message encrypted in adolescent experiences, feelings of being misunderstood, and harsh, critical judgment
Ambiguous visions help to clutter the mind
Choices are crucial; Which path to take?
The long, narrow road of righteousness? Or the easy, flashy street of destruction?
A split begins to take place due to the lack of decision
One side is erudite, wise, and expressive, the other foolish and naive
Both have equal pull and soon the individual as a whole begins to crash
Neither side wins, all lose
The internal conflict remains and the cycle repeats itself continuously
There is no rescue, no salvation
Thus, I am still a genius trapped

Karena Everett, Grade 10
Kirby High School, TN

Rain

Looking through the window, I see the rainfall; I see the damage it makes, all the love it washes away.
It is like the tears we cry that fall upon thy cheeks, wiping them away, making a clean slate.
The rain makes most sad but I am not like few, when I see the rain it reminds me of you.

Autumn Dye, Grade 12
Moore County High School, TN

From All Things Past

I'm from toy cars
From brightly colored converse and unkempt Crayola crayons
I am from the home of Elvis Presley and Mud Island on the mighty Mississippi
Falling asleep listening to ocean waves crash gently upon the beach at midnight
I am from the gum balls
Fallen from the trees in the forest behind our apartment I collected for my mother
I'm from camping trips every summer and loud, drunk laughter
From Great Aunt Petra and Grandma Koceja
From it's only a game and treat others how you would want to be treated
I'm from being baptized Lutheran as an infant to never attending church at all
I'm from Memphis, Tennessee
Macaroni and cheese and peanut butter and jelly sandwiches
From grandpa and grandma meeting over ice cream on a summers day while he played an accordion
Dad growing up just a small town country boy working hard for his pay
Under my unmade bed in a small wooden box I made at the age of eight
Reminiscences of loved ones passed
And childhood memories that will forever be preserved but never relived
Smiles created from looking back
And tears from missing how great things once were
But loving every second of it while knowing you would never change a thing

Ashley Grubb, Grade 11
Germantown High School, TN

Where I'm From

I am from gently used Ticonderoga pencils,
From Corky's BBQ sandwiches and crushed Coca-Cola cans,
I am from the house with red hard-wood floors and beige walls,
Transforming into a wintery wonderland of lights and snow during Yuletide.
I am from the deciduous trees that line the backpacking trails,
The poison oak that seeks to impede unknowing hikers braving the dense forests.

I am from the warm M&M cookies beckoning weary students after their first day
And wittiness together with insight.
I'm from the thirty minutes late to church and snap-happy photographers,
From He was pierced for our transgressions and always do your best.

From my *a-cun-cun*, my Chinese grandfather who spoke little English, with whom I
Traded high fives for saltine crackers.
From my grandmother whose sweet tea, potato casserole, and dressing can sate any
Hungry soul on Thanksgiving.

I am from hard bound scrapbooks gloriously decorated to commemorate past joys,
Meticulously designed and displayed to showcase creativity and connectedness.
I am from portrait upon portrait, tacit evidence of change and continuity.

Eric Ruleman, Grade 11
Germantown High School, TN

Flowers

The flowers smell like perfume,
The sweet scent that fills the room.
They are as pretty as a picture,
Lovely by themselves or as a mixture.
They are one of the many gifts God has made,
The beauty they have will never fade.

LeAnna Chambers, Grade 11
Seymour Community Christian School, TN

The Storm

The Spartan looked down the mountain below
The storm had passed but the flood still raged on
What they were dealing with, no one did know
A fog came down from the flood which was gone.

Danny Morrow, Grade 10
Union County High School, TN

Changed for Good

I hurt, I laugh so much
I am soaked, stung by tears
I lost something and don't know when to find it
Singing on the subways, discovering harmonies
Four natives
Three not too far
Two from the South
And one across the world
Brought together by a dream
No one else could understand
Remembering the brain power
In a spoonful of chocolate peanut butter ice cream
Remembering the last hug
And how you never thought it would end
Remembering the applause
When you showed your product
Remembering the sparkly blue nail polish
You bought when you got stuck in the rain
Remembering and never forgetting
New York City; three weeks in a camp
And changed for good

Zoe Zelonky, Grade 11
Germantown High School, TN

Come In, Come In

Welcome, ghosts
Am I your current host?
I've been expecting you
Ready for you to flow through
Come in, come in
Let the loneliness begin
Take over my eyes
So no one will see my desperate cries
Smash my heart
It's already torn apart
Break me already
Before everything gets steady
Am I taking this well?
Or is my soul about to swell?
Where's the rest of me?
Where's the fire within me?
Oh, it has run away with you
Now what am I supposed to do?
Somehow, some way, the loneliness will mend
And in a twisted way, the pain will end

Jenna Anthony, Grade 11
Centennial High School, TN

Coalesce

Rise, effervescent
through caverns and atolls do
bubbles meet their fate.

Alex You, Grade 12
William G Enloe High School, NC

The Amazing Gift

The Amazing Gift on Christmas Day,
Is not the ornaments and tinsels hanging on the tree
Or the snowflakes that come to the ground.
More than the excited children.
It's not having a lot of presents,
The joy and moments that we share.
Not the pretty wrapping or shiny bows.
It makes my heart jump with peace and joy,
That will give my soul a lift!
What can possibly be the most amazing gift?
But in our hearts there is a glow
When we think about Jesus' birth
And the purpose for Him to be on Earth.
He came to save mankind from sin
As shepherds watched their flocks by night,
Angels came to Earth that night,
Announce the birth of Christ Jesus
Sweetly sang praise to God
Magi came to give gifts to the Savior
Let us all praise God in unison!

Therese Poole, Grade 10
Holy Angels Academy, KY

Senior Blues

The panic of college life draws near
Like a prison school is escape proof
Oh please let graduation come soon
But months are left, tests to take

No sleep for many nights
I've become an overworked computer
Letters and keys are lost on a blank screen
How can my fingers still be moving
When months are left, tests to take

Deadlines, pop tests, and time crunch
The smelly feet and smacking of lips
Only push me to the edge of sanity
Because months are left, tests to take

Freedom calls as the end comes near
The sun burns red in the year's final hours
Oh wait, it was only a dream, calculus rolls on
Still months are left, tests to take

Jared Dmiszewicki, Grade 12
William G Enloe High School, NC

To Love, and to Lose

Now I know that to
Love also means to lose, and
I am so grateful.

Rachel Brown, Grade 11
Bearden High School, TN

The Death of Perfection

Speak to me my Sleeping Beauty
Come to life again
Fill this space with your carefree laugh
Prove this isn't the end
Touch my face my radiant angel
Make your frozen heart beat
Return the joy to this world of mine
Fill this winter with heat
Hold my hand my constant daydream
Rise again and walk
Motivate this world to turn
Become once more my rock
Brush my skin my darling flower
Open your tightly shut eyes
Keep my lonely heart fast beating
Brighten these dark skies
Kiss my lips my perfect ending
Break the seal of death
Tell me this coffin is a lie
Affirm it with your breath

Alyssa Palmer, Grade 12
Havelock High School, NC

Peaceful

Cherry blossoms bloom
In the late spring day.
A cool wind blows
And the trees begin to sway.
The clouds drift slowly
Across the blue sky
Like cotton candy puffs
In a child's lullaby.
The smell of the flowers
Is rich in the air;
Its sweet fragrance blossoms
A blush on the fair
Skin of the young
Who play all day
And soak in the sun
As if to store it away.

Nichole Lay, Grade 10
Havelock High School, NC

Twin Sisters

Two faces and two hands to clean.
Two heartaches to help when they're teens.
Two tempers to avoid with grins.
Double trouble when blessed with twins.

Best friends by choice sisters by birth.
Thank heavens being born on Earth.
Like the sign of Gemini love
They're the best of all from above.

Samantha Wilms, Grade 10
Spring Valley High School, WV

Ode to Promises

The Promises we made as children
running through fields of our vivid imaginations and
losing ourselves in the summer sun.
Those secret time bombs that littered our youth and our dreams.
Seeming like nonsense, to those on the outside.
They thought they knew the outcome.
They thought they were the only ones that could see the difference.
Though we seemed to pay them no kind of attention,
We knew.
Like an unexpected storm, it smashed itself in front of our faces.
Blinding us...but at the same time making us see the difference.
Now those long hot days, of playing in the fields,
seems like another life I never lived.
Those sacred gifts,
that bounded our everlasting friendship together...are gone.
The memories wiped away, like the history of a piece of land after a war.
So I ask you, my far away friend,
Will we Recover?
Will our bruises ever mend?
Or will our promises be left broken until all...
Ends.

Kimbra McCargo, Grade 12
Enloe High School, NC

If You Only Knew

If you only knew what it meant the way I look at you when you walk past me,
I imagining a world where we understand each other and our hearts meet,
A place where we see eye to eye, without even having to try,
Our feelings and emotions combined, as if we could read each other's minds,
With a missing piece, my heart bleeds,
And I wonder, are you the one to make it complete?

...Ha!...some fantasy...dream...

Many have asked this question a million times,
I mean, I don't want to be a nickel chasing a dime,
Life gave me lemons, but I like limes,
So would it kill to let this question shine?
WHY???
Do all the good ones have to be taken?
Every time I see you with her, my heart becomes shaken,
Disappointed, that I couldn't have you first,
Well since it's too late, may your friendship quench my thirst?
Well I don't know if you're in love, but if so,
Do you think your heart is capable of loving me too?
...Boy If You Only Knew...

Tiara Dickerson, Grade 10
Overton High School, TN

Southern Dependence

I came from a creek bed's
generous and capable hands in a
land where the flowers bloom
and the ice consumes the lifeless
buds spawned late.
Where the trees are the brewers
and their blend is an intoxicating
and delightful smell
which forever reminds people
of where they are.
This is the place where
everyone knows everyone
from the past or the present;
from the owner to his dog.
I came from a creek bed's
generous and capable hands
from which I might leave,
but to which I will
most definitely return.

Kurtis Smith, Grade 11
Oak Ridge High School, TN

Fear for It

I'm in love with grief.
Confessing my soul to it.
Negative thoughts cloud my mind
She tried to help, but
It didn't do any good.
What's so wrong for falling too hard for the unpleasant things in life?
Why must the innocent become scolded for its beauty?
No wrong deserves this extent of its mankind.
It's swallowed me whole,
Tightening its grip against my soul.
Forcing the cold air to become its breath.
How can someone keep a hold of it when it flies freely through the air?
Humans breathe it into our systems
Every day and within every second,
It consumes a life without
Regret.
Its twisted fate is enough to
Make you want to curl into a ball.
It harasses me every day.

Courtney Brooks, Grade 11
Western Harnett High School, NC

My Window to the Soul

My window to the soul is open,
for everyone to see,
for you to look inside my mind,
and read through inside of me.
My window to the soul is open,
waiting for the chance,
to show somebody who I am,
to make my spirit dance.
My window to the soul is open,
for you to read my mind,
but right now I warn you,
you never know what you might find.
My window to the soul is open,
to understand the lies.
Just take a look and read in them,
my bright and gossiping eyes

Harley Watters, Grade 10
Coffee County Central High School, TN

Westward Bound

With the body of a goddess and a voice of an angel you are most divine,
Beautiful girl, if I was lucky enough to know you better, I would make you mine,
The stars in the sky aren't as bright as the twinkling stars in your eyes,
I want to spend more time with you girl because in your presence time flies,
To say that you were anything other then amazing would be a fallacy,
And to any who does say it, I'll make sure they know of their blasphemy,
As seasons change and time passes, only will my love grow for you,
It's as if my life's a play and all this time you've been off stage just waiting for your cue,
It has to be that this is where my life has been heading,
The paths I have followed and choices I made have been creating this setting,
There is a song that says that everything is dust in the wind, but I say not my love,
For my love is as strong as steel and as pure as the feathers on a white dove,
I am simply saying that like in *The Princess Bride*, your wish is my command,
And like Romeo was to Juliet, I would love to be your man,
If I were to make the claim that I was the perfect guy, it would be a lie,
But heaven above knows that for you, I will most certainly try,
I will fight off the evils that will put my love to the test,
And I will finally reach this beautiful girl when I am heading for the West.

Richard Styers, Grade 12
William G Enloe High School, NC

The Holocaust

Born as a human
Thought of as a dog
Persecution's selected victim
Because of one man's ideologies

There was no escape
There was no hope
Nothing left up to fate

Born as a human
Only to die as a number

Nathan Henderson, Grade 10
Coffee County Central High School, TN

We Call It Night

I stare into
the midnight sky
as I wonder
what the future
holds, I begin
to notice the
beauty of stars
sparkling in
the coal abyss

Rachel Frye, Grade 12
Oak Ridge High School, TN

This Is the Life

This is the Life.
Waking before the crow,
Working from dawn 'till dusk,
Making little to nothing.

Weekends no longer free,
Work, work, work
Consuming my every thought.
This is truly the life.

Brandon Szakasits, Grade 12
Heide Trask High School, NC

The Perfect Game

The stadium appears with empty seats everywhere
Time stopped on the mount
Roars slowly become deafening,
Till silence roams in the ear

The ball in your hand
Becomes light as a feather
As it leaves your fingers,
The speed transforms into light

Motion becomes motionless
A thud diffuses throughout the air
A sudden yell stretches the sky
Strike three you're out of here

Time begins to speed up
Laughs, cries, and smiles burst the air
Dog pile on the mound
At the bottom I stand

A miracle has happened
As the scoreboard reads
Zero runs, zero hits, zero walks
And twenty-seven outs

Sujay Sahoo, Grade 12
William G Enloe High School, NC

Books

I'm Elizabeth Bennet, slowly falling for Mr. Darcy.
I'm Alex Cross, trying to solve my wife's murder.
I'm Harry Potter, going through seven years
of hunting down the one who killed my family.
These are the lives I live.

I'm Maximum Ride, leading my flock to save the world.
I'm Scout Finch, trying to understand life.
I'm Alexander Cold, dragged on an expedition to the Amazon
to help save my mother and the legends of the forest.
These are the lives I live.

I'm Frodo, looking to destroy the ring.
I'm Rukmani, reliving the hardships of my life.
I'm Matt, rejected from the world for what I am;
a clone for my master.
These are the lives I live.

I'm Jason, searching for the Golden Fleece.
I'm Jack Forman, trying to outsmart artificial intelligence.
I'm young Fiver, trying to save my warren
from the blood-soaked fields.
These are the lives I live.
These are the lives my books let me live.

Cassandra Meyle, Grade 11
First Flight High School, NC

My World

My world is a world of dance
a place where my troubles disappear
my sanctuary where I find peace and joy
and escape from anger and fear

A place where music and body become one
a refuge from life's storm
where my spirit shines like the sun

When I am in my world of dance
feeling so carefree
I express my emotions
and dance like no one's watching me

Dancing excludes me from my worries and strife
There is no fear in sight
dancing is the story of my life

Kelsey Nowlin, Grade 10
Coffee County Central High School, TN

Second Chance

You doin' all this talkin' like you want a second chance
But why should I give you that when I've already got a man
You never showed me love the way I needed you to
Yet and still, for some strange reason, I can't get enough of you
Even when I'm with him, I can still see your face
It's like when I was with you, I was in a happier place
Even though you never treated me the way you know you should
It was always by your side that I proudly stood
I can't lie to you and say that I've moved on
It's just that I thought the pain from you was gone
But here you are, yet again, asking for my love
Something that I'm not so sure that you're deserving of
But I'm only fooling myself if I don't do what my heart tells me to
Because I know that my heart will always belong to you

Cierra Paige, Grade 11
Overton High School, TN

Friendship

Friends are always there for you.
They know what you have been through.
Friends love and care.
They are the ones you have secrets to share.
Friends are like family but not by blood,
They will stand beside you even during a flood.
As years pass, we become closer and closer.
In the song of life, you are my composer.
To you I will be true,
Because life would not be worth living
If it wasn't for you.
Our friendship my dear friend,
We will have until the end.

Katherine Gable, Grade 10
Coffee County Central High School, TN

History Is For The Victors

All are weak, and cannot compare,
to the hate and anger within its stare.
Your penitent blade, and shattered shield,
they will rend the whole world bare.

A glowering darkness, now come to light,
is now and forever embraced as right.
The Devil's companion, the Reaper's sickle,
oh, cruel Fate! how thou art fickle:

To take the greatest heroes of yore,
to rip and twist them by the score.
Fallen angels, forgotten glories,
grasp upon their former stories.

Alas, true things must soon be twisted,
so damned is the nature of history.
To mangle the past of those defeated,
and partake in the spoils of victory.

Steven Richards, Grade 12
Heide Trask High School, NC

Eternal Lullaby

Old dirt path high in the woods.
Try to climb up but thought I never could.
Made it to the tip top with every stone in place.
Different names on the front even the birth date.
Flowers yellow, pink, and white scattered on the ground.
Every memory but never any sound.
Young and old they lay there still.
Never knowing how to feel.
The cold wind blows but they don't budge.
So lifeless there they cannot judge.
I sit and watch the memories dance.
Think back and wonder of their past romance.
The love loss and tears they used to cry.
They fall asleep to an eternal lullaby.

Jordyn Smith, Grade 10
Spring Valley High School, WV

Scars

Walking down that road was tough.
Unfriendly faces and angry words.
Feeling like all I could give was never enough.

Inhaling love, and exhaling hate.
The time will come to accept our fate.
To look our mistakes straight in the eyes.
To feel the love of Him, which never dies.

To live your life, so dead inside,
Is such a miserable thing.
Never feel, and do not speak of the undying pain,
The scars of the past leaving the deepest of stains.

Rachel Caudill, Grade 11
Lynn Camp High School, KY

Wrinkled Love

There is a reason
the clothes in my closet hang motionless.
Dresses that don't flatter anybody,
skirts that don't know how to live.

They are hard to clean, easy to get dirty.
Uncomfortable.
They are special, when in reality,
there is nothing extraordinary about them.

They have no memories
except quiet graveyards, fake smiling,
and people I don't really like.

If I were my clothes
I would not want to hang in the closet,
Dignified, beautiful, and jealous.

I would want thrown on the floor, stuffed in the dresser.
Smiling and blushing
with dirt stained memories,
wrinkled love.

Ferin Neff, Grade 11
St Joseph Central Catholic High School, WV

Death's Answer

Shall I compare thee to a knife through the heart?
Or a dagger, driven straight through the back?
A love once complete, now torn apart;
From a love so warm and bright, now cold and black.

My hope, my life with you I shared,
Completely lost to what could be;
Now I'm left alone and scared,
Like a ship in a storm lost at sea.

The promises you made, like lillies full of life,
But the finest of foliage must wither and die;
Promises of comfort through the misery and strife,
Now my heart shatters as I'm left alone to cry.

With six never ending feet between us, love, what can I say?
Death answers us in such peculiar, unexpected ways.

Rachael Waters, Grade 10
Loretto High School, TN

Gum

My feelings for you are like a piece of gum
Though hard and glitzy on the outside
After chewing a while your true feelings show
Though unlike gum your flavor never goes away
I just keep chewing and chewing
From many flavors there are to choose
But I'd always choose you.

John-David Gunther, Grade 10
Loretto High School, TN

My World, My Planet

My world, my planet,
You hold pulchritude in each step I take,
Vast oceans and open valleys,
Green trees and blue skies,
Colors of your face and rainbow halos.
Pioneers, oh pioneers, thank you!
I raise my heart for those who built these towns with bricks.
Respect the soldiers for who I will soon join,
Guns and bombs but my planet will withstand,
Smile for war and frown for the ones who rest,
Never will my planet be torn, thanks to the help of its fellow man.
Mighty ones yes you pioneers,
I learn from you to have Amor Patriae, to fight for peace.
Don't wait for better times work for better times,
Farewell to luck and hello to promise.
Whether with good grace or bad my planet shall rise.
Lost in a blunder victory is never absurd.
I direct never follow, while I breathe I hope.
I consider the end the end crowns the work.
I love my world, my planet!

Kwandre Croom, Grade 11
Knightdale High School, NC

Shall I Compare Thee to The Perfect Moment

Shall I compare thee to the perfect moment?
The feeling of absolute simplicity is what I feel.
People say it is crazy but I do not comment.
But my love for you makes me kneel.
Some haven't had the moment so they wait.
They wonder if it will ever fade.
You won't forget when it happens, it comes by fate.
My time has come like a raid.
Why am I unable to control my love?
It is something that you can't keep at bay.
It is like a flightless dove,
Which I never want to fly away.

Nothing will ever change from the start.
You will always have a spot in my heart.

Zak Kleinke, Grade 10
Loretto High School, TN

Beautiful

Have you ever sat outside at night,
In the silence and the darkness?
Listened to the quiet,
The world around you sleeping?
Only the songs of the crickets,
Only the whisper of the wind;
The stars above you glistening
Against a blanket of black.
Surrounded by all of these beautiful things,
There is only one thing in the world more beautiful;
That one thing is you.

Kelsey Adams, Grade 10
Coffee County Central High School, TN

Inspiration

Walk alone when no one will follow.
Take a deep breath when it's hard to swallow.
Breathe easy and clear. Every last trouble, every unwanted fear.
Unique is subsequent. Past irrelevant.
Slow down and walk tall.
When you stumble, know you won't fall.
Light at the end of the tunnel.
Even when your life is in a downward funnel.
Everything happens for a reason.
This too will pass, just like the season.
And when you feel lost.
Realize you're worth whatever the cost.
No matter how big or small. You stand skyscraper tall.
Your journey, your path.
Breathe in again and take a laugh.
When the going gets rough. And yes it is always tough.
Just know you are not alone.
Always waiting at the other end of that phone.
Rise as high as you can.
Even if it is alone that you stand.
Don't lose your way. Tomorrow is a new day.

Todd Bernstein, Grade 12
Knoxville Catholic High School, TN

A Town Called Carcross

Tucked away on a pinnacle of the golden Yukon,
A small workingman's town dwells,
Born from the age of greedy madness,
Do the dogs that drive the sleds still howl at the moon?
Snow blankets the mountains and the lakes and the trails,
Unrelenting, even in summertime.
Spring flowers push from the earth, fighting for an existence,
Sprouting gloriously before eminent frost ends the struggle,
I walk beside the train tracks of the tiny Alaskan town,
Sharing the homeliness and empathy,
For a treaded earth.
The sky above me is eternal space,
I fear losing myself in the power of the vastness.
Carcross skies are unlike no other,
Seemingly expanding,
blanketing days and nights with clouds and stars,
Breathing whispers onto the snowy footprints of the caribou.
A clever little namesake for a dreamy town.
Where the caribou cross,
The natives call this place
Carcross.

Caroline He, Grade 11
Germantown High School, TN

Nighttime Sky

As I look up at the beautiful sky
The stars twinkle and the moon shines very bright
All I can see is your amazing eyes
Our love is together for a short while.

Tony Strevel II, Grade 10
Union County High School, TN

Mein Zimmer Is Alive

My best friend is Mein Zimmer.
We have sleep overs every night, and it always lets me play my favorite music.
It lets me talk about whatever I want and never interrupts.
Sure, it won't win the award for cleanliness; although I'm sure it's not unsanitary.
Sure it sells out all its principles regarding authority on cleaning days;
It's always trying to impress my mother, so I can go out and buy more clothes to carpet it with.
Sure! It's not a Martha Stuart Catalog special with draperies and bed skirts that match
The scallop-trimmed edges of the bedspread. But it's me.
Every cubic centimeter of Mein Zimmer has my name stuffed inside letter to letter.
My mother says, "It's just a square, a small square, and you have to take care of it."
I pause for a rare, brief moment of teenage reflection.
I look at Mein Zimmer, and I'm sure, if it could, Mein Zimmer would look at me.
Then, I reply, "It's perfect!" and go about my business.
It's loud and friendly. It's crazy but trustworthy.
It's a seemingly unorganized stockpile of everything I've ever had and wanted to keep.
It's a lucrative safe haven from all the Why?s and Seriously?s and Oh My God!s of my life.
It's arguably the coolest, most interesting square on Earth.
And — I swear! — Mein Zimmer is alive.

Kara Bledsoe, Grade 11
Germantown High School, TN

The Attacker

Every day, every week, every year,
The bottoms fiery pit keeps dragging in
I find happiness...
And what happens, the Satanic Angel
Just burns me up inside
There must be a reason why I smile to the stranger,
It's because I don't want to show my heavyhearted, wishful, and despairing feelings to an endured soul
I just want to fly free with the birds
Spread my heavenly wings as the wind blows underneath my feet
I can't, please...
No more, there's no more room in my heart
It is full of all the weaknesses I have cherished
But I have chosen to let those things go and stand up to my attacker
Let him know who is in charge
And that is me!
A proud African-American and I will stand up for my equal rights of my human being.

Ebony Knight, Grade 12
StudentFirst Academy, NC

Blessed

Blessed is the one who walks with God, for his life shall be great.
But woe to the one who strays too far, for he will struggle in coming back.
Blessed is the one who believes Jesus died for his salvation, for he will be welcomed at the gates of heaven.
But woe to him who says that his deeds are the reason for his salvation, for he will be cast into the fire.
Blessed is the one who loves the Lord with all his heart, mindless of those who curse him, for he shall be rewarded.
Blessed is he who is faithful to his spouse for he will have a happy life.
But help the one who is unfaithful for he will live with his guilt for the rest of his life.
Blessed be the name of God for he is great.
But aid the one who takes it in vain.
Blessed are those who do not lie to the Lord for he will not be struck dead.
Blessed are those who are kind for they will be liked.
Blessed are those who love, for they will be happy.

Katherine Harris, Grade 12
Providence Academy, TN

Thanksgiving

Thanksgiving,
A wonderful time of the year,
Leaves a falling,
And roasts a roasting,
And full gravy boats,
Ready to cover them.

Thanks Giving,
A time for thanks,
A time for gratitude,
A time to be thankful,

Thanks Giving,
A time to give *Thanks*,
For those who are *Giving*,
Giving their lives for our country.

Thanksgiving,
Not just a time for feasting and merriment,
Or gaining a few more pounds;
But rather,
A time to be Thankful,
For all those who make our country great.

Brent Sivori, Grade 10
Holy Angels Academy, KY

We Wear the Mask

We wear the mask that looks away
Not caring about what people say
Only worrying about our cares
Looking away from foreign affairs
And never looking back

We hear all the problems
And plug our ears
Only to see the tears
We wear the mask

We have problems and so do they
Whose is worst depends on what you say
The pain builds up, soon it'll
Be shown little by little
Let the world think otherwise,
We wear the mask

Joey Anderson, Grade 12
Berkeley Springs High School, WV

Snow

In the winter time,
Snow falls very heavily.
It is freezing cold.

McKenzie Edds, Grade 10
Union County High School, TN

A Simple Poem

I'm offering this simple poem, for it is all I have to give.
Though, full of infinite heart and soul, all of my love is within it.

Please keep this poem, keep it close to your very heart.
Though it's just a simple poem, it will keep us from fading apart.

Keep it like a shield of course for your protection.
Keep it as your treasure, or if you're lost and need direction.

Keep it oh, so close, for it is sure and true.
Keep it like thick socks in winter, so no cold can bite through.

For all you have done for me, this would never suffice.
You gave me warm love, and I treated you like dry ice.

I'm here to apologize for all I've done and did.
And for all I have is just this simple poem to give.

One day I will be free and with you through the stormy weather.
But know what this poem holds, while I'm gone it's holding us together.

So here it is, my love in this simple poem, it's all I have to give.
However, I believe, it's something you may never willingly forget.

Simple things can mean big things if you're like me.
So just know I love you so and will for eternity.

Keep this simple poem as a simple memory to remember.
I do and always did, I love you mom.

Michael J., Grade 12
Audubon Youth Development Center, KY

Our Miracle Izzy and Our Angel Lizzy

She started a family one day, herself, a hubby and a 3 year old little boy
She felt her boy needed a sibling, someone to be close to
Someone he could share secrets with, instead of a Buzz Lightyear toy
Soon this eggo was prego, and symptoms of being prego had occurred
There was not only one, but two, TWINS…twin girls!
The family was ecstatic, hoping they would have their mamas curls
Time went on…the doctors needed to give us a talk
This mama bears cubs had a diagnosis that sent us all into shock
These angels had a disease called TTTS, a new trial for them to endure
They had many questions, like was there a cure?
They needed a special doctor, they needed one quick
They packed all their bags and took a long trip
They had to perform a procedure that might cost them a life
Sad to say, but there was a cost, one of the girls, Elizabeth was lost
But baby Isabel was a fighter, she was strong
They said she wouldn't make it, but they were wrong
On June 16, 2010 Isabel was born, she did win, she was weak at first
But after much care, she made it through, having lots of love to share
Isabel is our blessing and because of her, her mommy got her wish
One happy, healthy, baby, but the other is missed…
Baby Elizabeth lost her life to TTTS

Corinna Maxwell, Grade 12
Jack Britt High School, NC

Cycle

Greens excite to brilliant yellows
As they fall and fade to fire
At last done and gray

Lying dormant still and cold
Wet with mornings dew
Stiff under nights frost

Till their patience proven
Their entrance into mother earth
Slowly permitted

Till spring awakes
Lying deep within Mother Earth
Who takes gray

And makes green
That will flourish
Until time allows

New green will fade to old
Greens will excite to brilliant yellows
As they too will fall and fade to fire
At last they too done and gray

Maximillian Perdue, Grade 12
Enloe School, NC

The Kitchen

Strings of hair escape defiantly.
My hands are blurs.
Steam rises.
The oven screeches.
Beep. Beep. Beep. Beep.
Four times it gives its angry warning.
Hurry! It's almost too late!
I grab the pot of boiling noodles.
My knuckle singes on the rim.
It pours into the waiting drainer.
Steam fills the kitchen.
I smile as my face is gently warmed.
The knives and forks sing.
The table is set.
Creamy sauce joins the noodles.
Vegetables lie in bowls nearby.
Too-sweet tea glistens in its glass home.
A dinner is made.
Hands join.
We say a prayer of thanks.
No one speaks.
They only smile.
At the meal made by my own hands.

Amy Tanner, Grade 11
Germantown High School, TN

Rejuvenating

One Mississippi, two Mississippi, three Mississippi.
Countless times I have anticipated an upcoming storm.
Thunderbolts crackling in the distance,
confirm the morning's prediction.
Sunshine shamelessly hides
behind the immense gray and black thunderheads.
Wind whistles through the trees,
the sudden drop in temperature peak my senses.
Wind chimes sing the song of the approaching storm.
I shut my eyes tightly,
inhaling the fresh, distinct aroma of the impending rain shower
permeating the air.
Large, cold raindrops plummet from the clouds,
pelting the thirsty ground.
As the wilted leaves are quenched,
it is apparent that the looming thunderheads would leave us no blight,
instead,
a rejuvenating,
new dawn.

Sarah Wages, Grade 10
Germantown High School, TN

Sunset Nostalgia

Kingdom of clouds chasing the sun:
A vast dome of possibilities floating just above my mind.
I gaze up, struck by awe.
Never has nature proven so magnificent.
Oh, why!
Why do so many spend their days among the earthworms?
Why do they refuse to acknowledge such majesty?
If they would only displace themselves from the mulch: the lowest point of progress,
They would find that beauty is real,
Sensation is real,
Improbability is merely a mindset,
Possibilities are
endless!
Oh, Sun, do not sink into that uncertain skyline!
Oh, Clouds, do not be chased
away.

Samantha Sparks, Grade 12
Davidson County Extended Day School, NC

Watch Out for Evil Gum!

Chew, chomp, snap, boom, love is like bubble gum of doom.
Choose your flavor, but be wise, the wrong choice will lead to your demise.
Cinnamon flavored, warm to hot, will burn you, and care? It will not.
Spearmint, alive at first, it will lie to you the worst,
Because at first it bursts with flavor, sweet mintiness that you savor,
But after just a minute or two, the flavor leaves, it's bored with you.
Fruit flavored isn't bad, but the thing that makes me mad,
Is though at first it's yours to keep, you friends will notice, and they're cheap.
Then they will take all your gum, and leave you feeling empty and numb.
So what exactly can you do? Without love, like gum to chew?
The evil gun needs to be stopped, so go and get some lollipops!

Kelsey Graves, Grade 10
Loretto High School, TN

Calligraphy

These miniature drawings
blur together,
composing a picture
I have learned to recognize.

I see two curves,
merging molehills.

An arrow without a line,
vivid valleys.

A few curling marks,
slithering snakes.

And these little images,
seemingly insignificant,
dart
across my college-ruled page.

Rachel Enders, Grade 11
St Joseph Central Catholic High School, WV

Death of My Grandfather

I was in 4th grade
grandfather was really sick
from a decision he made to smoke
in the hospital
he had heart surgery
now in 6th grade
cancer had attacked his body
didn't believe in God
would have realized God had a plan
got put in hospice
forgot people
middle of 8th grade
my brother, sister and I got the sad news
God has a plan
my grandmother turned her life around

Andrea Willhite, Grade 12
Middle Tennessee Christian School, TN

Just Another Season

You know Fall is coming
when you hear the birds humming.

The beautiful trees are no longer growing,
the green grass no longer needs mowing.

Summer is over,
and there are no more clover.

When Fall time is here,
you know Christmas is near.

Steven Kenney, Grade 10
Holy Angels Academy, KY

Across the Ocean and into Germania

Walking by places that I've been,
places I've shared memories with you.
I gaze upon those places as if I can see us standing there on the outside,
looking in.
Seeing us standing there,
I miss you more than ever.
Knowing I might not see you,
see you for a very long time.
I relish on those memories,
trying to keep them strong and alive.

I remember everything you've ever said,
some of those things,
causing my cheeks to turn red.
So very kind and sweet,
without you, I feel incomplete.
The Atlantic Ocean and two thousand dollars,
are the only two things keeping me here,
And not going over to be with you.

Darian Seese, Grade 11
Morgantown High School, WV

Where I'm From

I am from the city, from busy streets and bright-lit nights.
I am from the Pepto-Bismol pink bedroom,
(bright and cozy, it smells of Cool Water Febreze.)
I am from the thorn bush, the roses, whose thorns are there for protection,
but do more hurt than good.
I'm from the Christmas family reunions and green eyes,
from King and Meade.
I'm from the constant chaos and fast-food restaurants.
From, "Reach for the sky," and, "Dreams do come true!"
Form the country land my Nana has received from her dead mother.
From the death of my cousin form cancer.
I am from the thousands of pictures on vacation,
the moments of thrill on Christmas morning,
I am from the Thomas family tree.

Lauren Thomas, Grade 11
Germantown High School, TN

Forever

Long has it been that I wanted something real.
Feeling I have meaning,
I've always wanted the true meaning of love.
Good God, you have shown me the true meaning of love I longed for,
I've hungered and thirsted for.
Now my eyes truly open, my soul's scars are gone,
The holes in my heart filled with your love for me.
So I'd give my heart away,
For you and I to have our bond back again.
So I'd give my soul away, now we can truly be together.
Good God, your love forever you'll offer, forever I'll give all I am,
Forever you'll always love and forgive, forever I'll never understand you.
Lord, forever you whisper to me, forever.

Andre Garcia, Grade 10
Lee Christian School, NC

Chaos

The forceful impact makes me leave all I know
How could this possibly happen to me?
The bright light is calling for me to go.

At first, everything was moving so slow
Comprehension only to a slight degree
The forceful impact makes me leave all I know

Crash! Spin! Whirl! Chaos after the blow
I can hear, but no longer can I see
The bright light is calling for me to go.

My companion vigorously screams "Hello!"
My mouth is locked and I don't hold the key
The forceful impact makes me leave all I know

Chilling blood on my skin as cold as snow
My young soul merely yearns to become free
The bright light is calling for me to go.

No longer do I have a chance to grow
I'm done. My mind, soul, and body agree
The forceful impact makes me leave all I know
The bright light is calling for me to go.

Ellie Romes, Grade 10
Notre Dame Academy, KY

The Commerson's Dolphin

Sitting in the sand, the wind in my hair,
Comes a blowing breeze of cool salty air.
The icy cold water, lapping on my toes
A grain of sand blows by my nose.

I hear a faint noise across the sea
Something there, it speaks to me.
I see the water as it makes a splash
Is it just a wave beginning to crash?

A black and white object way far out
Splashes through the water, in and out
A dorsal fin and tail so swift
Moving without current nor drift

Its shimmering skin, reflecting the light
A breathtaking and wondrous sight
Then it was gone, gone so fast
Disappeared into the ocean so vast.

I sat and thought of what I had seen
Was it true or was it really a dream?
The breeze slowed and the sun sunk low
And so the ocean was silent, and silent it was so

Erin Lester, Grade 12
William G Enloe High School, NC

As I Run

As I run
Whether it be under the stars or under the sun
I like to look around
And marvel at the wonders surrounding me.

I see the trees
And their changing leaves.
I gaze up at the sky
And see a huge, beautiful mystery.

I feel a gentle breeze
That blows against my face.
I breathe the fresh, clean air
And feel awake, open, and ready to release.

What do I release?
I release my energy
My anxiety and passions
And my ambition

I discover joy and peace
Beauty and love
All that has been given
From our Creator above.

Christina Norton, Grade 10
Holy Angels Academy, KY

ironic love

how ironic love can be
as he took you with him
away from the world
away from me

for 54 years they were together
and just in a matter of three days
they will last their eternal lives forever

so into you this last goodbye
and into me, another cry
for you will always be in my heart
for its obvious god never wanted you to apart

and forever they will last in god's promised land
for strangely enough this was what she wanted
as she stood her final stand

for she could not be without her love, her best friend
so now she's up above together with him again

i will see you again, maybe others before me, but i will see you again
and forever again we all will be, and forever we will be family
we will all be together in the end <3

Amanda Stevens, Grade 12
Wheeling Park High School, WV

Xue Yan

Images fly across the screen
Accompanied by sounds:
Bam, Blast, Boom
Detailing the story.

The program runs smoothly
Unlike the sweat on my forehead,
Gathering on the tip of the nose
But nothing more than a distraction.

The mouse moves quick
Under the guidance of my skillful hand.
But the ball of the mouse is creaking
And the edges of the mouse are beginning to feel wet.

Hands splashed the keyboard
Fast, precise, and loud.
I look up at the screen —
Two minutes left.

Xue Yan, Grade 12
Germantown High School, TN

Harris*

He can loop...
He can shoot...
He can dribble...
He can block...

He lives in the Bronx.
He loves basketball.
He always will.
He wants to get out.

His name is Harris...
He can do it all...
All he needs is a ball...
That's all!

Anthony Saunooke, Grade 11
Cherokee High School, NC
**Based on the book "Slam" by Walter Dean Myers*

I Remember When

I remember when things were simple
I remember when sorry fixed everything
I remember when hugs and kisses were all people needed.
I remember when scraped knees were
easier to fix than broken hearts
I remember when high school was all about Friday nights
I remember when respect was a virtue
I remember when things had a meaning
But now looking back I remember that the
simple hugs and kisses that mended my scraped knees
and broken hearts was a sign of respect
and molded me into the person I am today.

Jessica McCoy, Grade 11
Cherokee High School, NC

My Room and Me

In my room, you see
A place that stands out to me
As large or as small as it may be
It's a part of me

Countless times and moments untold
Have been spent in this lil abode
Often warm, sometimes cold
As I sit, time flows...

On and on
Till the breaking of dawn
Sometimes, I feel as though I have been shunned
Because of the excess time my room has won

Providing safety, comfort, and security
Which did not always occur to me
But in the end, I truly see
That it's just my room and me.

Morgan Johnson, Grade 11
Germantown High School, TN

Two Sisters

There were two sisters
People thought they were the same
Such much that they were called by the same name.

But one had blue eyes
The other had green
But no one noticed the difference between.

The blonde one had made a name for herself
The brunette's name was in her bookshelf.

Though their aspirations were different, they loved each other
Because of the separation they hid from their mother.

The separation was maturity.

Britney McFadden, Grade 11
Lynn Camp High School, KY

Wolves

People are confused
Hopefully amused
Marching by chime
Following in the line
The leader uses propaganda to control said masses
But he too is as ignorant as the lower classes
He is a puppet to the puppeteers, no way to be free
But I have no strings on me
The people will rise and finally see
We can soon begin to be free
The weak become the strong
But nothing ever lasts for long

Ian Grice, Grade 11
Lee County High School, NC

A Change in Season

Crisp leaves
tumble to pale grass.
Their vibrant colors
shrivel as the air chills.

Rigid pine cones
are sorted sprucely on the ground,
waiting to be bagged.

All summer's splendor
dissolves as cool breezes coil through trees,
conveying a change in season.

The ground seems lifeless now,
bugs no longer busy.
Acorns apparently absent.

All that is left
is a foggy haze
that backgrounds a mellow moon,
as the night is framed by frost.

And a lone survivor
withers away
in a cracked
flower pot.

Aaron Cowan, Grade 11
Germantown High School, TN

Sounds of Change

I love the way that music
Changes with me like the seasons
I listen to many different types
For many different reasons

For when I'm feeling down
I listen to some old Hank
And I listen to Lil' Wayne
When I want to rob a bank

When I'm feeling awesome
I know what just to do
I put on some Pantera
To put me in the mood

I head bang to those battle cries
I end up on the floor
I start to wonder why
But I just want some more

All in all this music
Makes me feel like I can fly
All I know is I will listen
Till the day I die

Garrett Adams, Grade 10
Coffee County Central High School, TN

Playroom

There is a place abundant with eternal and everlasting memories,
Where enough of the sun's rays are let in for warmth,
And enough light is let in for the magnificent illumination of the room,
Where children's laughter and mirth once filled the space in between its four white walls,
And the sound of quick scattering footsteps could be heard from the floor below,
Where imaginations would take flight among the sundry array of bright shiny Legos,
As aircrafts, ships, and fortresses took impressive shape after hours of complex engineering,
Where plastic plates and tea sets were laid upon a picnic blanket,
As small cousins would pretend to diligently prepare the aged Fisher Price grill to cook,
Where stories and action scenes came to life with dolls and figurines,
And where playtime seemed forever endless,
From time to time,
Its old visitors will visit once again,
Cousins of all ages return for family gatherings,
Reminiscing of the fond childhood memories,
They come to this room to play like young children once again,
There is a place that will always hold dear memories,
There is a place that will always be known to us,
As our one and only playroom.

Rebecca Fong, Grade 11
Germantown High School, TN

Tired

I'm tired of people treating me differently because who and what I am.
I'm tired of hateful people wishing me bad.
I am tired of the jealousy from people who were suppose to be my friends.
I am tired of the pity from people who need it more than I do.
I'm tired of people fearing me because they don't know any better.
I'm tired of people talking behind my back when they don't think I can hear.
I'm tired of people throwing sharp words at me because I'm different.

I'm tired of people hating me because I do what I have to do to survive.
I'm tired of people being my friend only to throw me away when they are done with me.
I'm tired of people seeing my intelligence and stopping there.
I'm tired of people ignoring me because they think it's what I want.
I'm tired of people wishing they were me and they don't even know my story.
And yet I do nothing to stop them.
...but they don't see the tears I cry

Kianna Hamilton, Grade 10
Oakland High School, TN

Beauty

Her beauty is like the sun, blinding you but keeping you warm
Her tears are like the morning rain, making everything around her bloom with life
Her voice is like music, soothing me as I admire her
Her soul reminds me of the ocean, sparkling with purity
Her eyes are like a rare flower, stunning you with its grace and beauty
Her body is like the rolling hills, beauty continuing as you look upon her
Her smile lifts the weight of the worlds of my shoulders
Her touch is a tingling sensation, like being paralyzed
Her laugh will bring light to the darkest days
I am blinded by her beauty, but it is only her I can see
I'm astounded by her, such beauty should only belong to a god
She is my world, She is my only, she is beauty

Ryan Sevier, Grade 11
Lynn Camp High School, KY

The Thoughts

I take the first step
The music starts
One, two, three more steps
Faster it goes
More thoughts roam my head
Oh no losing balance
Be strong
Hold
Five, six, seven, eight
They're all staring at me
Breath
A minute more to go
Not so heavy
Dance with the floor
Remember what's next
Here comes the lift
Perfect
Three seconds left
Three
Two
One

Destiny John, Grade 12
William G Enloe High School, NC

Girl Who?

Girl Who?
She is my sunshine, my world
She is sweet
Like a warm summers rain
She is always on the run
I never get her to myself
We don't always get along
Yet, she always makes me happy
When we are together
Time stops just for us
She is a friend
The sweetest anyone could be
Although she is not from here
I see her as just like me
Her parents are sweet and strict
Like that of a lion
They scare me a bit
But I still love her
I am so blessed
To have an amazing girl
Girl Who?

Lucas Smith, Grade 10
Spring Valley High School, WV

The Fall

Green leaves stay attached
Yellow and orange leaves fall
Fate to be trodden

Kristen Asbury, Grade 10
Union County High School, TN

Gone

Everything I have is gone yet
I still feel the need to stand strong.
My world is in shambles
and I don't know how well I can handle
anymore tests or trials to face,
when inside my heart still aches, from seeing the pain
and hearing the screams
all I can wish for is a place that is serene.
Like the heaven promised to me from the people who have come to help,
but all it seems they are doing is helping themselves.
When will their change become reality?
Where is the hope that they promised I would see?

So Lord if you're out there hear my cry
help me no longer to ask "why?"
Please let there be someone there,
whom with this burden I could share.
Help me not to feel far away and alone,
that when I wake everyone won't be
gone.

Ashley Colemon, Grade 10
Smyrna High School, TN

Absent

Didn't your mother teach you to clean up your mess when you're done
You left me with a broken heart and tears that will forever run
I feel abandoned and lost without you
Radiant skies of sunny days, are now forever blue
My tears run as deep as the dark oceans floor
My heart cries out for you...day after day
Night after night, and lonely years forever more
Many replacements, but none will ever match
Those hurtful things you said...you did
I'm now laced in them
PLEASE TAKE THEM BACK!
Those are the only memories I draw back to
But if time truly heals the scars, it's been years and years
16 years to be exact...why am I still going through!?!
The same exact hurt, from when it all started...
It's hard...but I'll move on. Our hearts forever parted.

Jade N. Mitchell, Grade 11
StudentFirst Academy, NC

Temptations

Temptations, yeah I know about those,
Sometime they are high and the others are low,
Either way I hate them all,
Know why? 'Cause they're here to make me fall,
Most of them are so sweet, so hard to defeat,
I wish temptations were not here, not here so I will not have to fear,
Fear the knowledge of getting into trouble,
Guilty pleasure should be called double-trouble,
I guess I have to stop making excuses, I have self control, guess I have to use it,
How hard this is to do, but somehow, someway, I know I can make it through

Erica Ross, Grade 10
Overton High School, TN

In the Theatre

The theatre is the place I call home
It gives me a new place to roam
Every time I act out a part
I perform with all my soul and heart

When I say my lines
As the character and I intertwine
With the different emotions upon my face
On the stage I can find my place

In an elaborate costume
As my character begins to bloom
It all becomes whole
When I assume the role

When I connect with the audience if only for one show
It lets their imaginations begin to grow
If a standing ovation is what I get
It will be something I will never forget

When I take my final bow
All I can wonder is how
I made it through the night
Without any stage fright

Haylee Eaton, Grade 10
Coffee County Central High School, TN

Love

Love is a burning candle
With an endless amount of wax
It burns bright
For every eye to see

Love lives on forever
Even when it physically dies
It still thrives from within the heart
The observers who see are mesmerized

Love is a box of chocolates
You never know what you're going to get
It's sweet
And fun at times

Love is an apple tree
There are lots that fall to the bottom
They are easy to pick up
But there are few and perfect ones at the top

Love is a journey
There may be a few troubles on the way
But if you bear through it
In the end you will be satisfied

Caleb Williams, Grade 12
Providence Academy, TN

Sour and Sweet

Sitting in his sweat pants and my old shirts,
He giggles with an echo that can fill the house.
Quoting his favorite TV shows,
He is waiting for a laugh in return from the characters.

My worst enemy, yet my favorite comedian.
The tattletale I can't understand.
He eats only corndogs and Halloween candy,
But he remains the skinny, fit one.

Saying silly, random jokes that don't make sense,
He is a ball of energy begging for attention;
He flies as if attached to helium balloon,
Yet just as much, stays grounded on Earth.

Playing with those animated video games,
Or listening to his beloved audio books,
He is always busy daydreaming on his baby blue bed,
In his unfinished light yellow room.

There he is spinning,
Unaware of my thoughts surrounding him.
I'm scared to leave him in the future,
But my love for him will always remain.

Annya Shalun, Grade 11
Germantown High School, TN

Playing the Mind Game

If you've fallen far behind,
what scares me most is my own mind.
If you look, then you may find
that we are two of a kind.

The first thing that hits me is fear.
I'm really scared when I get here.
I'm stuck in the headlights, I've become the deer.
That's made me want to hide for a year.

The second thing that strikes is hate.
It seems that life is just cruel fate.
This issue isn't up for debate.
You can kill. You can't create.

The final thing that bites is spite.
It makes me scream. It makes me fight.
Adrenaline makes me reach new height.
Watch the dog. It just may bite.

Insane asylums will not notice.
If they do, they'll just add doses.
You will never diagnose this
once your mind has reached psychosis.

Shane B., Grade 12
Audubon Youth Development Center, KY

Dancing Demons

Tell me you love me,
If that's your fix.
Make me plea,
To get your kicks.

But your demons don't dare,
To dance with me.
Because my demons won't care,
If they hear you scream.

Behind my mask I see you,
Waiting, wanting, and wishing.
Or could it be true,
That those feelings have gone missing?

Oh! The angel, the pure holy angel,
Will not lay his eyes on me.
For I am from the devil's loins,
And Hell's not his cup of tea.

So I'll let you in on my reasoning,
Of why we cannot be.
Your angelic form is so completing,
But Hell hath no key.

Sam Michael, Grade 11
Berkeley Springs High School, WV

Counting Falling

Counting falling, here I'm watching
Doubt I'm chasing, fear is stalking
Almost there, your gaze it lingers
Standing there, your ice cold fingers

Blood it races, as I trace this
Your face it hardens, dark eyes soften
Running from the world that's crashing
Bare the soul that you're unwrapping

Pelting in this land of rain
And watch the water stream down your face
Here I kneel and pray a fool
On the ground my tears they pool

In this love I find is weaker
Secrets stowed and dams concealing
Is it worth to watch this die?
We struggle through the stormy lies

Counting falling, here I'm watching
Doubt I'm chasing, fear is stalking
Almost there, your gaze it lingers
Standing there, your ice cold fingers

Jessica Graham, Grade 11
Berkeley Springs High School, WV

Memories of Home

At night, I look up at the sky, while memories seem to just go on by.
All day I walk and talk, but now I see Little Rock.

The reminiscence is black and white. It wasn't blu-ray but still all right.
The pictures just repeat themselves, while I'm whisked back to my former self.

On Saturday mornings, I would awake; just hours before the day would break.
My dad and I would go to climb, and we'd reach the peak at sunrise.

The wind over there had a breeze that took my tensions and made me free.
Every day was a good day; black and white but never gray.

When I was told that we were shifting, my head went blank and I went drifting.
At first, I was very defiant, but soon I had to comply it.

The day came for me to go, and time froze just like ice and snow.
I didn't want to leave my friends even though I knew it wasn't "the end."

I kept in touch with my friends, so that our bonds would never end.
But things are not the same now because they've changed somehow.

Now I'm in Memphis, "Land of the Blues"
Roaming around the place with no clue

I may be gone from Little Rock
Confused, lost, and a little alone
But I'll always have my memories
And I'll always call that place home

Tej Anand, Grade 11
Germantown High School, TN

Egotistical Teachers

I try to avoid egotistical teachers;
the ones who prance around like Peacocks and Kings,
look down their noses at us like we are their subjects,
and expect us to bow down on our knees and praise them as the Almighty.

The ones who act as if they know everything; who think we students
are incapable of an intellectual thought.
Ones who yell, scream, and pose rhetorical questions;

"That's an MR!" "Where is your homework?" "Are you paying attention?"
Like children, they throw temper tantrums, markers, and pencils,
and from them we are supposed to learn?

MRs and detentions are their favorite words.
We can't sing, we can't slouch, we can't sleep,
you might as well tell us we can't breathe.

I look for the teacher that takes the time to get to know us;
who tells the truth on Parents Day, and doesn't sugarcoat to please.
The one that gives meaningful tests and quizzes,
instead of busy work, just to pass the time;
I only wish the perfect teacher exists.

Nicole Yearwood, Grade 12
Baylor School, TN

Megan Who

Megan who is the light of my life
Who has eyes as blue as the deep blue sea
That rain raindrops when she takes care of me
Whose hair is as yellow as the sun
it makes me sad when she says goodbye
Who lives far away
She needs to be here every day
Three times a year isn't nearly enough
But we've got to be tough
Who is a dirty softball
She's always been one of the boys
She is also a pair of ballet shoes
Who is a girly girl too
Who screams "Come watch me."
She is fearless in any way possible
Who always smiles, never cries
She's such a special person inside
Who is a rainbow, a starry sky
Who is my sister
I hate to say goodbye

Natalie Ross, Grade 10
Spring Valley High School, WV

Donna Who

Donna who is a stone
Who loves being outside
Has always been there for me
Whose thumb is green
Who loves to listen to rainstorms
Is a great cook and baker
Who is strong-willed and hardworking
Is very forgiving to the ones she loves
Who loves the ocean and to tan
Is always rooting for the Steelers
Who hates messes
Is like a firecracker
Who is very talkative and loves to tell me about her day
Is a teller at a bank
Who is loving and caring towards kids
Is a Christian
But is also a sinner
Who loves cows and to drink milk
Is my caregiver
Who is like a best friend!!

Kristan Davis, Grade 10
Spring Valley High School, WV

You Taught Me How to Fly

You taught me how to fly
You showed me how to spread my wings
You taught me how to care
You were my lighthouse by the sea
You have been my driving force
You showed me to spread my wings
You showed me where to fly
You said be safe and aim towards the sky
And even at this moment
Without you I would be lost
My father and my teacher
You are my example
To be honest, true, and caring
To stand on my own feet and on solid ground
And to let my voice be heard
From the mountains and the streams
Daddy, you taught me how to spread my wings
You taught me how to fly
I'll show you I can use them
I'll never fall from the sky

Jessica Dotson, Grade 11
McMinn County High School, TN

Summit

The climber set out on an ordinary day
With a mission impossible in more than one way
They'd said not to bother, they'd said not to try
The face was too steep, the mountain too high
Yet here the climber stood, quiet and tense
Gazing up at what was so real and immense
The climb started slow, hand for hand, foot for foot
Special attention being paid to where each one was put
Soon their body cried out, their muscles on fire
Yet somehow they managed to keep climbing higher
The air was too hot and the climb was too long
They were tired and thirsty; gravity was too strong
They were drenched in sweat, almost making them slip
The blood on their hands made it difficult to grip
Everything was an obstacle; every crevice, each crack
But the climber hadn't come this far to turn back
So with pain in their body and sweat on their brow
They kept climbing and climbing without quite knowing how
They ignored the fear they might fall; they might plummet
Thus the climber climbed and reached the summit

Ashton Carrick, Grade 10
South Mecklenburg High School, NC

Posture

Broken slouchiness,
Smiling from outside my spine —
Sit up straight for once.

Devin Collins, Grade 10
Union County High School, TN

Rain

The rain pouring down
the thunder and lightning roar
the frightened kids hide.

Tyler Duncan, Grade 10
Union County High School, TN

I Wish I Could Have Danced with Cinderella

I wish I could have danced with Cinderella that day,
She looked as pretty as the month of may,
But I was sad because I had to leave the next day.

I wanted to be the king and she could be the queen,
But I was not even price charming

She danced like there was care
But all I could do was stare.

I like Cinderella she is a wonderful person I think I might love her
But she doesn't notice me, but still I don't bother

Cinderella always looks so pretty
But she doesn't like me;

What a pity.

Benny Balderrama, Grade 10
Overton High School, TN

Here You Are

Here you are, slowly drifting away and away,
Sometimes you do not even know your own name;
I'd heal you now if only there was a way,
I'm so tired of playing this horrible game.
I miss when we used to play together,
When I think about it I want to cry;
I do not want you floating like a feather,
I will really miss you if you ever die.
But Little Daniel, just keep trying and you'll get through,
Don't let this frightening thing bring you down;
With your family you'll know what to do,
So, come and let's turn this thing around.
This life does terrible things in many ways,
How do you put up with it, all these days?

Daniel Cooke, Grade 10
Union County High School, TN

I Have Seen Many Things

I have seen many things.
But none will every erase that day from my mind.
The blood, the glass, the flames.
They are forever engraved in my memories.
They pop up when I least expect them.
I can't help it,
It just happens.
And every time, no matter how many times it happened before, I cry.
I see them lying there,
Their eyes open but unseeing.
Never shall they breathe crisp mountain air or hear the rain fall.
They are gone now.
To a better place?
I honestly do not know.

Catherine Watson, Grade 10
Berkeley Springs High School, WV

I'm Torn

Shall I compare thee to a thunderstorm?
At first so peaceful, then so hostile.
You leave me confused, all withered and worn,
But when my sadness shows, only you can find my smile.

My thoughts spin round and round,
I don't know what to do.
I'm dying inside, but making no sound.
Do I love or hate you?

It's wrong to say I hate you,
Even if that's how I feel.
But I can't say that I love you;
Who knows if these feelings are real?

You leave me confused, all withered and worn.
Do I love you or hate you? I'm torn.

Emily Cothren, Grade 10
Loretto High School, TN

Pressure

To be the best
Outsmart the rest
Make a perfect score
On every test
To be the strongest
Work the hardest
Stay up late
Last the longest
To be quite bold
To what you're told
Have a heart
That's made of gold
To know that there are thousands all over the world
Who are trying just as hard as you

Cayce Dorrier, Grade 12
Enloe High School, NC

A Summer Sunset

It's not seeing the sunset.
It's not watching the
Cloud's golden lining
Turn a deep maroon.
It's not the sky turning
A deep violet. It's
Seeing the rays of sun
Breaking through the clouds,
Highlighting the blend of
Yellow to orange, pink,
Red, purple, and violet
That makes the sunset
Across the lake so
Beautiful from my hammock on the eastern shore.

Matthew Zalesak, Grade 12
William G Enloe High School, NC

I Wear the Mask
I wear the mask that hides the hurt and the pain
The cover hides all of my fright and shame
You make me so mad, but I can't let anyone see
You hurt everyone, but especially me
That is why I wear the mask

The slaps in my face and blows to my arm
You were never supposed to bring any harm
I sit alone so no one knows
I wear the mask

Harassment and yelling is all I've known
But smiles and laughter is all I've shown
I hide it all inside
No one has seen the tears I've cried
I'll always hide
I wear the mask

Cassidy Watson, Grade 11
Berkeley Springs High School, WV

My Ship of Dreams
In this world, I live my life
My home is bloody and full of strife.
In your world, I strive to go
Solemnly, you tell me "no."
Confused, I say "I don't understand...
It's in my reach, it's in my hand."
You turn to me and speak with regret:

"I do not think you're ready yet.
My life is still teaching me,
You cannot defy reality.
Yours still has more for you to know;
It forces me to make you go."
I dropped my smile. Pride no longer beams,
It appears I must respect what fate deems.
My perfect world may have imperfect seams,
But I am still the captain of my Ship of Dreams.

Joe McLaney, Grade 12
Polk County High School, NC

Moving
Moving away
Why would they do this to me?
Start all over again
Rage and sadness
Leaving friends and family
Never moved before
Only place I knew
Everything was falling apart
But
Happiness is coming
God's plan is beyond
Keep waiting.

Haley Williams, Grade 12
Middle Tennessee Christian School, TN

Misfortunes Arise
Gentle doves soar into the somber night,
each so captivated with the other,
that grim clouds become draped with amber light
which strokes their feathers as they flutter.

All night long she waits, the languishing moon,
amongst her jubilant friends in the sky.
For her golden sun to come to her soon,
but he coldly, heartlessly shines on by.

Watching the doves, the moon softly laments,
endlessly distant from is she.
When suddenly a friend himself presents,
bewitched me have you says the wondrous sea.

One must not fret when misfortunes arise,
true love may be a marvelous surprise!

Rabeetah Hasnain, Grade 12
William G Enloe High School, NC

What Shall I Compare Thee To?
Shall I compare thee to a winter day
Pure and white with the beautiful snow
Cold winds blow by while the squirrels play
It reminds me of your amazing glow

Often too cold for my skin to bare
Sometimes I cannot stare into the snow for the sunshine
One day I wish to hold you, to show you I care
I want to run through the snow to make you mine

The soft flowing snow like your hair
My eyes see two loving deer run together
Winter will soon fade but don't you dare
Stay with me forever

I cannot live without you
Without you my world would be blue

Tays Robertson, Grade 10
Loretto High School, TN

Seize the Day
Sometimes we run
Sometimes we walk
Sometimes we listen
Sometimes we talk
A time to laugh
A time to cry
A time to live
A time to die
Look at the future
Not the past
We never know
How long life will last

Victoria Holmes, Grade 10
Coffee County Central High School, TN

The Ocean's Secrets

As the ocean waves crash before me
I admire the shells the currents left behind
Before the water retreats back into the sea
I place my feet in the waves one last time

The waves bring in treasures not many can duplicate
They are rough from their travels on the ocean floor
Smooth to the touch of the things they create
They always seem to hold something more

The sun sets below the ocean's surface
And the waves seem to grow higher as the tides roll near
They view seems to leave me speechless
This is when the ocean is everything that it appears

I hear the sounds of crashing waves
My footsteps leading away from the shore are like farewells
The shells in the sand are almost engraved
Forever against the ocean will they rebel

Lorelei Pentifallo, Grade 10
Coffee County Central High School, TN

Lost

A cold raindrop plopped onto my forehead
just as the sun dipped behind the trees surrounding me.
The moon served my only light then,
and I was hopeless to find my way home.

Recklessly abandoned by my comrades,
I delved deeper into the impending darkness.
Without directions, I stumbled within the
overwhelming shadows which flooded my vision.

My warm breath was frozen in the still air,
as I crashed down in the forest mud.
I laid my head down slowly, closing my eyes
in hope that when my eyes opened again,
the sun's light would guide me home.

Ashley Culler, Grade 10
Providence High School, NC

Once Again

Here I am in front of you.
Broken and crying.
Begging to be yours.
But you only begin lying.
Telling me it's not right.
That we never were and never will.
You tell me you want someone else now.
It's like a stab to the heart, and you went for the kill.
Which is why I am here again in front of you.
Broken and crying.
Begging to be yours once more.
But, once again, you only begin lying.

Becky Norton, Grade 12
Berkeley Springs High School, WV

Friends

I used to have a friend I talked to every day
but now I barely see him to even say hey

We are a great distance apart
but I told him I would stick by him from the start

We have a lot of memories, good and bad
but I never knew it would be so sad

I knew he was sick, but not how severe
when I heard the news I had to adhere

This school year has not been the same
without him here, it is quite lame

He used to keep me laughing all day long
but sometimes now it's hard to keep strong

Even though there is a high chance he will live
there is always that question, "What if?"

He gets to come home every now and then
while he is here, it's just like back when

It is difficult to think of things that rhyme
because so much has changed, in such little time

When he returns home for good
will be when everything is the way it should

Taylor Bush, Grade 10
Coffee County Central High School, TN

My Love

I never make a sound
when you are around
you fill my heart with love
so I feel like I'm soaring above
I want to be with you
but I don't know if it will be true
so my mind tells me to move on
but my heart says stay strong
now I must choose
who will lose
will my mind come out on top
or will my heart not be able to stop
I want to go with my heart and stay strong
but I wonder if I can hold on long
for now I will wait
and see what's my fate
but it may be over-turned
or it may be burned
'cause my heart burns with fire
so it needs to be free from these imaginary wires
so Amber does your heart burn for me

Daniel Blackmon, Grade 11
Western Harnett High School, NC

Confusion

Confusion.
Choosing between two things,
That are both loving,
Not knowing where you're going.
There are two paths,
Yet none of them will last,
Just keep walking.
You see a door,
But you fall to the floor,
Fearing what's on the other side,
Just run and hide.
Feeling alone won't break your bones,
Just your pride.
Your expression can't hide,
The pain you feel inside,
Get off the floor.
You see a crack of light
And you take that flight,
By choosing the path,
You want to last.

Reem Alawar, Grade 12
William G Enloe High School, NC

A "Normal" Life*

In the first week of august
She said to a toad
"I'm going to run away," ...Winnie Foster
Only 10 years old

As she wandered the woods,
So innocent and sweet,
She came across a spring...
And a boy she happened to meet

But what she didn't know
With utmost certainty
Was the boy who drank that water
Was granted immortality

In the end she must decide
To live on endlessly
Or to have a "normal" life...
Just like you and me.

Athena Sadongei, Grade 11
Cherokee High School, NC
**Based on the novel "Tuck Everlasting"*

Summer Love

Our feet in hot sand;
By my side, Dylan's standing;
With my heart in hands.

Emily Wilson, Grade 11
H L Trigg Community School, NC

Shattered

Blanketed by love and affection; I felt alone
The sun shining in the middle of the sky; I felt frozen
Broken into a million shards of pain, yet still intact
Cowering behind my mask of "I'm okay"

Emotions locked away inside my stolid shell
Drowning in fear for what seemed like forever
Loved ones, showering me with hugs
Always longing for the set of arms over 500 miles away

Flashbacks overwhelm me; the memory of your goodbye forever burned into my brain
As my mother backs out of the driveway and blows to me, a kiss
A single tear rolls down my cheek; I must quickly collect myself
Because everything is fine, I promise you

Slipping away; I am losing myself, unable to reach the surface
I have no thought to where the old me could be hiding
And this constant search of the past has me so very tired
It is very possible that I will never be the same

The pain from your absence will never be forgotten
As I wander around this world unsure of where exactly it is that I'm headed
Just one broken soul in a universe of billions
Crying out silently for help, desperate for something familiar

Rachael Phillips, Grade 10
Coffee County Central High School, TN

Southern Ways

I'm from cowgirl boots and sun dresses,
From George Straight and Brad Paisley.
I am from a house of class and southern, traditional values.
Conservative and tasteful
Shining as bright as stars on a cloudless night.

I am from the sunflower,
Cheerful and full of happiness.
I am from a strong willed and whole-hearted family.
From being Daddy's little princess
And "Have a great day! Make a big ole' A!"

I am from Christianity.
The belief in a God that loves me and sent his one and only son to die for my sins
I'm from Memphis, Tennessee,
Barbeque and sweet tea.
From the father who ran away at 17
And smashing into the trash can when I learned to ride my bike.

I'm from Saturday nights with incredible friends.
The moments of creativity, adventure, and excitement we share.
I'm from the place where personality runs purest and love runs deep.
I'm a country-fried-chicken lovin' country girl
Born and raised in the south.

Phoenix Pope, Grade 11
Germantown High School, TN

A Gift from the Heavens

An angel came and touched my face
And gave a precious gift to me
A miracle from a higher place
It's a baby! Yes indeed!

Dear unborn baby I have loved you from the start
Such endless joy fills my heart
I wonder what your name will be?
This miracle inside of me,
As I bow my head each night
I pray that you will be all right.

I love you so very much
Thank you God, I will forever sing your praise
I yearn to see your face and feel your sweet touch
And to say, "My precious child, I'll love you always"
I hope that you don't grow too fast,
I want these precious memories to last

This mystery inside of me
Has built up my curiosity,
Will I wrap you in pink or blue?
Oh look at that! There are two!
Two times the joy, two times the fun, two times the love.

Sarah Wells, Grade 10
Notre Dame Academy, KY

Life in a Fast Lane

You've been there when I needed a friend,
You've been there to catch my tears,
You've been there when I needed a shoulder,
You've been there through all these years.

You were there when I first saw Earth,
You were there for my first laugh,
You were there when I learned to walk,
You were there in all the photographs.

You're in all my memories,
Seeing you laugh and play.
You're there for me always,
Especially when skies are grey.

But the years went by,
And we grew older.
You left home for college,
So I lost that shoulder.

Facebook connected us,
As well as the phone.
Thanks for being my big sister,
You're the best I have known!

Heather Anderson, Grade 10
Musselman High School, WV

Seasons

Does anyone realize how quickly things will change
We hold our heads high and grip our personal restraints
From the moment we enter, the seconds chase seconds
Time draws thinner, and we trade presence for presence

Does anyone want to resist this new form of life
Instead of living a patterned routine to survive
Distracted by difference and generic alike
Have you also accepted that things will never be right

Does anyone completely come clean about their thoughts
Our greatest crimes establish themselves within those walls
In those chambers are where we will leave our last words
Of heartbreak and conclusion and things of no known cure

Because those are our real secrets; those are our seconds
Those are our real seasons and where lies our true presence
Where our temptations are strongest and our sins perform
The rituals that we will all later adorn

Does anyone feel helpless against these same crowds
Trying to convince them of things they cannot figure out
Simple to say that we have all had the wrong reasons
When it is always the same price from season to season

Mayleen Mincher, Grade 10
Coffee County Central High School, TN

Solace

Midnight nears in this loft,
The only sign of life emits from floors.
Wooden steps reveal a chance,
That I may be returning home again.

I slumber down into my cotton adobe,
Reunited with R.E.M.
After the fearful attacks of the day,
My room is the only place I wish to be.

The cold blue walls and the whitewashed ceilings,
Even the floors ridden with deep amber varnish.
Atop a mountain of comforters,
The tensions of the day divide away.

I know this is the only place for me,
A room just tucked away.
The tranquility provides solace,
To the weary soul I retire with every day.

In a universe surrounded by others,
It seems hard to find a moment for one's self.
I find myself adrift in a world of lost thought,
Returned on my arrival at my place at home.

Collin Hutsell, Grade 11
Germantown High School, TN

Reflection In the Mirror

I stare closely at the one looking at me
Many things in this reflection I see

I see a girl but also a young lady
I see a future of promise, hopes, and maybes

I see one who has overcome but is yet overcoming
I see someone eager of whom they are becoming

In this reflection I see tears but also a smile
I see the significance and the results of trials

Each day the reflection grows stronger
Moving from the past the reflection is blurry no longer

Greatness is this reflection I see
But It is not my own greatness

Jasmine Marsh, Grade 10
Lee County High School, NC

Temptations

He has a smile that is like the sun,
All bright and shining in the sky,
And those around him have such fun,
That when he leaves they know not why.
When he speaks all will hear his voice,
The sound so confident and strong,
So if you choose you must make a choice,
To follow in good or choose to do wrong.
The path is wide and the road is long,
For each one to decide which way to go.
In order to travel you must know here you belong,
For without the trip you will not grow.
Move on, move on and find your way,
For each path we travel takes us to another day.

Rianna Watson, Grade 10
Loretto High School, TN

Love and Bubblegum

You could say that gum and love are the same,
Comparing the two they fit well.
After awhile they both get lame,
They both just begin to fail.
Love is great, so it seems,
And bubblegum can be so sweet.
But love is harsh under certain beams,
And gum doesn't always stay so neat.
Love, sometimes, can hurt at times,
It makes you want to forget it too.
Gum, you know, goes good with this rhyme,
For the longer it's there, the less you can chew.
Gum, to me, is just too cheap,
And the price of love, they too can keep.

Emilie Andrews, Grade 10
Loretto High School, TN

The Undisclosed Mask

I wear the mask that you choose to see
I fake the smile so you'll accept me.
Yet, as my heart breaks, and I'm torn apart
To you, I wish, I could impart.
But slowly, I begin to sunder.

You'll disregard, but I'll fall slow.
I'll drift out of your life, you won't even know.
But still, I'll smile, continuing the lie.
I wear the mask.

Tortured from within.
Will it change in the end?
My hope has gone astray,
If only you'd meet me halfway.
No. And in the end, death will conquer.
I wear the mask.

Brady Smith, Grade 11
Berkeley Springs High School, WV

Imagination

Scenarios I can fully create
Are tiny little worlds inside my mind
But to those in them, it is vast and great
It is the largest world seen by their eyes
I can imagine them worshipping me
If I so choose, I can make their lives end
I can do whatever I want, I'm free
To make them think me a foe or a friend
And when I stop thinking about that world
Does it suddenly cease to have a breath?
Or does it still exist yet still unfurls
With times of trouble, evilness, and death?
Through my time on earth I have come to know
That it could be like this world of our own

Dan Irving, Grade 10
Middle Creek High School, NC

Butterflies

Those that boldly put on a show, it seems,
Tend to always want, but never need, that,
Which we, the true to heart and love, you see,
Have worked for, given our best, and for what?
The transformation of a butterfly
Is a sightly wonder; from legs a-many
To valiant wings atop. We wonder why,
Most new beginnings are rather tinny,
But when one realizes that which is
The result is often not as cheery.
For we tend to live a book full of lies.
This, many have found as much more merry.
Therefore, live your life with ones you love;
They may be gone like the flight of a dove.

Lucas Nicely, Grade 10
Union County High School, TN

Monster of Darkness

Monster that comes from the darkness,
monster that comes from my mind,
monster that is not so kind,
please, please spare me this one time.
Monster that creeps and crawls,
monster that I cannot control,
over me you like to stomp and roll.
You are different in others,
some you like to smother.
Some you make cower, and some you make small,
Some you give fear and tell to take cover.
Monster of Darkness you are my arch enemy,
no battles have I won yet,
but with each one I bet,
that I come closer to seeing you.
Monster that will never leave,
Monster that likes to push and heave.
You have many enemies, and we outnumber you,
We over power you,
And we will destroy you.
We will destroy the Monster of Darkness.

Jeremy Hearn, Grade 10
Scotts Hill High School, TN

Life

Lost
In my field of wonder.
Surrounded
By dark clouds and thunder.
Crying
Because there's nowhere to go.
Naked
With all my sins to show.
Hurt
Blood stains my white sheets red.
Running
From all the voices in my head.
Dying
Just let the world go cold.
Forever
Will be the pain in my soul.

Emilie Anne Tucker and James Scott Tucker Jr., Grade 10
Coffee County Central High School, TN

And There Man Fell

He reaches out with inventive hands
He pours the waters. He sculpts the lands
From the dusts of Africa; Two He rose
Tall, black, without shame and without clothes
Two to have of all they see
Of all fruits, but one tree
Then came The Snake of Man and spoke
Beguiled Her so the vow was broke
And there man fell, too

Brendan Cooper, Grade 12
Western MST Magnet High School, KY

Where I'm From

I am from keyboards,
from Kawai and Yamaha.
I am from ballet flats, broken in and worn,
from clumsiness and uncontrollable laughter.
I am from Virginia, Sicily and Chicago.
(Vast landscape, rich culture; home sweet home has many names.)
I am from the hibiscus, the palm trees,
whose friendly exteriors epitomize vacation and relaxation.
I'm from swinging on the front porch of that old yellow house
and never failing to arrive unfashionably late,
from Phillip and Hyung Mi.
I'm from the military obligation and driving like a maniac.
From "always try your best" and "life's not fair."

From my sister's hair caught on fire,
and always knocking over the glass of water.
I am from the photographs, bringing memories so fond,
and family keepsakes scattered throughout the house:
under beds, top shelves of closets, and living room cabinets.
I am from everlasting familial love — felt though not spoken —
the acceptance of imperfection.

Sarah Jackson, Grade 11
Germantown High School, TN

Rage Against the Machine

As you read this poem,
Do not judge it
But instead ask yourself
What is it that I can do?
To make the world a better place?
Where there is no strife between others
Where there is no fighting between one another
But where there is love between neighbors
Ask yourself what you can do
To make this world a better place?
The answers to this question
Can be found within our hearts
But in the end
Questions don't matter
What matters is
That in the end,
We chose the easier way out...
Instead we should always be who we are, no matter what
Because in the end that's all that matters
And don't regret anything
That ever made you smile.

Irene Kangara, Grade 12
William G. Enloe High School, NC

Always

I always look out my window in search,
All day I look out and see you there.
I run down to you, we sit on a bench,
You aren't there, I'm wishing you were here.

Allison Brown, Grade 10
Union County High School, TN

Talk

He said, she said.
It's all
Talk.
Screaming, yelling, arguing.
Happy family photos
Faded away.
As doors slammed
And size 12 feet
Stomped away.
No, no
Nobody's mad.
Divorce?
No, never!
It's just
Talk.
He said, she said
Talk.

Brittany Kay Bridges, Grade 12
Jack Britt High School, NC

Recurring Daydream

You, you startle me so deeply
Shaking me from
My pleasant nights
Slumber. My fear.

You, you comfort me in times of
Need, watching me
With dream-woven
Wild eyes. My friend.

You, you show me secrets unknown
To mankind, through
Sanity and
Madness. My mentor.

Kyle Poteet, Grade 11
Oak Ridge High School, TN

Treasures

Waves crashing furiously on the shore
I was frightened
For I have never seen anything so horrid

Flashes of lightning
Shooting across the sky
Thunder booming
Like a million explosions
How many people tremble inside

These waters bring me
Shells and pearls
Who thought something fierce
Could bring such treasure

Lauren Fuller, Grade 10
Spring Valley High School, WV

You Are My Sun

Shall I compare thee to the sun
Warm and bright
Till the day is done
Life without you would be like night

You light up my day
Like the sun in the sky
I can't find the words to say
And I don't know why

How could I ever
Go on without you
It would be so much better
If only you knew

You are my everything
And you make me sing

Alex Carrick, Grade 10
Loretto High School, TN

Alien

Humans desire superiority
I desire equality

I desire to leave this place
to somewhere with diversity
without prejudice

No conflict, no war
no pride, no jealousy
no negativity, no curse
only love and respect

If these people are considered human —
I am not a human being

Jorge Flores, Grade 12
Heide Trask High School, NC

Indian Summer

The orange tint to the empty fields.
The midnight rush of warm wind.
Running hand-in-hand.
With the one you love.

Laughing until you cry,
And then falling down.
Gazing at the stars,
With that dreamlike wonder.

That midnight spark.
That October breeze.
We all remember.
That Indian Summer.

Cassidy Matano, Grade 10
Boyle County High School, KY

Grades 7-8-9
Top Ten Winners

List of Top Ten Winners for Grades 7-9; listed alphabetically

Kate Brady, Grade 8
Wren Middle School, SC

Eileen Collie, Grade 7
Providence Academy, TN

Stephanie Jill Davis, Grade 8
Swampscott Middle School, MA

Natalie Drury, Grade 7
Lebanon Jr High School, Grade OH

Lynzee Linnarz, Grade 7
Heritage Middle School, ID

Joanna Liu, Grade 8
Bret Harte Middle School, CA

Kianna Matthews, Grade 7
Eagle Point Middle School, OR

Hannah Ritchie, Grade 7
Sailorway Middle School, OH

Austin Siegel, Grade 9
Saint Stephen's Episcopal School, FL

Celeste Watson-Martin, Grade 7
Landisville Middle School, PA

All Top Ten Poems can be read at www.poeticpower.com

Note: The Top Ten poems were finalized through an online voting system. Creative Communication's judges first picked out the top poems. These poems were then posted online. The final step involved thousands of students and teachers who registered as the online judges and voted for the Top Ten poems. We hope you enjoy these selections.

My Dad's Off at War!

My dad's off at war,
And I am at school,
Fearing my dad,
Will be shot,
While I try to stay cool.
My dad's off at war,
I had little notice,
Before he was gone,
I spent the day with him,
Which was the shortest.
My dad's off at war,
Hopefully safe,
For he's shooting people,
Hurting people, bad people,
Who live in that place.
My dad's off at war,
And he has returned,
But he has changed,
And he isn't the same,
I'm hoping my real dad will come back.
My dad's off at war.

Jennifer Sixtos, Grade 7
Ramsey Middle School, KY

My Lovely Ocean

Forever changing,
Always moving, never still,
My lovely ocean.

You are full of life,
A mystery to humans,
My lovely ocean.

You give me kind gifts,
But take what men value most,
My lovely ocean.

My lovely ocean,
How wonderful you can be,
Don't leave me alone.

Corinne Schnadelbach, Grade 7
White Station Middle School, TN

I Am From

I am from the white house on Rosemary
I am from the wooden playground
I am from the bricked basketball court
I am from the crowded streets after a game
I am from the nights chasing my cat
I am from the Old Well
I am from Sunrise Biscuits
I am from the Dean Dome
I am from a college town
I am from Chapel Hill

Stephen Smith, Grade 8
Westchester Country Day School, NC

To My Mom and Dad

I love you so dear,
and I am always very happy when you are near.
You are always there for me when I need you,
and this is why I love you.
I can always talk to you about anything
even though what we talk about can be many things.
When you get mad at me when I do something wrong, I get kind of scared,
but it just shows me that you care.
You send me to a Catholic school to get a good education
even though it is expensive.
You run me everywhere I need to go,
to dance, swimming, volleyball — you never know.
At the end of the day you may be tired,
but for what you do you are admired.
Mom, you stay home and you are as sweet as honey,
while Dad is at work making the money.
When you go shopping,
the things you bring me back leave my eyes popping.
I will always LOVE you with all my heart!
Even one day when we are apart!
Love, Cassie

Cassie Collins, Grade 8
St Agnes School, KY

Papa's Window

Inside looking out
I see my papa in his hospital bed,
I hear the cries of my family as heavy as a ton,
I smell the oxygen tank as it helps my papa keep going,
I feel him hug me for the last time,
I taste the tears drifting down my face,
I will never look at that window the same again.

I will never forget looking into that window,
I will never forget my papa,
The memories in that window are priceless,
I feel the warm embrace of my family as we pray for my papa,
I feel the tears dripping down my face,
I watch my papa as hard as a bull to stay alive.

When I walked into the house for the first time without my papa alive,
I went to the window where he spent his last moments and sat there and cried.

Brandon Eschman, Grade 7
Mount Washington Middle School, KY

Happiness is...

Happiness is the tears on a new mom's face when she adopts a baby.
Happiness is when a little girl opens a birthday present.
Happiness is the smile on a child's face on Christmas morning.
Happiness is when a girl goes on her first date.
Happiness is a look on the dad's face when his little girl gets married.

Holly Everman, Grade 8
Boyle County Middle School, KY

Foods

This is a poem about food I like,
From chocolate pudding to roasted pike,
I'll start with PB&J,
Who doesn't like this classic family fave?

Another food is a turkey sub,
Preferably from Subway or The Hub,
The Hub also has hot chocolate,
I'll drink it until my pants don't fit!

Applesauce is always hot,
Either homemade or Motts,
Pudding is of the same type,
Chocolate or vanilla, it gets all the hype,

Once I had an amazing pork chop,
Of all my favorite foods, it's on the top,
I like my ribs with barbecue,
But I'm always willing to try something new.

These are some foods that I like to eat,
From peppermint bark to barbecued meat.

Austin Anderson, Grade 8
Boyle County Middle School, KY

Grandpa

I feel the room go black
And pain run down
Into my body tears running
Down my face landing
On my mom's hand
My life has just gone bad my
Grandpa is dead
He was the one when I walked
Into the door he would say here comes trouble
My grandpa was the one who made my day
When I was upset
My grandpa walked me down
Stairs because I was scared of his dead fish
Hanging on the wall
My grandpa would snore like a bear
Trying to fight
But that's what made me
Love him even more
One day I will walk up into heaven with him someday
when god says it's my time to go
And I want my grandpa to say
Here comes trouble

Kenzie Miles, Grade 8
Hebron Middle School, KY

Stones

Solace is a quiet, near-unattainable thing
That never attends honest funerals.
While grief roars
And flings itself against the parameters of the heart
Sorrow of the oldest sort curls within,
A networking of tender, subtle wounds.
We watch consolation drift away on nameless winds
Hoping the beloved soul is carrying its warmth,
Despite knowing that it means
We may never be consoled again.
Silence is not a balm —
We hear the emptiness, but we feel
Loving voices long gone to ground.
It is a bitter reminder of loss, worn smooth
And round
With constant tight grip.

Hannah Bledsoe, Grade 9
Middle Creek High School, NC

Love

Warm blood flowing though my veins,
searching for where my heart lays.
I finally found what I am looking for,
something hurts me deep in my core.
I am here now knocking on your door
while the rain pours.
Looking at the moon makes me want you more.
Your eyes are green,
her skin is like vanilla bean.
If you can only hear the sound of my heart,
we will never be apart.
Every time I see you my heart pounds stronger and stronger.
Every time I sit close to you the
further I fall.
Hoping for you to open the door,
when you do you should lead me down the hall.

Ahmad Hadariya, Grade 7
East Millbrook Magnet Middle School, NC

Blue

Blue symbolizes sadness of a lonely soul
Frozen but yet warm with a calm, steady flame of brightness
Deep, blue, cold water with the scattering and reflecting silver fish.
Frozen icebergs float as monsters all big and scary.
The light blue sky filled with soft fluffy clouds
Filled with deep tears of wet emotions
When I think of blue I think of bright, cheery, crazy, beautiful color
Blue is the color of his eyes

Taylor Sandifer, Grade 8
Montgomery Central Middle School, TN

Father

Our Father, an amazing God,
He is there when we are weary.
He sees us when we feel invisible,
But looks upon us and tells us
"I have made you beautiful in your own ways."
He gave us gifts beyond compare.
We have everything and even more.
What more is there to ask for?

Brenna Williams, Grade 7
Providence Academy, TN

Gone So Fast

It was all so soon
It was that one day
When he had left
I felt great pain
It was all so soon
On only one day
My heart is solid like a rock
But when I see him my heart just stops.
It was all so soon
It happened one day
He just comes and goes
But when we will never know.
It was all so soon
Only on one day
I fill up with pain
Because when he comes back he is not the same
It was all so soon
It was that one day
Although he left I will never forget
The day he left I wish I went.
(It was all so soon)

Junathean Cunningham, Grade 7
Ramsey Middle School, KY

Joy of Happiness

happiness is playing your favorite sport
getting ready for the big game with all your friends
friends are happiness
having fun on the beach or at a house
happiness is getting good grades
being able to go home and show your parents
that you did good in a school there paying for
knowing that you're smarter than you were
knowing that you were the best is happiness
happiness is helping a friend when there in need of it
helping them with a family problem
happiness is materialistic too
getting the newest phone
having the best equipment
happiness can be anywhere
happiness can be anything

Cutter Jackson, Grade 8
Baylor School, TN

Sunshine

You shine bright in the sky
And give us light each and every day.
Keep us warm when we are cold.
Are always there, even when we cannot see you.
Your yellow rays fill up the sky.
You are a beautiful thing.
You make me happy when I see you.
You give me the feeling of a great day!
Oh, sun please never go away!

Erin Walsh, Grade 9
Bearden High School, TN

Phobias

People are afraid of a variety of things,
Snakes, spiders, heights, and even clowns.
Sometimes people are afraid to talk in public or to sing.
All of these things can make you scared, or want to frown.
We all know somebody who is afraid of shots.
Friends and family that don't like the dentist or the doctors,
Who panics from things like knots and spots.
Fears of riding in ambulances and helicopters.
Little kids are afraid of monsters and the dark.
Others get nervous walking through places,
Going through alleys, forests, or even parks.
It really scares them when they see unfamiliar faces.
Some people are afraid of drowning or fires,
Or funnier fears of objects like mannequins.
Older people fear they will be forced to retire,
While some fear the dangers of pencils and pens.
These fears, or phobias, can be pretty scary,
That makes your heart race and feel off track.
The fears could be for something regular, or out of the ordinary,
They can even cause you to have a panic attack!
So, close your eyes and pray that it won't come back!

Tiffany Workman, Grade 8
Petersburg High School, WV

Hide and Seek

Writing is like playing a game of hide and seek.
The worst ideas have easy hiding places,
and are always the first found.
But the best ideas last through a few rounds.
Writing hides on the top shelf of your closet
locked away in a box of forgotten dolls.
It hides under your bed
among clothes, notebooks, and shoes.
It hides in your old Disney princess dresses
or inside the tree house.
Writing jumps into pictures
and hides in the smile on a friend's face.
It can climb all the way to the top branch
of the redwood
waiting for you to discover it.

Caroline Duggan, Grade 8
Baylor School, TN

One Rainy Night

One night, my dad and I were walking outside of some stores.
It was softly raining that night.
I told him I liked it when it rained.
We kept walking down the sidewalk, talking.
My dad told me a few stories.
Some were funny.
After a while, we stopped in front of a store that I liked.
Then, I showed him an outfit.
He told me we'll go to that store another day.
This is a time I'll remember with my dad.

Alexa Salazar, Grade 7
Freedom Middle School, TN

Lie

Lies, you hear them in the hallway
You see them
You say them
You pass them on
You live through them
You hate them
But still you always start them
They may be small
But eventually they grow
They keep growing and growing
But do we want to stop them?
NO
Do we think about the consequences?
NO
Do we care about who gets hurt?
Never
To some people lies are just lies they come and they go
So that new ones can begin
But for others they can ruin a person's life
Even stop it
So why do they exist…

Katie Kelly, Grade 8
Camp Ernst Middle School, KY

Seasons

Summer is hot,
But it's a lot of fun,
Playing and swimming under the sun.

Autumn gets cool,
Orange and red leaves falling to the ground,
Enough turkey and pumpkin pie to go around.

Winter is frigid,
Fluffy white snow would be nice,
But it seems that we only get ice.

Spring is my favorite,
All the flowers are in bloom,
Time to go and get out of my room.

Lucy Hoard, Grade 7
White Station Middle School, TN

Hi I'm Scott

I am special, weird, hyper, amusing.
Who cares about our troops.
Who intends to get a job.
Who wants to be known as that person.
Who wants to respected for myself.
Who fears the world blows up.
Who wants others to laugh at me.
Who gives tips to waiters.
Who dreams of dreams.
Who believes in the words of Gen. Patton — "Nuts"

Scott Gauld, Grade 7
Meredith-Dunn School, KY

Friends Forever

I am looking outside a window,
I see my friend doing nothing.
I am looking at my good times with him,
Playing Uno is his favorite game.
I see his new home,
Where he will be forever.
I wave to him.
Even though he can't wave back,
I see him in my heart waving back at me.
Even the trees are waving at him.
As I say goodbye,
My heart feels like a volcano about to explode.
My eyes are water guns,
Spewing out water.
I hear people crying.
I smell the roses.
As I leave,
I taste the bitterness of sadness,
In my mouth.
This is the last time I will see his face.
I am looking at my friend Corbin's grave.

Morgan Vaughn, Grade 7
Mount Washington Middle School, KY

Still I Stand

Still I stand,
Even though days are dark,
And everyone takes a part,
In the bad doings to make pain,
But still I stand to gain and gain.

You may look like the prettiest girl,
And you think you can rock anybody's world.
Some people think life is a game,
But still I stand as the same and same.

Some people are rich and some are poor,
But soon the poor will see an opened door.
Some animals fly and some animals walk.
But still I stand to walk and talk.

Destiny White, Grade 7
White Station Middle School, TN

The Lake

Around the dock, the water sits
Below the clouds, the fish eat bread bits
Under the boat, the motor roars
Behind my board, the water soars
Above my head, the birds will fly
Around the clouds, so very high
Before the sun sets, I go for a swim
With my brother, we race, but I always win
Back to the dock, with minutes to spare
After such great sights, there's happiness everywhere

Lindsey Basham, Grade 8
Heritage Middle School, TN

Unhappy Art

Sadness comes, right to my heart.
It's not a piece of happy art.
It's a piece of extreme depression,
and does not leave a good impression.
It feels like the world is no more.
Nothing and no one at any door.
It's a loss of work and time.
Nothing else but shame and hide.
It happens to both positive, negative,
Mean, nice or anyone sensitive.
There is no one to help and cure.
My body doesn't feel pure.
My tears fall down.
Which build a town.
Then they blast.
My heart pumps fast.
I will fall until I am on the core.
I will rise until I am on the floor.
All the happiness is sucked out.
There is nothing left to be happy about.
You lose yourself in water and fire.
Everything else gets expired.

Maryam Ali, Grade 8
Reedy Creek Middle School, NC

Realization

I watch you with fascination.
With all my admiration.
I have this temptation.
This wonderful sensation,
To start a conversation.
Yet, I have hesitation,
To get to that destination.
I need more information,
About your education.
What is your expectation,
Who is your inspiration?

I have this combination,

Of my realization,
That you are my motivation,
My dedication.

So, that is the situation.
In abbreviation,
I love you, with desperation.

Vicky Huynh, Grade 8
Rossview Middle School, TN

The Sound of Nothing

I call out for life,
and wonder why I am here,
in the lonely wind.

Tyler Adkins, Grade 9
Spring Valley High School, WV

Grandma

This is a poem to my grandma
Who was there for me no matter what,
Even when you were far away.
When I was afraid,
You comforted me and told me everything was okay,
And it always was, because you were with me.
You were there for all the milestones in my life
And sometimes you were just there,
And you have no idea how happy that made me.
You read me stories,
And the sound of your voice always made me happy.
But then things took a turn for the worse,
And your condition worsened.
As you got sicker, the hole in my heart was bigger.
And I thought I would never get through it.
I wished I was there for you,
Like you were there for me.
But now I know that you're here with me,
Just like always.
And now I have one wish; that I could've been around a couple years earlier
Just to spend a few more with you.

Isabella Ramicone, Grade 8
St Agnes School, KY

Love

I look around me, flowers at their bloom
Birds singing, people laughing, me remembering
What a bad place we were living in then.

I wonder to myself, "What went wrong?"
Watching the news I see things happen.
September 11, crime, theft...
No one to help stop it; yet no one trying to.

There are people dying
So we should land a helping hand
This could be the greatest gift of all.

The cool crisp air brushing through my hair
Looking around noticing our home, our country, getting better.
People giving that helping hand, love is now in the air, there shall be no hate!

Kelia Wilson, Grade 7
White Station Middle School, TN

Golfing for a Lifetime

Well, I remember a time around last year in the summer of 2009
That I went to visit my grandparents, aunts, and uncles in Mississippi.
Every time I go to visit I play golf with my grandfather, (he taught me how).
I never was really interested until last year.
One Saturday I went and played golf with all of my family who were golfers.
And we played thirty-six holes of golf that day!
After we played golf we went to Ben and Jerry's for ice cream and that was fun too.
I will always think of this moment in my life.
Because I will always love and cherish my grandfather and family.

Christian Blackwell, Grade 7
Freedom Middle School, TN

If I Were a Bird

If I were a bird,
I would fly across rainbows
To find what's at the other end.
If I were a cloud,
I would float around the world
To see all there is.
But I'm just a girl,
Locked in the reality
Of the real world.

If I were a mouse,
I would walk without worry
Of a cat nearby.
If I were a wild cat,
I would roam the mountains and jungle
The queen of all animals.
But I'm just a kid,
No time to live the dreams
I long to escape to.

Gianna Rini, Grade 7
Grey Culbreth Middle School, NC

Questions Unanswered

Asking questions,
Some answered
Majority unclear.
Curiosity covers the brain
Like a comfy blanket
Covering a newborn,
Nothing can open the key
To the unknown.
Finding the answers
Will not work for
You have to have a key.
When you find it
You will have relief,
Knowing that you
Have answered the unknown,
But that day will never happen
For only death can provide
The answers.

Mya Thompson, Grade 7
Center for Creative Arts, TN

My Little Brother

My brother is annoying,
As annoying as can be.
He is always in my way
And can't stop bugging me.

He messes with my stuff
And sometimes breaks things, too.
And when I tell him to go away,
He just runs to mom and cries, boo hoo!

Then I get in so much trouble,
But he just gets away with it.
He doesn't get in trouble,
Not one bit!

But even though my brother is annoying,
As annoying as can be.
I love him very much,
As much as he loves me.

Maggie Childers, Grade 7
St Vincent De Paul School, WV

Windows

Your golden green eyes look down at me.
They shine like the sun,
And they sparkle like the stars.
Your eyes glow in the darkness.
They gaze intently upon me,
Penetrating the depths of my heart.
Your eyes are windows,
Paths of light down into your soul.
They remind me of waves,
Ever crashing on the shore.
I can see the mountaintops,
Glistening in the morning sun.
Your eyes mesmerize me,
Putting me into a state of
Complete trust and peace.
I see a small patch of heaven,
Through the windows of your soul.

Victoria Pearce, Grade 8
Veritas Christian Academy, NC

Nature

Trees swaying in the wind, snowflakes
Are falling so fast it will make
The scene a blur, each one different
The snow sparkling quite brilliant

Red gold leaves in autumn falling
Flowers blooming in the late spring
Horses with grace and majesty
All of these things are quite lovely.

Torie Wellman, Grade 9
Spring Valley High School, WV

Downtown

When I look downtown,
I see all the people,
In rush hour.

When I look downtown,
I hear car engines racing, roaring,
The siring sounds of sirens.

When I look downtown,
I smell barbaric bourbon,
The smell of gross gas.

When I look downtown,
I feel protected,
Like a bulletproof vest.

When I look downtown,
I feel unstoppable.

Griffin Rogers, Grade 8
Bondurant Middle School, KY

The Mark

On the paper,
On your arm,
On the floor,
On the door,
They are everywhere.
An accident or on purpose,
They happen every day,
By marker,
By pencil,
By paint or pen or mud,
The mark is everywhere.
Look around you,
Don't you see it?
A spot here,
A dash there,
Maybe even a stain,
The mark stays with you,
Forever.

Isabella Lyons, Grade 8
White Station Middle School, TN

The Eyes

I feel as though
I am being watched.
In my bed, at night, when the door
Shuts tightly, and the blood-red curtains
Seal off all light, the eyes
Peek around the corner
And stare.
When I am alone,
And cold,
And scared,
And I feel as though the air is closing in on me,
Sealing me in like a Ziploc bag,
They are there.
And they stare.
Regardless of where I go,
From the unbelievable height of the tallest mountain,
To the unfathomable depth of the deepest ocean,
To the pitch-black darkness of the darkest, dampest cave,
They follow me.
They search for me, they find me,
And stare.

Quinn Mulroy, Grade 7
White Station Middle School, TN

Grandmother's Attic

Outside looking in
The room is quiet
I hear the silence in the air
Above the stairs is a doll
A doll with short, cut hair and dirty, smiling face
Across the room I see a closet
Full of clothes, they whisper to the bed
Telling all their stories of their adventures
Through the door is a room
A room full of my grandmother's toys and books
It's a jungle
Of boxes and more clothes
And more excellent stories
Another closet
Like a cave it goes way back to the wall
I smell the Christmas feast
Come up the stairs
I feel the warmth of my friendly family
I join them
I taste the wonderful food
Now inside the glass

Amber Coleman, Grade 7
Mount Washington Middle School, KY

Sunflower

I am five,
Skipping through a field of sunflowers,
taller than the Great Wall of China.
The sunflowers are like a canopy above me.
They make me feel safe.
I notice the sun-kissed butterflies landing on my shoulder.
They open their wings to show me their colors.
Sunflowers are as bright as the sun,
and as smooth as Mamma's hair.
I pick a sunflower chanting,
"He loves me. He loves me not?"
I wonder why the yellow flowers are so tall,
but I am only five.
I also wonder what the flowers taste like?
I wouldn't dare try them cause Mamma would get mad.
Mamma says, "you never listen," but I guess I will this one time.

Makala Shankle, Grade 8
Baylor School, TN

Where I Am From

I am from the yellow house on the hill
From the thick forests of West Virginia
I am from eating cereal every morning
From the toy cars and action figures
I am from wooden bunk beds
From soft green grass
I am from a turtle shaped sand box
From a little tricycle
I am from Hand in Hand Day Care
I am from drinking orange juice like there's no tomorrow
I am from going to church every Sunday
I am from the nasty school lunches
from memorizing all the books in the Bible
I am from stealing snacks from the day care
From playing in the mud with my sister
I am from the yellow house on the hill

Steven Hairston, Grade 8
Sissonville Middle School, WV

Red

This red I see is the fall of the human race
This color gets brighter every second
It leaves its mark on the lives it takes away
This crimson trail leaves the warning for all to see
As the warning is given the more we refuse to stop
But the more we refuse the desire for vengeance greatens
If this continues any longer what is to come
The end of time, or punishment for our stupidity
What is to come of this life of crimson red

Zachary Haston, Grade 8
Montgomery Central Middle School, TN

Me

While smiling all of the time
I still have things to hide
Never showing my emotions
And always keeping things inside

I keep my goals set sky high
I'm prepared for anything that comes my way
Never waving to my friends good-bye
Makes them all want to stay

Savannah Clark, Grade 8
Montgomery Central Middle School, TN

Peaceful Rain

The cool drops fall as light as a feather.
I walk over the slippery stones
And hear its sound.
Pitter-Patter Pitter-Patter.
The damp breeze sweeps through and through.
Yet it's silent, almost unheard.
As it wraps around me, it feels strangely
Calming.
The overcast clouds make my surroundings
Become satiated shadows.
It dulls the colors and glazes it
With a gloom.
As I'm overtaken with peace I notice the details:
The quivering of the grass, trembling of the leaves,
And the fresh scent of a rainstorm
Soon to come.
The pitter-patter of rain, the silent sweeping wind,
The overtaking gloom, and the fresh scent of rain
All lead to peace
My peace
Peaceful rain.

Todd Stetler, Grade 8
Bondurant Middle School, KY

Sailor's Anguish

The captain of the mission
looks for someone to hand the precious jewel to.
But when he did, he gave it to a bandit in disguise!

The captain's head hung low,
as he walked to the cabin.
Furious with himself. Furious like a lion,
cursing under his breath.

The would-be escort kicked himself mentally,
also cursing himself.
He went to a separate cabin,
and completely collapsed on the boring bed.

The bandit cheered loudly.
His friends, tackling him with joy.
The war was over. They ran off in victory.

The enemy won. The homeland had lost.
Going home in defeat.
No prize.

Evan Hatter, Grade 8
Bondurant Middle School, KY

You Don't Know Me

You don't know me
You don't know where I come from
Who I am
Or what I do
You don't know where I was yesterday
Where I am today
Or where I'll be tomorrow
You may look at me differently than the others
But I am me and you are you
I'm Whitney Aliese Nicole Mason
And I don't care if you like it or not that's me not you
And if you don't like me say it and then shut up
Because it's my turn to talk
Not yours
Get it
Got it
Good

Whitney Mason, Grade 7
Ramsey Middle School, KY

Clear Pool

Inside looking out
I see a large crystal clear pool
I hear birds humming, chirp, and chirp
I smell the strong chlorine
I feel the rough smooth layer of glass of the window
I taste the bubbly bubble gum-pop-pop

Without my window
It's just a dark wall
It is as dark as a night
It's like nothing was ever there
But something was there

Out the window was
A melted ice cube
Waiting for
To jump in it

Prescott Goodman, Grade 7
Mount Washington Middle School, KY

Red

Red is envy, love, and passion.
Flames of love spark between lovers.
Two hearts beat together as one.
Volcanoes erupt in madness.
But at the same time young love is everywhere.
Hugs and kisses all around for the new loved ones
They have recently found.

Kelsea Bulmer, Grade 8
Montgomery Central Middle School, TN

My Dad and I

I remember in the winter in 6 in the morning.
When I went to Illinois with my dad and my two other uncles.
To watch a soccer game it was really fun.
That day the stadium was really cold.
When I came back to Tennessee I played soccer with my cousins.
Later that day I went to Pueblo Real.
This was a day, I will never forget.

Humberto Angel, Grade 7
Freedom Middle School, TN

Seasons

Autumn leaves fill the ground.
The summer air turns colder.
The children laugh and play in the leaves.
Autumn comes once a year.
The tree became bare this time of year.
Autumn leaves color the ground — orange, red, and yellow.
Big trash bags sit in front yards filled with leaves.
Halloween is around the corner.
Children fill the streets with bags of candy.
Dressed up as Superman, Spiderman, and witches.
They run and play with friends and family.
Thanksgiving comes and you celebrate the Pilgrims.
Adults cook good ol' pumpkin pie.
Children stuff themselves with food.
Family comes from different places.
Then winter comes, and it's cold.
It snows. and children play in the snow.
Then summer comes, and we all have fun.

Christiny Seagroves, Grade 7
Elkton School, TN

The Spot

Inside looking out
See the bright summer season
As hot as the glowing sun
The burning heat melts my skin
No worries
Chocolate flavor bounces throughout my mouth
Sweet smell of nature lurks through the room
Birds chirping, bees buzzing, wind chime clinking
When I'm here I float off to different world
Where my mind is free
No worries

Eliza Love, Grade 7
Mount Washington Middle School, KY

Basketball

Basketball is the best sport ever played
I do it for a passion not just to get paid
I can drive it in, shoot a 3, or even lay it up
Take a dunk, free throw, or even throw it up
Now I'm here, Championship Game, about to get my first ring
I can't remember how it started but it all was my dream
Now I'm here playing ball, getting paid with my team
Couldn't do it without practice or even self-esteem
Now I'm done, scored points, broke records, did it all
And remember my sport, the only one standing tall,
And remember what sport it was, of course it's basketball.

Jarlen McDonald, Grade 8
StudentFirst Academy, NC

Where Might I Be?

The woods
So cold and dark
I sat there alone
And watched the rain kiss the leaves
I could not find my way out
I screamed for help
My flashlight darkened and darkened
As I became closer and closer
To a river of dancing waters
I could not see where I was going
The moon hid behind the dark clouds
So I lay there by the riverside
I cry Mommy, Daddy!
Come find me!
But all I hear is crickets and the whistling of the wind
I had not seen the sun for days
How did I get here?
Does anyone know that I'm gone?
I saw a light in the mist, so I chased it
Then suddenly, I became face to face with…

Faith Wright, Grade 9
Robert C Byrd High School, WV

I Wonder, I Wonder…

Her words cut like thousand knives,
Every word she says makes a deeper wound.
I hope and pray for the best, will it be true?
Some days I think it is, some days I just want to die.
Someone save me, but who?
I wonder, I wonder…But who?

Her words cut like millions of pieces of glass.
Each one of them shattering me more.
Her words are my worst enemy, the kind I can't escape.
Someone save me, I'm dying on the inside can't you see?
I wonder, I wonder…Can you see?

Her words cut through me like nothing has ever before.
One person I trusted, loved and cared about hurt me like this.
I hope one day it gets better, or will it?
I wonder if anyone knows, or notices?
Does my smile cover the pain and hurt?
Maybe there's someone who does and will come for me.
I wonder, I wonder…Who will?

Emina Proha, Grade 9
Atherton High School, KY

Clouds

Clouds are
Gray, clouds are white,
Clouds float feather light,
Clouds look down at us
And cry, we call it
Rain, clouds call it pain.

Nicolas Monnet, Grade 7
Grey Culbreth Middle School, NC

A Colorful Beginning

Darkness surrounds me as Daddy and I walk down the boardwalk
Camera in hand
And sit in the soft white sand
We begin to wait as the waves gently crash
"Splooshhhh. Splooshhhh. Splooshhhh."

As the sun climbs into the sky
Sand crabs scuttle to their holes
And seagulls dip in and out of the sea
Hunting for their morning prey
The sun was climbing higher and higher
Into the sky
That was when the colors appeared
Every color, every hue, a rainbow across the sky
The sky was becoming a painting
As the artist added the last details
Daddy was snapping pictures
So we could remember the beautiful scene
The sun was high in the sky
As we packed up to leave
With the perfect start, to a perfect day

Hannah Webber, Grade 8
Bondurant Middle School, KY

Football

The smell of the freshly cut grass
The sound of a last minute touchdown pass
The practices 5 days a week
Getting a win is what they seek
Lacing your cleats up tight
Hoping you do the drills right
Wearing your jersey on game day
Listening to what your coaches say
Running out of the tunnel, helmets gleaming
Looking in the stands, fans screaming
Your school's band is playing
Not listening to what the other team is saying
Watching TV, all the playoff drama
Bandaging up all your battle trauma
Making fans scream and shout
That's what I think football is all about.

Zach Thompson, Grade 7
White Station Middle School, TN

Splash!

Outside looking in
I see myself fast as a cheetah, graceful as a swan
I hear the water beating on the backs of people at work
The smell of chlorine fills the air
I can feel nothing but the heat from the boiling waters of the sun
I taste Gatorade trickling down my dry and dehydrated throat
The water smiles as I hear myself diving in,
SPLASH!
Without my window hard work would not exist

Sydney White, Grade 7
Mt Washington Middle School, KY

Melissa Who

Melissa who is beautiful
inside and out.
Who has hair as dark as
the tip of a pencil.
Who has hair as long as two
rulers put together.
Who smells like a rose just
after it has rained.
Who is hardworking and strong.
Who is oceans and sands.
Who is pencils and paper.
Who has dark skin from going
to the tanning bed.
Yet her skin is as soft as a
horses' nose.
Whose voice sounds like a
choir filled with angels.
Who demands that I clean my room.
Who works as an accountant in Huntington.
Who still after all of that
says she loves me.

Haley Petitt, Grade 9
Spring Valley High School, WV

I Refuse!

I turn in circles, looking around me.
I flip on the news, but nothing excites me.
I witness the heartbreak, grief, and strife;
Meager emotions of our life.

They seem to draw you right into despair.
You'll moan "Nothing is right!" and "Nothing is fair!"
You become depressed with every word.
They attack your soul as does a penetrating sword.

Guess what, world? I refuse!

I refuse to let this life take me down,
To cry such a melancholy sound.
I refuse to be the compromise
Of horror, distress, and the devil's demise.

I refuse to let my happiness go;
I'll let the writing shine and the music flow.
I refuse to depress while in the Lord's great arms;
If needed, I'll be His shining star.

Destinee Siebe, Grade 8
Zoneton Middle School, KY

Beautiful

Some things you see are too beautiful to put into words,
or paint a picture of,
because God already spoke the world into existence
and painted the picture of where we live.

Becca Sellers, Grade 8
Sellers Home School, KY

My World? Cheerleading...Enough Said

Cheerleading
The ultimate sport.
The only thing that puts a smile on my face.
Cheerleading. My Love. My Life.

Screaming cheers and dancing like a star,
doing toe touches and bringing my team far,
leading at least 16 girls,
Cheerleading is my world.

Wearing orange, blue and white
on every Tuesday night,
Waving pom-poms and cheering on the crowd,
Cheerleading makes me so proud.

Saying "Never Say Never,"
before every game and practice,
making so many new friends,
I hope Cheerleading never ends.

Erika Hart, Grade 8
Hebron Middle School, KY

No Basketball

I love basketball
It's the best of all
Hanging with friends
Chilling with homies
Nothing can't end
Unless someone told me
You can't shoot
You cant' score
You can't do nothing
Get out the door
Then I'm sad
Now forsaken
No more basketball
There was no mistaken

Grace Ntangu, Grade 7
East Millbrook Magnet Middle School, NC

My Life in General

My life is about riding and family
I live with all girls
Sometimes I feel left out
I'm the only guy in my house
My dog is one of my best friend's
I often feel as if I'm a burden in my household
My life for me is often very hard
But then I think to myself and know god is just testing me
That way I can become something more
I always wonder why my father left me alone
Then I do something fun to hide the pain for awhile
Someday I know I will have to fight the pain, but that's one day
Until then I'm trapped and deserted in a cold world

Trey Young, Grade 8
Montgomery Central Middle School, TN

Le Coup de Foudre

Love at first sight.
When I first saw you.
You looked into my eyes,
it was love at first sight.
Just the way you looked at me,
I could tell you were looking deep into my eyes,
through my soul, to my heart.
Your gray-blue eyes are the color of sadness,
with my love I can turn them to gold.
The color of love and happiness.
We spend each day together,
playing in the surf.
You look in my eyes,
I look in your eyes,
it is sure to be love.
There is a reason I married you,
because,
I loved you the second my eyes set on yours.
I searched through your deep innocent soul,
to find you felt the same,
for me.

Delaney Goldberg, Grade 9
First Flight High School, NC

Peace

Peace is the sun in the morning and the moon at night.
It's the grace of rain,
sparkling as it falls to the ground.
Peace is true silence as you sleep.
It's the music that floats around in the air
through your ears and into your soul.
Peace is freshly cut grass in the morning.
It's a dream in the eyes of children.
It's the purple frosting on a white cake.
It's simple and glistens in the light.
Peace is crowded with joy.
It's the sunset over the ocean.
It's snow on a Christmas morning.
It's the shine of a star in the dark sky.
Peace is a smile in the eyes of a child.

Laura Beth Hellerstedt, Grade 8
Baylor School, TN

Life of Blue

The beautiful depths of the sea
To the highest reaches of the sky
That unhappy miserable feeling
Coming from within
Blue is the brightest sapphire
Or the stunningly magnificent yet uncontrollable blue fire
Blue goes beyond the reaches of our planet
Past our marvelous light blue sky
To the biggest blue that crosses my mind
Neptune

Seth Wild, Grade 8
Montgomery Central Middle School, TN

Bedtime Woes

"Mommy! Daddy!" cried little Mary,
"I'm all tucked in and I see something scary!
There are monsters in my room!" she said.
"I hear them in my closet and under my bed!"

"These aren't monsters!" her parent insisted,
But this was the time that Mary resisted.
"I see them!" she shrieked, "all over my room!
They're coming to get me, I'm destined for doom!"

Her parents flipped on the light, and what she saw,
Was stuffed animals and chairs, not monsters at all!
She saw her pink pony with beads for hair.
She saw her dresser and her princess chair.

She went back to sleep, the evening was through.
Now, you're wondering, what does this mean to you?
It teaches you, even when things are wild and scary,
You can get through them, even if you are wary.

The burdens in this life may not seem so small,
But they really are when God is carrying them all!

Eileen Collie, Grade 7
Providence Academy, TN

Dear Someone

Dear Someone,
There is a God who died for our sins,
Then rose again to let us enjoy
This beautiful world he made for us.

And it's sad we poison each other with drugs.
And kill each other over a color.
To me it makes no sense.

But me, I was told to be a man.
Be for anything.

But the time will come,
When all the drugs are gone,
And all the racism will stop,
And we'll all unite.

Tyler D., Grade 9
Taft Youth Development Center, TN

Football

It is hard and challenging
It is quick and intense
It is fun and satisfying
It is rough and tough
It is sore muscles and smelly cleats
It is late night games and early morning practices
It is trips to the doctor and x-rays the next day
This is football

Jacob Weise, Grade 8
Boyle County Middle School, KY

Running

I run from all I have
I carry all my hurt
I run blindly, leaving no footsteps
I bump into others
I get knocked down
I don't know where I'm running
My heart takes me there

Finally people start to hold me back
But my heart is too strong
It feels too much
Then they take it
They throw it in my way
I'm blinded by my tears
I feel myself fall, and then I'm stopped

He cradles me in his arms, they're soft as daisies
I know not where I've come from, but where I've gone
He shushes my sobs and wipes my tears
Then he throws my pain away
He loves me, a love like I've never known
I finally found where I was running to, to the Love that saved me

Zoe Corus, Grade 8
J Graham Brown School, KY

An Author Is Me

An author I am to be,
I love to write, I hope you see.
My inspiration is my teacher,
I am so glad to be taught by her.
My parents encourage me to do my best,
And stand above all the rest.
An obstacle for me,
Is that I might not get the job you see.
A way I could prevent this is,
To try to be an "author-wiz."
And if I get the job and I don't know what to write,
I could read some books and get some insight.
As I reach high school I'll begin to make my mark,
By writing to help kids stay smart.
I would try to change the world by letting all kids know,
How to write and let imagination and creativity show!

Madison Rivera, Grade 7
East Millbrook Magnet Middle School, NC

Ups and Downs

Families go through ups and downs.
You don't know what's coming
If it is good or bad.
But the good thing is they love you no matter what.
Your family will always be there
For you because you are there for them.
Even though you get angry at them
They love you.

Jase Brown, Grade 7
East Millbrook Magnet Middle School, NC

A Lone Star Night

Down in Texas on the ol' cattle ranch
I put my boots on and I do a little dance
It's a western party on a long summer night
With my daddy's arm around me, it feels just right
He spots the Big Dipper as the sun fades from the sky
And asks me if I like a land so arid and dry
So without a thought I quickly reply
The city is too crowded and the mountains are too high
I need a place for dancing, just to clear my mind
The only way to free oneself from the long day's grind
Grandpa plays the fiddle and Grandma cracks a joke
Mama starts workin' 'cause the fear of being broke
I stomp my heel and tap my toe
Moving to the rhythm of that ol' banjo
The 'skeeters start biting and gnats get in my ear
But as long as I'm dancing, I have no fear
The tumbleweed tumbles
The deep thunder rumbles
And Mama begins to find that in these dry Decembers
Do a little jig and the worries, Mama no longer remembers

Virginia Douglas, Grade 9
Ravenscroft School, NC

Music Is for the Soul

Music affects your ears, your soul, and feet
There are many different types of music
But all have a unique number of beats
Tapping your feet sort of like a bomb's tick
Music can make emotions happy to mad
It can calm you just like a wave
Or it can start a good party, be glad
It is also found in nature or a cave
From a bird's hum and tweet to a lion's roar
There's genres, such as pop and also country
There is something for everyone and more
Music is for the soul, if gone we'd die
It fills the soul with its harmony
Music empowers you, it is the key

Kylie Gilbert, Grade 9
Spring Valley High School, WV

My Smile Will Never Fade

I let my tears run down my face
Just to see where they go.
I wish we were face to face so I could let you know.
Things are torn up since you went away
"He'll come back." Is what Momma would say.
Mission Impossible, on ship Nine
Years pass but not the time.
We are separated by oceans, land, and air.
But you're in my heart telling me, "I'm still Here"
I let my tears run down my face, and let them go to race
Through my Sorrow, and slow pace
You still put a smile on my face.

Corbyn Harris, Grade 7
Overhills Middle School, NC

The Gray Shriveled Mat

A beard so twiddled it spindles down,
as he walks, it snags the ground.
The children play jump-rope
as they wish, for he is
unobservant, as a fish.
They ride its back like
a furry carpet, but
he will never know,
he is so far from it.
If one were to dive
head first to ride,
they would travel
like a slippery
penguin on a
slip and slide.
Matted, tousled,
tangled, and rigid,
his hair was his pride, his joy, his kid.
But when he looked back at the gray shriveled mat,
He decided to visit the barber for a chat.

Andi Kur, Grade 9
Bearden High School, TN

The Jungle

The jungle is an exotic place
Where you can meet animals face-to-face.
You see things you won't see at your house.
Maybe a tropical tree or even a mouse.
The bananas are almost everywhere,
In a monkey's tree and a tiger's lair.
The bugs in the jungle bite like crazy.
Mosquitoes suck your blood and caterpillars are really lazy.
Wolf Spiders can have a very deadly bite.
Watch out! They might sneak up on you at night.
From the canopy layer to the forest floor,
Dangerous and harmless animals are in store.
So as you read this poem you might see,
The jungle may not seem like the place for you and me.

Nick Nestor, Grade 7
St Vincent De Paul School, WV

A Change in Direction

Love is a blossoming tulip
That bestows Cupid's arrows
Upon both the loved and unloved;
It smells like a garden of red roses
The beautiful fragrance brings about peace,
It tastes like recently baked double chocolate chip cookies
That are so enticing to eat.
It feels like the angels are hauling you up to the heavens,
It looks like an assembly of birds soaring through the air,
It sounds like the delightful music
That's assembles breathtaking emotions,
It makes the foulest person approach life in a blissful manner.

Mirabel Ijeomah, Grade 8
Leesville Road Middle School, NC

Searching

Walking, walking
Down a never ending road
Sometimes everything, even my identity
To me is unknown
Questions about who I am
Swirl in my mind like a hurricane
Questions about what I'm going to do with my life
Are driving me insane
Searching in the darkness
With no end in sight
Searching for the light at the end of the tunnel
But this I can't find
So I pick up the pieces of my shattered heart
With the remedy of the tick-tock of time
Sometimes I don't even want to get out of bed
But I trudge out
And await the cape of ever flowing questions to drape over my head
Like this poem, life doesn't always make sense and rhyme
But when it does, it might surprise you sometimes
I will make my scene
Until then, I'm just another self-searching teen

Kelsey Cole, Grade 7
Herald Whitaker Middle School, KY

They're Always There

Friends are always there
No matter if you're down
They will turn your frown
Upside down.

Friends are always there
To laugh at silly stuff
To stay up all night long with at sleepovers
And to share all the new gossip with around the school.

Friends are always there
To tell you to get better when you don't feel good
To help you up when you fall down
And to share promises that could last a lifetime.

Friends will always be there!

Alexis Kerbaugh, Grade 8
Boyle County Middle School, KY

Game Room

Outside looking in
I see video games piled as high as a giraffe's neck
Begging me to come back
I no longer hear the soothing sounds that
Once filled the room
I can taste the sorrowful cold air
I can't smell the refreshing air that used to be there
I see games as old as my grandparents
Without my window I would never see the world again

Brandon Newton, Grade 7
Mount Washington Middle School, KY

Keeping Sanity

I've matters to handle before the day begins,
I've matters to handle until it ends.
Things I do daily, But commotion never fails me.
I go upstairs, and down, upstairs and down.
And yet my features rarely curl to a frown.
School does not depress me, for my studies interest me.
But people can be stupid,
So my annoyance becomes lucid.

I bring to mind the feeling —
The rush of harmony, The exhilaration of excelling.
My wordless testimony.

Rhythms make my day so much better.
Melody makes my day so much brighter.

Most don't understand, why I am the way I am.
They don't know how grand it is, playing in a band.

The music has grown within me.
The music will forever be what frees me.

Hallie Trader, Grade 9
Spring Valley High School, WV

Eyes from Above

As I look up into the nighttime sky
I see many pairs of twinkling eyes
They are watching over us with a wise gaze
Helping us through the world's maze
As I lay down tonight to say my prayers
I thank the Lord for those caring stares
They are there for us every single night
Including times of our greatest fright
Even during the day
There is still one eye ablaze
Keeping everything alive
With all its power and all its might
And then, knowing everything they do
It hit me as though I had been kicked with a shoe
The reason those eyes give off so much love
Is because they belong to God's angels above

Emily Parks, Grade 9
Bearden High School, TN

Gone Forever

Outside looking in…
I see a dark, empty, ghost like room
I hear the wind blowing the trinkets, allowing them to speak freely
I feel her ghostly body all around me
I taste sadness and pain that's not only from me
I feel the cold, closed off room
I hear the drip, drops of rain
With out my window…
I'm lost, confused and over taken by sadness.

Ramzey Noyes, Grade 7
Mount Washington Middle School, KY

Beauty Itself

It was early Monday, when the sun awakes. I didn't want to open my eyes. It was going to be a hard day at school, as I had three tests to write, and I knew all of them would be fiascos. I opened my tired sleeping-beauty eyes and there was a beam of golden sunlight fighting its way through my curtain. I got curious like a child getting a present from Santa and forced my tired legs to take me out of the bed. My hands parted the curtains, and the sun made my room shine like fire. The sun outside my room made my skin feel like it was burning. Fire filled my soul. The sky was glowing, and the clouds looked like smoke growing from the burning sun. The trees were dancing in the spotlight of the golden, show-stopping, heartwarming day star. The landscape looked like waves curving and dancing in front of my eyes. The scenery took my breath away, every little detail made this a special day for me. The sunlight warmed my soul with energy. All my worries, troubles and anxiety dissolved. People think of beauty in a lot of different ways. It could mean to be beautiful inside like kindness, dreams, love, emotions, or promises. It could also mean to be beautiful from the outside like lips, skin, smiles, sea, sun, nature, landscapes or blossoms. I now know that beauty itself woke me up. It made me realize, it made me believe, it made me understand that beauty can be anywhere if you just look closely and enjoy the moment.

Vivien Eckert, Grade 8
Baylor School, TN

Life Long Journey

No one said it would be easy, that's why there are always mistakes in life, and by those mistakes people learn by their failures. So we have people who lose and people who win so should be discriminate them from the successful, no because one day that could be you starving, cold or even homeless, so no 'cause one day that could be you on that losing side, that could be you. When I was young and spirited, things were very simple, my heart…it was just a beating heart, and my cuteness was only used to fool you. So soon I'm older now, then not as smart, things get very complicated, along, with playing angel I now get very frustrated, things are no longer as we dream. Hey, you could say who turned off the lights. First I was too young and then too old. But I feel like I accomplished my goal. Everyone thinks death is terrible, but all that's terrible is death before time, especially if I think of my 79 yr. old grandmother, even though she died I will always know that she is watching over me. Life is like a mountain before you. Death is when you've finally finished that climb. Energy is given at birth, taken at death, borrowed in the first, repaid with the last breath. Hidden by my own shadow, I just try to face the world. I am searching for that lost pulling voice trapped inside my thoughts. Revive the freedom within my mind, hoping to be free in my own little world!

Christion Cherry, Grade 7
StudentFirst Academy, NC

I Am Who I Am

I am a Libra from the stars and a rat from China, I am a sapphire from way down in the earth
I come from the South, home of hospitality and of course everything that is fried
I come from the "Tar Heel" state and little old High Point, where settled there is High Point University, the place my parents met
I come from New Hampshire and Vermont, where man and earth are friends
With lakes and mountains and camps, that is where I spent my summer days
I come from basketball, where I would be the top dog, but a couple years passed, that faded and it evolved into volleyball
I come from finger painting and stick figures that are now becoming masterpieces
I am at a high altitude and share the name of Sherlock Holmes' sidekick, Dr. Watson
Every day, week, month, year, and decade that goes by, it shapes who I am
And
I am me

Kayla Watson, Grade 8
Westchester Country Day School, NC

A Time I'll Never Forget

As my family and I went to the fair we would ride amazing, exciting,
wonderful, extraordinary, colorful, unique, and all different rides.
We saw an old man that was seventy nine years old get shot out of a cannon!
Afterwards, we all went into the Agricultural Center and ate funnel cakes, drank coke, and played games.
I also saw some friends by chance and we rode rides with them.
My mom and I rode on the pirate ship, both of us were scared, but very excited at the same time.
We went back home exhausted.
This was one day I'll never forget.

John Power, Grade 7
Freedom Middle School, TN

Fall

Cool fall days
so short and sweet
colorful leaves
blowing by my feet
tall bright trees
up so high
as if hoping
to reach the sky
and the pure white clouds
that float so free
the chilled wind blows through my hair
as if hoping to find a home there
ah these beautiful fall days
they are so great
each year, I cannot wait
until the wonderful date
its days begin
and pray they do not end

Noah Merritt, Grade 7
Coopertown Middle School, TN

Christmas Is...

A tree decorated beautifully,
a blanket of snow along the lawn,
and a warm fire.

It is friends and family
coming together
to celebrate.

It's being happy and being jolly,
having fun and playing,
and being good

It is waking up Christmas morning
and seeing what Santa Claus has sent.

Christmas is not all about the presents,
but about joy and family.

Delaney Mealer, Grade 7
White Station Middle School, TN

Things I Do in Florida

In Florida
At the ocean
Around the pool
On a boat
Beyond the resort
Despite the rain
To the store
Inside the resort room
By the restaurant
With my family in Florida I am
always happy

Jared Bowers, Grade 8
Heritage Middle School, TN

Tribute to a Friend

The more friends a person has, the more love they receive.
I'm realizing that having one best friend really isn't my thing.
It takes a really special relationship to be best friends with one person,
but right now I love the bunch of friends I have.
I appreciate you more than you know.
Sometimes I wish I could just say
how much you mean to me,
but then I would probably sound like a freak.
People say family over friends.
Friends are family.
Just a text or phone call from you can change my whole day.
Then when I want to talk to you and you ignore me,
I don't know whether to cry or scream.
Then you ask me what's wrong.
That's a friend.
From going shopping to eating lunch together,
I know you'll always be there.
I hope we can stay friends for a very long time.
Right now, I don't need only one best friend.
So I'll stick with what I've got...
I LOVE YOU GUYS

Claire Suetholz, Grade 8
St. Agnes School, KY

Perfection

As I stood there looking at the judges I thought,
There is no way I can do this; I'm too nervous
And there are too many people
But as the judge rose her flag and I saluted
Stepping out onto the floor, I realized that I had practiced for this,
I deserve this I thought, this is my chance to shine!
Standing there waiting for my music to start I thought, I can do this!
At the sound of the "Bleep" I started jumping and flipping and twisting all around
Nothing was going through my head except "PERFECTION!"
First pass, nailed it!
Second pass, stuck it!
Last pass, perfection!
As I saluted back to the judges with a huge smile on my face
I had one thought on my mind and one thought only,
Perfection!

Krista Collins, Grade 8
Weddington Middle School, NC

My Special Day

One cool morning in May, my dad and I were off to Alabama.
My Aunt Sonya was going to spend the day with me for my birthday.
After she picked me up we went to Lifeway.
It still wasn't open, so we went to The Dollar Tree and Target, we got a little crazy there!
Before we knew it Lifeway had been open for 30 minutes!
After we went to Lifeway, The Dollar Tree, and Target we went to Chick-Fil-A for lunch.
Then, we were off to the land!
We rode 4-wheelers for the rest of the day and had a blast!
When it was time for me to go home, we took a stop at Gi-Gi's Cupcakes.
After that my Aunt Sonya gave me a card for my birthday.

Jacqulin Sumner, Grade 7
Freedom Middle School, TN

Life

Life, live life right
It is a beautiful thing we have
But it can be taken faster than given
Do not let anyone turn your life around for the worst
Life is the living soul inside of you
Life, full of death
Life, full of hatred
Life, full of sadness
Life, full of laughs
Life, full of happiness
Life, full of accomplishments
Life, keeping your eyes on the prize
You can have a good life
You can have a bad life
Just live your life
Because life is short
You may not be able to see tomorrow
Life, enjoy it to the fullest

Jamonte Grant, Grade 7
Weldon Middle School, NC

Rain Falls

I love the dreary days
When the rain falls
And I don't go about my usual ways
I answer to sleep when the rain calls

The water floating in the air
Like a bird soaring
I go on without a care
And the day is just great, just by being boring

Out the window, I can stare and look
Not worrying about having to do with anything
And passing time with an interesting book
Thinking about the rainbow that the rain could possibly bring

My favorite days are the ones that bring rain
Where I can relax and forget the pain

Allie Stephens, Grade 9
Bearden High School, TN

What Is Love?

Love?
What is it?
Hearts, flowers, chocolates?
Is that what love is, or is love something of our imagination?

No one knows what love is, but everyone will experience it.
Hearts
Girls
Boys

Love, what is it?

Nick Roberts, Grade 9
Oldham County High School, KY

My Loving Mom

This poem is dedicated to my mom
who walks in any room with a loving smile,
who always sees the inner good in people.
Although we don't always see eye to eye,
we make it through the hard times together.
You are my comforter when I am sad and gloomy,
and I try to return the favor.
What I'm trying to say is I love you with all my heart
and you brighten up my life every day
from sun up to sundown.
The fights we get into mean nothing because
our friendship can make it through anything,
even the strongest storm.
Please take this to heart and know that I mean
every single word I have said so far,
And you are my creator better yet...my mom.
Mom, I may not be the best at expressing my feelings,
just know that I am always thinking of you
and most importantly I LOVE you.

Cooper Theobald, Grade 8
St Agnes School, KY

One-Man Race

On the track field, I step up to the line;
Although no one is there, I need to start on time.
I conjure a position to start off the race;
My watch is held steady, to keep up the pace.

"Click!" I began the race with a little jolt;
The little machine had made me want to bolt.
But I've recovered now, and am on my feet;
To try to turn back now would be defeat.

I fly along smoothly, hairs blowing as they please;
But the air is too chilly, my leg start to freeze.
I must hurry home now, before things get worse;
But I will come again, and next time, get first.

Sam Fluty, Grade 8
Boyle County Middle School, KY

Who Are You?

This world is made up of decisions,
Some are small and some are large
Choices we make shape our character
Define who we are
Will we turn out good,
Or will we turn out bad?
The answer to that question is this:
Who you are right now,
And how do you look at your circumstances?
It's not about the mistakes you make,
But what you do after you make them
Always remember, it's not who you've been,
But who you are becoming.

Fred Slusher, Grade 9
Lynn Camp High School, KY

Shopping

Shopping iz fun
Shopping iz kool
I luv to shop what about you?
I shop everyday n everynite
I never get sick of shopping cuz its what I like
I shop everywhere n all da time
Shopping iz just so exciting it helps clear mi mind
My favorite things to shop for iz shoes n clothes
Cuz I like to luk gud everywhere I go
I kant be luken a mess cuz it's just no my style
I like to set gud impressions so wen people luk
They give me a big smile
I like to shop with all my friends
My mom never comes she just give me da money n my hand
I spend it all cuz mi clothes its just so expensive
Especially at da mall
I see da clothes on the mannequin it catch mi eye
So I knw exactly wat I have to do
Go luk n buy
You see what I like to do which iz shop cuz its like a hobby
I can't stop!!!!!

Aniya Davis, Grade 9
StudentFirst Academy, NC

Through the Owls

Owls fly around my dining room.
Spreading their long wings,
Hooting,
Trying to catch my attention.
There are a variety of them,
Golden, wooden, ceramic,
Smooth, rough, textured.
They were once my mysterious grandmother's.
I was never able to meet her,
Yet I feel her presence and have a connection.
Because she is like an owl,
Always watching me, making sure I'm all right.
The owls, one big family of misfits,
Were brought together by my grandmother, a collector.
She will be remembered through them,
Through the owls.

Shelbi Shultz, Grade 7
White Station Middle School, TN

Fire of the Mind

In the center of the earth there is a flame.
A flame, that in everyone's mind there is a spark.
A spark, that is your inspiration,
Used to lead you on this path of life.

The spark is influenced by your choices.
So let your spark burn bright,
Let it not be of destruction,
Let it burn to spread your light.

Bethany Schull, Grade 9
White Station High School, TN

Nerf Wars

Click, Click
My five darts are loaded
I fire them against the wall
A perfect hit!
I hear him creep into the living room
Game On!

I try to sneak out of my room
As quietly as possible
It doesn't work that way

Plan B

I'm racing into the living room
My heart pumping
I shoot two darts
Direct hit
I run to retrieve them
I'm hit on my back
My skins stings as if I were stung by a wasp, not a foam dart
I roll behind the chair reload and run

Courtney Woodyard, Grade 8
Bondurant Middle School, KY

Myself as Me

I'm a gentle whisper of dust,
That loves this world of adventure,
I travel in my mind to change the lives of others,
Only change the way of how I inspire the world,
Grasp myself for the air I breathe,
Love myself for loving me,
Meet someone I will always love,
Break away from the sorrow,
Grow something that I had already hadn't become,
Run my time of life shortly,
Transform into a creature that destroys the badness of itself,
Haught my past history of life,
Bit the recharging life of my skin,
Struggle with the fear of messing up my chances,
Die with the pain I swallow at night, as I close my eyes,
Myself as me.

Luciey Garland, Grade 7
Highlands Middle School, KY

The Tumble

Looking at the mats ahead…
Listening to peers cheer for you…
Stretching and thinking about how fast to move…
Looking then running the two steps you take…
Letting your hands glide across the mats…
Landing jump back into a handspring…
Stick the landing then up, up, up…
You jump, open your eyes…
Then tuck, it's over…you did it

Chelsee Colyer, Grade 8
Boyle County Middle School, KY

I Wiped My Hands

I wiped my hands
I'm done
I feel like I'm being blinded,
But not from the Sun.
I wiped my hands
I'm tired
Tired of being talked about
I wiped my hands
I'm done
Done with being on the outside looking in;
I wanna be on the inside looking out
I wiped my hands
I'm tired
Tired of being verbally and emotionally abused
I wiped my hands
I'm tired
Tired of being tired
I wiped my hands
I'M DONE!

America Hilton, Grade 7
Roanoke Valley Early College, NC

Junk, Junk, Junk

In my basement there's
bins full of old toys when I was a kid
Old rounded up baseball cards
Some old bounce balls that lost their bounce
Old pictures of me when I was chubby.
In my closet
Old coats and shoes
My old transformer backpack I got on my first day of first grade
Old costumes of a bumblebee and a dinosaur when I was 6
In my old regular Xbox
Old blankets when I was a baby first born
A stuffed animal monkey
Some old Legos that I haven't touched in years
And the oldest thing ever is the house that holds it all.

Daniel Lawson, Grade 7
Meredith-Dunn School, KY

Family

This is a tribute to my family
who never lets me down.
You always love me no matter what,
even when things get hard.
Thank you for always being there
and showing me that you care.
Thank you for all the opportunities that you give me
that I will never forget or regret.
I know some friends don't last forever,
but family always does.
I know I don't tell you I love you enough,
so this is for you who have taught me
to never ever give up.

Annie Kramer, Grade 8
St Agnes School, KY

Window

Outside looking in,
I see myself growing up fast,
Getting better at sports,
Baby-sitting cousins for money,
Watching the days pass by.
I hear my newborn cousin crying,
The heart monitor beeping,
My grandmother waking up from a coma,
The cries of my family at the hospital,
The sound of the nurse walking in the door,
The taste of tears dropping in my mouth.
I feel the cold skin of my grandma,
The couch was as cold as Antarctica,
The fake pillows in the hospital bed,
Hugging her for the last time,
The tears running down my face.
I smell the awkward scent of the funeral home,
The perfume and cologne of the adults,
The roses that sit next to her casket,
The food that was in the basement,
Without my window.

Corey Plahuta, Grade 7
Mount Washington Middle School, KY

Mister Death

Soft are his footsteps on the pavement
You may not hear him but he is coming
Calming the tone of his voice
You may not recognize him but he is watching
He brings news of loss and sorrow
His features sharp and hideous
His eyes are cool and clean
He will offer his condolences
He knows where you are
He knows where you're going
So free are his subjects
For he is freedom
He is the whisper in the wind
Watching us all like a hungry bird
He waits, he watches

Tim Roszell, Grade 7
J Graham Brown School, KY

The Pasture

Across the woods and grass,
Under the blue sky,
Around the corner lies a pasture,
On the land used to be a farm,
Beside the flowers I sit,
After night falls I leave,
Past the woods again,
Through the grass,
Up the gravel road,
In my house I wait for the next time to come.

Lori Sykes, Grade 8
Heritage Middle School, TN

Snow

Snow, Snow,
Shoveling,
Shivering,
Blustery,
Accumulating,
"Keep it going!"
"Stop the Process!"
Come from Fall,
Go to Spring,
Stay in Winter.
Maybe fast forward to Summer.
But everybody loves you, snow.
Without you there would be no fun in winter.
So stay for awhile and go away.
I will be sad.
Or maybe glad.
Because whatever I decide,
Will stay by my side.

Joesph Minor, Grade 8
St Vincent De Paul School, WV

The Nefarious Emotion

Jealousy is a sudden bomb:
You don't know that it's coming
And then it hits you,
It smells like the sweet aroma of warm chocolate brownies
That you want to enjoy so bad
But you aren't allowed to
It tastes like bittersweet chocolate;
Remembering all those sweet memories
Yet doubting he remembers them at all
It feels like having the wind knocked out of you
Wondering if you'll ever be able to live or breathe normal again
It looks like a fluorescent lamp to a tiny bug
You can't look away
But then you get burnt
It sounds like our song
The sweet melody now sounds like fingernails on a chalkboard;
The screeching sound you despise
It makes me wonder why I wasn't good enough.

Grace Taylor, Grade 8
Leesville Road Middle School, NC

Trust

"Should I trust you?
I don't know.
Friends aren't supposed to do what you did."
"What did I do?"
"Friends don't back stab each other.
They don't leave one another behind.
They have fun and unwind."
"I'm sorry.
I didn't know I hurt you so bad.
I'll try to be a better friend.
Can you trust me?"

Lachelle Weathers, Grade 7
Center for Creative Arts, TN

A Ride Through the Country

A ride through the country is like
Hanging your head out the window,
Of an old Chevy truck driving
Down old dirt roads,
Listening to an old Hank song.
You feel like you are at peace with the world.
Like all your worries are gone.
You feel that breeze of fresh air,
That flows through your hair,
Thinking to yourself,
This is where the heart is.

Lindsey Bowers, Grade 8
Weddington Middle School, NC

Life

I show happiness on the outside
On the inside I feel sad
I wonder what's going to happen next in life
I've been in the worst mood lately
My friend has been on my mind every second of the day
Wondering if she is going to be okay
Undecided if I should show my feelings to someone
Maybe it would make me feel better
Or maybe make me feel worse
Going to try to show my happiness to get through the day
Maybe tomorrow will be better

Lee McGehee, Grade 8
Montgomery Central Middle School, TN

True Friends

True friends are there until the end
They have your back all the time

True friends are always there to mend a broken heart
They're with you through all your climbs

True friends care about how you feel
They cheer you up when you're down

True friends are an amazing deal
They're the best things in town

Kailee Rogers, Grade 7
Elkton School, TN

Lost Battle

Inside looking out
My gaze falls to him
Like a magnet.
He tries and tries again.
It's Parkinson's disease,
The dragon that can't be slayed
I hate it, so does he.
Still, he works in the yard.
The flowers are his friends, they love him as much as I do.
He's like a mouse after cheese,
Caught in this trap.
I taste the sadness, tears.
They race down my cheeks.
Tap, tap, tap
I hear them hit the window.
I love my grandpa,
I care for him. I'm losing him.
Hearing him fall,
Flinch as I see it.
Itching to save him,
Knowing I can't.

Haley Steinmetz, Grade 7
Mount Washington Middle School, KY

Pain

Pain is all too familiar with me.
A tear runs down my cheek.
I'm glad no one will see.
As I feel shamefully weak.
Nobody can see my fear.
As I walk and silently cry.
I won't let anybody near.
And the tears come faster if they try.
So as I get shoved, and hit in the head.
They will truly never know.
That on the inside, I'm already dead.
They just keep up with the flow.
Surrounded by a crowd, I never felt more alone.
Throughout the pain and tears.
I have never let it shown.
But now is the time to stand up to my peers.

Amy Ott, Grade 8
Signal Mountain Middle High School, TN

Me

I smile all day as if trying to prove something.
But on the inside I am a kind mix of sweet and sour,
I am chocolate but also lemons.
I am generous yet selfish sometimes,
You see happy, joy, and laughs,
But I am also weeping and tears.
My family is my life but my friends are too.
I am bossy, but in a good way,
I am amazing — so they say.

Marlana Roberts, Grade 8
Montgomery Central Middle School, TN

The World in Eight Ways

A place to learn, a place to grow
A place to see what you know
A place where kids are forced to go
Drop out and say, "So," get a job with pay so low
College bound, knowledge found
Where no one has to hound for you to wear a cap and gown
Drop out is not ok, especially in this world today
My family needs the extra money
My mom says, "Sorry Honey"
Can't wait for the day I graduate
Mom and Dad oh so glad, I just think I'm that bad
Working minimum wage, with all this rage
Can't get ahead, stuck in bed
Should I go? Should I stay?
In state or out of state
UNC or UNC-G

Home at Burger King, doesn't make my spirit sing
Flipping burgers, mopping floors
Oh why am I so poor?
Now I see, things I want will never be.

Lady Johana Cuervo and Raziyah Farrington, Grade 8
Charles & Lucile McDougle Middle School, NC

The Fighting Brothers

The fight brothers
Two brothers always fighting
Separation would not be bad
But one
Always tend to sneak out
And aggravate the other.
Picking back and forth
Day after day after day a non stop world. The parents get very mad
Sometimes they try to ground us.
But we always find
away to get out of it.
By being the cute little kid
That mommies and daddies like us to be.
But then were off the hook
And the whole thing starts over.
That is the art of a mastermind.

Cody Street, Grade 8
Bondurant Middle School, KY

School

Pencil, markers and erasers
The new school year is about to start
Many bells ringing causes you to dart
Math, science, language arts and social studies
Hours and hours of studying time
Trying to pass tests and get good grades
Gym, life skills, art and music
New related art classes to be creative in
Some of them you have been in

Kori Martin, Grade 8
Boyle County Middle School, KY

The Benguin

Across the daisy-filled meadow,
Through the thick forest,
There sat a petite little creature,
With stripes of black and yellow.

With the features of a penguin,
And the black and yellow stripes of a bumblebee,
It was a funny sight that anyone should see.

Crackle...Snap...Crunch...
The confused little Benguin begins to rise,
Wondering what he would find,
And looked around in such surprise.

Quack...Chirp...Peep...
The forest began to gather around,
And look at this curious thing
Which they had found.

Brr...Brr...Brr...
The little Benguin began to sing,
And flap his little flappers,
And tap his little feet.
Even though he is strange,
He really is very sweet!

Madison Hinson, Grade 8
Weddington Middle School, NC

Girl to Media

Dear whoever runs the media
Dear whoever runs the advertising
I'm insignificant to you, I know
But there is something I think you ought to hear

From a very young age
You've been my self-appointed guide
To show me what I should be:
As pretty as my doll, just as perfect
As the girls in the catalogs

You said that if I looked
That way
I would be loved
So why do I feel like I'm trying to be the impossible?

A mule that wants to be a stallion
A stallion that wants to be a Pegasus
They are told they could be better
They believe it
But should I?

So are you also my mask:
Is what I am inside really too hideous to be given a chance?
You seem to be misunderstanding me.

Emily Parker, Grade 8
Deerstream Learning Center, NC

The Wreck

It was a dark and scary night
Down that old windy road
When all of the sudden
The brakes started to scream and I
Heard the glass of the window break into pieces

I sat very still in the back seat
Not knowing weather to move or not
Listening to the frantic screams of people yelling
"Call 911"

Then about five to ten minutes later
I heard the sound of sirens crying like babies
In the back of my head.
As it started to get louder and louder
I knew it was real

When the man who smelled heavily of after shave and coffee
Got me out of the car
And into the ambulance
I started to relax I knew I was going to be ok.

Christina Wray, Grade 8
Bondurant Middle School, KY

Trust

Trust
wins the crowd.
It struggles to get out
of the disobedient child.
The taste of trust is country fried chicken
your new neighbor cooked.
It fills your belly with a sleepy-after-church feeling.
But trust sometimes fools you,
and leads you into a dark unknown.
Millions of Germans trusted Hitler,
and their trust killed millions of Jews.
Trust is the smooth smile that starts a friendship.
Death is the struggle of trust.
You know it will come, like how salmon trust their
instincts and swim swiftly up the narrow stream without sleep.
Trust is frightening, but you have to accept it
or else you will be paranoid for life.

Ryan Smith, Grade 8
Baylor School, TN

If Teenagers Ruled the World

If teenagers ruled the world life would be a mess
We'd run around breaking things causing people stress
If we ruled the world life would be bad
The whole world would go mad
However
If teenagers ruled the world
Life would be pretty fun
Not for you, not for me, but for everyone

Kaylan Durham, Grade 8
Weddington Middle School, NC

"Daddy Don't Go."

"Daddy don't go
Don't leave my side,
What if I need you
Here with me tonight?"
"Baby don't worry
You have mommy with you tonight,
I have to go to war
And make our freedoms right."
"Daddy don't go
I'll miss you too much,
It just won't be the same
Without you with us."
As I watched him leave
Tears rose in my eyes,
He walked away slowly
As I started to cry.
I would not know
If I would see him again,
It's hard to think about it
But this could be the end.

Hannah Figg, Grade 7
Ramsey Middle School, KY

Libby

This is a poem to my best friend Libby,
who is always there for me,
As I hope I have always been there for you.
You cheer me up when I am sad
with your smiles of pure sunshine
and your laugh of bubbly song.
You solve my problems for me
and show hope when there's despair.
And you stand up for me
when people hurt me
just as I hope I've done for you.
I know that I've probably hurt you,
and you've done the same to me.
But I know that you don't mean to,
And of course, I don't either.
There's so much I could say
about all you say and do.
And I know that you love me, friend,
and to that I say
ditto.

Rachel Peavler, Grade 8
St Agnes School, KY

Springtime

As the spring wind blows in my hair,
I think of the harsh winters ahead.
But I am grateful for the time I have
to feel the sunshine, the breeze in hair,
and prepare for the winter.

Sierra Witt, Grade 7
Elkton School, TN

The Fire Within Me

The smell of smoke stings my tongue and makes me feel dizzy
My mind is telling me to run run as far away as I can,
but my heart tells me that I must stay —

So I close my eyes and step silently into the cool ash
letting it swallow me completely,
In that moment I realize that everything is gone,
my whole world destroyed by the raging flames

My home
My family
My memories
My life…gone
and I am lost questions are torn from answers that will never be found

and all the tears that I had been holding in spill from my eyes,
letting me know that this is real,
and not a dream.

Emily Poteet-Berndt, Grade 8
J Graham Brown School, KY

Tears

My tears slither down my face as snakes of sorrow
Somber and gentle as thoughts race through my head
Slowly I lift my hand to wipe away the tears
The action was useless

Wiping them just made the emotion explode; though quiet and calm
Like a baby sleeps through the night

Raging though peaceful the feeling lingers on
I close my eyes and the eery silence deafens my ears as I sit there crying;
My somber tears

Kirsten Powell, Grade 8
Davidson I B Middle School, NC

Movies

I have a wonderful movie collection. It is always ready for inspection.
There are many to choose. How could you lose?
There are many great ones, literally tons.
Some to watch if you're feeling blue, and some even leave you a mystery clue.
I have twenty-three James Bond. Those I am really fond.
I have a lot of old movies. Even some about the silly Three Stooges.
I have movies for all ages. Even some with read-along pages.
There is even some from TV shows. It is a hard choice to make, I suppose.
Walt Disney movies are always great to see. They are wonderful; don't you agree?
Cartoons are always great to collect. There are so many to be checked.
I am proud of the movies I have collected. I worked hard and have them perfected.

Zach Daniel, Grade 7
Elkton School, TN

Off to War

Off to war
She goes again
Leaving us alone
Off to war
She goes over
As she leaves
I cry on Daddy's shoulder
As she's off to war
She calls every night
I'll ask her
"When are you coming home?"
She'll say "Soon, Baby."
Every time
One night
Someone called Daddy
And tears swelled in his eyes
She was gone
But this time she's not
Gone off to war

Bethany Mattingly, Grade 7
Ramsey Middle School, KY

Off to War

The feeling I felt when you left
Was unbearable I tried to be brave because
You thought it was adorable.

The fact that you left when I was
At school made me angry with you
Having my dad go to Afghanistan made
Me realize he was a brave man.

I knew I wasn't going to see him a lot
But the sad part is me and him were
Like two pees in a pot.

Oh daddy why did you have to go
You left me nothing but pain and
Sorrow I'm always going to feel
This way even tomorrow

Deaja Drewery, Grade 7
Ramsey Middle School, KY

My Basement

What is in the basement
My Xbox 360 that is fun
My TV that is old
My games for my Xbox that are new
My Wii that I sort of play
My DSi that has a broken button
My sister's slide that is sticky
My green chair that you spin in
My couch that is uncomfortable

Jake Taylor, Grade 7
Meredith-Dunn School, KY

Middle School Drama

As soon as I arrive I find
That Mark has just dumped Sue.
Katie and Savannah are fussing
About the friends they choose.

Cassandra is with Markus
But she is also with Jim.
Everyone is deciding for her
Don't choose him, choose him!

Everyone has homework
It is driving them insane.
And everyone seems to agree
That all the stress is lame.

Matt and Susan are together
And Reagan and Jenna aren't friends
And all of this is well before
First period will end!

Callie Effler, Grade 7
Heritage Middle School, TN

Blue Moon

Could it be
a blue moon I see
They are so rare
I can't even bare

It is so bright
like it's not even night
could it be true
with it so blue

It is, it is
a blue moon I see
I hope it comes back
for all to see

Taylor Falls, Grade 7
East Millbrook Magnet Middle School, NC

I Am Sorry Mom

You take care of me each day and night
I realize I don't have the right
You deal with an unselfish boy
Who only wanted a toy
I'm sorry for what I've done as your son
Will you forgive what I've done

3 words that are hard to say
Will not forgive what I've done
I'll need your forgiveness
To feel good inside
Will you forgive me I'm sorry

Mark Thieman, Grade 7
Meredith-Dunn School, KY

Dogs

Dogs, dogs
can't name them all
some are short,
while others are tall.

Some are skinny,
some are big,
most dogs
even like to dig.

Some dogs work,
some dogs play,
some even try
to run away.

But of all the dogs,
that I like to see,
the Jack Russell Terrier
is the one for me.

Kayla Phifer, Grade 7
Elkton School, TN

The Nature of This Earth

From Nature's beautiful wonders,
Astonishing landscapes,
And to its tiniest plant
Nature is amazing

Its lakes, streams, and oceans
Is a world of its own
So are it's forests and jungles,
With all kinds of life

Mother Nature controls this world,
Making it do whatever she wants it to
What if nature is not truly amazing,
Then what else on this Earth is?

Avery Guerrero, Grade 8
Boyle County Middle School, KY

The Whistle in the Night

On a clear starry night
The light chilly wind whistles
Through the tree tops as the
Moon shines down on the ground
To light up a path for all the night
Creatures that creep and crawl
And hoot and howl until
The morning sun rises above the
Horizon and the night creatures
Sleep in all day then they dance
And work to the whistling wind through
The tree tops working by the moonlight

Elizabeth Gordon, Grade 8
Hebron Middle School, KY

In My Dreams

In my dreams you were not there,
In my dreams you did not care.
In my dreams it was all so dark,
The only things left were scars and marks.
In my dreams you left me alone,
You left me there I should have known.
In my dreams I thought you would stay,
That's what I get for thinking you just walked the other way.
In my dreams we walked hand in hand,
In my dreams we sat in the sand.
In my dreams we stood by the sea,
In my dreams you really loved me.
In my dreams you always made me cry.
In my dreams I always asked why.
In my dreams it lasted for so long,
In my dreams I thought what we had was strong.
In my dreams you always crossed my mind,
In my dreams you left me blind.
In my dreams you meant a lot to me,
But in real life it just wasn't meant to be.

Sierra Linkous, Grade 9
Robert C Byrd High School, WV

The Coming Fall

The colors change from green to red and all
The little creatures go in their own homes.
The crisp air bites my flesh with coming fall.
In the morning new frost coats every dome.
My breath comes in billowing clouds of steam
as I wait on my porch to catch the bus.
The graceful deer run through fields and jump streams.
The cold air helps to wake up all of us
and school is still boring as in the spring.
The ponds get their first layer of new ice
and first gentle flakes cover everything.
The beautiful mornings could have no price.
All lands prepare for the winters new rest.
These times of year are always the very best.

Caleb Stanley, Grade 9
Spring Valley High School, WV

Spring Day

Love is the first day in spring,
Where the sun shines bright and the daises bloom,
It smells like freshly pruned roses,
It tastes like freshly baked chocolate chip cookies,
Warm, rich, and gooey,
It feels like a warm, soft sweater,
All cozy inside;
It looks like a field of blooming yellow daises
When the sun shines bright,
It sounds like a symphony of harps,
Love is the bond between people,
And the thing that holds us together.

Katie Elks, Grade 8
Leesville Road Middle School, NC

The World Through Angel Eyes

feels as if I'm falling apart
sewn together
seams down the middle of my heart
and as I'm falling
drowned in acid tears
people keep watching
my smile hiding the secrets of my fears
waiting, hoping for my chance to bloom
alas, I stand still stuck
trapped in my cocoon
banging on the walls
only to be pushed
thrust into the freefalls
never knowing what to expect
plummeting until no end
no one willing to protect
me, until splat
splashed in the fountain of youth, the puddle of love
I wear my halo proudly atop my head
watching the world's evil from above

Adelina Salcevski, Grade 9
Robert C Byrd High School, WV

My Great-Grandfather

In the beginning, he was doing fine
The only one I could truly call mine
We used to play around
Till the day he fell down

The story from there didn't go too good
He couldn't walk but, one day he thought he could
And down he fell
Then he really wasn't doing so well

He'll be hospitalized
For the rest of his life
Nope, the doctor lied
For the next day, he died

Alyssa Houston, Grade 7
East Middle School, NC

I Am Green

I am fresh, and crisp
Natural and leafy like ivy
I am both the frog and the lily pad it climbs upon
I am the color that symbolizes envy and jealousy
I can be full, of new life;
Or dark like sea snakes
I can be in the Northern sky dancing with auroras
I am rain forest bliss
After a nice long shower,
I sparkle, glisten, and glow
I can be a shy, shallow olive
I am Green

Dalton Eatherly, Grade 8
Montgomery Central Middle School, TN

Christmas Day, Christmas Day
Christmas Day, Christmas Day
So full of joy and cheers
All the children laughing
All the parents smiling
Oh Christmas Day, Oh Christmas Day

All the colorful presents
All wrapped up in wrapping paper
Under the big Christmas tree
With the shining star on top
Oh Christmas Day, Oh Christmas Day

All the family together
All exchanging presents cheerfully
So glad they got together
To be here on this special Day
Oh Christmas Day, Oh Christmas Day
Maria Boldt, Grade 7
East Millbrook Magnet Middle School, NC

Fort Knox
Fort Knox brave but true
Strong loyal dedicated determined
Too

What it does for this
Country is important
And needs to be admired
Just as soldiers do

When I went there
You see the flag
Red, white, blue stands for
Loyalty, determination, freedom
Just as soldiers do
Brave, courage, trustworthy
Loyal Fort Knox Fort Knox
Where would we be with out you?
Robbie Olson, Grade 8
Bondurant Middle School, KY

Choices
It's your choice on the decisions
You make.
What you decide will
Stay with you every day you wake.
Life's hard,
But it's something you have to
Face.
But it's your choice
On how you take it.
Make the world a better place and
see where the choices you have
made take you.
Morgan Sevier, Grade 9
Lynn Camp High School, KY

Off to War
Off to war.
There I stand,
Fighting for our country,
No food, no home, no family

It started when I was 18.
I joined the military.
I had everything,
Now, no food, no home, no family

I stood there in Iraq.
BOOM-BOOM-BOOM!!
Fighting for what's right.
No food, no home, no family

Now a veteran;
For it feels good to be home.
But now that I'm back,
No food, no home, no family
Madison Coleman, Grade 7
Ramsey Middle School, KY

Basketball
Running up and back on the basketball
Court; trying to catch up without a fall
Thinking of a quite magnificent thing
Something that's a really important thing
To me; that is practically my life
Each day I am with it like man and wife
It is always there for me when I'm down
It always bounces up back to the crown
Of my hand; now when I want a fun fit
The basketball will be brought out from its
Place on the floor near my bed; I really
Need to get back from my water break by
The fountain and join my team in the game
Now I wish I was a player of fame
James Keyser, Grade 9
Spring Valley High School, WV

Beautiful, the Color Is
Orange is the color of fall
The color of a beach sunset
Of pumpkins ripe on Halloween night

Orange is the color of
The number one football ranked university
Auburn University

Beautiful, the color is
A color of a fierce fire
Orange is my favorite color
The dominant color of a lion's mane
Beautiful, the color is
Lauren Calhoun, Grade 8
Montgomery Central Middle School, TN

Farewell to the Day
"Farewell," whispered the sun,
Its fractious light struggling,
With the night's darkness,
A dog gave an ilk of a huff in diatribe,
As it saw the day's life,
Slowly elapse,
"Leave soon!" moaned,
The dying day to the moon,
"My brother shall come tomorrow,"
Quietly wailed the day,
The light now only nominally showing,
A placard perfect moment this would be,
Irresistible,
Like an artist next to the sea,
The horizon almost gone,
No light left to show,
The day's final words,
Were said to be,
This light no longer glows.
Diamond Benson, Grade 8
White Station Middle School, TN

Halloween
Halloween is full of candy.
People smile but I'm full of fear.
I trick or treat with my aunt Sandy.
A girl sees a ghost and is full of tears.

I get Snickers, Reese's and Kit-Kats.
Ghouls and ghosts fill the streets.
My sister runs around like a rug rat.
All goblins have big feet.

Witches fly through the air.
I look at them in awe.
The monsters will even scare a bear.
And tear off its claw.
Hannah Miller, Grade 7
White Station Middle School, TN

Ribbons
Landing so graceful
Seeing the lights make every thing
Coming to life
But only one thing caught my eye

It is the glistening pink ribbons

I don't know why it just does
Maybe its because it's the soft pink
Makes them pop out
Or because they make the show

It is the pointe shoes themselves
Emma White, Grade 8
Bondurant Middle School, KY

The Glory of the Morning

Golden Sunlight, glistening Dew
What an unlikely pairing of two
Glancing out the window it occurred to me
This is a special and strange thing to see

Every morning that seems to be what they do
As I peer outside at the exquisite two
They are very careful when they convene
The Moon might see and think it obscene

So shrouded with Mist, the forbidden lovers meet
And the two rejoice as they cheerfully greet
But this joy they share doesn't last long
The heat of the Sun cuts short their cheerful song

Then the Sun moves away, mourning for his lost love
Sailing, retreating into heavens above
Then shadow is cast over his glimmering crown
And the Dew creeps back trailing her silvery gown

The long darkness finally breaks
And the Sun in his splendor brilliantly wakes
Golden Sunlight, glistening Dew
Long live the love and glory of you!

Elizabeth Earnhardt, Grade 8
Deerstream Learning Center, NC

Behind Closed Eyes

As I lay down in my bed
Exhausted from the day's labors
I reflect on what is
And what could be.

Soon, my eyelids droop downward
And darkness falls around me.
I make one last turn
And drift into peacefulness.

I plunge into a pool of thoughts, and
Swim to each end several times.
I hope that I will take in all of the values and lessons
That this water of ideas has to offer.

Here my imagination springs into action.
Short stories play in my head
Like movies.
Their scripts write themselves in front of me.

I remember the last vision, and take it to thought.
Once I finally understand it,
My world changes.

Austen McKinney, Grade 7
White Station Middle School, TN

My Very Best Friend

I have a friend that you can count on;
He will never leave your side;
He carries you through your pain and strife;
And sees you in his eyes.

I have a friend who won't take no for an answer;
This friend makes no mistakes;
He knows who you are when you don't know yourself;
Talk to him he will listen.

I have a friend who's happy when you've done the right thing;
I have a friend who loves it when you sing music upon his name;
His heart smiles with excitement when you dance to his praise.

Not only do I have a friend;
But a very best friend;
Whose name is Jesus Christ;
But never forget He carries you through your pain and strife.

Bre'Anna Best, Grade 9
Union High School, NC

Perfect Picture

Inside looking out
I see an open field; it's full of animals,
And there's a bright sunny day
Outside my window is glowing real bright like the sun
Every time I look out the window I
See the grass and its perfect money green
My window is a perfect picture that pleases
Everyone who sees it
Outside the window the grass waves at me
Without my window, I have no perfect sunny day,
The grass no longer waves at me, and I have no perfect
Picture

Ethan Henley, Grade 7
Mount Washington Middle School, KY

Summer Days

The wind was blowing hard.
It tried to knock me over.
The sun was climbing the sky.
He was smiling, too.
Somewhere else the moon and stars were sleeping.
The clouds were running.
The trees were fighting.
The animals were playing.
The flowers were waving at children.
Before the day ended, the sun said,
"Good night, Savannah. See you tomorrow!"
"Good night, Sun," I said.

Savannah Jones, Grade 7
Leland Middle School, NC

A Good Morning

The calming sound,
Of waves as they crash.
The silence of nobody,
But me on the beach.
The orange of the sun,
Shimmering on the water.
Without but a few,
Clouds in the sky.

The seagulls coming,
To eat their breakfast of crabs,
As they scurry on the beach.
Running around,
Like the color of sand,
Not knowing where they are.
The giant pelicans,
Looking for fish,
As the waves break.

Such a good morning,
Knowing I will have to leave soon.

Brooke Pulliam, Grade 8
Bondurant Middle School, KY

Does That Mean I Do?

When the seasons change,
When people change,
Does that mean I do?

When style changes,
When the world changes,
Does that mean I do?

When everyone goes one way,
When everyone picks one thing,
Does that mean I do?
When everyone does one thing,
Do I do another? Do I go with them?
Do I follow the crowd?

Or do I hold my head up and move along?

Kaylee Jacobs, Grade 7
East Millbrook Magnet Middle School, NC

Afraid of the Truth

The smile is spread across her face
As she dances down the hallway
You always lead her to this place
Never wanting to leave; she stays

Her heart pounds as she gathers near
Wondering "If only he knew."
He's the one she wants to call "Dear."
She's scared to admit this, but it's true.

Lana Blake, Grade 9
Spring Valley High School, WV

To My Mom

You've always loved me, Mom,
from the time I was a baby, when you sang me to sleep in bed,
1and you will always love me, even after you are dead.
Your love for me forever grows, you know that it does.
Every day when I come home you're full of more kisses and hugs.
You're the one who encourages me to do the right thing and to always do my best,
and you always help me study for any sort of test.
You're the one I can go to for help with any situation,
You will always be there to help me through all my frustration.
Whether it is difficult homework or a challenging project,
you will always help me through it, and that's why you've earned my respect.
If I ever need help making a choice,
you will always give me wise advice with your friendly tone of voice.
Sometimes you seem like my very best friend,
if I'm ever sad you'll be there to cheer me up again.
You say you'll always love me; I just wanted you to know that I will always love you, too.
I would say that I love you more, but we both know that couldn't be true.
I know you're very proud of me, for all the things I do,
but I know I couldn't have done it, if it hadn't been for you.
Thank you, Mom.
Love, Skyler

Skyler Koch, Grade 8
St Agnes School, KY

There Was Silence

I approached my mother with a glittering smile.
Then, words hit my ears; the kind that astonish you at first hearing.
AND THEN, THE SILENCE.
This silence was exquisite, yet saddened my heart.
Thoughts raced, and at the moment, I was so overwhelmed with emotion, I burst into tears.
Screaming, "WHY?!" I remember.
Memories of her with her tartan at the Scottish festival.
Her smile which outshined the sun and most powerful: her youthfulness.
Always having positive energy, extremely spontaneous.
The joy she brought to holidays described the meaning of holiday cheer!

I sobbed endlessly as I ventured back through our lives together.
My photographic memory brought me joyful sadness.
My sleep was an interminable struggle.
School was endless drudgery.
My friends were now annoying, and my teachers irritated me until…
I had to let it out…I cried: remembering my amazing grandmother.

Alexis Pelton, Grade 7
White Station Middle School, TN

The Best Year Ever

Time is so slow time is so fast now that 8th grade has ended I can't believe it has passed.
Going to school is so dull and homework is so hard day after day it makes me very tired.
The friends I have made the things I have done O Wow that was so much fun.
Looking back looking forward I can't believe middle school is almost over.
What once was the future is now the present looking back it is not what I imagined.

Gabriell Shumate, Grade 8
St Gabriel the Archangel School, KY

Chicken Coop

Out side looking in,
I walk out and see
The sun going to sleep
The feather puff balls are
All waiting for me with
Their excitement that I can feel
I walk in and tell them "hello"
I can hear them saying "we have missed you"
I step in and give them grain that
smells like corn. They jump
all over me like a bunch of fish when
They get food, which I love to see.
I go over to the box
And collect the gorgeous golf balls.
I put them in the basket, tell them good-bye
and that I will see you in the morning.
Morning comes and I love the
Taste of fresh eggs in the morning and
The sound of
COCK-A-DOODLE-DOO.

Gabby Wasson, Grade 7
Mount Washington Middle School, KY

As the World Is Spinning

As the world is spinning,
I am calm;
Peaceful as I can be.
I am taking everything in stride.
The petty complaints in the media
Will make me roll my eyes.
Do they not know?
Life is meant to be lived to the fullest.
Life is about making each day count.
Life isn't about arguing.
And people say this world is ending.
Guess what? I don't care about that.
Life should be spent with loved ones.
In the end, no one cares about the money we make.
It doesn't matter who won what football game.
What matters is we live each day with no regrets.
We should never go to bed angry;
I know these things for sure.
And as the world is spinning,
I intend to make every day count.

Megan Munson, Grade 9
First Flight High School, NC

Who Am I?

I am serving our country around the world.
I am missed by my entire family and friends.
I am associated with the Marines, Air Force and Navy.
I am the strongest group of men in the world.
I'm looking forward to being home soon.
I am the Army.

Eric Hirschhaut, Grade 8
Westchester Country Day School, NC

Nature's Wonders

Do you hear the whispers of the wind?
Do you feel the kiss of the sun?
Do you see the puddles from the rain?
Do you taste the sweet air?
Do you know all the senses of nature?
Can you feel more than just cold or hot outside?
See the falling, colorful leaves of fall
See the bloomin' green leaves
Watch the crystals of snow fall
See everyone enjoying nature
The birds peeping waiting to be fed
Children playing in the streets
Stopping to watch nature do its work
Winds twisting, rain pouring
Everyone running inside to hide

Nature is extravagant, but dangerous
It has turned into a massacre of crying clouds
Take away the noise and nature is beautiful
Now the clouds are happy and puffy with joy
Nature is a wonderful sight and you should love it

Maya Robinson, Grade 7
East Millbrook Magnet Middle School, NC

The Scream

It was a dark, dark night,
All about me, I had no sight.
All I could hear,
In my ear
Was the sound of a scream

The faster I walked, the faster it came.
As if chasing me was a game.
I dodged the branches, stumbled over rocks,
Lost a shoe, and ran in socks.

Up hill, down hill, all around
The screaming followed me, the same sound.
Finally, giving up, I sat down with a moan.
Just then I remembered — a scream was my new ring tone.

Tyler Brandstetter, Grade 8
Meadow Bridge High School, WV

Stuck in LaLa Land

She waits.
Waits for something to go wrong.
Perhaps it's too perfect.
Or maybe she's waiting for him to sing her song
Because she's stuck.
Stuck in this place she's started to call home.
Before he came along, she'd been all alone.
But to tell you the truth, she likes it there.
When it revolves around him, why would she leave?
So she waits…

Bailey Nykole Holcomb, Grade 9
Dickson County High School, TN

Off to War

"Daddy, daddy, please don't go
Instead stay with me"
"No baby, no for I must go
Children are starving
People are dying
Afghanistan needs me."
"But I will miss you so
Don't go there are too many hurtful deaths
You must not go!"
"Daddy, daddy, please don't go
For I fear you not coming back
And play video games with you."
"I swear to you if anything more
But, daddy look at the sky."
It is so gray and dull
"Daddy, daddy, please don't go
Because of you there are tears coming from my eyes
I'm so scared that you will die!"
"You must have faith in me
As I fight I will be thinking of you."

Abigail Rowe, Grade 7
Ramsey Middle School, KY

The Court's Beauty

The court seen as the nature of beauty
The wind rushes, blows,
From fence to fence.
The net swaying back and forth, back and forth, from side to side.

The tennis balls walking slowly through the court
That enthusiasm as you pick up that shiny bright orange racquet.
That "Slash!" As you hit the yellow striped ball.
The racquet slowing the pace
After it hits that ace.

The sun beaming, court glowing
Trees casting the shadow among the concrete court.

The court is the nature of beauty
The green grassy grassland, that lay restless before
That unexplainable feeling as you walk away.

The everlasting court
What a wonderful place...

Abaiz Shahid, Grade 8
Bondurant Middle School, KY

Shoes

If boots were made for walking, these shoes were made for talking.
If shoes could talk when they walk, I wonder what they'd say?
"Let's go dancing or how about prancing.
Add some bells and we might jingle all the way.
Stomping, romping on our merry way, tip toeing all the day.
Heel-to-toe, dosey doe." I bet they'd say, "Let's go, go, go!"

Emilee Hudsmith, Grade 7
White Station Middle School, TN

In Remembrance*

So far away you went to be.
Every day I wish you'd stay with me.
I think about the time we had,
and sometimes it almost makes me glad.
I know that you are safe with him,
and you'll always look down on us and grin.
I know that you are free at last,
and that all of this is just your past.
I know you did all you could do,
and you lived your life till it was through.
So many deeds and favors done.
So many lives you've filled with fun.
Every now and then I'll shed a tear,
but still I know I have nothing to fear.
I know that you've saved my place with you,
and someday when my life is through,
I'll find my way right back to you.
And together forever we will stay,
in the heaven above so far away.

Tabitha Ruble, Grade 9
Parkersburg High School, WV
**In loving memory of Viola Ruble*

Off to War

It all happened so soon
Daddy was gone again
He'll come back then leave again
Just like every other time before.

When he's here we do a lot,
Play games, cards and stay up late.
Then it all happened so soon
Off to Afghanistan again.

I didn't know much about it there but
It all happened so soon
I found out about that place.
A sandy place, not knowing he's safe.
People shooting at him and him shooting back.

It all happened so soon he's back!
Better than ever.
No more going back,
He's done.

Taylor Sparks, Grade 7
Ramsey Middle School, KY

Weather

Sometimes it rains sometimes it's sunny
Sometimes it's cloudy I think it's funny
In the mountains sometimes it snows
In the mountains sometimes the wind blows
In other places it is warm
In other places snow forms

Francisco Delacruz-Hernandez, Grade 8
Central Wilkes Middle School, NC

Everest

A man,
His face weathered and scarred,
Breathes in deeply.
Staring up at the
Challenge of huge
Proportions waiting for him,
The unavoidable moment of
Hesitation arrives.
Turning,
He faces what he is leaving.
All he has ever known
Is
Waiting for his decision.
Slowly,
Almost painfully,
He turns back to face
The challenge,
And, after an extended pause,
He takes a step
Towards
Everest.

Madison Zehmer, Grade 7
Lexington Middle School, NC

Melodies

Music is poetry.
Speak to me
between each beat
With each lyric
bleed into me
Flood my veins
with your rhythm
Scream into each brain cell
make me sane
Intoxicate my mind
with every rhyme
Shake me with your bass
empty my thoughts
Let it remain wasted space

of silent melodies.

Amber Douglas, Grade 9
Bearden High School, TN

Wings of Doves

The dove is flying 'round and 'round,
I close my eyes then hear the sound,
Of crying souls around the globe,
Tears of people that have no home.

They don't have much, not even drink,
These poor people are on the brink,
They ask of you nothing but love,
And peace that comes on wings of doves.

Bobby May, Grade 9
Spring Valley High School, WV

Companionship

Friendship is trust and love
Friendship is a nonrenewable resource,
it comes as naturally as the heartbeat of a newborn baby.
Friendship is your phone ringing 24/7,
only so they can say "Hey, how's life?"
A real friendship lasts forever and ever
like in a fairy tale. Risking an MR in class,
just so you can doodle a picture
of their name to tape in their locker after class
Friendship is a "You scratch my back, I scratch yours" type of thing.
A dedicated friendship is as hard to maintain as
sprinting with 12 inch high heels on, unity is friendship.
Friendship is close, caring, compassionate,
and has more chemistry than the black and white on a zebra print purse.
A friendship is like a pair of sandals,
they help each other step by step to get to their destination
and never leaves the other behind, I smile as I witness
an ant carry a dead ant on it's back to it's resting-place with love.
That is Friendship.

Emani Moon, Grade 8
Baylor School, TN

My Sister And I

It was early one Friday evening.
I was super excited about getting to spend the night with my big sister.
She was excited, too.
It was going to be just us at the sleepover.
No pesky little sisters or nephews.
Just us.
We baked our own pizza then watched a movie that only we would like.
Afterwards, we played card games and my nephew's video games (Shh! Don't tell him).
Before we knew it it was 2:00 am.
We were both exhausted!
But that didn't stop us.
We hopped in the car, in our PJs, and went to buy some coffee.
That kept us awake and we stayed up until 5:00 in the morning!
After that we slept and slept and slept.

Hanna Smithson, Grade 7
Freedom Middle School, TN

O the Beautific

O the Beautific
Heaven so gracious, He let down His arms.
Allowed me to see what was to be.
Step foot on paradise and witness the Lord, with enduring conversation and more.
Touching thy Lord He lifted me up to the sanctuary of life, giving me holy light.
There I stand at the golden gate, looking down from the light.
Onto the life, where I was and yet will be.
To only think he has chosen me.
Chosen me to be a saint for him
to carry his existence on and through.
To walk the earth and glory His name for all to see.

Jessica Emmons, Grade 9
Western Harnett High School, NC

Santa's Horse

It was Christmas Eve and all was silent in the barn, as I remember. All my stall mates were asleep except me. My owner was talking to me earlier. She said that Santa Claus was coming tonight. She told me that he gives presents to all the good boys and girls. This made me wonder if maybe Santa had a horse. It was about midnight and my eyes were starting to close. Then my ears picked up a sound. I heard hoofs clomping on the pavement outside my stall. When I looked out there was a white horse that smelled heavily of peppermint. I pretended to sleep and next thing I knew there is an unwrapped candy cane hanging from my stall door, in fact there was one on everybody's. Then he walked out the barn door and disappeared. It was Santa's horse.

Madi Armao, Grade 8
Camp Ernst Middle School, KY

Jo

I once knew a cow name Jo
Who loved to drink cocoa,
Jo was really nice,
And loved to crunch on ice.

He had a friend dinosaur
Who to him was a really big mentor.
The dinosaur's name was Dingo.
Together they played with arrows and a bow.

Jo shot an arrow in the air.
It landed in my dad's hair.
Uh oh
You should have seen him go.

Jo lived on a farm
The barn had a big alarm.
That would ring loud and clear
While the Farmer John was drinking some beer.

The alarm gave Farmer John such a fright
That he ran out of sight.
Jo was a scared one too
That he started crying boohoo.

Now he is the Farmtown's mayor, Jo is the best cow ever.

Tallis Herron, Grade 7
White Station Middle School, TN

They Say

They say you shouldn't cry over what is past,
But if that past is present in your mind,
Is it wrong to cry?

They say you should forgive and forget,
But if you can forgive but not forget,
Is it wrong to remember?

They say what doesn't kill you makes you stronger,
But if only part of you feels alive,
Is it wrong to remain as you are?

They say you need to move on,
But if every time you try to leave you find a reason to stay,
Is it wrong to stop trying?

Who are They to say what should or shouldn't be done,
What you need to do or not,
Is it wrong to not let Them choose your path?

What if you can't help crying?
What if you can't forget?
What if you can't get stronger?
What if you can't move away?
What if you want to live your own way?
Is it wrong to ignore what They say?

Alexis Ridenour, Grade 8
Heritage Middle School, TN

Spring

Spring, spring
It's almost here
The time to see the fawn and deer,
And watch the bees go buzzing by
In the pretty sunset sky,
The flowery gardens scent the air
While a soft breeze ruffles my hair.
I taste the honeysuckles that hand from a vine,
Gee they taste mighty fine.
Ding, ding, ding went my dad's chimes
And look at the animals of all kinds!
I feel the morning spring time dew,
Don't be surprised if you feel it
Too!

Skylar Hope Peterson, Grade 7
White Station Middle School, TN

The Traveler

Step by step, stumbling o'er sidewalk cracks and
Through alleyways, cross streets, over bridges
As time runs on the hourglass shifts its sand.
Distant clouds beckon me saying, "this is
Freedom, escape to me." I trudge onward
Body worn from rain and snow. Might I fail?
Brush off the grime and keep moving onward
Ahead and above, no man should prevail
No longer will I strive and struggle on
Fighting what aims to hold me back from life
All I have ever known has come and gone
The pain and aches cut like a cold, dull knife
So step by step fantasies call for me
Swallow the taste of pride, be what you can be.

Jacob Maddox, Grade 9
Spring Valley High School, WV

The Event of the Day

The World Equestrian Games
Held outside of Europe for the first time
And in Kentucky, my home.
Rising early Tuesday morning
Riding a Lextram all the way there.
Hanging on tight to the bar above me.

All around me I hear Spanish, German and French.

As we arrive workers dressed
In Equestrian gear stamp tickets.

Here we are. Once in a lifetime opportunity.
As we take our slick, silver seats,
I'm in awe at what greets us. The first horse was the best.
As the magnificent beast jumped the first of many hurdles,
It was as if it froze in midair
It was silent like there wasn't a soul on Earth.
Just me and the clop clop of the hooves.
The crowd goes wild. A perfect run.
Here we are, a once in a lifetime opportunity.

Emilee Agee, Grade 8
Bondurant Middle School, KY

Gone

I see him standing there
My pappy.
I see the smile on his face, the grease in his clothes.
I see the nails.
On his block of wood,
Our names printed in sharpie, Tyler, Kelsey, William, and Wesley
Can you hear that wonderful sound?
His laugh, but I hear it no more.
Oh lord, I hear it coming.
The water, a snake coming up in waves.
Snickering at my pain.
I taste the creek water,
Drowning me.
Sour with rage, like a bull,
Destroying everything in its path.
Now I hear the bulldozer,
Destroying his life work.
He's no longer there.
No window to look into.
But now all I see,
Is that forbidden land, looking back at me.

Kelsey Mattingly, Grade 7
Mount Washington Middle School, KY

Fear

My fear came alive as you took your last breath,
I knew that day that you had come to your death,
My heart started to pound,
As all my tears fell down!

Faith Johnson, Grade 8
Lashmeet/Matoaka Elementary School, WV

Night Sky

Inside looking out
I hear the soft, gentle, wind
Brushing against the thoughtless clear glass
I munch on Granny's cookies
Freshly baked
I watch the jewels in the night sky
As they shimmer and shine
I notice the ball of cheese
As it floats it the empty space
It looks lonely and sad.
I smile at it,
It smiles back
Sitting with Granny
I smell a new batch of cookies
Being crisped in a box of heat
As I think the sweet thoughts of my glass,
I begin to fall asleep slowly
I take a last glance at the sky jewels
And then I silently lay in bed
Thinking that if I had never looked past my clear glass
I would have never met a new friend.

Miranda Green, Grade 7
Mount Washington Middle School, KY

She Is Gone

Inside looking out
I see my great grandmother's name
Surrounded by an ocean of colors
I hear nothing absolute silence
I am there alone, I hear the wind whispering
I feel empty inside, I feel hollow like a tree
Standing there waving its branches slowly in the air
As if saying goodbye for the last time
There is one difference between the tree and I,
I didn't get to say goodbye
I feel the soft warmth of the blanket she made for me,
wrapped around me, holding me, protecting me,
Telling me that things will be better
I am sitting in the floor of the church
Her love still lingers here
I taste my tears running down my cheek and into my mouth
I am remembering the stories that granny has told me
About her and how wonderful she was
I am in front of her window
The stained glass window dedicated to Agnes Hicks,
My great grandmother, wishing she was here with me now.

Cassidy Tinnell, Grade 7
Mount Washington Middle School, KY

Blue

Blue is the color of the sky on a sunny day.
Blue is the color of the ocean as it moves off the shore.
Blue is the color of blue jays that fly through the sky.
Blue is my favorite color.

Johnny Rayburn, Grade 8
Elkton School, TN

Sunshine

What brings such warmth
May hurt our eyes,
What can change colors,
That would be sunshine.

What comes in the morning
To shine so high,
To settle back down,
That would be sunshine.

When water is hit
For everyone to see,
It turns into a rainbow,
With the help of sunshine.

It comes from God
With His beauty it shows,
No brighter than angels,
The sunshine it glows.

Hannah Reimer, Grade 8
North Raleigh Christian Academy, NC

The Fair

I went to the fair one day,
And all my friends said "hey."
I walked up a trail,
to ride a Ferris wheel.

I later got off,
And then coughed.
This big ride,
Made my heart slide.

Off to the emergency room we went,
My dad's car got a dent.
But we got there just in time,
The doctor said I would be fine.

Eli Sholar, Grade 8
Boyle County Middle School, KY

My Thoughts

On the outside, I am loud and outgoing,
But on the inside, I am quiet and shy.
I fear nothing,
But am scared of many things,
I hold my head high,
But I am clouded in shame,
I possess many friends,
But on the inside I am alone,
I am funny when I want to be,
And furious when I don't,
I hate to be crowded,
But I dread being alone.

Christian Harrison, Grade 8
Montgomery Central Middle School, TN

When My Dad Left

When my dad left,
I was okay for a bit.
But the realization,
Of him gone had hit.

When my dad left,
Something strange had occurred.
I was nervous and upset,
My stomach was stirred.

When my dad left,
My life turned around.
I was more helpful.
But my heart was full of love by the pound.

When my dad left,
Was I sad or mad?
I guess I was both,
But my dad is the best the world ever had.

Matthew Crowe, Grade 7
Ramsey Middle School, KY

Failure of the Dictator

Derogatory impositions
Clearly things you should not mention
You of all the people should know
What to hide and what to show.

Jeopardize insanity
For clearly it adds to your vanity
Such a beautiful person you could be
Too bad beauty includes personality.

Annihilation holdup
Figures that all your plans would blow up
You should have known whom to choose
To light your ignition fuse.

Failed communication
The story of the nation
Too much of your relationship
Cradled on your dictatorship.

Whitney Westall, Grade 9
McDowell Early College, NC

Don't Give Up

As the tires spin
And the lights flash
Closer every minute,
To save Granddaddy.

They're stopped at the gate,
Trying to get in,
While in the house
He's fighting for his final breath.

Break the gate down!
Pummel the fence!
Don't give up!
You have to get in.

Finally they arrive,
To find it's too late.
If only they knew then
How much I would miss him.

Adam Cruthirds, Grade 7
White Station Middle School, TN

Since He Left

Since he left
I feel so alone
I just want my daddy
To come back home

When he left
The last thing I said was
"Daddy don't go"
But all I heard was, "I'll Be back home"

When he left
I was filled with anger and still so sad
I may never see him again
I feel so bad

After he left
Mom got the call
And started to cry
Because my daddy had died

Madysan Brinley, Grade 7
Ramsey Middle School, KY

Hannah

Entertaining, enjoyable, extremely athletic, reliable.
Who cares about animals, family, friends, and sports.
Who intends to go to college to become a teacher, a vet or a nurse.
Who wants to be known as someone who people look up to, and know they can come to me for anything.
Who wants to be respected for who I am and not what other people want me to be.
Who fears death, criminals and getting sick.
Who wants people to understand that I love my life and the person I am and do not want to change a thing.
Who gives because I like to make people smile and be happy.
Who dreams of world peace and fairness.
Who believes in the word of John Mason, "You were born an original, don't die a copy."

Hannah Mockbee, Grade 7
Meredith-Dunn School, KY

When I'm Sick

When I'm sick I lay in bed
When I'm sick I cough and sneeze
When I'm sick my mom calls the house and I answer when a weary voice and she says are you okay
When I'm sick I get out of bed and see the kids play sports outside
When I'm sick I turn on the TV and put the soup in the microwave that my mom set out for me in the refrigerator
When I'm sick I go to sleep and wake up and my mom calls again and she tells me she is on her way
When I'm sick I lay in bed until my mom comes ome
When I'm sick I hear the car door shut and know it is my mom
When I'm sick my mom checks my temperature and asks did I eat the soup she made for me.
When I'm sick I go to sleep and hope I feel better in the morning

Terrance Bardlavens, Grade 7
StudentFirst Academy, NC

Good Times

It was early in the afternoon, when Barbara, my dad's girlfriend, and I decided to go shopping.
The cold wind hitting our face heading for the car.
Highway jammed, not ruining our good time, going to Starbucks to warm up.
Stores all over the mall filled with customers young and old.
Bright colors attracting young customers.
When thrilling movies called our name, we left, bags in our hands, smiles plastered on our faces.
Salty popcorn, and soda quenching our thirst and lightly satisfying our hunger, we left, the hunger over powering.
My dad waiting for us at the restaurant, darkness filled the sky ending a great day.

Kirsten Curry, Grade 7
Freedom Middle School, TN

It Happened So Soon

It happened to soon
I was so happy just knowing you were OK but I heard a knock at the door and I knew you were gone it all happened so soon.
Me and mom just sat there saying what are we going to do I wanted to cry so so bad but it all happened so soon.
I just could not believe the words I had just heard I kept saying it was not you but it still all happened so soon.
I couldn't take any more so I burst into tears now my daddy is gone how could this be now all I can say is
It happened so soon.

Christian Murphy, Grade 7
Ramsey Middle School, KY

One Thing: Writer

I grab a pen and a notebook and my loopy cursive writing takes me away. Somewhere terrible, somewhere amazing, somewhere where my imagination is in control and I'm just there for the ride. Then I see things through the eyes of another person entangled within my words or as someone watching from afar, knowing everything about everyone, but still wondering what will happen next. I am a hundred different people in a hundred places in a hundred different stories. But I am one thing for sure: writer.

Jessica Nienaber, Grade 8
Nienaber Home School, KY

A Life Well Lived

Not worrying about a thing,
Even when times are hard,
Popping bubbles with my gum,
Even at school,
Snapping pictures with my camera,
Even when it's almost out,
Stopping to smell the roses,
Even when I'm terribly late,
Listening to music loud,
Even when I'm almost deaf,
Racing through the streets,
Even if I'm being led nowhere,
Comforting my sick friend,
Even if they're contagious,
Standing in the rain,
Even if I have no umbrella,
Watching through the window,
Even when I can be on the outside,
Doing what I want,
Even when I could be following in the footsteps of others,
This is a life well lived.

Elly Wiegert, Grade 7
White Station Middle School, TN

Winter

Winter days are coming soon,
Autumn's coming to its end.
Say goodbye to the harvest moon,
Say hello to cold weather trends.
Snow days are coming,
So we can have snowball fights.
On candy canes, we will chew,
And stay up late on Christmas Eve night.
New Year's will be soon after,
And you will see the ball drop in Times Square.
That's when you will hear the young children's laughter,
And everyone will show love and care.
This season may be crisp and cold,
But I still love the feeling.
This time of year never gets old,
Because it makes all our heads go reeling.

Shawna Whiteman, Grade 8
Petersburg High School, WV

Echo

What is an echo?
Some say it's the reflected noise.
I believe that it is nature.
Nature whispering back to you,
the sweet hum of your own voice.
Over and over, they murmur,
until the words are embedded into your head.
Damp cave walls say so much,
without saying a single word.

Chloe Starr, Grade 7
East Millbrook Magnet Middle School, NC

My Parents

This is a poem to my Mom and Dad
whom I have hurt many times.
Who always forgive me,
and are always there to
talk and to listen.
When I am sick you stay by my side
to lift my spirits and take care of me.
I hope you know I love you
even if I don't say it.
I could never not love you,
for when I'm upset you comfort me.
You have never told me I cannot succeed.
I just thought you should know
how I really feel about you both, Mom and Dad.
I try my hardest to please you
and make you proud every day,
and to really show you that
I love you.

Taylor Berling, Grade 8
St Agnes School, KY

"Riverdance," an Irish Tap Dance

Light becomes dark
Black shoes of night
Skirts of color make a wonderful scene
Nature and people act as one
With the music of generations

Timeless as ever
Unnerving with powerful beauty
Changing in the darkness of the stage
Sweet and all-powering glory arises
Never challenging itself

Making crowds cheer with delight
With awe and fascination
Ganging up against one another in a tap dance war
This poor, lonely soulless dancer
Taps his way towards victory against others

Jordan Morgan, Grade 7
White Station Middle School, TN

Dove

sometimes I think you were sent to me for a reason
from a dove
a present for me from up above
but I ain't teasing the season
cause that is just plain wrong
but I know you're going to keep us strong
together we can be anything
so why not fight for what we stand for
why not for our own true love
so now you and me both should say our thanks
to that precious dove not love

Anna Delacruz-Hernandez, Grade 9
Wilkes Early College High School, NC

Off to War

We dropped him off at the airport
We said goodbye
In a flash he was gone
My mom and I pray he won't die, I miss my dad
We just left the airport
It was so hard to say goodbye to my dad
When he made it safely
My mom and I were so glad
I miss my dad
When my dad got on Skype
I was so glad to see him
We weren't sure if we lost him
He made a great friend, Jim, I miss my dad
We got a call from Jim
He said my dad died
My mom and I were so sad
All I could do that night was cry, I miss my dad
Every night we look at the photo album
We try so hard not to cry
After every night we say a prayer
We try so hard to keep our eyes dry, I miss my dad

Adam McDowell, Grade 7
Ramsey Middle School, KY

Green

I love green!
Almost everywhere you look, it can be seen.
From the color of trees to the color of grass,
green is a color you can't bypass.

You can see it when you look into someone's eyes.
By mixing blue and yellow, you'll get a surprise!
There are so many shades that you can see.
It's funny how they all came to be.

From forest green to neon lime,
all shades of green are quite sublime!
From granny smith to the color of moss,
without green, I would be lost!

Green is a color that makes me smile.
As I look outside, I can see it for miles!
It make my heart sing and eases my mind.
I adore greens of every kind!
I love green!

Shaniya Bellefant, Grade 7
Elkton School, TN

My Heart

My heart means a lot to me.
My heart lets me love others.
My heart gives me courage.
My heart gives me hope.
My heart makes me feel that somebody loves me.

Tahmeek McKoy, Grade 7
Leland Middle School, NC

Off to War

When I gave my last good-bye
He walked out the door
And I couldn't help but cry
We may not see him anymore
He left in a heartbeat
I wish he could stay
Now he's gone to defeat
For long long days "Daddy! Daddy! Don't you see"
"Please don't go for you and me"
"Daddy! Daddy!
Wait don't go"
"You might not be back
And I'll be alone"
Off to protect
The U.S.A.
He is ready and set
To save the day
Mom is upset
So am I
Hopefully he will be home soon
We hope he doesn't die.

Miles Ellis, Grade 7
Ramsey Middle School, KY

What Am I?

Some call me the ruler,
Others say I'm cooler
Others say they're wrong.
Some call me beast, with my steady beat,
Others say I am no such thing as unique.
What am I? And some call me this why?
I am your life, strong, why yes, I take no rest.
Have no fear, for if you will listen you will
hear...that's right...ME.
Still you wonder what I am?
What could be strong?
And do no harm?
Well, I am something that will never part...
Your heart

Katie Schoondyke, Grade 7
Providence Academy, TN

Night Sky

In the air, no sound but little bugs flitting around
Through the creek, a snake wades into the still yet moving water
Up in the tree tops, the leaves brush against each other
Within yourself, you find who you really are
Under the night sky is where I long to be
Out of the blue, the lightning bugs come out to play
With the fire burning, my heart starts to sing
Except for my sister, who has fallen asleep
Until we find, it is almost midnight
As soon as I retire to my bed to rest,
I realize this is the place I love the most

Madison Barnes, Grade 8
Heritage Middle School, TN

Give Thanksgiving

As we close our eyes and bow our heads,
Let's thank God for what he has done,
He sent his son, Jesus Christ to be our Lord and Savior,
For that let us give Thanksgiving.

For God has prepared us a home for eternity,
We can live with the creator of the universe,
That is so cool!
For that let us give Thanksgiving

He has sent communication to us through prayer,
We can go to God for anything because he loves us!
God gives us another breath and another day,
For that let us give Thanksgiving

Through every breath we take,
Through every day we go through
Through the struggles life throws our way,
We should give Thanksgiving!

Julia Little, Grade 8
Boyle County Middle School, KY

Every Being Knows

At this day and age,
It took over the world,
It's all knowing as a sage,
And this whisper is rarely heard.
From the time it entered
my life, it changed my every thought.
For now, it's centered
around me, like a favorite item bought.
Love's meaning is feared by most,
And rarely touched,
But is as humble as a host
And can be needed just as much.
How the feeling engulfs you, as it ebbs and flows,
Leaves heartache, but also happiness, as every being knows.

Madison Phillips, Grade 8
Danville Bate Middle School, KY

Imagine

Imagine what it would be like to soar above the clouds.
Imagine you are with the one you would love forever.
Imagine never having to let go.
Imagine dancing in the stars.
Imagine having everything you have always wanted.
Imagine singing in front of a million people.
Imagine walking on sunshine.
Imagine.
Just imagine.
What do you imagine?
I imagine,
You.
Imagine.

Savannah Brown, Grade 8
West Middle School, TN

Imagine My World

I imagine winning every cross country race like Jan Gautier,
scoring the winning goal like Mia Hamm,
and making that last minute shot like Michael Jordan.
I imagine having the leading role in the play,
being the lead singer, somewhere other than the shower,
or playing the tuba in a marching band.
Skydiving or plummeting from a plane is what I imagine daily.
What if I had brown hair and pale skin or if I liked reading?
What if I was a yellow lab? Is a thought, I like to imagine.
I imagine what it would be like to live when Jesus did.
I love imaging if I were a superstar or married to one.
Click, snap, shoot.
My imagination brings me to having straight A's
and never having to correct papers.
I imagine a world of no hunger with world peace
and people who love one another.
My imagination takes me on voyages
across the ocean to foreign countries.
Being only fourteen years old, I can only imagine these things now,
Bippety, Boppety, Boo.
But when I get older, I hope they come true.

Sydney Gautier, Grade 8
Baylor School, TN

Outside of My Window

When I look out of the window...
The gleaming sun shimmers up upon the glass,
And the powerful wind blows my hair back.
I hear the displeasing sound of the train miles away,
And the basketball pounding right in my driveway.
I am alarmed by the lusty sound of my dogs' bark,
And the sound of cars darting past the busy street behind me
Zoom, zoom, zoom.
When I look out of the window...
The drab color of the sky depresses me,
And the rain pounding up against me.
I see the smoke billowing from my neighbor's cigarette,
And the lightning bolts across the sky, along with a crash of thunder.
I see the Christmas lights twinkling across the street,
And I realized the unity in my cove.

Emily Thorpe, Grade 7
White Station Middle School, TN

Meadow

Near where I live
Through the woods
Beside a trickling creek
With soft, green grass and trees that blow
In the cool breeze
At this area I sit and think
Within the mountains listening to the birds sweet, soft music
Below the bright blue sky
Of all the places I could be
Along here is where I find peace

Katlyn Aistrop, Grade 8
Heritage Middle School, TN

Courage to Love

You are everything to me,
You make me who I want to be.
I have been loved and I have been left,
I have been hurt by the best.
You are like the sun,
You outshine everyone.
You are like my north star,
I will follow you wherever you are.
This seems too good to be true,
To think I would have ever been loved by someone like you.
I hope you feel the same way,
I don't want this to go away.
Please don't take it from me,
This feeling is so amazing, can't you see?
You are the one I want to hold,
Please don't leave me in the cold.
I sit here by the phone,
while I wait alone.
You are as free spirited as a dove,
You give me courage to love.

Mercedes Luzader, Grade 9
Robert C Byrd High School, WV

Legacy

In a meadow, a tree stood.
Mammoth in proportion to the other
Inhabitants that resign there
Powerful limbs stretch to the sky

Strength kept it growing,
The tree's seeds in its fruit kept its line going

Resilient as it is, its final day comes.
With a deafening shriek of machinery
To the sickening thud of death

But the tree is still here
No, not stretching to the sky
But replenishing itself it its sapling counterparts
The seeds hold the trees existence
But the tree created its legacy

Danielle Underwood, Grade 8
Campbell County Middle School, KY

Swirling Water

The swirling water stands on air,
I don't know how it can stay there,
It tumbles and whirls while cupid sings,
Some are pink and some can look like anything,
Some are wild and some are tame,
It's something your hand can never claim,
There's no way you can name them all in a day,
Because if you tried you would find,
Some vanishing while you briefly closed your eyes.

Madeline Bonner, Grade 8
Deerstream Learning Center, NC

Deployed and Sent Away

Deployed and sent away from home
Where you grew and became a man
Educated and supported every day
You hear the call to help your land.

Deployed and sent away from family
You want to stay,
But have to go away
In a mission to end the war

Deployed and sent away from friends
You wish you could be there thinking of them
Wherever they are, praying for their sorrows
Hoping to meet again.

Deployed and sent away for awhile
Getting homesick for my kids
Wishing to return home
And be a family again.

Deployed and sent away for home!

Shayne Howell, Grade 7
Ramsey Middle School, KY

Volleyball Legend

Sensations of nervousness run down my back
Butterflies fill my stomach, while it flips
Sweat covers my palms
Memorized plays run through my mind
As coach calls my name. My eyes close
Running once more over the drills
Being setter I call my roll
The ball rises
The crowd becomes silent
I realize the ball coming toward my face
My arms lift automatically
I set the ball. Perfect.
The hitter runs, jumps, and spikes
Other players gasp as I save the faux pas
Passing the ball over the net

Alexis Burton, Grade 7
White Station Middle School, TN

Basketball

On the court
With my team
Among the cheering crowd
Out comes their screaming voices
Under so much pressure
From across the court the ball comes to me
Past the other team's girls I go
Down the court
At the goal
In the basket the ball goes, my team is filled with joy

Ivy Russell, Grade 8
Heritage Middle School, TN

I Am Running to Stand Still

I am running to stand still
I wonder why time flies slowly around me
I hear the footsteps of my future
I see their mouths moving
I want to hear their words
I am running to stand still

I pretend that I am a bird
I feel as if my wings are clipped
I touch the metal bars that separate me from being set free
I worry my time will run short
I cry when I become lonely
I am running to stand still

I understand why the sun rises
I say my day will come
I dream about the wind of the world beneath me
I try to grip reality
I hope I never do
I am running to stand still

Payton Boyd, Grade 9
Bearden High School, TN

Sadness

Crystal water silently is absorbed into clouds,
So many clouds,
So many hearts,
Rain occasionally carves trails and rivers into the Earth,
So much land,
So many faces,
These storms strike fast and quick,
So much thunder and lightning,
So much sadness and hurts,
Precious little sapphires of cleansed and salty liquid,
So much rain,
So many teardrops,
Clouds let out rain,
We let out tears,
Clouds create showers for nature,
Hearts temporarily douse our pain,
Our hatred,
Our angers,
Our sadness; only to swell up inside us,
Once, twice, and more again.

Serena Thaman, Grade 7
Villa Madonna Academy, KY

I Wish for a Star…

I wish for a star
to brighten up my life
I wish for a star
to shine up in the sky
I wish for a star
to change my heart

Kayla Dunn, Grade 9
Hickory Ridge High School, NC

Ode to My Guitar

When I see you I see beauty
I see gold
I see art
I think of a bond between two objects that will never set apart

When I hear you I hear harmony
I hear music
I hear sound
I feel a sense of happiness when no one is around

When I play you I play my favorite songs
I play my passion
I play myself
I feel like I play to the world even though it's to a shelf

When I feel you I feel happy
I feel safe
And I feel free
I feel a sense of love that will always stay with me

Kramer Miller, Grade 9
Bearden High School, TN

Horrible Fate

WHEN I woke up one day,
The smell of smoke and the sound of sirens filled the air.
My mood turned a shallow gray,
In a way that is troublesome to share.

I jumped out of bed,
And touched the knob on the door.
I let out a single cry of dread,
Because without any warning I slammed to floor.

The sound of an explosion rang in my ears,
A horrible heat passing me by.
Suddenly the situation became crystal clear,
I was about to die.

War is not a favorable thing,
For it does nothing but destroy and kill.
No one knows for sure what victory would bring,
Except for a horrible fate that the deaths fulfill.

Lydia DuBois, Grade 8
Signal Mountain Middle High School, TN

The Darkness

In the darkness I see
Pain, fear, and terror
I see what no one else sees
There is darkness and fear
There are children with no parents
Parents with no children
Everyone is heartbroken about the truth
Because everyone is afraid of the darkness

Kashanus Hunter-Fleming, Grade 7
Weldon Middle School, NC

Baby Room

Outside looking in,
I feel the glassy surface,
Pushing harder against my face,
As I grow more excited,
I smell something,
I think it was the weird hospital,
Filled with nice people,
A taste in my mouth,
Almost like a cookie,
But no,
It is happiness,
A new sound,
I hear her,
Like a wimpy whistle,
The first sound,
Without my window,
I'm an only child,
Lonely,
Curious,
They leave me,
Without my window.

Lauren Perkins, Grade 7
Mt. Washington Middle School, KY

Soar

I want to fly high in the sky.
And watch the rolling clouds go by.
I want to feel the wind on me.
To soar and just be free.

I want to soar over open waters.
Not being heeled back by collars.

Not getting filled up with sorrows.
Acting like there are no tomorrows.

Getting a view from different eyes.
A most wonderful surprise.
The wonders of the land.
Are both spectacular and grand.

I want to see things from up high.
View what can only be seen from the sky.
Get a brand new view.
Doing what the birds can do.

Lyndsey Sebourn, Grade 8
West Middle School, TN

The Night Sky

The sky is twinkly at night
This is a beautiful sight
The stars' twinkle are so bright
Nothing could feel more right
I love the sky at night

JoElle Thompson, Grade 7
White Station Middle School, TN

The Sad Fate

Why don't you love me anymore? Why don't you care about me anymore?
I thought I was your number one
I thought I was your best friend ever you even said
You said I was a faithful and loyal friend then why are you ignoring me?
I remember when we used to play fetch
You used to feed me your food
I especially remember
The thunderstorms were strong and violent you would comfort me
And tell me everything would be all right
Now I'm sitting here out in the cold
I'm watching you from the window with a sad, heavy heart
You seem so happy with your new puppy your new best friend
Is it because I'm older? Is it because I'm tired all the time?
When a thunderstorm approaches
All I can do is cuddle up and hope it's not too strong
But please remember that I still love you with all my heart nothing could ever change that
I ask for one last favor
Please don't throw your new best friend outside like me

Christina Dotson, Grade 8
Andrew Jackson Middle School, WV

The Special Time Spent

I heard it.
The sound of the RV rolling down the road.
On the way to the Camping World, I saw it.
The go-karting track.
I asked if we could go go-karting and my dad said if we have any spare time we would.
What we had to do took a while but, that was alright.
We ended up having some time, so we went.
When we got to the gate of the course, just watching the people going was fun.
I knew this was a special moment.
When it was our turn all I could say was thank you.
It was the most amazing personal time I ever spent with my parents.

Tyler Reilly, Grade 7
Freedom Middle School, TN

A Choral Calamity

Fear and trepidation fill my mind; my stomach churns as my heart races.
I stand at the culmination, the climax of months of practice and rehearsal,
And yet I hardly feel prepared.
The narrow corridor, with its soaring ceilings and stark white walls,
Makes me feel small and insignificant, like just a face in the crowd.
I step forward into a room.
I prepare myself to sing, to be heard and be judged
But alas! The words don't come, the notes don't flow,
And I falter and stumble.
I leave downtrodden and embarrassed but with experience
And knowledge more valuable than victory.

Aaron Parker, Grade 9
White Station High School, TN

I Have to Serve My Country

"Hey, Daddy, where are you going?"
"I'm going off to war."
"Oh, Daddy, please don't go.
Without you it's such a bore."
"I have to serve my country.
I have to leave once more."
So he packed his bags and said goodbye,
And off to war he went.
I don't think anyone will ever know
What those few words meant.
I long for the day that he comes home.
Every day, I pray he will.
Every day all I do is worry until I'm ill.
When he comes back,
He's tired and his patience is very thin.
But when he's gone, he's gone.
I just can never win.
"I have to serve my country."
Those are the words he said.
I don't think I'll ever want to
Get those words out of my head.

Samantha Benjamin, Grade 7
Ramsey Middle School, KY

Greatest Grandma

Outside looking in,
The blinds blink open,
I see her,
Beautiful and calm,
She's an ocean on a hot day.
She was the greatest grandma.
I hear her voice,
Pure, gentle, and soft.
I smell her perfume,
As sweet as rain kissed leaves.
I feel her hug,
Stiff and tight,
She never lets go.
Without my window
I would never see her again.

Brianna Elmore, Grade 7
Mount Washington Middle School, KY

The River

Below the water
In the river
On the rocks fishing
With fishing rod in hand
Through the water we swim
Beside the cave we walk
Up the hill we go
Into the car
On the road we leave
In love with the river I am

Logan Clark, Grade 8
Heritage Middle School, TN

Goodbye

Inside looking out
Though I seem happy on the outside,
My cry of sadness inside is that of a mourning dove.
Moments ago, my laughter filling the air was like a zebra
Now, the dreaded sound of the moving van screaming
Vroom, vroom! is echoing in my ears.
These well-meaning people surround me
And hold me back from the place I love.
I still see the beautiful painted flowers
Covering my walls and my bookshelves
I hear the Sunday morning sausage
Sizzling in the frying pan from the kitchen below,
The rough bark scraping against my hands,
Bare feet, and back as I conquer the front yard Magnolia tree.
I breathe in the sweet, fresh, homegrown raspberries
But now, I taste the salty tears
Welling up in my eyes just as they did on that horrible 4th of July
Without my window, life would be much better.
Without my window, I would not have to endure these painful memories
These painful memories, which I love as much as
The Home and FAMILY who built them.

Reilly Fields, Grade 7
Mount Washington Middle School, KY

A Life Short Lived

In the beginning of life there is sometimes death,
However I have also heard in the beginning of death there is sometimes life.
Her life was if anything, not enduring,
Because the minute she entered the world she died.
Death came and grabbed her from her mother, and sibling, and from me.
Death only doing his job came into the world, picked up the small bundle,
and carried her away.
The creature laid lifeless on the chilled concrete floors of my basement.
I cried softly, quietly as my father gently rid of the small kitten,
in which breathed no breath. Death's dreadful darkness took my dear kitten,
To live in a place far better than this harsh and hurtful world.
Tulula was my dark and beautiful black and gray haired kitten,
She roamed the nights with joy, for adventure she always sought,
She was the mother, she too now gone from here.
And so it went that way, that there was one living,
And one dead.

Katie Watts, Grade 7
J Graham Brown School, KY

Orange Feelings

The color orange is happy and calm
Orange is the color of life
Always illuminating brightly and large
This reddish-yellow color is relaxing to me
Orange in my mind makes me calm and happy
It shows me the nice things in life
Orange also makes me think about giraffes in Africa grazing in the sunset
To me orange means happy and calm

Shane Sims, Grade 8
Montgomery Central Middle School, TN

Poem

I'm thinking up a poem,
Oh what should it be?
I have to write one soon
Or Mizz Fizz'll be mad at me.
Her eyes will start to bulge,
An'er mouth will start t' gear,
but I have nothin' to worry 'bout really
until she wiggles her left ear.
So I'm thinking up a poem,
Oh what should it be?
Should I write about a person?
Maybe you or maybe me?
I once wrote a poem,
About my good friend named Liz —
But when my teacher saw that poem, well,
That's why her name's Mizz Fizz.
Yeah, I'm thinking up a poem,
Oh what should it be??
I think I'll just flop down,
And sit and wait and see.

Anna Loring, Grade 7
James Graham Brown School, KY

You

This earth used to be a sphere of sadness,
But I didn't know the full extent.
I used to be dreary,
But my life has been bent.
You brought this change upon me,
I owe it all to you.
You've changed my life in many ways,
Really, it's true.
You're the center of my world,
Though I doubt you'd understand.
You've been oblivious of the love I've had,
Since the first touch of our hands.
It's time you know,
What is alive and true.
What I must say now is,
I'm in love with you.

Jared Bonee, Grade 8
West Middle School, TN

A True Mountaineer

God must be a mountaineer.
He painted the sky blue,
He made the sun yellow,
A true mountaineer he is.

God must be a mountaineer.
He made daffodils yellow,
He made heavenly blue flowers,
God is a true mountaineer.

Lauren Harman, Grade 7
Petersburg High School, WV

Never Stop, Never Stuck

There may be no place to go in life,
but back home,
Nowhere, maybe to run,
Nowhere at all,
In life there are ups and downs,
bumpy rides, hills to climb, or mountains to get around,
But…sometimes you have to hit rock bottom,
To ever reach the top,
Sometimes you must start over, your life that is,
You can't get distracted so easily,
Can't let words hurt you, can't let anything stop you,
Through the thin you still go through battles, and you must fight, but…
Through the thick, you still can win,
If believe in God, you must pray,
To get through your sins,
All I'm sayin' is, don't give up,
Don't let go,
hold on to what you got,
appreciate everything you have,
hold on tight, embrace with strength and faith, and don't let go of hope.

Johnathan Crutchfield, Grade 9
Caneridge High School, TN

Childhood Fairytales

Childhood fairytales are extremely inviting.
They welcome you to journey into what once was.
When venturing into this engaging chamber of past hopes and dreams,
all that is thought is…
I wish.
I wish these childhood fairytales were true.
The ones with Prince Charming and the beautiful
princess with the angelic face and stunning blue eyes.
I wish those childhood fairytales would never stop
the ones with the villain who could always be defeated
by the prince's love.
I wish I could become part of these fairytales
the ones with the sweet fairy godmother and the pumpkin.
I wish childhood fairytales would become real.

Grace Corinne Terhune, Grade 7
White Station Middle School, TN

The Special Trip to Florida

One hot evening me and my mom went down to Florida.
It was as hot as a boiling mad volcano.
My mom and I had a great time.
We did many fun things like swimming in the ocean with a wild manta ray.
I will always remember the time my mom woke me up in the morning.
The morning was so bright that I couldn't see anything,
but with my sunglasses on I got to see a baby turtle no bigger than the palm of my hand.
So cute!
But how could I forget the zoo we went to.
It wasn't like any zoo I've ever been to.
You drove though the pens and the animals would walk right in front of the car.
My trip to Florida was the best time I've spent with my mom.

Emma Catlett, Grade 7
Freedom Middle School, TN

Princess of Mine

I'm on a journey,
A journey to find;
A wonderful girl,
The princess of mine.

I've looked all around,
High and low.
Soon I'm bound
For her to show.

I'm not giving up,
I'm not giving in.
I will fill my cup,
And I will win.

But where is she?
Here or there?
Is she pretty?
What does she wear?

She will show,
That I know.
And I will find
That princess of mine.

Ilyas Nazarov, Grade 7
White Station Middle School, TN

The Immortal

The immortal,
In an unchanging sky;
I watch her rise,
A gleam in my eye;

The immortal,
Regal even behind a cloud;
Blinded by the beauty,
Down below we are wowed;

The immortal,
She's bright in our eyes;
Reigning above mother earth,
With her years she must be wise,

The immortal,
Warmed by her grace;
Forever seeking,
Wondering about her face;

The immortal,
Forever up high;
Our brilliant sun,
Lighting up the sky.

Brandi Tungett, Grade 8
Hebron Middle School, KY

Happiness

Africa is orange
Orange is bliss
bliss grows
And it glows

In Africa
In the morning sky
Birds like God
In Heaven

I see the heavens
As pure as day
Look up at the sky
And ask yourself why

The sky is orange
In the morning sky
The sun gives us
A sight to see

When in Africa
Look up and ask why
Orange is contentment
And Africa is orange

Johnathan Williams, Grade 8
Montgomery Central Middle School, TN

Like Playing Chess

I could dream,
Of your ultimate scheme.
And make it seem,
As if you haven't done a thing.

I could find peace,
In a final release.
And ultimately disband,
From your master plan.

I could run very far away,
To a place where night never met day.
But still I stay,
A pawn in your hand.
Writhing but never taking my stand.

Got to find a way,
Got to run.
Not giving up yet,
The battle isn't won.

My kings and queens are yet again safe.
I can still win, it's never too late.

Brittny (Britt-Brat) Williams, Grade 7
White Station Middle School, TN

Growing Up

We couldn't wait to grow up
We were ready to drive
Be one of the "big kids"
But back then we were only five

Well look now
Here we are
All grown up
But we haven't gotten far

Drama and pain
The things people say
The way they look at you
Like no one's the same

Violence and teasing
Our whole world has changed
It used to make sense
But it's been rearranged

So much to take in
Life has gotten tough
We've been pushed down too hard
And we couldn't wait to grow up

Melissa Marsee, Grade 8
Sharon School, TN

The Ancient Royal Pastime

I feel the beating of my heart
My rival just sat down
The game is about to start
To compete for the crown

The army is prepared for battle
With the pieces all in place
Its knight is on its saddle
I'm about to start an endless race

A mistake cannot be made
If I touch the wrong piece
I will destroy my strong raid
And our battle will cease

The soldiers fall, one by one
His king tries to run away
As I capture everyone
There is no escape for him today

Checkmate young man
Are the words I say
What an impressive plan
On this auspicious day!

Benjamin Levine, Grade 7
White Station Middle School, TN

Rain Drops

I look out my window, seeing the water slide down the cold glass.
I don't smile or laugh or follow them with my finger.
Like I usually do.
I can't find the will to care.
I can't find the will to smile, laugh.
And move my fingers or my body.
I see the rain slide slower, almost begging me to play.
But I hide my eyes and begin to cry.
You don't understand how trapped I feel.
How I feel like someone is choking me.
I lay there and think of the good things.
And I begin to laugh
I rise from my bed and try again.
But I know it will come back.
But I try and dry my eyes.
You don't understand.
But that's the way it must be.
It's not easy to explain nor an easy matter.
Just you wait and see.
You will know the feeling.
Just come to me and I will help thee.

Leigh Causey, Grade 7
J Graham Brown School, KY

Friends

Someone that really cares
They never let you down
Whenever you are sad
They somehow fix that frown

From pinkies to super secrets
Swears are the best
And when your friends have kept it
They are none other like the rest

From morning to evening and then to the night
You have a true friend even when there's little fights
Friends are forever but some say it's not true
But if you keep a strong relationship
They will always be there for you

Erin Spinks, Grade 8
J Graham Brown School, KY

My Room

Across the walls there are posters and pictures
Over the floor is a fluffy carpet
Through two doors is my closet
Against the bed is a desk
Under my bed there is a box
Within the box are pictures of my family
In the closet are my clothes
Except for the closet, everything is clean
During the night it is where I sleep
Inside my room I will always feel happiness.

Colby Burkett, Grade 8
Heritage Middle School, TN

My Favorite Window

Outside looking in,
I see my self sitting like a bird,
I hear all the good times we had,
I smell as new from the first time I looked out,
I feel the glassy window that talked to me,
I taste fresh flower with joy when I look out,
Something is happening,
I can't stop
It's my favorite window,
I'll never get to see it again,
I am packing up,
Saying good bye for the last time,
Pulling out of the driveway,
I said "bye little window,"
And off we went,
Then we pulled into another driveway,
It had a window,
It was my new favorite,
Without my window, I wouldn't survive.

Nathan Leslie, Grade 7
Mount Washington Middle School, KY

In Memory

She looks at him and feels her heart flutter,
Surrounded by the light of her own self.
He talks to her; she melts like hot butter.
She thinks he puts her heart on a high shelf.
But maybe she will blossom in the sun,
Like summer daises in the air she burst.
She hears a voice inside; she is not done,
Cause she knows she won her father's heart first.
The girl is terrified of what comes next,
She listens to her heart longer once more.
She never goes by what is in the text,
But yet again she feels like she can soar.
Her father always told her she could dream,
And she still thinks about her father's beam.

Megan Morrison, Grade 9
Spring Valley High School, WV

Snow

Snow is like a blanket that covers the world.
It's layers fall and wrap around houses.
Down and down it comes and goes as it twirls
the white takes over and clothes us like blouses.
So gentle it pleases all who touch it;
even though it's ice cold it warms my heart.
But sometimes it throws a gigantic fit;
still some of us make it a piece of art.
But when it settles, the world is so calm
and people come outside to laugh and play.
The huge sheet grasps us in its palm,
the flakes fall to the ground where they lay.
When I see snow it warms my heart so.

Kendal Obregon, Grade 9
Spring Valley High School, WV

The Pain

The sparkling water,
Looks like the sea.
Waves crashing the shore,
That's like you and me.
Look at the tree lines,
Below the clouds,
Birds are chirping,
Loud and proud.

But I love your eyes,
And your smile.
And I won't wait another day,
Without you next to me.

I hear the sounds of nature,
Not your voice.
Can't stand your anguish,
Do I have any other choice?
To hear the waves,
Crash on the shore,
Then I cannot take anymore,
Of this pain.

Chrystal Pierce, Grade 7
Elkton School, TN

Why Does Love Hurt?

Why does love hurt?
3 words you want to hear
But once you do it turns to fear

The guy you think he is,
Is sweet, always there and
Would never hurt you.

Little did you know that
Was just a show.
And it was a trick to
Pull you in.

It worked
Now to him I'm just dirt.
Why does love have to hurt?

Anna Kathryn Campbell, Grade 8
Weddington Middle School, NC

The Sandy Beach

The sandy beach is a fun place to be
As I sit on the beach
As I watch the sun go down
I have my feet in the sand
There is no other place I would
Like to be sitting
On the beach with my sandy feet

Jamie Martin, Grade 7
Elkton School, TN

Just Wish

Why won't they stop!
He knew it wasn't right so why would he do it?
She wants to leave now!
They need to stop!
As I linger in my room waiting for the silence that has yet to be heard
I sit here and cry along with my brother...
Hoping and wishing they would stop!
She tells us get up we're leaving!
We say "but why?"
Just get in the car! She yells
Stop! Stop! Stop!
I am yelling constantly in my head
Why me? Why us? It's just not right!
Why would he do that to her, why would he do that to us?!
I wasn't supposed to know about it...
I supposed it is my fault I know...
I shouldn't have eavesdropped it's my own fault!
But I guess their yelling has caused most of my anger...
Stop, Stop!
I just wish all these thoughts should just float away like a leaf in the wind
Just stop!

Roni Pollard, Grade 8
J. Graham Brown School, KY

Forever Only Me

I am the focus of all your negativity
Me, I'm the one at fault it is always only me
You tell me to get out and leave, just flee

I wish I could just take that step to be
To be what I am and what I know maybe even to just scream
Let the world know how it feels to let a part of you die in glee

Alone and crying, desperate but dreaming
I am holding on to thoughts where I could have a smile just gleaming
A world where your words have no meaning

I am only me remember
Only one tiny glowing ember
And on the day you try to forget you will always remember

Autumn Huffman, Grade 9
Fairmont High School, WV

St. Louis Road Trip

It was one spring morning the air was cold but the heat of the car flowed through it.
I went in the car as hungry as Gandhi.
And me and my dad drove off to St. Louis.
We talked a little bit but, I could not miss the scene outside.
Trees like giants.
Lakes like ocean.
And faces blazing past my eyes in the cars on the highway.
I took a short nap or rather a long nap that lasted the rest of the road trip.
When I woke up we were there I could see the arch on the bridge we were driving on.
That's why I enjoyed this trip with my father who I love dearly.

JhaSun Ogle, Grade 7
Freedom Middle School, TN

The Truth

Cracked tombstones;
Among them stands a wicked old crone.
Her black shawl wrapped around
Her stooped shoulders.
Will nobody see the truth beneath the ground?

The raven's croak, can barely be heard
Through the cloak
Of the whispers of the dead.

The old barn owl,
The wolf's haunting howl
Rings and echoes through the dreary
Old, nearly ancient cemetery.

From a time long past
A stark contrast, to today;
In the old bone yard
The broken shards
Tell the story; Of the dead and the mourning
Will nobody see; the truth that lies beneath the ground?

Olivia Leathers, Grade 8
Bondurant Middle School, KY

Hunter's Remorse

We woke before sunrise, and walked out the door,
I brushed sleep from my eyes and said,
"Mom, we'll be back, no later than four!"
As we started on our way,
Just my dad and I,
We took note of the ground,
Guessing where the deer might lie.
On and on and on we trekked,
Spotting deer, some brown, some specked.
I never had a clear shot, don't you see?
But I was having fun, just my dad and me.
On and on again, we walked,
Finding more tracks, all the day we stalked.
But the more we went, the more I grew weary,
My spirits discouraged, my eyes they grew bleary.
When right behind us, wouldn't you know?
Came, seemingly out of nowhere, a great big doe!
My weariness forgotten, just a glimmer of hope,
I took careful aim down my long rifle scope.
My first deer I had taken, my eyes must've shone,
At least 'til I had to drag it, all the way home!

Justin Wilson, Grade 8
St Vincent De Paul School, WV

The Nature On Beach

Sunny day on sandy beach,
through slanted trees.
Sun shining through the sky,
behind the clouds, like of sunshine.
Golden color falling in the water,
leaving the golden waves behind.
Hot day and cold water in summer time.
Water looks clean and transparent,
like a glass.
When you step in,
you feel the beauty of nature.
The sun, the sky, the mountains, the clouds,
the trees, wind, water and sand.
The emotion of happiness and love was to feel there.
And that's it.
Sunny day, on sandy beach
through slanted trees, with the sound of silence.

Jenika Soni, Grade 9
Greenwood High School, KY

Peace Be With You

"Peace be with you."
"And also with you."
Isn't that what we say?
Then maybe people should try to
practice living those words each day.
Hateful things shouted in anger.
Mean looks from people on the street.
It doesn't seem like anyone wants to try and practice peace.
Just offer a kindhearted smile,
whenever you get the chance.
And, "Peace be with you, my friend."
I'm saying this in advance.
Because anytime I see you,
No matter where it may be,
I will offer my hand and open my heart,
To bless you with the gift of
PEACE.

Tony Vogel, Grade 7
White Station Middle School, TN

Rose

Red velvet petals, spiraling from the middle.
Crafted by angels, you are absolute perfection.
A trite symbol for beauty, you are beautiful yourself.
But just like all things that are beautiful,
You need to be left alone.
There are thorns running down your back.
They frighten me, so I stay where I am.

Laura Peck, Grade 9
Bearden High School, TN

Dreams

Dreams, the way you want your life to be.
Dreaming is your life in a show for you to see.
Your dream can be a reality or just another fantasy.
If you dream big and work hard, you will succeed.
A dream is a goal, a mission of what you want to take place.
Dreaming is automatic, but success takes time.
So let success come and your dreams shall fly.

Tare' Davis, Grade 7
Weldon Middle School, NC

Papaw Danny Who

Papaw Danny Who tells
jokes all day
works along the way
who is the sky
and the apple of my eye
is number one
world wide
who is a child at heart
and his is a work of art
who can fix cars
and has some scars
Who is an answered Prayer
and helps those everywhere
Who is nicknamed "Shorty" just smiles and says "Oh Lordy"
Who is my best friend even after the end
Who has a Pincher that doesn't whimper
Who preaches God's word and is loudly heard
who is a Christian even after the end
Who is the sea deep and free
Always supports me for the good things
Papaw Danny...Forever my best friend!

Alisha Sansom, Grade 9
Spring Valley High School, WV

What Is Forever Lost?

The smell of death runs up my nose.
The strong wind starts to pick me up.
People running for their lives,
As some decided to stay and treasure their home.
My body starts to fight the fear,
As the sadness eats me alive.
My body is like the dog's tail of happiness that shakes.
Cars flying across the sky.
I close my eyes and hoping that this nightmare will end.
I count to 5 and take a deep breath,
I open my eyes and this nightmare isn't going to end.
I can't take this anymore!
My body heats up and angry erupts.
I run and hide and stay in my place.
I'm all alone and cowardly to move,
Wait till it's all over.
Peek back and stand straight up.
My feet feel cool against the sad sorrowful blackness.
Tears fill up my eyes then pour out into a pool.

What was there then was now forever lost.

Jacora Warner, Grade 8
J Graham Brown School, KY

Flame

A candle sits before me,
And I behold its shining flame,
But this time I looked at it differently,
Like it had never been the same,
Just this one small light,
Could be thought of on such a wide range,
From happiness, joy, and delight,
To anger, sorrow, and pain,
A fire could keep you warm in the cold,
Or light a room by night,
But it has destroyed things more precious than gold,
And caused death, worry, and fright
It's amazing how such a beautiful flame,
Could cause so many to grieve,
But the real question will forever be the same,
Which fire will you receive?

Marideth Batchelor, Grade 7
North Raleigh Christian Academy, NC

Peace

Peace
is a lilac dancing on a sunset.
Peace, (he ping), la paz, la paix, frieden, and pacem.
It is silence dripping from a silver leaf
through the unknown darkness.
Peace is the dance of the swans
as they soar over emerald mountains.
Only peace can be so graceful as to dream of a distant world.
The wisdom of peace comes from Linus and Ghandi.
Doves caress peace, deploying it to the world,
but it never stays long enough to save us.
Peace is the equal balance of sun and moon,
dark and light, fire and ice.
Peace is like a windswept field that plays with the wind.
Peace drinks the violence
that destroys a blessing that we call earth.

Abigail Boyer, Grade 8
Baylor School, TN

The Titans Game with Dad

It was a loud Titans stadium that noon.
The smell of food that we ate, was so great.
We looked at the Titans gear.
We were on the Jumbo-tron.
No brothers to bother me that day.
Sitting on the away team side, was just me, my dad, and his friend.
The soda that I got was my favorite kind.
When the time had come the Titans were on top.
That is a special time that I had with my dad.

Andrew Beaman, Grade 7
Freedom Middle School, TN

Hide and Seek

Writing hides in my grandmother's rocking chair.
It hides in the cobwebs underneath the couch.
Writing hides in the old family photo albums.
It hides in dusty tricycle buried in the attic.
It hides in the fist of a baby.
Writing hides in rubber bands.
It hides in the beard of Abraham Lincoln.
Writing hides in the lonely kid no one wants to sit by.
It hides in the death of a loved one.

Will Jumper, Grade 8
Baylor School, TN

Life's Greatest Gift

A giggle, a smile, a hug
A sob, a gasp, a tear
They know my story
They know what makes me happy
They know when I'm about to cry
We give each other Christmas presents
And ride bikes in the park together
We're glowing whenever we're in the same room
We exchange secrets
Everything we own we share
Every time I laugh they laugh too
A second with them has more value than a million dollars
They're my shoulder to cry on
And hands to raise me up
They will always be there to stand by me
To comfort me if nothing else
And even if I won't admit it
I love them
They're my friends
And they love me too

Hallie Storms, Grade 7
White Station Middle School, TN

My Barn

In my yard sits my barn, my favorite
place
Behind my barn, I sit and watch the sun
slowly set
Inside my barn, my chickens roost

Along my barn, my horses rest

Within my barn, is a nice place to relax
and have the weight of stress lifted off
your shoulders
Toward the front of my barn, my cat
sleeps all day
At the corner of the front door, a spider
makes a beautiful web full of dew
Past the barn my dogs roam without a
care in the world
Among my barn, love to be with all my
animals
Across my barn lies a blanket of peace and love

Kailyn Norton, Grade 8
Heritage Middle School, TN

Snow

It feels cold when it touches me
Hear it crunch when I step on it
I see all the white flakes fall from the sky
Taste the great snow cream that Grandma makes
The smell of coldness floats through the air

Cody Hill, Grade 8
Boyle County Middle School, KY

The Real Deal

Everyone is on the field,
Waiting for the starting whistle.
Your heart pumping
Teeth chattering.

Start of the game;
You have the ball and you are on fire,
You look up and there is no one in front of you
You speed up, feel a smile coming across your face, Shoot.
SCORE!

Focus, get back in starting position.
Knees bent, eyes narrowed, now you are ready.
All you do is run.
You can feel the burning pain in your muscles,
But you ignore it and keep running.

You do this all for the sport you love,
The best sport and
The most active sport
SOCCER

Myrissa Druien, Grade 8
Hebron Middle School, KY

The Heavenly Window

Inside looking out
I see the cross by the field
Just standing tall and strong
I also see the birds twittering through the air
Tweet-tweet
I hear the preacher's loud booming voice
A loud clap of thunder
Ringing in my ears
The birds are sweet to hear
Like a child's laughter
I feel Jesus' soul rise
Throughout my body as I turn the pages
Slowly
The Bible speaks to me
As I have words flash right before my eyes
Without my window
I feel lost and insecure

Sophia Wright, Grade 7
Mount Washington Middle School, KY

My Family Is a Dolphin

My family is a dolphin intelligent, graceful, caring,
My dad is the blowhole that spurts every now and then,
My mom is the fin that leads the body,
My youngest sister is the nose that sniffs out danger,
My older sister is the tail fin that leaps for challenges,
And I am the mouth that catches the little pesky fish.

Monica Sellers, Grade 7
Sellers Home School, KY

Bubbly Bloom

I'm inside looking out
Children scattered before me like marbles
Each unique and bright
While the swing quivers with excitement
The whiny birds quarrel with sassy squirrels
About peanuts. While children giggle in glee
The flowers are being flattered by the Sun
And the spreading sweet fragrant is joy
The Sun tickles my fingers with a feather of warmth
While the glass' icy touch slides away
And the darkness is conquered
A rainbow flavored lollipop
With quickly melting clouds fill my mouth
Without my window the battle
Of cold darkness and warm brightness
May venture on
But for now
Life is a
Smiley face

Brooke Armenta, Grade 7
Mount Washington Middle School, KY

Choices

Choices.
You will make so many in life.
Some as small as what hairstyle to wear,
and others as big as who to make your
husband (or wife).
You may choose wrong,
as many people have done.
But you'll be able to fix it,
— or at least attempt.
If you make the wrong choice, don't fret.
Things will get better, I bet.
So the original choices you make don't count,
It's the choices that you make after that,
That can change things for you.

Blaze Herren, Grade 9
Lynn Camp High School, KY

The Foundation of Life

Happiness is an inspiring light,
surrounding your mind in spirit,
It smells like freshly baked bread,
filling your heart with joy,
It tastes like sweet, soft cotton candy,
making you smile with pleasure,
It feels like sleeping calmly on a feathered pillow,
giving you endless comfort,
It looks like a ray of beautiful colors,
making you gaze in awe,
It sounds like peaceful music,
a tune of laughter that tickles your heart,
the foundation of life.

Heather Thompson, Grade 8
Leesville Road Middle School, NC

With the Face of a Doll...

A tiny baby, with the face of a doll
Curls her small fist in a tight little ball
Her wispy blonde hair is as white as a dove
While her blue eyes twinkle like stars from above

A young girl smiles, with the face of a doll
She's grown quite a bit and is now quite tall
Her pale blonde hair is as soft as the sky
And she has beautiful, blue, sparkling eyes

A girl of sixteen, with the face of a doll
Smiles at a boy by the name of Paul
Her long, blonde hair sways in the summer breeze
And her eyes are the color of the ocean-seas

A woman in white, with the face of a doll
Raises a child with her husband, Paul
Her pale blonde hair is now streaked with gray
But her eyes remain blue as that very first day

Laura Campbell, Grade 8
Deerstream Learning Center, NC

The Joy of Joy

Joy is doing service for those who need it,
the feeling from it starts in one place,
and travels through the whole body;
It smells like a barbecue,
the aroma overwhelming all within its radius,
It tastes like a double fudge brownie,
soft and warm between your teeth,
It feels like a fire on a cold night,
warmth wrapping itself around you,
It looks like beautiful gems of assorted varieties,
glimmering and smiling back at you,
It sounds like the soft hissing of water,
as it cascades down a waterfall,
Bringing amusement and pleasure to all around.

Lee Pixton, Grade 8
Leesville Road Middle School, NC

The Dentist

It is now time,
To search for all my plaque
As I walk in the room,
I almost have a heart attack,
But I get rid of all my gloom,
And lie down on the pleasant, leather chair.
I settle and receive a whiff of the goofy latex gloves.
Sadly, Dr. Rover utilized a tooth of a bear,
And triggered tons of pain,
But finally, he polished my teeth,
For the pain began to wane.
"We are all done," stated Dr. Rover.
Finally, it was over.

Jarrett Rong, Grade 7
White Station Middle School, TN

Don't Go to War

When you first told me
You were going back to war
The only thing I could
Think of are tears running down my face?
I wish you did not have to go to that place
I can't wait until you come back
For I can see your lovely face
When my friends see the tears
Rolling down my face
They ask me what is wrong
I say you just won't understand
The pain I'm going through
This hurts
Every time
I hear a gunshot
My heart races like
It's you
In the battlefield
Dying slowly
But I hope it's
Not you.

Demauri Haskins, Grade 7
Ramsey Middle School, KY

What Soccer Is to Me?

People cheer when you score
Even if you're not adored
Some could laugh if you fall
But next time you're sure to take the ball
When you dribble down the field
You know you can't be beat
That's what offense is to me

Defense is just the same
They never should take the blame
Importance to the team
That's the key
Always be on your toes
Ready to take a blow
That's what defense is to me

Emily Jackson, Grade 8
Camp Ernst Middle School, KY

Long Lost Love

You are my sweetness and my life
Even if I won't become your wife
You shall always be my long lost love
Your eyes are like the stars above
My mind is going crazy for you
I hope you feel the same way too
You are the one I am longing for
Even though I met you in a candy store
I dream of the day we shall wed
So we can stay together until we are dead

Cheyenne Kent, Grade 7
St Vincent De Paul School, WV

To My Grandma

This is at tribute to my Grandma.
Thank you for being there for me.
I don't think you mean it when you yell at us (Me, Matt, Kevin), but
I like when you yell at us because it means that you care about us
I know you love everyone, but we're a little bit special because we give you a hard time.
You have always opened your arms to me and cared for me.
You always support me
and you will be in my life forever.
I know you love me and when we come over, we always have a good time.
You're always in a great mood,
and you always give good advice
and we can always trust you.
Thank you for coming to my games
and picking me up when I'm down.
You help me with things when I have a problem,
I love spending the holidays with you
and having great dinners.
Thank you for all the birthday wishes and presents.
I know you make sacrifices for me because it means you love me.
Even when it's a bad time, I'm still happy to be around you,
and I love you.

Jake Erpenbeck, Grade 8
St Agnes School, KY

Daffodil

A glittering speck gliding along the wind stream with all of its kind.
The journey of life has been an experience that weathered this speck.
It has been governed by generals and colonels never had freedom.
Doing the same thing day after day: the routine never thought to change.
But one day did change lives in every country the weather was cool.
Falling with the wind gliding under condensed clouds landing parachutes.
Glittering ocean: the perfect platform to land caught the speck in flight.
The daffodil scent relieving from the hard day distracting from pain.
They were sent from home from loving and caring hands made a soldier's day.
How did flowers live? Jumbled around for two weeks just like the soldiers.
Finally arrived in the correct location but not a good one.
Disappointment reeked. Rotting bodies, screaming, wounds but daffodil scents.
Brightened many days, but once that scent was absent: expressions of shock.
Gone for twenty weeks solemn and pained expressions all comfort was gone.
The beaming faces rejoiced on that twentieth back came daffodils.
Aromas filled camp the men shouted happily their country was free.

Mia Smith, Grade 7
Providence Academy, TN

Where I'm From

I'm from scraped knees in the summer and snowball fights in the winter
I'm from picking flowers in the spring and jumping in piles of leaves in the fall
I'm from the old oak tree with the long rope swing and the little lake with the huge catfish
I'm from walking the old trails in the woods and playing in the deep pools in the creeks
I'm from slipping and sliding on a frozen pond and making tracks in the fresh snow
I'm from watching cartoons on Saturday then getting up early for church on Sunday
Where I'm from is Sissonville, West Virginia, and there's no place I'd rather be

Crystal Hanshaw, Grade 8
Sissonville Middle School, WV

Never Forgotten

All the days of sadness and pain,
Can't be replaced by a single remain.
There's nothing left but memories to hold,
On these nights when my heart feels so cold.

I have nights where I feel sad and alone,
but I know you're better off with God in his home.
I pray that he takes good care of you,
Then I sit and hope my prayers get through.

Words can't begin to describe our heart ache,
I try to smile and go on, but everyone know it's fake.
I can still remember the good times we've had,
Up to the night when things went bad.

But why dwell on the past?
You're in a better place at last.
Now you sleep on a bed of cotton,
You're in heaven with God, and will never be forgotten.

Haley Taylor, Grade 8
Boyle County Middle School, KY

Meteors

Falling, raining like a fiery storm
Scorching heat but a deep cold
A feeling of dread for when that one single mass falls
You know the world will be crushed at its feet
And when those dark masses are cleared they leave a mark,
A mark that is unforgettable
Pouring, pouring, pouring
Down, down, down
It may be called a shower but in reality it's a storm
A storm of colors red, black, orange, yellow...black
That one storm that you'll remember forever
The darkness covers the sky in its shadow
Leaning over you, covering you
Until you cover yourself in your own blanket
And you see darkness once again
But now that feeling of dread and fear has lifted
And you feel safe
For you know that daylight will rain once again
And all will be at peace

Nahal Pahlevani, Grade 7
Villa Madonna Academy, KY

Party in the U.S.A.

Music playing
Children swaying
Teenagers kissing
Schools dismissing
Dogs barking
Fireworks sparking
What a wonderful day
It's a Party in the U.S.A.

Kathryn O'Leary, Grade 8
Kerr-Vance Academy, NC

Final Moments

Here I hearken in this darkened room,
This place where no face is shown.
Here I lie while I slowly die alone,
And wait until my fate be bones.

My mind, it dwindles, winds away —
But here I am, my body stays.
I lose all reason, but just for treason's sake,
I curse the Earth and it's worth, a fake.

My soul, it aches, as I watch a vole pass,
And I see as the vermin of life control the human mass.
How the beasts made a feast from my humanity,
And the guards beat me hard, oh hostility!

I do not hearken in this darkened room,
This place where no face is shown.
There I lay now, my days have ended,
And my soul was tired as it soon descended.

Savannah Toler, Grade 8
Meadow Bridge High School, WV

Friends

Friends are sweet and always there.
You can count on them no matter where.
They could be in the sky or on the ground,
But you can find them year round.

Friends can help you when you're down,
And can make you smile when there's a frown.
They give you a hand when you fall,
And they never doubt you, never at all.

Friends do no wrong in your eyes,
And can never tell you a lie.
They mean so much and everything,
With the everyday love they bring.

Friends make you laugh and smile,
And can fill you will love that lasts for miles.
You can count on them whenever,
And you'll love them forever.

Abigail Crosby, Grade 7
White Station Middle School, TN

Harvest Festival

The Harvest Festival is almost here.
Give a shout or a cheer.
Caramel apples and a slimy snake pit.
There are all kinds of goodies to get.
Do the cake walk or get a grab bag.
Please remember not to brag.
Come tonight there is so much more.
A night of all nights for goblins galore.

Kristen Williams, Grade 7
Elkton School, TN

I Had to Cry
I had to cry
When you said goodbye
You closed the door
Leaving for war

I had to cry
When you looked in my eye
You held me tight
And said it's all right

I had to cry
And lay there and sigh
Alone at night
While you're in a fight

I had to cry
If you were to die
Not knowing what to do
Never ever seeing you
Jacob Lush, Grade 7
Ramsey Middle School, KY

Fairy Tales
In the real story
The wolf ate the three pigs
In the real story
Rapunzel wore wigs

In the real story
The dwarfs were a little too late
In the real story
Hansel and Gretel never escaped

Stories with happy endings
Those are the only ones people tell
Those are in fact
The true fairy tales
Michelle Sotelo, Grade 7
White Station Middle School, TN

My Grandparents' House In New York
After a long time in my car
On the road
Out of my window I see a river
Past the river I go.
Up a long driveway
Into hugging arms
Inside my grandparents house I
escape the chilling air.
At the table I talk
With my Grandparents
Outside I watch the snow fall
slowly and joyously.
Liberty Denu, Grade 8
Heritage Middle School, TN

Best Friend*
From your beautiful smile to your gorgeous face,
you put me in awe with your God-loving grace.

I can trust you with anything and you will always be there,
friends like you are very rare.

We give and take but mostly give. I can always count on you.
You have so many wonderful qualities but I will only name a few.

When I am upset and things get too hard,
and when I am in trouble you will be my guard.

You are friends with everyone and are always kind.
I know friendships like these are exceptionally hard to find.

I know we fight sometimes, but never very long,
and I know you will always forgive me even when I am wrong.

You're so smart and are willing to help anyone in need.
You always go beyond the borders fighting to exceed.

I love you just the way you are, so don't you ever change.
You are the type of friend I want to keep; one that I'll never exchange.

I know this poem isn't enough to tell you how much I care.
But I know we will be friends forever, I promise you this, I swear.

Whenever you feel down and don't know what to go do.
I will help anytime because I love you!
Alex Smith, Grade 8
St Agnes School, KY
**A tribute to my best friend, Josie*

Happiness
Happiness
is sailing across the smooth sea on a sunny, blithe day.
When you catch big fish, like Ernest Hemingway, it is happiness.
Happiness is weekends.
Riding my bike as fast as Lance Armstrong with the wind in my face is happiness.
Happiness is getting stupendous grades on my report card,
and feeling for a moment, like Einstein.
It is a dream of graceful hummingbirds buzzing outside the window.
When your dog says hello for the first time in a week is happiness.
Happiness is rafting on the rapids of the Hiwassee, Ocoee, and Pigeon Rivers.
It's devouring a banana split dripping with hot fudge syrup.
It is sweet.
Lying on a grassy hill counting stars like diamonds in the sky is happiness.
Happiness is swimming in silence with dolphins in emerald waters.
Smiling for the first time after getting your braces off is happiness.
Happiness is an ice-cream-eating, game-winning, smile-making, milk shake-drinking,
skipping-everywhere, fun-with-your-friends kind of experience.
Flying a kite on a wide beach of glistening sand near sunset is happiness.
The happiest feeling in the whole world
is receiving blessings from our Lord and Savior, Jesus Christ.
Colton Holloway, Grade 8
Baylor School, TN

Gentle Giant

A quiet bark
a little kick,
My fifty five pound gentle giant

Wrinkled and soft
a single white streak,
On my fifty five pound gentle giant

A light,
ocean like,
breathing.
By my fifty five pound gentle giant

the burnt sunset haze,
Begins to fade

From the border of my memory,
Then she begins to wake,

My fifty five pound gentle giant.

Erin Chapman, Grade 8
Bondurant Middle School, KY

Magnificent, Marvelous Moon

The moon is striking
Floating in the firmament
Dotted with craters.

The moon in the sky
A heavenly reflector
Gives light in the night.

The moon in dark space
Interesting entity
A lifeless planet.

Celestial body
Is a magnificent sight
During an eclipse.

Cambron Johnson, Grade 7
Providence Academy, TN

On the Mountaintop

Skis race down the slope
Flashes of colored coats, scarves
Kids stop by pizzas

Flakes of snow float down
Onto the trees and branches
And melt on my tongue

The biting cold stabs
As I race for the warm lodge
Hot chocolate time!

Kendall Bard, Grade 9
Bearden High School, TN

School

Inside looking out
I see the world moving on,
Doing their daily things
Not even noticing I'm trapped in this prison 6 hours a day.
I see the bright sunny sky outside,
While I'm stuck in this dull, boring, gray room.
Listening to the clock mock me with its laughter.
I imagine the smell of the beautiful flowers.
I see bright colored trees and smiling faces on the outside,
But in I see sad, lonely, dull faces that do not want to be imprisoned any longer.
I hear the sounds of pencils around me
On the outside I hear laughter and playing of little children
And I think of how I want to be there.
The hinges on the windows and doors
Are like bars in a prison keeping me in here,
That's what this place is it's a prison
Again I hear the laughter of the clock
Taunting me Saying Ha, Ha, Ha, Ha.
I hear the rustle of papers and I taste the bitterness and want,
I know how they feel They want to be on the outside looking in
Not on the inside looking out.

Sarah Vincent, Grade 7
Mount Washington Middle School, KY

Where I'm From

I am from Sissonville, West Virginia,
from riding and running.
I am from the woods and mud.
I am from the soccer ball I kick,
from running and kicking to catching and punching.

I'm from the wind that catches my breath,
from sweat of my heart pumping to friends or family members death.
I'm from camping and time together,
from outside activities and campfire s'mores.
I'm from traveling the U.S.A.
with a car that fits all of us
and a camper behind us.

I'm from the Pittman and Mitchell's Branch,
campfires and terrific food.
From both my grandfather hearts stopping
and the time spinning backwards.
In the spare bedroom are scrapbooks and old memories.
I am from those memories before the family tree
is losing pieces and gaining pieces.

Chaz Pittman, Grade 8
Sissonville Middle School, WV

You and I

The snow,
So fluffy,
So white,
I don't know why, it makes me miss you,
I can't explain my feelings,
I don't know what's happening inside,
What are these feelings,
That I don't recognize,
You are funny,
And so sweet,
When we are together,
We can beat anything,
When you are here,
I notice nothing,
I love your smile,
Your soul is beautiful,
I love you!

Candy Johnson, Grade 8
Heritage Middle School, TN

Northern Lights

Far, far in the northern lands
Farther where breath turns to ice
Farther where there are no sands
Farther where coats do not suffice

There are lights in the sky
When the sun sets they rise above
They move as if they could fly
They appear to be just like a dove

They never ever fall
The shades are changing, always flowing
Colors like paint strewn on a wall
Never ending and always glowing

They light up the sky
Far, far where the land is frozen dry.

Jason Woodworth, Grade 9
Bearden High School, TN

Change

Coming out of this hard place,
Showing my own face,
Playing my way,
Showing the way.
Life is full of twists and turns,
Winding in and out,
Waiting for life to mix it up.
Got to smile and move on,
So my heart doesn't break any more.
I can't find the same old things
That used to make me smile,
But that's change.

Monica Spritzky, Grade 8
Villa Madonna Academy, KY

The Kingdom

My heart is soaring like the Eagle above me,
The Eagle, precious Eagle,
Has welcomed me into its Kingdom.
A world that knows not of trees, but only of rocks and small wildflowers
Oh Eagle, My King,
Thank you for sharing your Palace with me.

Peaceful, so peaceful
A burbling, babbling river flows over smooth, smooth rocks
The air is sweet, filled with the relaxing scent from the purple budding blossoms.
Soft crunching of rocks dying beneath my boots,
The King cries out, a blessing for their souls.

I'm hopeful, oh how I am hopeful.
The clouds up above,
Let loose a soft, white blanket, covering the, hard, hard rocks.
I stick out my tongue. A sweet, pure snowflake falls onto it.
A miracle, it can snow in the Middle of July,

I have to leave the Kingdom.
I am sorry my King, I will be sure to return soon.

Hannah Metzger, Grade 8
Bondurant Middle School, KY

I Just Hate, Hate, and Keep on Hating

I hate homework, reading, messing up,
traffic on the highway like the president was in town,
green veggies, being underestimated, being overestimated.
When my mom gets that leave-your-sister-alone-attitude.
I just hate, hate, and keep on hating.

I hate this dark, smelly bus, when my backpack cracks in the stairs.
I hate war, not understanding the teacher, when my pen leaks in the middle of tests.
I hate people that do not respect Martin Luther King's ideas.
I just hate, hate, and keep on hating.

But there are a few things
I don't hate.
I love my family, chocolate, waffles,
going to Baylor, having two homes, my friends,
And I hate haters.

Maxime Santisteban, Grade 8
Baylor School, TN

Orange in Nature

What is orange?
Orange is a radiant burst of a blooming tiger lily surrounded by fallen leaves.
It is stuck between hot and cold,
And between the brown spots of a giraffe roaming the African plains
Where the setting sun's tangerine colored rays shine.
The clementine pumpkins that line the homes on Halloween,
glow a calming carrot colored flame resembling the brightness of a parrot's beak,
and the coat of a fox in the still forest with apricot leaves resting on the ground.
Orange is energy.

Nicki Baggett, Grade 8
Montgomery Central Middle School, TN

I Wonder What's in Your Head

What's In Your Head?

I wonder what's in your head
When you're off to war
Shooting at someone, holding a gun
When you're gone it's no fun,

I wonder what's in your head
When you're getting bombed
If you ever stay calm
I really miss you mom

I wonder what's in your head
Does leaving for war make you mad?
Does missing us make you sad?
Does going back make you feel bad?

I wonder what's in your head
Does killing make you cry,
So much that you ask God why?
Just make sure you don't die.

Isaiah Johnson, Grade 7
Ramsey Middle School, KY

Daddy, Daddy Please Come Home

Daddy, daddy, please come home
It's becoming hard to see
The fact that you're out at war
Fighting for you and me
Daddy, Daddy please come home
Mamma misses you too
It's becoming hard for her to see
Cuz you're not here to guide her through
The nights are dark and weary,
it's hard to see the light
And when you're not here
I feel the urge to fight
Daddy, daddy, please come home
I need you here with me
To help me through everything
That I will never see

Amber Appleby, Grade 7
Ramsey Middle School, KY

I Miss You!

I miss you
I miss your smile
And I still shed a tear
Every once in a while
And even though it's different now
You're still here somehow
My heart won't let you go
But I need you to know
I miss you!

Aubree Whiting, Grade 8
Boyle County Middle School, KY

Florida's Warm Summer Breeze

After the long drive
I stepped out of the car
Greeted by Florida's warm summer breeze

As we carry our bags inside
I see that the once lonely house
Is now full of life

I grab a bike and explore the town
Shops are filled with people of all ages
The small streets are crowded with people riding their beach cruisers
Going place to place

But one little shop stands out
The Sugar Shak

I walk in,
The sweet smell of homemade ice cream fills the tiny "Shak"
Bins and cartons of candy
Waiting to be eaten by the little kids hovering over them
Old-fashion drinks light up the big Coke coolers
Along with a small porch on the other side of the room

The smiles on everyone's faces make me realize
How much I am going to like this little town
Surrounded by Florida's warm summer breeze

Haley Rainwater, Grade 7
White Station Middle School, TN

What the Sun Is Hiding

The sun rises, at first a pink rose
Then gradually the rose gives way to an orange glow,
That is so mysterious, so secretive as it hides all thoughts of the night
By swallowing the dew; like bugs that turn this beautiful orange glow
Into a lemony yellow, that has to float in the vast blue sea of the sky
And just like it hides the thoughts of the night, it hides its sadness
For its unappreciated work from the day before

It's sad that few people experience the event that starts each day
But it doesn't matter how early the sun actually rises
Because some people would still take such a simple thing for granted,
And I'm sure that if the sun could feel how truly unappreciated
Its work was, it would be very disappointed that not many people
Even so much as acknowledges everything it does for us

At the end of a long day, the sun begins its graceful descent
By first turning from its lemony yellow to a fiery orange
Then comes the fire engine of red that puts out the day
And when you think that there is nothing left to change,
The fiery sun changes into a cool, milky moon
But the sun's ways are reflected in the moon's: both must
Feel people's thoughtlessness to the feelings that are found deep inside

Kyra Kocis, Grade 7
Grey Culbreth Middle School, NC

Lost in My Own Reflection

Who is this scrawny girl?
Staring straight at me
Must she make me feel so uncomfortable?
Her tanned skin clashes with her chocolate hair and eyes
Flattering as her navy dress may be
She feels like a lowly turtle in its shell.

Why, that awkward girl is me!
Those narrow eyes drift over to my sibling.
How is it that she looks so naturally gorgeous?
Jealously creeps into every part of my body.
How dare she!
Why must I suffer while she doesn't even have to try?

Turning back to my own reflection,
I stare into those dark eyes of mine.
The wooden door creaks open
My mother clunks in with her shiny, high-heeled shoes.
I see her eyes water as she tells us what beautiful girls we are.
I smile and turn away.
Not once did I look back.

Lana Singer, Grade 7
White Station Middle School, TN

Sports

Sports,
Played on fields, diamonds, and courts,
Soccer, Cross-Country, Biking,
This is the occupation of my liking.

Being outside in rain or shine,
This obsession of mine, is mighty fine,

Sports, they're what I love,
They give me greater enjoyment than all the above,

I spend my time enjoying myself,
Every day from 12 to 12.

I may not be the best on the mound,
But I keep a good spirit, and that's what counts.

Patrick Leahey, Grade 8
Boyle County Middle School, KY

Art

Art is full of imagination,
Full of lines, shapes, and things,
People talking, people laughing,
Sometimes gets on my nerves.

Pencils, pens, and all kinds of paper,
Paint, brushes, and messes on tables and chairs,
Glue and scraps of paper layered on cardboard.
Art is a wonderful thing.

Austin Meck, Grade 7
Petersburg High School, WV

All I See

I look out the window and all I see is snow
The trees shiver without their jackets of leaves
I swallow the hot chocolate as it runs down my throat
It is winter time and that's all I see

Leaf after leaf is falling down
Orange, yellow, red, and green
The smell of nature rises in the air
It's fall, and that's all I see

Drip-drop, the rain comes down
The flower on their branches have a frown
The flowers blossom in the wet rain
It's spring, and that is all I see today

In my bathing suit as I jump in the pool
Sweaty and hot even with a glass of lemonade
School is out with excitement on our faces
It's summer time, and that is all I see

Sophia Wilhelm, Grade 7
Grey Culbreth Middle School, NC

Hillside Nursing Home Performance

It was a big dining hall,
There was no color on the wall.
The room was very warm,
But, I still had to perform.

The brown piano was out of tune,
It looked like something from an old saloon.
The keys got stuck so it didn't play loud,
Maybe that's why they were such a sleepy crowd.

I played them my hymn,
Then I walked up to them.
I was a little sad, but didn't let it show,
They were young like me, not long ago.

Kathryn Cowsert, Grade 7
Cowsert Christian Academy, NC

The Last Day of Winter

A fairy tale full of wonder and color
Sights and sounds of every kind
Filled the ears of weary travelers
Through the night and starry sky.

Animals here and there
Wander through the trees
Flowers that are so bright and have uplifting spirits...

They unravel their beauty to the world
As rays of sunshine, shine upon them.
Morning has come and a cool breeze blows
Telling all that spring has come!

Loren DuPont, Grade 7
East Millbrook Magnet Middle School, NC

The Obstacle
Run and jump you
will always
find
something in your way
may come to
bind
troubles and tricks
might persuade
you to make a
fall in your parade
try to stay away
and true
let this poem tell you
If you find one of
these don't beg for mercy please
don't make a fret or a bet on one of
these obstacles
Jason Holt, Grade 7
East Millbrook Magnet Middle School, NC

Red
Red is like a river of tears that flows
like the blood in my veins.
It's like fresh embers from a blazing fire
that is slowly burning out.

Red is like a rose that sways faintly
in the wind as it rages through the trees.

A perfect silence runs through the air
as tears fall from the sky.
It gently kisses a crimson rose
as it lays over.

The dark gray skies bring out its
beautiful candy red color
hoping that one day, it won't be
so alone.
Kiana Ledbetter, Grade 8
Montgomery Central Middle School, TN

Beautiful
Beautiful is the day
When Jesus was born
Beautiful is the day
When children don't have to mourn
Beautiful is the day
When angels fly
Beautiful is the day
When mothers don't have to cry
Beautiful is the day
That the blind can now see
Beautiful is the day
When God made you and me.
Destini Harney, Grade 7
Elkton School, TN

Winter's Noose
Open. Swoosh!
Down the steps.
Frozen feet.
Thick sweatshirt.
And rosy cheeks.

Into the car,
hop on in.
Feeling a draft?
Turn on the heat!
Away for a second,
the cold I fear…

Finally here.
Going back out there.
Wind phlegmatic,
like death itself.
Shivering again.
Caught in winter's noose.
Colin Abbott, Grade 8
White Station Middle School, TN

My Life as a Twin
My life began with one egg
Unknowing to everyone, it split into
Grew and developed to term
And "Surprise Everyone!" There are two!

From the beginning of time
Our bond with each other
Is amazing and unique
That of myself and my brother.

My life is so special
Knowing this will happen again
So few of us in this world
Are the miracles of a twin.
Jesse Northcutt, Grade 8
West Middle School, TN

Winter Nature
The sky drops frozen water,
Called snowflakes.
Each and every one is different,
They cover the ground.

Some hibernate.
The trees lose their leaves
And they are bare.

It is cold outside.
Then the season changes
And all the winter fun,
Happens next year.
Abigail Dean, Grade 8
Boyle County Middle School, KY

Up Against the Wall
Up against the wall
A girl stands hoping not to fall
To fall in love
To fall in doubt
To fall in a situation that she can't get out

Up against the wall
She stands and tries to hide
Hide from you
Hide from them
And definitely hide from him

Up against the wall
She stands and decides
Decides her life
Decides her dreams
And decides what life really means

Up against the wall
A girl became a woman
Jhone Egerton, Grade 9
Roanoke Valley Early College, NC

My Beloved Grandmother
Standing here all alone,
Not a tear I shall cry.
I loved you so dear much, Grandma.
Now, there is nothing else to say.

When that last second of breath came,
You struggled to say a word.
I rushed through the entrance
Because I knew it deep down inside.

Even though we were going separate ways,
You managed to give one last smile
And told me that you loved me.
When the time finally arrived,
I knew I would be thinking of you
For the rest of my days.
Katie Han, Grade 9
White Station High School, TN

Basketball
My favorite game
My best sport
My whole world
My special talent
My social outlet
My friends all play
I practice every day
I hope to go all the way
I love basketball
Tyler Newmeyer, Grade 8
St Vincent De Paul School, WV

Skiing

On the cold December day,
I ride up the ski lift.
On the Rocky Mountains,
There I sit and wait.

After waiting, waiting, waiting,
I finally reach the top.
Now staring down the snowy trail,
I prepare to travel down.

I push on my ski poles,
And off I go.
Speeding down the mountainside,
I glide across the snow.

On my skis my poles in hand,
I fly down the run.
Moving at great speed,
I soon reach the end.

I stop at the bottom,
And head into the lodge.
I drink hot chocolate,
And celebrate my feat.

Garrett Schaffer, Grade 8
Boyle County Middle School, KY

Outside

The sky is blue.
The clouds are white,
What a sight,
You can't see at night.

The stars are white,
And oh so bright,
What a night,
With stars a flight.

The ground is wet,
The dew is there,
The grass so green,
I love to stare.

The sun is yellow And full of warmth,
that fills the air,
I love the sun,
With lots of care.

Nature is beautiful,
As you can see
It's very special,
To you and me.

Jessica Duncan, Grade 8
Hebron Middle School, KY

Bundle of Joy

Big eyes,
Sparkle at me,
While she lays upon my shoulder,

Nobody can handle how cute she is,
She can be a little jumpy,
At the end of the day,
She's right back into my arms.

Sometimes she can be loud,
She barks at the sunrise,
Not a day goes by without her barking
But I learn to love it.

When I come home she greets me well,
She just loves her master,
When I see her she brings joy to my eyes,
She's my puppy Maxie,
And she will always be my bundle of joy.

Alita Reed, Grade 8
Bondurant Middle School, KY

Special to Me

Golden hair and emerald eyes,
Really funny, kind of wise.
A gleaming smile that shines brightly,
And when he hugs, he hugs tightly.

He laughs, he smiles, he talks to me,
When he's around, everyone is happy.
He lets me cry on his shoulder,
He is stronger than a boulder.

He always knows what to say,
And what will brighten up my day.
He'll be here 'til the end he swears,
And that's how I know my best friend cares.

Macey Berzak, Grade 9
Bearden High School, TN

Breathe

For we were meant to breathe.
Everlasting, breath never failing.
For we were meant to breathe.
Silently, the breath forced out so happily.
For we were meant to breathe.
The feeling aware, alert.
For we were meant to breathe.
Slowly now at loss.
For we were meant to breathe.
Now ever so ending peacefully.
For we were meant to breathe.
Life and breath, short you see.
For we were meant to breathe.

Armante Horton, Grade 8
Central Wilkes Middle School, NC

Life

Here I am
Where my life is going as planned
I have things I'm not happy about
But I don't walk around and pout
I have things in my life that are good
I live life to the fullest like I should
I don't want it to end until it's time
I have more adventures of mine
My friends are what make my life mine
I have a life
And it's all mine, not yours
It can get deep into the core
But I won't give up
My life is what I live for
What is so great about life?
It's only yours and you make it what it is
There are things we might miss
But that's life

Alexis Ulerick, Grade 8
Camp Ernst Middle School, KY

I Am Wonder Woman

I am me
I am super
I am independent
I am wonderful
And I'm
Intelligent
I do not let anyone put me down
And I never will
They can try
But they will not succeed
You give me respect
And I will give you respect
I am me
I am Wonder Woman

Jazmin High, Grade 8
Roanoke Valley Early College, NC

Daddy Please Don't Go

Daddy please don't go,
I wait for you in the cold
Hoping you would come back home.
Daddy please don't go,
I wish you weren't so bold
To leave me and Mom home…
Daddy please don't go,
You're all I got
And all I need
So come back please.
Just come back Daddy,
Without you I feel like I'm dying
You're always gone
I feel like crying.

Tessy Lutes, Grade 7
Ramsey Middle School, KY

Life of a Leaf

Leaves, leaves,
blowing through the air.
Where will they end up?
Over here or over there?
Summer, spring,
winter, fall.
Changing seasons,
having a ball.
Red, orange,
yellow, and green.
It's like they're in
a time machine.
Always moving,
making friends.
Too bad this season
has to end.
Fall, oh
it brings so much cheer.
Too bad they have to wait
'til next year.

Kathleen Jusko, Grade 7
East Millbrook Magnet Middle School, NC

Bubbling

I am bubbling
My insides are turning
I'm starting to feel queasy

I've practiced and practiced
I know I am ready
But then I look around and see
People so much better than me
Doubts rush through my mind

When I sit down to play
all my doubts run away

The room silences
And my name is called
I am ready.

Sarah Baxley, Grade 8
Signal Mountain Middle High School, TN

God's House

In His house, He is near
Throughout the church, the spirit lives
On the stage, God is praised
Across the sanctuary, His word is preached
Among His children, His love is shared
With my friends, we celebrate
Instead of sorrow, we feel joy
Of the choices, we choose Him
Inside the church, His spirit overflows
Into our hearts, God shows

Andrew Wigdor, Grade 8
Heritage Middle School, TN

As If It Would Help Any Ways

The world is full of so many people, so many places, so many memories.
We never stop to think about the individuals. Just ourselves.
Yes it's true, we think about how many people there are and what they may look like.
But do we think about what they've been through?
Perhaps we do if they don't have water or food or a crew.
But there's more than that. Each person has a story and each story has more.
But instead of thinking of that, we think of what we wore.
There are so many secrets and so many happenings that have taken place in this world.
But we never uncover the most mysterious things.
Certainly we could, if we tried. But why bother when our ideas are fried?
The world is so full but we are too self-absorbed to notice.
So we just stay inside the box. Never outside.
It's almost as if we have a blind side.
We're made like this and we can't change who we are.
So if you want, just stick to yourself.
Stick to the memories if it's all you can hold on to.
Because you can't hang without something to reach out for and grab.
When we mess up, there's not always a napkin there to make a dab.
As if it would help any ways.

Thea Henry, Grade 7
J Graham Brown School, KY

Life's Not a Breeze*

Well I'll tell you:
Life for me ain't been no breeze
It's had bypasses where I have lost friends
And family because of death
And hardships with family
But all the time I let the wind go by
And kept on turning cheek after cheek
And forgave and forgot
And living my life to the fullest
So don't turn back keep moving on and
Don't you be mean to people you don't like
Don't give up when life's hard because I know you'll make it through
Don't be like your friends be original (without getting in trouble)
But even though that breeze keeps telling me to give up
I turn my cheek and keep moving forward to the end of the line
That's where I want you to end at so keep turning your cheek
No matter how much you want to give up keep moving forward to the finish line.

Lindsey Cook, Grade 7
Meredith-Dunn School, KY
**Patterned after "Mother to Son" by Langston Hughes*

My Special Place

Near my home
On the patio
In the swing
Under the arbor
Beside the flowers
After dinner
At my special place
Before I leave
Across my body I feel peace

Trevor Perry, Grade 8
Heritage Middle School, TN

Robbers

Tearing down many kinds of doors,
Not even making a loud noise,
He took it all from old and poor,
When sirens sound he keeps his poise

They see him and he runs away,
He hides in the hills until night,
To come again another day,
But he will wait until it's right.

Kyle Fischer, Grade 9
Spring Valley High School, WV

The Everlasting Delay

My heart is aching,
When will I stop faking?
When I'm around you,
I'm not me; I want you to see too.

When my eyes meet yours,
I want my feelings to pour,
But instead, it can't find its way,
So I say silly things to delay.

The delay never comes to an end.
I try different ways to send the message I always send,
But it doesn't come out how it should.
Everyone laughs as I'm misunderstood.

As my feelings stutter,
And my butterflies flutter,
You will never know,
In my heart, you glow.

Mattison Domke, Grade 7
Elizabeth City Middle School, NC

Beyond Awaits Wonders

Inside looking out
Waiting for me
As the misty fog rises I see the curved knob turn
The house shrieks with joy
The woodsy scent of the
Old rocking chair on the front porch
The smooth wind rushes through my hair
Waiting for my grandma's arms
To embrace me
Back home at last
Her hair is cotton candy
Great Papaw's voice is like a roaring lion
When dinner is on his plate
The steamy air rolling down my throat
As I step outside the door
I am covered in hugs and kisses
Without my window
I would be blocked from the
Wonderful wonders that wait.

Cassie Beaton, Grade 7
Mount Washington Middle School, KY

Cycles

When a flower blooms in the meadow
A fish dies in the sea
When you have a moment of silence
A baby cries as he's brought into the world
Life is like a cycle always turning
So live your live like you mean it
Listen to your own heart not someone else's

Maley Wagner, Grade 7
Grey Culbreth Middle School, NC

The Sky

During the night I look up at the sky
and see a bright star.
The brightest star is a friend or family member that
you cared about, that just recently
passed away.
The moon is Jesus and God watching over
you.
The sun is also Jesus and God watching over
you.
The clouds that pass by are the friends and
family cheering you to
go all the way.
They watch over you and everything that you
own.
Cheering you on so that you can see them
one day.
Everything you see, you'll see them and know
they are cheering
you on.

Crystal Pike, Grade 8
Swansboro Middle School, NC

Growing Old

As the trees wither their leaves,
The human sheds his youth and life.
Winter approaches and besieges joy
With frostiness.

As the sun dissipates in the dark of night,
Wrinkles and creases gather on the smooth surface.
With the luminous moon and shining stars
Comes weariness.

As the railings rust and fade into nothingness,
Spiteful demons shred and rip the internal body.
Pain and agony wrest control of the mind and soul
Along with hopefulness.

As the sun lightens and reveals itself in dawn,
A hope for a better day rises and takes hold.
Once young and bright,
Now dull and full of gloominess.

Haatef Pourmotabbed, Grade 8
White Station Middle School, TN

Nighttime

Nighttime
Dark and calm
Gliding, blinking, shutting off
Sleep brings you to another time
Opening, anticipating, freshened up
Bright and content
Morning

Emma Burklin, Grade 9
Bearden High School, TN

Just You and Me*

There would be no more worries,
No more tears.
No more unspoken words except
I love you.
One of these days,
I'm going to speak.
I'm going to shout.
I'm going to ask questions.
I'm going to tell him the truth,
The truth of how I feel.
'Bout me,
'Bout him,
'Bout us.
The breath and words that are unspoken.
The wondering of what sends everyone
Speechless before their very breath.
The breath that lies between him and I.
The breath that tells what we should be.
Then I lay here wondering.
Would we ever be?
Just you and me.

Nika Jones, Grade 8
Carlisle County Middle School, KY
**Dedicated to Darin Richardson*

Why Was It Me

Why was it me
That went off to war
Without saying
Goodbye?
Why was it me
That wasn't there
For my comrades
Fighting the war?
Why was it me
That was not there
To see my first
Baby be born?
Why was it me,
That when I came
Home I saw nothing
But my wife at my knees?

Olivia Montgomery, Grade 7
Ramsey Middle School, KY

Jesus

Jesus is my sword.
Jesus is my Lord.
Jesus is the one everyone should adore.
Jesus is at the door.
Jesus is the one you can't ignore.
Jesus is the one I believe in.
But Jesus is the one I won't forsake Him.

Edward G., Grade 9
Audubon Youth Development Center, KY

Dream or Nightmare?

As I drift off into deep slumber
I enter the wonderful land of dreams

So many things beyond my wild imagination
A man with bunny ears is standing near
A small child is petting a black deer
The red moon shines so bright
Filling this world with gleaming light

But what makes a dream a nightmare?
Dreams aren't scary
But what lies beyond the horizon of a dream?

Nothing
Dreams just end
When you wake up from a dream,
There is nothing left but reality

Dreams can become nightmares because there's an end
You may have the best time of your life and never want your dream to end,
But sooner or later, we all have to wake up and face reality.

Jason Yu, Grade 7
White Station Middle School, TN

Move

I begin in my home, but I must leave
I am moving far, too far
I sit quietly thinking about where I'm going, through the window I look
This way and that way, I see great places
But they always have to go, I will not forget them
Even if they are not my friends, left and right
Each turn takes me somewhere new, I want to get a better look
But I'm locked to this small window,
The window sits with me, letting me see what I can
One direction I can look, one direction I am going
I know where am I, this place is like a pancake
Where are the mountains, I can't seem to find them
I have to stay and can't leave, thinking that like the others it will go
But unlike the others, this one doesn't have to be seen
Through a window

Ethan Froeber, Grade 7
Mount Washington Middle School, KY

An Epic Day in California

It was a hot summer day in California.
We were going for some mini golf.
My sister and I wanted to do something before I left.
Her and I played for a few hours.
After we were done, we went to the go-carts.
At first sight of my sister, they made an excuse to let us cut to the front of the line.
She and I had fun.
When we finished, they let us cut again!
I thought it was hilarious.
Tiana and I had a fun day.

Zachary Kalamar, Grade 7
Freedom Middle School, TN

Sarah

This is a poem to Sarah,
my big sister,
whom I love very much.
You help me pick out clothes,
and you help me when I have a problem.
You visit me on the weekends,
and I hope you never leave.
I tell you my secrets,
and you tell me yours.
You always tell jokes,
and you always make me laugh.
You always listen to me,
and you try to cheer me up when I am sad.
You are my only sister,
and I don't see you very much anymore,
so I miss you a lot.
This ends my tribute to you,
Sarah.

Emily Kreutzjans, Grade 8
St Agnes School, KY

Stuck in the Middle

Inside looking out
The light of eternal life
A light like the sun
But under you
Its booming tremendous screams
Terrible screams attacking you
But above again
There's singing
It was a dove of joy
Evil below and joy above
Two roads one small one giant
One hard one easy
But you can't choose yet
Because you are stuck in the middle

Zachary Neace, Grade 7
Mount Washington Middle School, KY

A Step Above Anger

Fury is a demon
that makes you lose control,
it smells like an animals breath
laced with rotting meat,
it tastes like pepper spray
burning every word,
it feels like burning coals
pressed deeply in the skin,
it looks like total darkness
turning good men blind,
it sounds like a tremor
rattling every bone,
it dredges up painful memories,
never meant to be found.

Daniel Koenig, Grade 8
Leesville Road Middle School, NC

Dandelions

I am eight,
I run barefoot out into the dew-coated, stick-to-your-feet grass,
unmindful of ants and other creepy-crawlers.
Out to the dandelions ready to be plucked and scattered through the air.
Everything below the sun is scorching.
I focus my eyes on the challenge,
the enormous boulder awaiting to be climbed in my front yard.
Now standing on top, knowing I have conquered
something, in my eyes, as big as Mt. Everest.
When I awake Mama says my hair is as messy as a bird's nest.
Come play with me. I gallop to the end of my driveway,
going out of my way to crush a few crispy leaves. CRUNCH!
We play hide and go seek, but no peeking!
I dash towards a bed of fiery and golden brown leaves, as if I was Rambo.
No one can see me now.
We also play like we are fairies and run around with Pixy Stix's touching everything
and it turns to candy. I seen what my mama's car did to my kitty
and I wonder what kitty heaven is like.
I imagine there are plenty of treats and balls of yarn.
Mama says she is in a better place now.

Annabel Kisling, Grade 8
Baylor School, TN

Kentucky Bluegrass

I am seven,
The Amazon rain forest surrounds me as I listen to the yellow joy,
standing on a wide open plain.
Holding my first pigskin,
there is no staying up past nine.
I am seven, I am big, I am curious.
I wonder why mommy's tummy is so gigantic?
The school building on a busy day, the clashing and banging of lockers,
reminds me of a white lily being consumed by bumblebees.
Mama says "It ain't polite to stare."
With my stepfather soaring over me, like the Empire State Building
I am seven.
I feel like a bull in a china shop.
I wonder what eight feels like?

Cole McMahan, Grade 8
Baylor School, TN

Morning

Sleep covers children's eyes,
Like the layers of dew on newly freshened grass.
The great sun awakes from its slumber,
Peeking ever so slowly from the mountains peak.
Plants stretch out their limbs towards the morning's warm embrace
As smells waft from the kitchen, bringing wake to everything
From the forest,
To the wild dog, lying on the ground, hungry for just a bite of human life.
New troubles begin as old ones disappear like moon does
But for now,
No one or nothing seems to care.
Just let morning come.

Rebekah Alvey, Grade 7
J Graham Brown School, KY

Snow

It was freezing outside
and we were weary
when she finally said
"Let's go play
in the snow."

So we dressed,
layer after layer,
like Eskimos in the arctic.
We flew out the door
And it was as cold as
ice on a hot summer day,
but we still played
and made snowmen and snowballs

until we got tired.
We went inside
and crashed in the bed,
until late in the day
when the sun was out
and it was all gone.

Darby Taylor, Grade 8
Bondurant Middle School, KY

Autumn

Fall is here
Let's all cheer!!
Beautiful as a rainbow
Glorious flavor,
Rich red,
Bright orange,
Shiny yellow.
Swish, whoosh, wow,
Rustling leaves,
Kelly green grass
By the morning sun.
Do you see it too?
Feelings of overwhelmed,
Leaves and more leaves
Heavy winds blowing me away,
But protection is the key
From this old tree.
Full of life,
But still so peaceful
Never forget the memories
Of this old fellow.

Ashton Chaney, Grade 8
Bondurant Middle School, KY

Hunted

I see glowing eyes,
The tiger is stalking me,
I am his prey. Help!

Hannah Voyles, Grade 9
Pleasant View Baptist School, KY

Our Meadow

You and me,
Feeling free,
Dancing in our meadow.
Soon the moon will rise,
And bring the fireflies.
We will just say hello,
As we jump in our meadow.

Lying in the flowers,
Hoping no one will find us.
Wasting away hours,
Eating pizza crusts.
Laughing in our meadow.

A loud! crash abruptly breaks me from the effects of the love potion!!
I was daydreaming while the class was causing commotion...
Seeing him sit back down in his seat fills me with emotion.
Playing with my hair,
I relax in my chair.
I wish we were back in our meadow.
Dancing, jumping, laughing in our golden meadow.

Hannah Manis, Grade 8
West Middle School, TN

Homework

Homework, ugh, nobody likes it but there's just one thing. We have to do it.
Sometimes it's hard, sometimes it's crazy but that doesn't mean we have to be lazy.
The teachers might give a lot but that doesn't mean we can't take a shot.
No violence used, this is homework you see. It's a requirement for you and me.
I don't like homework, I'd rather be free, but there's a place at school where we have to be.
Home is blah, but we're haters. I do the work because it makes me better.
Homework is graded and always hated, but we still do it to get 100s.
We are all very smart and different in ways.
We use our brain from day to day, to make straight A's.
When we don't do it, we don't start acting like babies.
We are taught better so we try again, then the next time we just might win,
Homework isn't punishment; it's not to destroy you.
Homework is available, but it doesn't control you.
This is my homework poem and I hope that it informed you!!
HOMEWORK!!!!!! Nike: JUST DO IT!!

Kelton Cherry, Grade 9
StudentFirst Academy, NC

My Story

One time two snowy years ago,
I took a trip to Oklahoma,
It was as long as a person walking the trail of tears.
When we arrived my grandmother had a warm, hot meal on the table for me and my mom.
We saw my Aunt Judy, my Uncle Edward, and some other family that I hadn't met.
Me and my cousin went to a game place like Dave and Busters but more fun.
After a fun filled week my mom and I needed to head home before the weather got bad.
We got to the hotel and ended up staying there an extra night because of the snow.
The next morning me and my mom got up super early to go home,
Twelve hours later we arrived at home safe and sound.

Rachel Burger, Grade 7
Freedom Middle School, TN

Stranded

Stranded,
like on an island; But at Bondurant instead.

The thought of basketballs dribbling,
fans cheering, and buzzers going off.

Then reality kicks in —
The sound of nature and the wind so pure.
The fresh air full of life and joy,
meanwhile, we're both full of fright and fear.
We run, we sit, we laugh, we play,
wasting away this long-lasting day,
with giggles and moments to cherish.

Mournfully, the day is ending
and our ride is near, So we hop in the car,
Laughing, laughing, laughing,
about what a unique and
extravagant summer Saturday, spent
stranded
at Bondurant, rather than the Lady Braves basketball game.

Destiny Hyatt, Grade 8
Bondurant Middle School, KY

The Taste of Gold

Outside looking in,
There is a tray dotted with mounds of chocolate,
The timer sounds — tick, tick, beep!

As I open the gateway to goodness,
Joy fills the air
And my face is flushed with heat.
The doughy rounds are lumps of gold,
Taunting me, until they cool.

At last, I taste
Luscious, rich, satisfaction.

As they slither down my slick throat,
I think,
"Without my window,
I wouldn't know when perfection would be done."

Layne Cutler, Grade 7
Mount Washington Middle School, KY

Christmas Tree

See the tree glimmer against the Christmas lights
Colorful ornaments reflect such a beautiful sight
On top lies a shimmering star
That shines an aura very far
Below lies a skirt full of presents
That waits for the children to spot its special surprise!

Mariah Mook, Grade 7
East Millbrook Magnet Middle School, NC

Not a Ray of Hope

Sadness is a thunderstorm,
It may only last a while,
But can always return tomorrow,
It smells like white carnations,
The petals of grief and gloom,
It tastes of the ocean,
Salty drops flood your face,
It feels like a relentless monster prodding at your broken heart,
Knots twisting your stomach inside out,
A lump rising in your throat
Making you choke on your own sorrow,
It looks like a gray sky,
Without sun for days,
Not a ray of hope to be found,
It sounds empty,
The silence echoes off the walls of a desolate home,
It leaves you numb and disconnected,
Hollow like a tree,
No one ever cares to stop and admire

Davis Raynor, Grade 8
Leesville Road Middle School, NC

Ode to the Moon

She sits on high in the starry night sky
And spotlights the lives on the graveyard shift
For those who look, her face will they see
And her luminescent grace shall awe them
She drove us to trek the final frontier
And our feet to touchdown on her splendor
She provides the bats their headlights to fly
And the wolves, their primal urge to howl
And when the horizon lights up the sky
All the region knows that she must now leave
But we all rest assured, for we all know
The mistress shall return on coming night

Cody Hastings, Grade 9
Bearden High School, TN

Happy, Happy Mourner

You stare at the box
  that's hidden in the corner
You look at the locks
  you're the happy, happy mourner
The house is in your hand
  you twirl it in your fingers
The itch you cannot stand
  and the memory still lingers
So sit in your chair
  and stare at that corner
You just don't care
  because you are the happy, happy mourner

Sydney Rymer, Grade 9
Center for Creative Arts, TN

Basketball

The feeling in the locker room
Heart, passion, determination and dedication
As I lace up my shoes I go into a different world
There is only one goal...WIN

During warm-ups I see all of the Panther fans
Filled with smiles and laughter
Pumped up and excited for the game
If only they knew how I felt...

As my name gets announced for the starting line up
It sends chills through my body
I suddenly feel that everyone's eyes are on me
It's a wonderful feeling that puts a smile on my face

High fives, cheers, fans yelling...
That's the sound of victory
The sound that makes you feel complete
The sound that makes you feel like you're on top of the world

At the end of the day when the buzzer sounds
I know I've performed at my best
That I gave all I had and I'm proud of myself for that
Basketball...It's more than just a sport
It's a part of me

Jordan Vorbrink, Grade 8
Hebron Middle School, KY

Whispers

I whisper in the night...
"Are you still up?"
Hoping an answer is coming.

I whisper in the night...
Shhhhhh!
To all the scurrying I hear in my head.

I whisper to the monsters...
"Your beauty is present, but I don't want you now."
Begging that they won't come back.

I whisper in the night...
"I love you."
To whom I don't see anymore; as if they can hear me.

I whisper to myself...
Songs of enjoyment that make me feel better.

I whisper to my sister...
"It's okay they will stop."
But just like every time before they don't stop

Whispers are like wind they are felt, but barely heard.
Can you hear my whispers?

Carlyn Causey, Grade 8
J Graham Brown School, KY

Finally Reached

The whistle echoed off the walls
As I walked up the steps
The pressure started to beat down on me like the sun
Take your mark, then the buzzer blared off

I dived into the onslaught of cold water and bubbles
I heard a voice in the back of my head telling me to kick
And not even think about slowing down
Reach the end, flip, go back
Kick kick kick kick kick

I reach the flags
Put my head down and sprint into the wall
But the wall isn't the place to stop
I have to keep on swimming

The clock kept tick tick ticking away
Then below it next to the number seven
My first "A" cut
My only goal for the entire season
Finally reached

Jacob Silvernail, Grade 8
Bondurant Middle School, KY

Tori's Cat

It's hard to pick a place to just begin
On explaining this cat of my old friend's.
She's just so small, and vile, and strangely thin —
Sure, she's cute; except for the fact she tends
To bite and scratch without any reason.
You'd think her to be a bit more grateful,
But purr turns to yowl — And then just treason.
To me, it would seem, she's oh so hateful.
With her blank cat-ish stare, and menacing
Air, it's no surprise we brawl when I'm there.
Yeah, Zoey has claws — they hurt and they sting
Once she gets me; but I forget to care —

Because she curls up in my lap, all nice;
It's not a 'sorry,' but it'll suffice.

Montana Gatens, Grade 9
Spring Valley High School, WV

Winter

The cold winter is near
Snow is falling
The ground is covered in white flakes
The smell of warm, hot chocolate
Presents are under the tree
Christmas lights are all around for you to see
Kids waiting for Santa Claus to come and visit
Leaving gifts for the good girls and boys
Waking up their parents when they get up
This is why winter is my favorite season

Nick Belcher, Grade 8
Boyle County Middle School, KY

Daddy, Please Don't Go!

Daddy isn't here,
When he is gone
I feel he'll never come back
"Daddy, please don't go."
"Honey, I'll be back soon."
I fell to the ground
"Daddy don't go; I'll be so sad
You're the best daddy anyone's ever had."
"Daddy, please don't go."
I saw a tear
Shed from his face
"Everything will be OK."
He started to open the door
My emotions dropped to the floor
What if I won't be able to see
My daddy anymore?
All these questions
Were running through my head
As I was up and in my bed
Could we be a family again?
Or is this the very end?

Madeline Brocato, Grade 7
Ramsey Middle School, KY

Longing for Summer Vacation

I desperately long for
Summer to come…

Day after day I hear
The school bell hum.

With all the teachers
And all the work,

Time with my friends
Is the only perk.

But I'll keep on going
Although it's a pain,
Because school's the only path
To fortune and fame.

Noah Christianson, Grade 7
Elkton School, TN

The Ones Who Run

Together we beat as if one
Through valleys o'er hills we shall run
Hearts softened with each others love
She is the gift sent from above

Hoof after hoof they hit the ground
Thud after thud her heart will pound
The raging spirit flushes out
What little ounce of fearful doubt

Brandi Caldwell, Grade 9
Spring Valley High School, WV

Vetch

I am six,
A nose-picking, go-with-whatever six year old.
Waiting outside into the brutal-sun, not thinking about the sunburn I will be getting.
Outside observing the grass grow
which seems as slow as watching molasses move,
and have no friends that live close to me.
I have my silver Nike football,
so I can play by myself and not with friends.
The brutal sun reminds me of the beach,
but with no sand or waves crashing.
No one is allowed to leave except me
because I will have the skin color
of a peach if I don't.
I am six,
I wonder why so many people die of old age.
Maybe the older you get the harder it is to live.
I wonder what living the moment taste like
because mama says the memories that last a lifetime are the best ones.
I guess living in the moment will wait until I am older.

Tyler Seaberg, Grade 8
Baylor School, TN

Lexington: The Town That Built Me

I am the product of:
A small southern town
Known to most for BBQ and formerly furniture
But, sadly, to residents as a dead city
Struck down by the bad economy, leaving large plants abandoned and dilapidating
With a main street which is a snapshot of the 20th Century
Where everybody knows everybody and the term, "everybody and their brother" is true
Where news travels faster than the speed of light
Where cold fall nights are spent at the county high schools watching football
Where country music is heard playing in most public places
Where most folks own a gun but maintain a Christian lifestyle
And where Southern hospitality is a prerequisite to live there

Yeah, I have been raised there…

David Cowan, Grade 8
Westchester Country Day School, NC

Locked Out

I slid down the hot, green plastic
My hair filled with static, like a lion's mane.
The shrill pitch of a whistle cut through the screaming children.
I bolted inside, frigid school air chilling me to the bones.
Everyone bounded to the water fountain
Except a fiery red-haired boy and me.
Three loud bangs on the door cut through the silence
I glanced out of the glass, smudged with sticky hand prints of six year olds.
There stood three girls with tears staining their faces.
The boy with the blazing hair shoved open the door.
The abandoned girls gave him thanks
Hugging and playfully running their fingers through his flaming scarlet hair.

Bella Golightly, Grade 9
White Station High School, TN

On Stage and Alone

Here I am again
On stage
Alone
No one here
But me
The silence destroys my sanity
As the empty chairs laugh at me
Here I am again
On stage
Alone and cold
Like winter that never ends
No one to guide me through rough times
Through the snowy
Iceland
With no one as a friend
No one to catch me when I fall
Nor anyone to answer my calls
Here I am again
On stage
Alone
I'm alone

Serena Stoddard, Grade 8
J Graham Brown School, KY

True Love

Roses are red
Violets are blue
Sugars are sweet
But not like you
When you walk in the room
You make my heart beat
Your eyes sparkle like the
Sun and the heat

Roses are red
Violets are blue
You are the shine
In my sunshine
My love for you
Is like how a fat boy loves
Chocolate cake

Loris Lawson, Grade 7
East Millbrook Magnet Middle School, NC

White Wonderland

Waking up to white wonderland
Singing along with my best friend
Looking out my frosty window
Seeing snowmen in the meadow

Getting ready for all the fun
Sledding down the hill one by one
Playing each minute of the day
Wishing it wouldn't melt away

Sammy Brody, Grade 9
Spring Valley High School, WV

Papaw's Window

Inside looking out
I see pretty landscaping, as pretty as a bird singing
I smell the flowers every time I walk past that window
A sound fills the room
Papaw's voice is candy, it brightens my day
Answering my question, "Did he live through the night?"
I taste that old person smell, as I kiss him on the cheek
The touch of sadness,
It rises upon my shoulders
I feel the super softness of those blankets as I sit on his bed with him
Once again, when it is time to say goodbye,
I walk past that window
The flowers parachuting in the air
Without that window
I would surely cry
All that joy leaving my body
I leave those nursing home doors
Every night I pray, "Dear Lord, please let Papaw Cliff wake up every morning saying,
"Thank you Lord for letting me live another night on Earth." Amen."

Sierra Waddle, Grade 7
Mount Washington Middle School, KY

Game Day

On one hot Sunday afternoon I was going to my baseball tournament with my dad.
In the tournament my team would have to win two games to win the championship.
We ended up winning 1st place.
On our way home we stooped at Arby's to get something to eat, I got a roast beef sandwich.
It was delicious!
When we got home my dad said "Do you want to watch the Sunday Night Football game?"
I said, "yes."
So we got out 2 fire pits and had 2 fires.
I roasted marshmallows and made s'mores.
The worst part was at 9:15, when I had to go inside for bed.
I had so much fun with my dad that day.
I'll never forget it.

Chris Keivit, Grade 7
Freedom Middle School, TN

Life

When I lay I look up at the huge sky.
I wonder, think, and rest. I take a breath of goodness.

Reasonable thinking about how great life is.
Trees, flowers, us, we all make up a given reason for life.

When I think about life I ask myself,
"What makes me a part of life? What makes me same and different?"

I put my best into life in order to do well and learn all I need to know about life.
Life is an amazing thing and we should enjoy life as much as we can.

Mikayla Brown, Grade 7
East Millbrook Magnet Middle School, NC

Grandma's Garden

Inside looking out
I see vibrant colors
I feel the smooth glass beneath my palms
It separates me from the glory
I love this window
Through it I see heaven on earth
Grandma's Garden
I smell sweet scents
Honeysuckle
It fills me with a shot of excitement
Flowers singing songs
Praising me for my company
I hear bird chirps
Taste the fresh morning air
Many memories in this garden
Childhood in the playhouse
Tea and cookies on the bright mosaic table
Without this window I couldn't see
Grandma's Garden
As I look through the window I feel
Home

Breena Frazier, Grade 7
Mount Washington Middle School, KY

Music Is Alive

Have you ever wondered?
Wondered about music?
A deep thought,
Stuck in your head,
Whispering is music,
Sounds like the ocean,
Footsteps is your beat,
Don't you forget it,
Thump, Thump,
Like a heartbeat,
As if music can move,
But really moving you,
Listen closely,
It is living,
It has a life,
Music is alive.

Kelsey Nguyen, Grade 7
East Millbrook Magnet Middle School, NC

Fallen Leaves

The fallen leaves dance solemnly
To silent music tragically.
They seem to understand my heart,
And how it hurts to fall apart.

They flit and flutter about the ground;
I was forgotten, never found.
I lay beneath this lonely tree,
With dancing leaves for company.

Hannah Smith, Grade 9
Spring Valley High School, WV

Thanksgiving

After all the Halloween decorations are gone, and the leaves have all fallen
And when its windy and cold,
Then Thanksgiving will soon come to be
Thinking of our loved ones,
Memories of all the good times we had,
Then Thanksgiving is finally here!
On Thanksgiving never a fall morning, never leaves blowing by,
Never a golden harvest, never a still, gray sky…
Never a crisp November or bright Thanksgiving Day,
But someone thinks of someone in a warm and happy way.
The kitchen has a scrumptious good smell, the dining room looks nice,
Decorations with pilgrims and turkeys,
And now we are ready to eat!
Napkins placed down on our laps;
Now we say a prayer for the meal to be blessed,
Make thanksgiving last for more than a day.
Enjoy what you've got; realize it's a lot,
And you'll make all your worries and cares go away
We are all full now,
Our grateful hearts find new delights
And we hope for all food to digest!

Lucrecia Mathodi, Grade 7
East Millbrook Magnet Middle School, NC

I Am…

I am a girl who loves to cheer.
I wonder if I will ever be a UCA cheerleader.
I hear myself cheer all the time.
I see our stunts getting better with each practice.
I am a girl who loves to cheer.

I pretend that I am a cheerleading coach.
I feel lucky to even be on the cheerleading squad this year.
I worry that someone will get hurt during practice.
I want to be the world's most known cheerleader.
I am a girl who loves to cheer.

I understand that in cheerleading you have to work as a team.
I dream of becoming a Georgia Bulldog cheerleader in college.
I try to stretch and practice every day.
I hope to become a captain of the University of Georgia cheerleading team.
I am a girl who loves to cheer.

Arianne Gerasimchik, Grade 8
Elkton School, TN

The Shark

There I am standing on the beach with my 7 foot pole that could catch a whale.
The sun beating down on me and cooking my skin while I try to catch a monster,
"Zzzzzzz…" the line is screaming,
I could feel by strike that there is something bigger than me on the end of the line,
This huge sea creature is pulling me into a shiny blue DEATH TRAP!

Philip Fincher, Grade 8
Weddington Middle School, NC

Ode to My Lost Friend

My stomach flips as you,
Sputter and crackle to life.
Fighting back song and dance as,
You suck in that
Big black tongue.

The crinkly tape sprints through you,
Like dark ink through a pen,
Your aging species,
Has such an,
Ancient charm.
For you,
I pine for the velvety feel of your buttons.

You are my VCR.

Such as life,
All good things come to an end,
So 'till next time,

My dear lost friend.

Simon Holden, Grade 8
Bondurant Middle School, KY

Ten Seconds

I inhale the air.
It relieves me
with its salty scent.
I look up towards
the horizon;

It is sunset.

With only the moon
to guide us.
Like a flashlight
in a damp, dark cave.

I stare at the
brilliant light.
Being forced down
by the shattered shadows
of the night.

10 seconds and
it will be dark.

Morgan Gay, Grade 8
Bondurant Middle School, KY

The Snake

The very cunning snake
Keeps trying to find his way
Back into his hole

Stephan Ramsay, Grade 8
Kinston Charter Academy, NC

Papaw

Every day I think about you,
and wonder what it would be like if you were still here.
I miss you more than anything, but I know that you are not really gone.
You watch me every day from above, but you are also with me.
You are in my memories.
You are in my dreams.
You are in my heart.
Everything I do I try to revolve around you.
You and Dad have told me all your stories
about carrying people out of a coal mine and all the things you did with Mamaw.
Then I think you might be in the coal mines or somewhere at your house.
I look at old pictures.
Ones of when I was a baby as small as your arm.
You are in your favorite brown chair that Mamaw hates so much.
I see your smiling face I miss so much.
I look at the picture from ten years ago
Embracing your bear hug with my tender arms
and always the sweet words
"I love you."
You are in every hug I give, and in the brown chair that is now in your basement.
You are everywhere in my life, and I want it to stay that way.

Trey Foshee, Grade 9
Baylor School, TN

Reality

"We all try to master reality" as the saying goes.
But the real matter is we can never face the awful truth.
We lie to cover things up, but we can't always hide what is really there.
The truth, the ugly, awful, and disgusting truth.
Sometimes, people do master reality, however, beyond their time.
Others around don't understand as they do things perfect, but nod as if they know.
They have yet to learn reality.
Also, reality is a way to say such a thing doesn't exist or can't be done.
People say a bumblebee can't fly because it is too heavy.
They also say that bat's can't fly.
Bees and bats still fly, don't they?
If we all just told the truth, listened, and believed we would all master reality.
Who knows?
The quiet person in the corner might be wiser than we think.
Maybe if we start listening, learning, and believing, we too could master reality.

Deena Notowich, Grade 7
White Station Middle School, TN

What Is Happiness

Happiness is like the sun, some days it shines bright and others not so much.
It can affect others around you, when you shine bright they will to.
It smells like a cake baking in the oven, great and wonderful.
It tastes like a glass of sweet tea, the best thing you will ever taste.
It feels like velvet soft and wonderful like nothing you have ever felt.
It looks like a masterpiece painted by Picasso or Rembrandt.
It sounds soothing, like a waterfall.
And somehow you can always tell when it's around like a sixth sense.
It does what's right, always willing to help those in need.
That's what happiness is.

Jc Zargo, Grade 8
Leesville Road Middle School, NC

Seventeen Pounds of Hard Work

"Err," the roar of the motor buzzes across the lake
The captain is trying to cause no wake,
No one knows where we are going
There are plenty of chances that people are blowing.

The hook was baited and ready to cast
Who knows how long it will last!
I cast and now we're trying to fight others wake
All that I know is that my bait was now in the lake

Two minutes passed and my line starts going out
Right at that instant, the captain starts to shout,
"Fish on, Fish on, set the hook!"
You don't know how long it took!

It took about fifteen minutes and the fish was tired
I was the one that the captain admired,
We finally pulled in the seventeen pound beast
All I know is that salmon was not being released!

Corey Rogers, Grade 8
Bondurant Middle School, KY

Yellow and Red

Y ellow leaves and fresh cut grass
' **E** ver more the warm breezes pass
L ower and lower the warm sun will sink
L onger shadows and a sky stained with pink
O ut in the evening one still sees
W here leaves hang, on stately trees

A nd out in the night comes a howl
N ow the soft hooting of an owl
D own the sun sinks and high the moon rises

R evealing what the shadow disguises
E ven now the wolves start to run
D ivine is the red of the setting sun

Lydia Gwaltney, Grade 8
Deerstream Learning Center, NC

Typical Days

Woke up, six in the morning,
So darn clumsy that I tripped on the flooring.
Jumped in the freezing cold shower,
Used Herbal Essence — berry tea and orange flower.
Brushed my teeth 'til they were sparkling white,
Mom didn't like my clothes so we got in a fight.
Man I was starving; I burnt my toast.
Car's outta gas so I slowly gotta coast.
Late to school, as I ran through the door.
Teach was giving homework and she gave me more.
Finally got home, on the couch I lay,
Can't believe I made it through another day.

Adair Broome, Grade 9
Bearden High School, TN

I Can't Believe

I can't believe
That this day has come
When you left your home behind
To fight for your country and save all those lives I can't believe
That since you left the nights and days have been dark and gray
It scares me to wonder
Where is my brother? Has he gone away?
I can't believe that you're in Iraq
Risking your life for everyone
I have no clue, what should I do?
Please, please come home soon
I can't believe my days go on So sad but mad
I yell and hit things when I'm thinking of you
I care to wonder where you are at
I can't believe its been a year since you left
I hear the door Mother screams
I run to the hall I see you
Am I dreaming? I can't believe my brother is home
Not hurt on the outside
But Scared on the inside
Of what you have seen I can't believe

Glenda Farrow, Grade 7
Ramsey Middle School, KY

Football Sunday

As all the players kneeled
It was silent on LP field
Number eight was hurt
With his face in the dirt
As the player shook off the hit
He got closer to the sideline bit by bit.
As Vince Young went back to throw
Kenny Brit made the catch with two yards to go
It was fourth and two
Coach Fisher was thinking what he should do
Should they punch it in on a run
Or throw a pass and make it fun
As the clock got shorter Jeff Fisher flipped the quarter
And Chris Johnson busted through the hole for a touchdown
I'm pretty sure there were screams from the whole town.

Christopher Feemster, Grade 8
Signal Mountain Middle High School, TN

Choices

Sometimes you are put in situations.
Which decision should you make?
There's not always a good side to it, but there's a choice
you have to make.
Is it decided at random or put a lot of thought into?
What should you do?
Try to decide the best, or try to impress.
Try to do for your own good, no matter what you choose to do.
Try to make the choice best for you.

Rachel Cox, Grade 9
Lynn Camp High School, KY

Melancholy Melodies

My musical piano made the meager
Notes tell tales of a miserable
Man whose heart had been mashed
To a million pieces.

The man always played a mellow
Violin during the
Misty Monday mornings just resting
And mourning over the sorrow-filled
Melodies shooting memories of his
Mistress of midnight.

Soft as marshmallows, deadly as
Malaria, squeezing the man
Out of you like a vampire-like
Mosquito.

'Malady murdered my love' the
Man would moan, remembering
The misfortune that tortured his
Misled mind.

Bryanna Miller, Grade 8
Coopertown Middle School, TN

Whiskey Window

Outside looking in,
Nightmares scattered before me
Old trash, empty bottles, shammed beauty
I hear the laughter of a madman
A strong whiskey scent fills the air
The madman standing before me,
Taller than a skyscraper,
Smiles like the devil
Whiskey stench teases my tongue
I swallow hard
A streak of panic runs through me
I feel sympathy for the madman
Without my window, his flaws are invisible
But nothing can be done for the madman,
For I am on the other side of the window.

Haylie Stopher, Grade 7
Mount Washington Middle School, KY

River

Above the ground
in the water
outside my house
over the street
around the corner
beneath the bridge
along the road
near the school
during the day
through the great moments

Gloria Young, Grade 8
Heritage Middle School, TN

Growing Up

When you're a little kid everything is just so good,
you never get broken or bruise, and you don't have guilt on you.
You get angry when you don't get ice cream, and you think you're misunderstood.
The only thing that ever bad happens is you might get the flu.

On Christmas you wait for Santa to fill your stocking.
And on Easter you let the Easter Bunny give you candy.
You love happy surprises, because it's so shocking.
Your mom has to go to work, and you're thrilled to see your Nanny.

The second you get home, you find your dog and give him a kiss.
You're favorite thing is to go outside and play hide and go seek.
The biggest honor is when someone calls you miss.
Who cares if you walk inside and your sister tells you that you reek?

Being a little kid is great in almost all the ways you can think of,
But there is always a reality check and it's kind of all done.
When you start to grow up and you don't get the same kind of love.
The day you don't think tag is the best kind of fun.

Growing up your mind starts to change a little bit.
You have heavy regrets that pound on your chest for a lifetime.
The worst kind of pain isn't being pricked when you're attempting to knit.
Goodbyes last until tomorrow, and stealing someone's eraser is the biggest crime.

And the worst part of it all...Is when you grow up, you never grow back.

Sarah Hoffmann, Grade 8
Signal Mountain Middle High School, TN

Waking Dream

Swirling surreal mist slinks alongside the slow ribbon of creek
Ancient silver columns rise from the earth and soar skywards
Hundreds of feet above, a white translucent roof supported by these living pillars sways
Stones of soft anomalous shaping flow with the transparent ribbon, molded by time

Faint whisperings float down from the canopy sky
Almost as silent as the haze, water purls down the natural stairs of rock
The quiet hum of silence brings on the overwhelming song of the life of the forest

Fresh airborne moisture enters my lungs, purifying the body and soul
The crisp scent of living air, unspoiled by chemical contaminants whirls through the forest
Mingling with the crisp smell like biting into a hard apple is the potent smell of damp earth

Sitting by the creek, you can taste the magic of the age-old timberland
Sweet minerals are present in the liquid crystal of the stream
Fresh sensations fill the senses

Gazing upon the unspoiled sanctuary,
I think only of the beauty of nature.
As it should be,
Should have been,
Will not likely be.

Celia Maddy, Grade 9
South Charleston High School, WV

Freedom Rings

Free as
the American flag soaring sky high,
a butterfly flittering from flower to flower,
an untamed stallion running wild to an unknown place,
or a cheetah standing at the zenith; the almighty king.
Freedom wraps its arm around me
and helps me feel relieved of my stress.
Freedom is the sensation when all the car windows are down
and the wind glides through my hair.
I feel
freedom when the ten-pound weights on my shoulders
are lifted after finishing a harsh test.
I taste
freedom at the edge of my tongue
on a frisky Friday night.
Freedom
is a wish that has been granted.
Freedom
was declared on July 4th, 1776
by the United States of America,
Home of the Free.

Jennie Kwon, Grade 8
Baylor School, TN

His Words

Blistering stabs penetrate her fragile mind
The thought of him now makes her cringe with ire
She asks why she continued to listen to his senseless words
His words once soft and comforting
Now a constant reminder of her own specific stupidity
Words from his arrogant mouth burn her flamboyant soul
Her magnanimous identity is now a pile of phlegmatic dust
She must venture out from his prison
Hoping she won't be recaptured by his condescending charm
Her new desire of freedom guiding her reformation
His stare chilling to any mortal creature
With the exception of a rare, slight crack in his malevolent being
She is apprehensive about her feelings toward him
Her mouth might say that she is done
But his words can change her purgative in one quick syllable

Jazmine Kelley, Grade 8
White Station Middle School, TN

Rocks

We are rocks as you can see
Some call us dull, but how can we be
We make up your buildings, and were never told "thanks"
Considering we even house money inside of your banks
Some of us are made into "tools"
You guys call some rocks diamonds and jewels
Those rocks are expensive when we aren't worth a dime
Explains why people step on us "gravel" all the time
Us rocks deserve a little bit of respect
Rather than suffer from this abusive neglect

Devin Yuengling, Grade 8
Deerstream Learning Center, NC

I Just Can't Rhyme

I try all the time,
But I just can't rhyme.

When I look at my work,
I tend to huff, puff, and smirk.
And when I write again,
I want to break my pen.

I try all the time,
But I just can't rhyme.

I read many other writings,
And lose my mental lighting.
I look for inspiration by walking through the park,
When, oh my word, I lose it to a bark.

I try all the time,
But I just can't rhyme.

I studied works of Seuss,
But got distracted by a moose.
I write this poem to you,
And hope you are laughing too.

For I try all the time,
But I still can't rhyme.

Lauren Brown, Grade 8
West Middle School, TN

Invisible Boy

Who is the boy who never gets praised
Is he just a little person who is afraid
He feels as if he is alone
He believes his fate is written in stone

Who is the boy who never gets any praise
Lonely is how he will spend his days
He feels he doesn't have any skills
He can no longer feel any thrills

Why doesn't he get any glory
He tries to get out and share his story
He is drowning in a pool of fear
He misses the ones he once held near

Who is the frightened little boy
He is treated like a child's play toy
He has no one to love
He thinks of beautiful doves
He feels too much pain
It drives his mind insane

The little boy died without knowing who he really was
Sadly, he drowned in his own tears

Marquis Jones, Grade 8
Roanoke Valley Early College, NC

Horror...An Act

Knocking on the door tentatively,
The noise echoes in the lonely corridor,
Knock, knock, knock,
Hearing a scream and evil laughter,
Almost seeing what was going on,
Behind the heavy metal door,
Almost hearing the blood dripping,
On the floor of realistic horror,
Drip, drip, drip,
Hearing the step of steady shoes on the floor,
Tap, tap, tap,
Excitement surges through my body,
The door slowly opened, revealing,
A bloody face and worn out body,
Lips turned up in an evil smile and hand motioned
In a mysterious gesture, inviting me in,
Confidently, I step to see what was behind him,
What I saw didn't surprise me:
A well lit, wood floored, high leveled,
Stage...Applause.

Meera Patel, Grade 7
White Station Middle School, TN

Rainy Days

You think it quite strange to go out
And stand in the rain, just walking about
I say that rain is for having some fun
To jump and splash in, to dance in and run
You may believe storms keep you up at night
You lie in your bed tossing in a fright
Me? Why, I think they're cozy and dreamy
I tell you this but you don't believe me
On rainy days I curl up with a book
And on days such as these I don't like to cook
I love the feeling when it rains all day
In fact, I wish it would rain today
I realize you hate when it rains a lot
But compared to oceans, what's one small drop?

Hannah Raines, Grade 9
Spring Valley High School, WV

The Choice Is Yours

You can go through life like a speeding train,
Never stopping for sunshine, wind, or rain,
Or maybe like an ever changing wind,
Never following any known trend.
But whichever way you choose,
There is something you will lose.
Choose the first and get all life's wants,
But at what price will there be taunts?
Choose the next and have all life's pleasure,
But what success can you measure?
Life's choices can change and shift,
But what you choose is what you must live with.

Cassi Lee Smith, Grade 9
Lynn Camp High School, KY

Journey of Friends

Friendship is a journey we go through,
A bond that brings together me and you.
I can remember the day we met,
It was kindergarten and I told you not to fret.
We sat side by side at story time and show and tell,
I told you to shut up when you got excited and started to yell.
Then came first grade and before we knew it, sixth,
We've been through a lot even through our first kiss.
Then all of a sudden you moved away,
At that moment all my blue skies turned to gray.
But not even that could separate us,
Because a friend is a friend no matter what.
We alternated summers so much it was like joint custody,
We got wild and crazy and just wanted to be free.
After graduation we will go our own ways,
But we will talk on the phone every single day.
Someday when I get an invitation in the mail,
Saying that you're getting married I will silently yell, "Hurray!"
Friends for life from the first day,
I promise I will be there when you're old and gray.

Elizabeth Runyan, Grade 9
Robert C Byrd High School, WV

Outcasted

The mockery and hatred of them all
They had no wish, except for us to die
"We're only different," we would weakly call
But we were shunned, no one would hear our cry
Although the people treated us like swine
Our chins were up; we looked toward the sky
But why would we forgive them for their crime?
We all would ask, and all would question why
And so we came out of our hiding holes
We marched the streets and started to rebel
Then finally persuaded their black souls
Our difference is something we cannot help
Hesitantly, our people lived with theirs
And made a new era of love and care

Jake Davis, Grade 9
Spring Valley High School, WV

What God Is Mine?

I can soar through the air
Like a bird in flight,
I can fly through the water,
Like a fish swimming from its hunter.
I can jump from the ground and fly sky high away —
I am wise,
Like an old turtle,
Who lived for a hundred years.
I am sharp like an arrow and just as fast too.
Who am I?
Where did I come from?
What god is mine?

Thomas Jackson, Grade 7
J Graham Brown School, KY

The White Tiger

Its fur is like a blanket
of white snow.

It reminds me of a
snowy cold day
of play
Its intense rush gets this little tiger
EXCITED
Sensitive.
Calm and Sweet.

The loud ROARING
fills the quiet empty space
with a bang of noise
from this hungry
little creature

Its fur can brighten its own shadow
Just standing in the bright
Sun.

Cierra Graham, Grade 8
Bondurant Middle School, KY

The Florescent Light

At the beginning of a week
On a Monday morning,
It is the least favorite time and
Day of the week, especially because
Of that bright, white, and dull light,
Above your head all day.

It will create an eerie shadow
Behind things never seen before,
On top of all that, that tiny little
Buzzing noise all throughout the day,
Causing a horrible headache.

But by the end of the week,
This seemed to be the longest
Week of my life.
On a Friday afternoon, the light seems to
Vanish at the flick of a switch,
The headache goes away,
Just like that.

Drew Easton, Grade 8
Bondurant Middle School, KY

Bellyache

There once was a pelican who tried to bake
Dead fish, and then got a bellyache!
He did not know it was bad
And it drove him mad
So he quit for his own sake.

Mia Spicer, Grade 8
Home School, TN

Farming Fun

In a faraway town called Cropville,
lived many people who loved to farm.
They would get up every morning at 4 o'clock,
to attend to their crops with smiles all around.
Everybody of all ages loved to farm
from as young as they could start till the day they died.
However, there was one particular man who loved to farm the most,
who would farm until he fell down in exhaustion.
He had been farming for so long, and was so skilled,
that he would produce three times as many crops as the second best.
This man was named Maize for his devotion to farming,
and it was said that he never stopped to eat his crops.
One day, however, Maize died of too much farming,
and it was the saddest day that ever came to Cropville.
It was not known until a week later that he had a baby son named Soil,
who had been farming since one minute after he was born.
Now this was the happiest day in Cropville,
for Maize's farming could be carried on.

Luke Carrington, Grade 7
White Station Middle School, TN

Under the Orange Maple Tree

Writing hides in the crackling of the eucalyptus tree.
It's camouflaged like a frog on a leaf between the thick concrete walls of Hitler's bunker.
My sister's perfume has writing hidden in the pink smell.
The bottom of a pitch dark sea bed has writing all over it.
Unfit boxers hide writing under their unwanted fat.
Writing plays hide and seek in a tropical island full of coconuts.
Worldwide known spaghetti sauce has more writing than the unknown.
Vapor full of old spice essence leaking out of Julian's room.
Her eyes are full of forgotten but still remembered writing.
Neath, beneath, underneath in the orange maple tree
You will find all the writing you've been seeking this entire time.

Lucas Baker, Grade 8
Baylor School, TN

Falling Hard

My heart sunk, and eyes widened, fingers bounced along perfectly
as if he was born playing.
Déjå vu shot through my spine. Was he real or just a figment of my imagination? Should I hold my hand out and give away my heart like I had done once before, or stay bundled up
and keep all this love locked up in its own prison forever?
Questions like this drove through me and left tire prints on my brain, and gas stains on my heart. Was he too good for me? All this was just all too good to be true, I don't deserve him. "Stop with the questions already," I yelled in my head. You looked up, smiled and said,
"Bailey, you okay?" I started to zone back into reality, and realized that you were
waiting. I replied back with a giggly, "Yeah, totally."
But even though I knew deep down that I was falling hard for you!

Bailey Zane Gordon, Grade 8
Signal Mountain Middle High School, TN

Family

The ones who *love* us,
Who *care* for us,
Who *play* with us —
These are the people we *love.*
Family is like our blood stream.
We flow *together* forever.
When some are gone, we *mourn.*
We bring new *family* into the world,
But we never fill in the *gap,*
For it reminds us of those who are *gone.*
When some go, *others* come.
That is how *we* flow.
Those who *disrupt* the flow are gone.
When people are gone, we *mourn* forever.
We never *let* go of them.
We *hold* on until we are gone.
That is what *family* does for each other
When we go, we will be *mourned* by our children
And hopefully by our *children's children.*
When they *mourn,* they will *remember,*
And when they *remember,* they will *mourn.*
Sadness is hard to deal with,
But those who have to, will *be okay.*

Victoria Schaefer, Grade 8
Shepherdstown Middle School, WV

Haunted

The things that haunt me most are the things I like
Dark places
Quiet phases
And your sparkling eyes
I caught my breath
Didn't wish to see them again
But they follow me
They haunt me

I still don't believe
The things I can't see
Where are you, hun
Can't believe you're gone
My phone's ringing your number
Maybe feeling watched is a blunder
But you follow me
You haunt me

I know you're gone but I feel you
I know you're gone, I hear you, too
If you really left, you left way too soon
Because your spirit haunts me
You haunt me

Ivy Jones, Grade 7
White Station Middle School, TN

Sensory Lake

The cool, blue lake water slaps against the dock
The thick, plush grass quivers in the breeze
Jet skis glimmer in the sunlight
Delicate, fluffy duckling clumsily waddle behind their mother

The ripple of the water strikes the rocks
Fish flip and slap into the water
The large flag whips in the wind
Ducks quack and shake themselves dry

Slimy plants submerge beneath the water
The fishy dock stretches across the lake
The burning of the barbecue prepares for use
The icy breeze slices through the air

The cool, heavy breeze greets the morning sun
The bitter lake water sprays across my face
The tiny rain drops begin to fall

This is a place to never be forgotten
Every child should experience a place like so
The happiness here will always be cherished
I will share its greatness with many

Rachael Day, Grade 9
South Charleston High School, WV

I Am Me

I am athletic and energetic.
I wonder about my future.
I hear the blaring music
I see mounds of clothes on my bedroom floor.
I want to be an honor student.

I am athletic and energetic
I pretend to be happy when I am down.
I feel the warm hearts of others.
I know I have two best friends in the world.
I worry about my loved ones.
I cry over the death of a loved one.
I am athletic and energetic.

I understand that no one is perfect.
I think that everyone should lie their life to its fullest.
I dream of no drama.
I try to be perfect.
I hope to be with friends and family forever.
I believe that there is only one God.
I know that the U.S. is in a great amount of debt.
I am athletic and energetic.
I am me.

McKenzie Marske, Grade 8
West Middle School, TN

Fast Forward

Winter
I'm inside looking out
I see the snow
The animals mock me as they sleep
It's a cold dark winter's night
Time flies by like a movie with a friend
Spring
I smell life
I see the animals waking
The world is a bright green
Summer
The air smells like ice cream
As I see the truck go by
The world is beautiful
Fall
The leaves are golden stars as they hit the ground
The world is golden and red
I smell candy
I hear the doorbell
Now I'm outside looking in

Seth Chastain, Grade 7
Mount Washington Middle School, KY

Battle Without a Fall

The pull of the leash makes my arm ache.
An untamed beast at the end of the line is yanking,
trying to show dominance over my powerful will.
She may see me struggle
but she will not see me fall.
In an instant a thunder clap roars,
freeing the lion from its cage,
sending wet needles down from the sky above me,
creating an obstacle I must overcome.
The once wild beast now quivers at the darkness that surrounds us.
I gently whisper reassurances in her velvet ear.
The storm may see me ache,
but I do not fall.
Reticent faces glare at me through windows,
taunting me for they enjoy the comfort of their own homes.
I stay strong,
like a soldier in combat.
I follow the path that will lead me to my own safe haven.
They may see me weaken and they may see me slip
but I never fall.

Sophie Leary, Grade 7
White Station Middle School, TN

Band

I hear the awesome sounds of the brass.
I see the vicious tune of drums.
I taste the wind zooming through my lips.
I touch the valves in a whirlwind of sound.
I smell the determination of our award winning band.
We make a beautiful symphony of sounds.

Brandon Goble, Grade 8
Boyle County Middle School, KY

Big Picture

Look at the Big Picture,
You're just one person on this world,
Not everything revolves around you,
Friends, family, plants, and friends,
It never ends.
So look at the big picture.
It's not about you, your coal filled stocking screams,
Now wake up from those silly present filled dreams,
Whoooshh, you wake up, up and your Christmas has fallen apart.
Because you tried to be arrogant and smart.
So
Look at the big picture
Your friends and family love and care,
So care for them, and be there
It's not that hard,
Now get your head out of the clouds.
Because it's not all about you,
Not then, not now
I hope this is where you see the snowy white light,
So say "Merry Christmas to all,
And to all a good night."

De'Quan Tunstull, Grade 7
J Graham Brown School, KY

Football

My name is football.
You can toss me, throw me, or run me.
There's even a game named after me.
My sole purpose is to make you famous.
I made Jerry Rice famous and many others.
When you're running the ball, and you break
one tackle...two tackle...
and running for the end zone...
the crowd goes crazy!
So, the next time you touch me,
don't be lazy.
So when you hear the crowd go crazy,
just remember, after all,
my name is
football!

Cliff Garner, Grade 7
Elkton School, TN

The Last Shot

The second the ball
leaves my fingertips
I know it will go in

My pulse is fast,
and my stomach flips and flops
making me feel nervous

But it's not until the ball swishes through the net
that I can sigh with relief

Haley Dean, Grade 8
Boyle County Middle School, KY

Where I'm From

I am from the back roads of West Virginia.
Living on a road called Derricks Creek.
Where I live on a farm,
With horses, cows, and pigs.

I am from nothing but Teletubbies, Blues Clues, and Barney.
That was something I lived by.

I am from a place where four-wheelers are legal.
To us anyway.

I am from a family that loves God.
That's what comes first.

I am from traveling to different states to see parts of my family.
Some are farther than others but family is important.

I am from yellow slicky slides,
in a backyard under a big oak tree.
Those were the days.

Whitney Monday, Grade 8
Sissonville Middle School, WV

Imagine

In my room there is a place where I like to sit and imagine…

What if I lived in the fields of Nebraska,
Or the frozen terrain of Alaska,
Or the bustling streets of New York?
What if they never invented the dinner fork?
What if music didn't exist?
Or if Dallas Clark hadn't injured his wrist?
What if I was a geese, a gander, or a salamander?
What if I didn't use an assignment planner?

And then I realize
If I didn't use an assignment planner,
I would have failed a while ago.

You know, we're lucky the world turned out the way it did.
What if the colonists lost the Revolutionary War?
Or if the South won the Civil War?
What if I failed that test last week?
You wouldn't want that last one to have happened…I hope…

Jacob Boughter, Grade 7
White Station Middle School, TN

Mercy

The clash of steel rings loud, just by my ear.
The rush of adrenaline, I feel.
The blood, pumped quickly through my veins, I hear.
I see a flash, so in raising my shield —
I block the strike, his life is in my hands.
I look into his eyes, so deep and bright.
I see, he is not of place to demand —
That I not end his life, with all my might.
I see his face, so young, wanting mercy.
He studies on my face, knowing his fate —
His grin becomes so wide, he's been set free!
His honour, mine, I had let him escape.
I've finished this battle, for it, I've won.
This quest for my courageous king be done!

Jared Workman, Grade 9
Spring Valley High School, WV

The Illness

Let the silence rumble still
Let the weakness wait until
Your faith dissolves away
Killing your soul within a day
Your eyes are bloodshot red
As you lay inside your bed
Hear the people that you love
You drift closer to above
Murdering your thoughts that show the past
Its disappeared you way too fast
The pains harder to bear
They can see it in your glare
Drifting off into the sky
Leaving this life with no goodbye

Halie Trueblood, Grade 9
H L Trigg Community School, NC

Where I'm From

I am from Sissonville, West Virginia,
From lumps of school to bumpy roads,
I am from Charleston,
I am from five houses,
I am from the honeysuckle tree to the apple orchard,
From rednecks to gangsters on the Westside,
I am the peacemaker of the family, I am from the know -it -alls,
To the not- so -smart ones,
I am the one who doesn't get yelled at,
I am the one who fights and argues with my brothers,
I am the only one who goes to school,
I am from memories of family and relatives.

Dean Baldwin, Grade 8
Sissonville Middle School, WV

Where I'm From

I'm from the people on the front porch
Men on the tractors
Cow manure smelling under the hot summer sun
Kids feeding the hogs
Learning the cycle of life
doing what they can for others and friends

I'm from the part of Earth
Where we know everybody
The women cook all day
Wood is burned for heat
This is the life in the country

Clint Marsh, Grade 8
Westchester Country Day School, NC

This Is a Tribute to My Mom

You're always there for me, caring for me, loving me,
and thinking about me.
I love when you have a smile on your face.
When you think about others before yourself,
it makes me feel wonderful to know you're my mom.
You're beautiful, smart, and filled with everything nice.
You're very encouraging and thoughtful.
I love you more than anything in the whole wide world!
Sometimes we disagree with each other,
but everything always turns out fine
because we love each other.
Thank you for teaching me right from wrong
and loving me more than Paul.
Our friendship is strong
and it's building stronger as we age together.
You are sweet and kind and always pushing me to do better.
Just another reason why I love you!
— Hope

Hope Thelen, Grade 8
St Agnes School, KY

Ode to a Butterfly

Silent, beautiful, you carry the world on your wings.
Petite and gentle, yet strong.
How much do you see? What do you hear?
Where have your paper wings flown you?

So small, but so wise.
You rise high above the earth
And drink of the flowers' beauty.

How is it that you are so small and fragile,
Yet you have been places I will never go?
You are tiny and breakable,
But you can soar above the clouds and into the stars?

The world is your flower,
You sit all day and watch,
You wait,
In silence.

Ashley Slimp, Grade 9
Bearden High School, TN

The Pain of the Outsider

When your life is in ruins
The invisible tears pulling down on me
The pain ripping through and
It's getting so hard for me to breathe
When I feel like the world hates me
Like I'm the only one who understands
How lonely life can be
Every day I try the best I can
But it seems like nobody can see
Who is really me

Hannah Reis, Grade 7
Campbell County Middle School, KY

Live Life

Live your life,
You only have one.
No one can change what's already been done.
So sing in the silence,
Dance in the pouring rain.
Ignore the petty violence,
And the sorrowful pain.
Listen to the silly laughter.
See every sweet smile.
Make life worth living,
It's all worth the while.

Kristen Oberlander, Grade 8
West Middle School, TN

I Am a Snowflake

I am a snowflake.
Drifting in the wind.
I'm unique.
No matter what anyone says.
There is no one like me.
So I can always be myself.

I am a snowflake.
I will land somewhere,
But no one knows.
But wherever that is,
I will make the best of it.

I am a snowflake.
When you touch me
I melt right in your hand.
You can see right through me,
Even if I don't want you to.

I am a snowflake.
I am so bright, I hurt your eyes.
But the sad part about it is
I only come out in a certain season.

I am a snowflake.

Alexis Smith, Grade 7
White Station Middle School, TN

The River

Down the road,
Beside my school,
Under the bridge,
With a splish and a splash,
To the rope swing,
Up the rocks,
Beneath the trees,
Through the air,
Into the water and over again,
During the day, I love to be at the river.

Katrina Rogers, Grade 8
Heritage Middle School, TN

Watching and Waiting

I sat alone
Watching and Waiting
Thinking of what
Things were unknown
Would I be
Successful or just,
Another drone?
These decisions I make
Now and later
Affect my life
Now and later.
Go to school?
Or stay at home?
Do my work?
Or play a game?
I now sit here
To Watch and Wait
To help decide
My own fate.

James Easley, Grade 9
Lynn Camp High School, KY

Just How I Am

I am bitter, sweet, but crazy at times
Have a heart of gold that over pours
Moments that are embarrassing
Like having your heart ripped out
Friends that care
Help me through the rough times
Stories to share
Stories to hear
Understanding is what they are
Nervous to what is to come
Or how to deal with it
I put my armor on to prepare
For anything to happen
Just like any other person

Yasmen Stinson, Grade 8
Montgomery Central Middle School, TN

Fun

The solid black vans.
The faded flair jeans.
The dirty, worn jersey
From a past or present team.
The silver hoop earrings.
The squared up silver watch.
The funky little bracelet,
The best friend has the match.
The peace sign necklace.
The hair up in a bun.
The smile on my face.
The life I'm living,
Fun!

Faith DeWolfe, Grade 8
West Middle School, TN

Until Next Time

A bridge I have trodden so many times,
Sometimes to just escape all of my personal crimes.

You can peer over the edge to see the dry river, or how it was,
When the rain falls upon it, you seem to forget your most terrible lusts.

It is a comforting privacy,
Yet you can hear all of the voices of the wispy rain whispering to me.

When the fog gathers and surrounds the world,
Me, on the bridge, always forgets and twirls.

Like a tattoo of ink, the rain embedded the wandering bridge in my mind.
I hear the rain and yearn to resign to my bridge outside the grapevine.

Silent pitter-patters of the millions of playing children,
They envelop me on that chilly morning.

The bridge made of constant stone absorbs them.
And I, kept the left over trims.

When the weary children readily resign to their beds,
I said good-bye, until next time, and locked the memory in my head.

"Until next time," I thought with a vibrant heart.
I kept that promise and carried it wherever I went in its own little cart.

Forevermore I will replay that reverie of the bridge in my mind,
Until next time.

Hannah Junkins, Grade 9
Robert C Byrd High School, WV

If You Only Knew

If only you knew how the light touched the Earth,
If only you knew the small of dawn.
If only you knew the song of the mocking bird,
If only you knew the colors of the wind.
If only you knew what it means to love,
If only you knew how Earth feels.
If only you knew the feel of the ocean,
If only you knew the smell of freedom.
If only you knew the feelings of people,
If only you knew how to believe in yourself.
If only you knew how the trees giggle,
If only you knew how to fly.
If only you knew what it means to dream,
If only you knew how to not spread hate but how to spread love.
If only you knew the meaning of trust and respect,
If only you knew all the joys in the world.
If only you knew all the joys in the world.
If only you knew how to be yourself,
If only you knew how to be honest.
If only you knew how to get a good education and respect your teachers,
If only you knew what it means to be free.

Dezirae McCauley, Grade 9
Robert C Byrd High School, WV

Love

It doesn't seem to be there
Every time you turn it seems to disappear
Yet you can faintly see it just out of reach
It sits there mocking you making you wish even more

You long for it
You reach for it
But it's too far away

The selfishness stands guard
No one comes out
And no one goes in

You have begged and pleaded
But it stays locked up
The hold is too strong
And love stays in

You see one solution to the pain
Giving up
It will lessen failing work and disappointment
But the problem still remains

You are desperate for love
You want love
You need love

Courtney Wright, Grade 7
White Station Middle School, TN

The Eighty-Eight

My hands slide over the black and white keys,
Pressing harder and harder.
Soon, everything around me starts to freeze.
Promptly, I feel much ardor.

The semblance of the tenebrous strings echo in my mind
Overwhelming my senses,
Every note on the paper becomes more and more refined.
On my brain, the music etches.

It seems as though I embark on the momentous journey.
Repeatedly, I whip through the score,
The sharp thrusts of my fingers on the keys look so blurry
This laborious songbook is done for.

The ambiance of the area is so rapturous.
The pulchritudinous music flows through the air.
The mellifluous harmony is vastly glamorous.
The sounds are remarkably and audibly debonair.

As the song comes to an end, my fingers slow.
They lay still, rested on the keys.
The peaceful piano emits a gleaming glow
I've finished the song with much ease.

Katlyn Eakle, Grade 9
Robert C Byrd High School, WV

Once a Player, Always a Player

I can't say I want you back
I can't say I can live without you
And every day I can't seem to forget your name
No matter how bad I want to
Your name is everywhere I go

You broke my heart once, twice, no, three times
But somehow I can't let you go
I keep coming back for more
But now I think it's really over

How can I forget about you?
When every day that went by and I was in love with you
How was I so blind to the way you treated me?
When every second that went by you ignored me

I know you're not worth all my tears
But I still cry, cry for you.
I cry because you didn't really care
I cry because you simply just weren't there
I cry because once a player, always a player

Erin Fritz, Grade 8
Elkin Middle School, NC

Life Is...

Life is a battle,
In which everyone faces rivalry and struggle.
Life is a building,
Beginning with a strong foundation while adding more.
Life is a stained-glass window,
Full of a variety of colors and lights.
Life is a prison,
Feelings like others have control over our lives.
Life is a puzzle,
Waiting for us to find the missing pieces.
Life is a roller-coaster,
Consisting of many ups and downs.
Life is a mystery,
Wanting to be solved.
Life is a classroom,
With many lessons to be learned.

Kennedy Walls, Grade 8
Boyle County Middle School, KY

Laundry

Doing laundry is moms' worse nightmare
But if they don't do it, you won't have anything to wear.
She uses everything from bleach to Tide
If my clothes aren't clean, I lose my pride.

Sorting out colors from whites
Putting Shout on blood when I'm in fights.
Waiting for hours for them to dry
Doing laundry is hard; I've tried.

Aaron Coontz, Grade 8
Boyle County Middle School, KY

Daddy

I'm only ten years old.
Suddenly my world's cold.
I patiently look around.
No one knows what I felt.

I remember your sharp face.
I remember the NASCAR race.
I remember the choice.
So why not your voice.

I'm only ten years old.
And even I knew you were so bold.
I walk slowly up to him.
Then the lights start to dim.

Tears flood my light green eyes.
In the end my dad's the one to die.
Whom we were wondering
Sad songs slowly sway.

I walk away with many thoughts.
It feels like my heart's been shot.
So I look at the memo.
In loving memory.
Michael Ray Scott, I love you Daddy.

Chelsea Scott, Grade 9
Robert C Byrd High School, WV

Joy Returns

Once upon a time
There was a boy
Who always wanted to learn
And never had any joy

Although his friends
Urged him to play
He just sat there
And learned to stay

One day his friends
Bought a ball
When the boy played
He was top of it all

So now, the boy
Has a ton a fun
You should really see
How much he runs

Ryan DeVasher, Grade 7
White Station Middle School, TN

Fine

They have worry in their eyes,
But look I can pretend
I'll be fine

They ask how I am,
Waiting for tears
But look I am strong
I'll be fine

They stare at me,
They think they know
But look I can handle it
I'll be fine

They are afraid,
Of a girl who's different
But look I don't care
I'll be fine

They have forgotten,
About the girl I used to be
But look she is gone
And I am fine

Fiona Sparks, Grade 8
Signal Mountain Middle High School, TN

If the World Ends Today

If the world ends today,
What would we regret?
That we couldn't end hatred in one day,
Besides it really wasn't a big ret.

If the world ends today,
What would you regret?
Who did you betray?
What did you forget?

If the world ends today,
What would I regret?
Nothing, I would've lived my life gay,
So I can drift into the sunset.

But if I said the world did end today,
That would be a lie,
For the world never ends,
Unless, we die.

Brian Nwokeji, Grade 7
White Station Middle School, TN

In a Valley

There I lay,
in a valley.
Sectors of flowers lie.
Nobody around but me.

I'm alone again,
feeling how I always do.
Nobody around to care,
not one creature has a clue.

As the sun rises,
I feel happy again.
Prancing around happily.
Welcoming my grin.

For the first time,
things seemed right.
Right for a short time,
right until night.

Now my sun is leaving.
It may never come back,
so say goodbye to happiness,
which is what I'm beginning to lack.

Jacinda Evans, Grade 9
Robert C Byrd High School, WV

Just a Kid

I'm just a kid
Why you walkin' away?
I'm just a kid.
My simple hello
Don't gotta be one-way.

I'm just a kid
So quit treatin' me wrong.
I'm just a kid.
All I wanna do
Is belong.

I'm just a kid
You wanna start fightin' already?
I'm just a kid, but
My words are stronger
Than your fists are steady.

I'm just a kid
All I want is in.
I'm just a kid;
All I need
Is a friend.

Sarah Smith, Grade 9
Central High School, TN

It All Happened at Night

"It all happened at night"
My dad just had to leave,
I was so sad I let out a heave,
When he shut the door I hit the floor

"It all happened at night"
I was scared he might die,
Although I hope it's just a lie,
"I hope he's still alive"

"It all happened at night"
I heard he was leaving,
But I still believe,
That everything will be all right

"It all happened at night"
As I start to fall asleep,
All you can hear is me weep
It was a sad sight

Justin Kirkpatrick, Grade 7
Ramsey Middle School, KY

The Fall of the Twins

Ash falls like snowflakes in the wind
So many lives come to an end

Tears and tears
Survivor's fears

Another sound breaks through the day
Another bomb? The people say

Cries lost
Buildings tossed

A light comes through
The clouds drop dew

So many lives are lost and gone
Endless cries go on and on

The laughter stops the feel of pain
What from this loss will people gain?

Lindsay Johnston, Grade 8
Davidson IB Middle School, NC

My Time

Hey this is my time,
It's my time to truly shine,
I outshine them all,
They do not stand a chance,
I will show off my talents.

Kaitlyn Bumgardner, Grade 9
Meadow Bridge High School, WV

Running Through the Wood

The Moon shines and the Wind is a ghost
I stand in the midst of dancing shadows
The emerald green grass, rustles underfoot
I turn around when the owl hoots
And they are standing together, the Owl and the Wolf

The Wolf runs and the Owl takes flight
They are my guides for the night
I follow them and trees rush by,
I'm panting hard, my mouth is dry
The stars glisten and the Moon gleams
Endless forest, or so it seems
But I'm still running,
Through the Wood

I'm never lost with the help of my guides
The Wolf sprints, the Owl glides
The trees are like a roof overhead
And a patch of moss is a deer's warm bed
There is a rustle of leaves and the whisper of the breeze
This place is Enchanting and I'll always be running through the Wood

Emily DeNigris, Grade 8
Bondurant Middle School, KY

Missing: My Daddy

I tried to hold my tears back as my daddy walked out the door
I just couldn't help it
The tears fell to the floor as loud as a shattered vase
Oh, I wish I could see my daddy's face
I'm in the war of my life I just can't stand the pain
An endless cycle of happiness, sadness, and anger
All of the pain is hard to maintain I just couldn't help it
Remember that all of our soldiers leave half of their hearts at home
Mothers, fathers, children, friends, and a lot of happiness
How'd you feel if you came home to no one?
The soldiers get awfully lonely in such a hot, lonely place because
They just can't help it
We are all waiting for an end to this war
All of the death, and horrible attacks
We just can't stand it anymore
We are just digging deeper and deeper into this war because we just can't help it
I am proud to be an American and this is where I stand:
"We hold these truths to be self-evident,
That all men are created equal
That they are endowed by their Creator with certain unalienable rights,
That among these are life, liberty, and the pursuit of happiness"

Zackary Holdreith, Grade 7
Ramsey Middle School, KY

I Wasn't the Type to Fall in Love

I have seen the blossoming of
Love like a deep, red rose. I have
Also seen its destruction, and I
Think playing it safe, alone, lonely is best
I stayed this way for so many years,
I knew I was safe, so I was happy.
Sometime during then I stopped believing
In love it's not true at all. I wasn't
Icy and cold just distant heartbreak
Is...risky. That was before I met
Him.

My heart always skips unevenly when he steps
In the room. When we see each other
We gravitate automatically our feet glide
Toward each other. He can be awkward
And strange, but so am I. Everyone
Asks if we're in love. We always deny. They think
They know best sauntering on. Are we in love?
I never wanted to fall in love, could I
Have avoided this? Oh well, I guess
We'll see what's going to happen.

Krysta O'Conner, Grade 9
Robert C Byrd High School, WV

Trust Is Lost

When you deceive
You make me believe
That all trust is lost
You go behind my back
Think of all the words you spat
Haven't you thought about all trust possibly lost?
Do you crave the pain
And all of the vain
That could make me go insane?
Do you want to put me on the spot
So that you'll feel like you're on top?
Do you know all trust is lost?
Will you go out of the way
Until there comes a day
That I tell you that I hate you with a passion
Don't you know all trust is lost?

Tamiya Chatman, Grade 9
Northampton High School West, NC

Bedroom's View

Inside looking out
I see the birds frolic and play
Their chirps are bells I hear
I smell delicious dinner almost done
I feel the glass as smooth as tile
I taste the glory sweeping my mouth
As I watch this nature's day
Without my window this day would be nothing

Tucker Gardner, Grade 7
Mount Washington Middle School, KY

Ocean!

Summer days hot in the sun
Where do you go?
Lakes, rivers, streams?
No, no, no there's only one more place to go
The ocean, that's right
Crisp blue water calling your name
Warm beach sand, ready to play?
Bright, hot sun ready to bathe?
Fun in the sun
That's what I say!
Forget the pools and video games
Get ready for water and a place to play
Summer's here and ready to go
To the lake?
No, no, no
Where is the place I want to go?
Go, go, go!
Go and float in the...
OCEAN!

Ashley White, Grade 8
Boyle County Middle School, KY

The Great Knight

The moon lighted the way
Of a small path by a large bay
The Great Knight comes to the site
His horse's eyes shine in the night
Away the animals creep
The kingdom is no longer asleep
The mighty sun peaks its head over a cloud
The Great Knight's horse whinnies out loud
The fight is on
As the Knight rides through the dawn
He waits, but through the light
Comes another Knight
They wrestle and fight until at last the Great Knight stands
The people celebrate the winner and play in bands.

Layne Skinner, Grade 7
White Station Middle School, TN

Ways of Life

Life can be like a butterfly —
Unknowingly — which way it'll fly,
Sometimes we watch one high in the sky,
Wondering which route it will take,
And knowing it could be a mistake,
Reminding of our very own life,
Knowing of people who will be divine,
Will go on and judge and criticize.
The choices we make today will reflect on us tomorrow,
Knowing we might have to deal with our own sorrow.
So be precise and choose your life well,
And tomorrow you probably won't have to dwell on it —
Tomorrow.

Jessica May, Grade 9
Lynn Camp High School, KY

Lie to Me

We are like a ticking time bomb.
I'm the explosive just waiting for you to reach zero,
to hit realization that I am more, and not that little kid you grew up with:
Just grasp that acceptance for me, and we will ignite together

You are in my veins now, and I don't want to bleed you out
Try as you might, but there is no denying
I've built a fire in you, and only I can dampen it.
It's a wild fire, this burning passion you cannot ignore

It's no use pretending, this was never just one-sided; you cannot lie to me.

We are partners in crime now, your weakness is mine to keep
Both of us know you're no longer invincible, you never were
Contrary to what you'd like our friends to believe, but allow me...
You try to be the safeguard here, but why can't I be the one to protect you?

Your skin is so soft, so warm beneath my finger tips, pressing your cheek into my palm
Those glassy green eyes capturing mine, the same way I yearn for your lips against mine
For just a moment you'll let me, won't you?
There's just the taste of your shaky hesitance on your breath, mingling with mine

And then you run away. "I can't." It's stuttered. "I'm sorry," you say.
It's a painful sensation, the heavy weight of loss and hope. Your lingering gaze, time resumes...
I feel your touch at the back of my neck, but turn and am alone.
You can lie with "I can't," tonight, but it won't allow you to cheat your heart in the day.

Mattie Davis, Grade 8
J Graham Brown School, KY

Money Makes Our World Go Round

If you look at the world the way that I do, I conclude that money makes our world go round.

What puts warm, fresh food on the table? Money of course.
What gives you your safe and comfortable house? That's right, money.
What makes most people jump up and down for joy? Right again, it's money.
From this I can say that Money makes our world go round.

Some people say that they control their own lives but this is a lie.
Most people don't control their own lives, money does.
I must agree that this is a depressing and hurtful truth but let me let you in on a little secret, sometimes the truth hurts.
But it doesn't make it any less true
The truth is that Money makes our world go round.

Money is the reason that everyone has things.
My family has this computer because of money.
You can buy those warm, sugary, fresh out of the oven cakes because of money.
You can buy that new, expensive, high-tech car because of money.
Just more proof that Money makes our world go round.

Without money people can barely get by, let alone prosper.
They may wilt and die like a frozen flower.
Or they might fight their fate like a raging bull.
But that will not change the fact that Money makes our world go round.

Walker Loving, Grade 8
J Graham Brown School, KY

Working

It was a late Summer way past my curfew in Tennessee.
There was my Uncle working on his car.
And the drill was as loud as a howling monkey.
The sun was really bright I was glad I didn't go blind.
Somewhere right behind us there was a loud engine roaring.
We were really surprised the car was a Honda Civic SI the color of the blue sky.
The man in the car told us to fix his car because the head gasket was broken in the bottom of the engine.
Excitedly we told the man old man ok we would.
My Uncle paid me $5 ever hour.
So I worked really hard.
We finished the car within 5 days and I earned $100.

David Hernandez, Grade 7
Freedom Middle School, TN

Happiness

I spoke to you but your mouth remained shut
I looked at you but your glassy grey eyes never meet mine
You sit in your house looking out the fog tinted window.
Questions seem to wrap around your neck and choke you.
Comments people throw at you seem to cling to your ankles like weights
Gossip people whisper about you seem to leave deep scars on your back
Suddenly I looked at your glassy eyes meet mine your words escaped your mouth
You said "I have seen God and he has traded me forgiveness for the broken heart I used to have"
For a new heart
I pondered your words when I looked at you again I saw what seemed to be a smile
Then I knew what true happiness is.

Ashley Monteith, Grade 8
Weddington Middle School, NC

Brothers

He called the house and, I didn't answer because I was in bed.
There was a knocking on the door.
There was a pause but I answered it and, my brother was standing on the doorstep waiting to go to laser chase.
We got there and 15 other people were playing, I thought to myself tonight was my night.
They explained the rules to us.
When pigs fly my brother probably said to him self.
The game started and we all rushed into the arena.
Though my brother broke the no climb rule and quietly climbed up to find sniping.
I sighed, Oh Daniel what are you doing now.
My brother got the best score and I came in seventh, I think I can't really remember,
But that night was full of action, drama, and courage.

Michael Cremin, Grade 7
Freedom Middle School, TN

Sacrifice

He runs to save lives, diving into holes while hearing bombs going off a house away. Running into fires, feeling the hot flames scald his skin
He mourns over the lost ones that were looking forward to seeing their families
They wish the bullets they shot were like the ones they played with when they were little. They think about taking their own lives
He knows the right thing but not sure if it's worth doing it.
Sacrificing their lives so we can have a good time
He thinks is it my last day fighting for my country
Water slowly drips off his face
They wonder is that sweat or the sign of fear?

Sadie Moore, Grade 8
Camp Ernst Middle School, KY

The Outdoor View

Inside looking out...
I see
Deer, rabbits, squirrels, birds
Even little chipmunks
Racing along like wild horses
The window is open
I hear
The crunching of leaves from the deer
I smell
The sweet, but crisp autumn wind
I am a bird flying free with no fears
The trees are dancing in the wind
I taste
Happiness in the air
My window is
The joy inside of me
Without my window
I would be in jail
Sitting in a dark cell
Alone

Emily Petri, Grade 7
Mount Washington Middle School, KY

Dominance

Maybe men have trouble seeing
The might of Duke
But we know the truth
You can't stop us!

We do not lie
About our dominance
You can't stop us!
We will rise and dominate!

You can't stop us
This is Our House
We will dominate all you nay sayers
We pillage you all our rivals
You can't stop us!

James Myatt, Grade 7
Deerstream Learning Center, NC

This Is Beautiful

This calm setting takes my breath away
The sun is a ball of fire
I can hear the wind whispering to me
Whoosh!

While the waves move up on shore
I slowly walk down the beach
Feeling the water weave through my toes
And I say to myself
This
Is beautiful

Hayley Johnson, Grade 8
Bondurant Middle School, KY

Summer Days

Inside looking out,
I can fell the rush of cars passing,
It's almost like a drop of adrenaline,
But it stops,
Dead silent for five seconds.
The taunting smell of food on a grill,
Laughing at me about how I can't manage to reach.
Inside I light a candle,
The taunting is replaced by growls of anger, I laugh.
As I set on the ledge, I can almost hear the melody of my writing drift,
I hear the birds singing, and young kinds having the time of their lives,
And then my little dog at the door.
He jumps and were on the ground, I can taste the excitement flowing between us,
And then it stops by the sound of a rock.
We freeze like popsicles,
I peer out and my friends are standing there laughing, of course at me and my dog,
I'm embarrassed but I laugh.
Night falls, I'm alone and everyone's asleep,
And that's when I see the twinkling stars winking at me,
And that's what puts me to sleep.

Blair Becker, Grade 7
Mount Washington Middle School, KY

All Me

I am from tree hugger to recycling
To loving animals to helping the earth

I am from art, the colors
The paint, markers, crayons, and color pencils, from canvas and paper

I am from swimming, flippers, goggles, and swimsuits
Racing with friends and family to swimming like a fish

I am from dance, twirling, leaping, jumping
Dancing in my room, letting myself out

I am from jumping on beds, eating at the table
To reading magazines and books to using skype with friends and family

I am from being clumsy, tripping over dog toys
Tripping over cat toys, stubbing my toe

I am from Timmy annoying me, playing loud music
Having a lot of friends over, barging in my room

Maddie Sumpter, Grade 7
Meredith-Dunn School, KY

Always Have You

A light breeze fills the trees and the leaves dance in front of the sun filled skies. The river as clear as diamonds with bright gold fish swirling around. We fear of nothing, and dream of everything; both of us young and well. We sit in the sunlight and dream about dreams, and I know I will always have you.

A light breeze fills the trees and the leaves are now gone and on the ground. The river is brown with mud, and the fish still alive and happy. Our fears are few, and our dreams are many; both of us middle aged and healthy. We sit in the cloud filled sky and dream about dreams, and I know I will always have you.

A light breeze fills the trees and the sky cries rain on the very few that still live. The lake is green from pollution, and many fish have died out. Our worries are many, and our dreams are few; both of us old and sick. We sit in the rain and dream about dreams, and I know I will always have you.

A light breeze fills the trees, yet all the trees have been cut down. The lake is gone and what's left is a swamp of pollution. You died last year, and I will too, sooner than I expect. My worries are everything, and my dreams are none; I am so old and half dead. I sit in the storm and dream about dreams, and I know I will always have you.

Abby Rader, Grade 7
Grey Culbreth Middle School, NC

Jaden Who?

Jaden,
who is the best brother anyone can ask for.
Who is a ballerina wannabe; prancing around in tutus and high heels.
Whose eyes are pools, and
whose hair is always a train wreck.
Who is a speck of red in a black and white picture;
never unnoticed, never overlooked.
Who is never going to be just Jaden.
Who is like an obtrusive butterfly, fluttering from person to person, bringing an unforgettable smile to each of their faces.
Whose scream is like an ambulance siren; a warning and an annoyance all in the same.
Who's never wrong, always right, and still struggling to prove it.
Who's that rare kid that saves all the other kids from the bullies on the playground.
Who's a cheerleader wannabe; jumping around in skirts and pom poms.
Who is still, the best brother anyone could ever ask for.

Maddisen Ellison, Grade 9
Spring Valley High School, WV

The Snow Has Fallen and Christmas Is Coming

The chill in the air, the fire wood crackling (pop, crack), the smell of hot chocolate.
I love to glide down the slope on a sleigh, the chill on my face, snow flying by me as I race down the hill.
I love to look at the tree, bright with so many ornaments, so many different memories.
My family and I love to bake cookies and pies.
My family and I love to go to church service, and the Christmas play, to remind us of the day our Savior was born.
I love to make a wish list that I put on the fridge.
I love to sit by the tree and watch Christmas movies on TV.
When the snows falls I know Christmas is coming.
I love on Christmas Eve, to wait up, and see what is put under the tree.
I go outside on Christmas Eve, and I look up, the stars shine and the snow falls, it's so magical.
One of my favorite things to do is to make gingerbread houses with chocolates and sweets.

When the family is all together, and Christmas music is playing, it warms my heart.
The snow has fallen and Christmas is coming.

Lorelei Jupin, Grade 7
J Graham Brown School, KY

Brandi Who

Brandi who gives me all the love she has.
Who is herself and doesn't hide a thing.
Who drives to my house just for a hug.
She tries so hard.
She won't give up.
Even after she said she was.
She is a picture of an open pasture.
Her love for horses known by all.
Who is a learner and a teacher.
Who is a lover of dorks.
I should know.
She shines in any situation.
She is my best friend.
She is my girlfriend.
She is my family.
She is the one who talks to me always.
Who is a daughter of God.
And I will see her in heaven when I go,
Unlike the deer she loves to hunt.
Together forever.
That's what I hope.

Kevin Coleman, Grade 9
Spring Valley High School, WV

Blind Faith

Tell me what to believe.
I can't think for myself.
Tell me what to say.
Put the words in my mouth.
Tell me who to pray to.
Tell me what to live for.
I won't ask questions.
Tell me who I am.
Tell me what the world is;
Tell me where it came from.
Tell me what is right.
Tell me what is wrong.
It must be the truth.
Tell me who to be.
Tell me who to love.
Tell me what love is.
Tell me what I'm hearing;
Tell me it's the truth.
Because I'll do anything
To believe
Your lies.

Casey McNabb, Grade 8
Center for Creative Arts, TN

Decisions

Decisions are made —
Bad or good, we don't know yet.
We live to find out.

Amanda Bowman, Grade 9
Lynn Camp High School, KY

Fun Without the Sun

I look outside, at the gloomy November day.
Only to find, to my dismay,
More and more rain.
The forecast was wrong.
Curse you, you dang forecast.
I was supposed to play outside today.

Might as well not mope around,
I'll try to find some fun without the sun.
Make something, bake something.
Something has to be fun.

Finally, I thought of what I was hoping for.
A game of hide-and-seek, with my little sister, and maybe even my brother, too.
As we begin, I start to count.
I skip all the odd numbers, because I never really liked them anyway.

Seeking them out, I find my brother, he can't hide from me.
Now to find my little sister. Where could she be?
At last we find her, in the bathtub.

I look outside, and the sun is shining brightly.
But instead of going out I suggest we play more.
Before we start, I tell my brother,
Maybe we can have fun without the sun.

Katie Kimzey, Grade 8
West Middle School, TN

Holocaust

Man's wickedness can never be known,
Fighting over unnecessary things,
And making life harder with wars and genocide.

Genocide, the murder of a race,
Doesn't occur very often,
Yet it happened only half a century ago,
Devastating the Jews and all of Europe,
This event is none other than the Holocaust.

It started out with a powerful leader,
Who used propaganda to lure his victims,
Once the sinister man got support,
He became a dictator called Adolf Hitler.

Slowly and slowly, he snatched rights away,
From Jews, handicapped and many others,
Concentration camps were set up to murder,
Those who weren't of his kind.

This continued for about many long years after which a war broke out,
Which ended this disaster,
Which wiped two-thirds of Jews in Europe,
History is all about learning mistakes in past,
Let's learn, so a catastrophe like this will never happen again.

Anwesh Dash, Grade 9
White Station High School, TN

You and I

I wanted to stay by your side
The night you saw me cry
But when I saw you cry
I got the worst feeling inside
I thought it was my fault
But we turned to God and to him we exalted
And when I'm feeling blue
All my thoughts go to you
And I smile
That smile carries on for miles
Never the less
To God I say I'm blessed
And even though the sky turns gray
I know you would be there to make my day
And as rough as the night is
I know I'll always be his
I used to ask God why
And stare into the sky
Hoping time would pass us by
Just you and I

Mallory Hanson, Grade 9
Robert C Byrd High School, WV

Running

I see kids running
To win the trophy.
I hear people calling out names,
And cheering their team on.
I taste the banana still
Settling in my mouth on the starting
Line from the morning.
I feel my heart beating fast,
And faster every second
Before the race starts.
I smell the new cut grass
The people cut the night before
So we can know our
Way through the course.
This is a cross country meet.

Nikki Coffey, Grade 8
Boyle County Middle School, KY

Night Fall

I watch as the stars
Dance around me

Crickets start singing a song
As night fall strikes
And my glow
Fills the dark
Sky

Bats yell, "Good evening,"
As they keep me company.

KeyAnna Johnson, Grade 8
Leland Middle School, NC

Seaside Solitude

As I stand by the water, coarse, wet sand squishes through my toes, and
The white foamy waves lap at my ankles.
I feel the water cooling my feet, a huge relief from the heat of the day.

My worries have gone away with the sun.
The moon, pulling the waves back and forth, casts my eerie shadow.
The darkness does not creep but envelopes me like a cool blanket.

In a state of complete calm, I take in the beauty
Of the moon reflecting off the gentle ripples of water
And listen to their sound, a sound more beautiful than a thousand songs.

The wind from the sea tangles my hair
And fills my nostrils with wonderful marine scents.
Every breath fills my lungs with the moist sea air.

The sun's golden fingers curling over the horizon
Awaken me from my splendid dreamland,
And I reluctantly walk back into the shadow of the city.

Mary Katherine DeWane, Grade 7
White Station Middle School, TN

Thanksgiving

Thanksgiving is a time to be full
Of turkey pie and everything else good
It is also a time to be full of joy
The joy of friendship, family, and the greats of food
When family and friends come to stuff themselves
They stuff themselves with food and happiness
Thanksgiving is a rare day in the year
Where one can eat as much as someone wants
Without a guilty conscience
Many people, though, have forgotten the true meaning of thanksgiving
The way people treat it now,
It should be named Thanks-eat everything in sight
Thanksgiving is a time to give thanks
The fact that the pilgrims did not starve that cold first winter
And that we are fortunate enough to be able to receive
Anything we would ever want in a quick visit at a nearby store
So before you embrace the glutton inside of you
Do as the name Thanksgiving implies
And give thanks for all that you have

Tian Liu, Grade 7
White Station Middle School, TN

The Reality

They're screaming, they're crying
They're grieving, they're dying
I'm seething, I'm writhing
You're bleeding, you're trying…

In the hands of fate we rest
Well aware that this life was a test…

Hannah Wayman, Grade 8
Weddington Middle School, NC

Summer Nights

Summer nights are the best
To share with friends and family
Even the one's you are not too fond of
Just being welcomed by campfires,
Summer parties, vacations to the
Sparkling crystal blue lake
Summer always makes the best memories

Armani Martin, Grade 8
Weddington Middle School, NC

Off to War

I just walked out the door,
I am going off to war,
Everyone is crying,
I tell them it will help stop the people dying,

I am on a plane ride at 9:34,
I am going off to war,
I am going to fight for what is right,
All day and all night,

I cannot take it anymore,
I am coming home from war,
I cannot stand the sound of gun shots,
Or a bomb's bright dots,

Here I am again walking out the door,
I am going off to war,
I hope I can see everyone again,
But remember to respect your service men and women

Mikie Klein, Grade 7
Ramsey Middle School, KY

What Am I?

I am an egg ready to hatch
I come from a big batch
Of brothers and sisters

I have grown older now I can swim.
I haven't any hair so I needn't trim.
I have a tail and a big head.

I now have arms and legs and still a finlike tail,
I can swim a bit better, so I don't wail.
I'm still small but I'll progress.

My tail is gone, I look for my mate
I realize it's my first date.
I grow no more.

I am an egg ready to hatch
I come from a big batch
What am I?

Samuel Ruben, Grade 8
Boyle County Middle School, KY

Balance

Light and dark,
Sun and moon,
A really good mark,
Perhaps, a bad one, too.

Perhaps in this life,
There is no absolute good or evil.
However, in the depths of night,
We try to cling to hope's light.

In hopes of repentance,
We pray to our god.
But is it that we truly believe?
Or, perhaps, we fear what's at the end of this fog.

Light and dark.
Sun and moon.
A devil that barks,
And an angel that gives up far too soon.

Chantel Kidd, Grade 9
Mount View High School, WV

Enclosed Room

Inside looking out
I see people roaming freely Crossing streets, playing games
But I'm stuck here living most of my childhood
In a place like a volcano
I hear a voice telling me to get out
This place is like a ghostly gallow
One day I'll get out
A man is taunting me
But I feel his freedom
I smell all the candy and soda
I want to get out
So I ran to the door
But it was locked
I taste the sourness of this place
I'm at a place worse than a dungeon
But I have to learn
That I can't get out
Because of this window
But without my window I feel alone

Conner Welch, Grade 7
Mount Washington Middle School, KY

My Two Sisters

I have two sisters
I have two friends
I have two angels
I have two guardians
I have two role models
I have two wonders
I have two beauties
I have two sisters forever filled with love.

Lucia Valentine, Grade 8
Shepherdstown Middle School, WV

In the Dark

In the dark I can't see.
In the dark I can't breath.
When I hit the light I will soon find out.
That all dreams come true.
The dark is a scary place to be.
The light is sometimes a wonderful sight.
Dark will never be happy.
It'll always be dark cold and cramped.

Xavier Milton, Grade 7
East Millbrook Magnet Middle School, NC

Elizabeth

This is a tribute to my Aunt Elizabeth,
You treat me with respect and love. You treat me as if I were your own child.
You know how to give me love and grace.
You are an example for me to look up to and without you in my life, it would be unimaginable.
You understand my feelings, and look out for me no matter what.
I love you so much and want you in my life.
You are a second mom to me and I come to you in need.
You teach me things in life that no one else could.
You give me life lessons that help me to be a better person.
I love coming to visit you, and I miss you when I'm not there.
I know you miss me also, and I'm so sorry I don't come visit more.
My love for you is true, and my respect for you is great.
I always remember that you have God's grace.
I know you love me with all your heart and would never let anything or anyone hurt me.
I come to you in need when I have an aching heart.
I know that God moved you closer to me, so that you could be my second mom.
I love you so much, and I won't let you down!
Always remember you are forever in my heart.

Josie Hammon, Grade 8
St Agnes School, KY

Ode to a Pencil

Oh, my tiny tree,
You bring so much joy, yet pain as well.
To the creative artists you are a means of escape,
But to your average school boy you are a meaning of torture.

Oh, my little sapling,
You are the cause of toil, yet you bring about tremendous deeds of good.
You have the capability of designing war machines that bring death,
But you give entire countries their freedom with the stroke of your head by listing their rights.

Oh, my waning branch,
You have developed so much over the generations.
For centuries you proudly stood as a wooden stub,
But were recently replaced with a reusable, robotic, mechanical version of yourself.

Oh, it's just a matter of time, my small twig,
Before a new competitor arrives at your doorstep and begins drawing out plans on how to rule the world.

Ashley Whitaker, Grade 9
Bearden High School, TN

Amanda Grace McGrath*

November 2nd, 2009, was the start of a whole new beginning.
One day after Grace's birthday she went to the doctor because she was complaining of numbness on the left side of her body, only then was she to be diagnosed with a brain tumor.
For the next 10 months family, friends, and neighbors devoted their time to helping Grace's family.
As time went on Grace went from being able to chase her brother and neighborhood boys around the yard to not being able to walk to then only being able to blink her eyes as a sign of communication.
And in the end Grace passed away August 8th, 2010.
Grace would have wanted you to not remember her as the girl in a wheelchair but as the spunky, light hearted girl she was even on the inside throughout her sickness.
For I believe that throughout her sickness Grace helped many people.

Devyn Szklinski, Grade 8
Weddington Middle School, NC
**In loving memory of Amanda Grace McGrath.*

Everyone's Dream

I see the crystal clear ocean
with fresh sand, and palm trees
all around with ripe coconuts.

I see the beautiful
colored fish as bright as a rainbow,
swimming through the sea.
The calm fresh air as cool as can be.

As I step out from the palm trees
I see the bright sun beaming
on my face.

I can hear the wavy wild waves
crashing into the shore,
while the wild exotic birds
sing to me, while I slowly
fall asleep.

Chris Kennedy, Grade 8
Bondurant Middle School, KY

A Life of Fear

Fear is a black veil
that covers all,
no matter how courageous;
It smells like acid,
the pungent odor burning everything,
It tastes like a cigarette,
once you start you can't stop,
It feels like getting shocked,
over and over,
It looks like a graveyard,
with darkness that suffocates you,
It sounds like lightning striking
straight into your heart;
the swarming bees of a timid life.

Addie Schmitt, Grade 8
Leesville Road Middle School, NC

Sarang (Love)

Something that one person can give
Something you can show
Something very precious
Something that can break easily

Can only be given once
Can show a lot
Can be very strong amongst two
Can be shown in many ways

Precious to a soul
Precious to one another
Precious to be taken away
Precious to be shown

Calvyn Sykeo, Grade 7
East Millbrook Magnet Middle School, NC

Winter Days

A jolly family
So loving so sweet
As they sit by the fire
Winter days

I hear the gulping and guzzling
As they drink Hot Chocolate
I see the sparkling snow
Falling from the roof top and sky

I see the Snowman
Standing out there
Smiling and waving at me

I see it with its big button eyes
Carrot nose
And the small buttons for the mouth
Oh the things I see
And hear on winter days

Miranda Gunn, Grade 8
Bondurant Middle School, KY

Forever and Always

The rocks slide
From under my feet
And then she reaches out and catches me.

She is there
To giggle with
To whisper secrets to and
To hug me when I am sad.

She peeks into my heart
And understands me
As if I was herself.

I can trust her
With everything that is mine.
So when I do slip
From those rocks
She will be there to catch me.
Forever and always.

Elizabeth Gonda, Grade 7
White Station Middle School, TN

Waiting, Watching, and Wondering

Waiting,
Watching,
Wondering.

Waiting for someone to stop,
For someone to give,
For someone to help.

Ignoring,
Just walking away,
Blocking you out,
Not hearing your shouts,
Overlooking your bouts,
Just walking away.

But you keep waiting,
Watching,
And wondering.

Ben Anderson, Grade 8
James Graham Brown School, KY

Mine

She drives me crazy in the way she moves
It's like I have been taken by strange pools
As we talk on the phone all evening long
I get lost in her innocence and want more
Yearning for embrace and touch of silk
I then lay awake and begin to wilt
She is something magical in theory
If I had known I would have been weary
Due to I have been willingly captured
She keeps my mind on the positive side
Because she is always extremely kind
I welcome her presence in my nightmares
She is the light during my darkest hour
That's why I'm not going anywhere.

Jaden Trent, Grade 9
Spring Valley High School, WV

Summer

In the summer I like to play
And swim in a pool during the day.
I like to see the hot sun
And eat a hot dog on a bun.

I like the smell of food on a grill
Also, riding on my bike down a hill.
I like to see the plants grow
Even if they grow a little slow.

And when it gets too late
I don't go on a date.
I like to watch the sunset
Even if the grass gets me wet.

Kayla Williams, Grade 7
White Station Middle School, TN

Outer Space

Outer space, so empty yet so full
So many things fill the heavens it is unreal to me
Huge things like stars and planets that are as small as an ant yet bigger than life itself
It is nothing from here but when you get nearer you can see it and hear the sun's whispering flames
The cool air passing you as if you are a soaring eagle
And you know it's there like an angel secretly watching over you
Outer space is an eyeball.
They are hanging over us constantly like our fears, hopes and dreams and a promise never fulfilled.
The planets know your fate and put it into place every day
They are watching us from light years away making us do things though we never really think about it.
Space is always changing and it has been since the beginning of time and beyond
If I only could join them up in the stars and flee this earth forever
And go beyond the boundaries of where the eye can see.

Hunter Grove, Grade 8
J Graham Brown School, KY

Mistress

A small, deathly, black widow.
Like a lovely, heart broken, mistress of fate,
sorrowfully dances around her web.

This mistress, in her youth, was like a dainty, yet disastrous feather.
Gliding through the gentle winds with colors beyond stunning black, and sharp, piercing crimson.

A miniature mark shaped on her back, harmless, though frightening enough
to steal the breath of others who so much glance at her;
even through the abyss of chirping crickets, and snapping branches.

As her prey struggles helplessly to free itself,
this mistress strikes! With such fatal elegance that some may think of this as a swift mercy, and an honorable death.

William Warren, Grade 8
Bondurant Middle School, KY

My Dad and I

Early Saturday morning just my dad and I went on a once in a lifetime trip.
It was my dad and I, and no one else.
I have eight siblings and we go on trips as a family.
We went to this incredible place called King's Island.
The best part of the trip were the rides.
When I saw the park I freaked with excitement.
Dad found some of his favorite rides, which were mine too, and we did those about three times each.
But the sad part was we had to leave.
On the way back I think I talked the most out of the whole trip.
All I talked about was how I missed my family and my bedroom.

Raegan McKelvy, Grade 7
Freedom Middle School, TN

The Wonders of Butterflies

I am a beautiful blue butterfly just hatching from my cocoon.
Soaring and flying through the trees with my sky blue wings seeing everything in front of me.
I feel like I'm invisible just knocking over everyone and everything in my past, feeling so strong.
Blasting throughout the trees fighting whatever is in my way, looking around just wishing it was all real. Thinking, thinking
I am here. This is real, this is real. Why though why does this feeling feel so powerful? It's like tumbling over everyone.
Strong powerful I say, seeing all of the beautiful butterflies smashing through them. Seeing them cry.

Jonathan Clark, Grade 9
Robert C Byrd High School, WV

Mirror Image

A plumber who washes off thoroughly
Who is a night owl
and watches the three stooges without a scowl
Sports are his best;
hunting and fishing are his rest
Who's kind heart would bring tears to your eyes;
but when he's mad, you'd be surprised
My brother and I are his life;
and we mustn't forget his loving wife
Who does the best she can to improve us by every strand
Who's dark hair is turning gray,
as he gets older with age
It makes you think...Why should such a good soul pass?
At least my dad will pass with class
Junk food lies in his body constantly;
who's chip crunching haunts me
When deep brown eyes squint tightly,
do not take what he says lightly
Who's memories will stick with me forever
Daddy who? I will always treasure

Cassie Adkins, Grade 9
Spring Valley High School, WV

Life

Comforted by what we know
Alarmed by what the light doth show
It's as if we are endlessly falling, falling!
But passion and adventure and LIFE are calling
So in the corner you cannot cower
You must live like it's your final hour!
Because what if it is? For that might be true
So we must be thankful for what we can do
And if opportunity knocks on your door
Be thankful for it to your heart's core
Because if we leave just one stone unturned
And one little secret we never learned
How on Earth could we rest in peace?
I'd turn in my grave like the regretful deceased
That I'd be; for we only get one life
And I'd never want to leave it in strife
I want to be peaceful when my life is complete
And to have completed some wonderful feat
And when the businessman goes to Heaven and has sadly sighed,
I'll stumble in, saying happily 'What a ride!'

Gabby Hubert, Grade 7
Parkwood Middle School, NC

Love of Winter

Oh my darling don't you just love winter
The cold winter chill gives me an odd thrill
Ice on the lake seems to queerly glitter
The snow gently falling peaceful and still
The winter night is chilly, dark, and long
The wind of old man winter whistles loud
Rarely can you ever hear a bird song
The snowman artwork makes the children proud
Icicles and snow drifts become winter's art
Inside from the cold grandma's stories told
The sound of Christmas cards warms the heart
In the living room the Christmas tree bold
And steadfast; hold onto winter my dear
Oh my darling the warm of spring is near

Andrew Scarberry, Grade 9
Spring Valley High School, WV

Dear Weather

The fall of raindrops caress my pink cheek.
They're feeling as cold as snow on winter ground.
It feels as if this could last a mere week.
The look, the feel, the taste, but most, the sound;
It finally ends, but disappoints me.
I love the feeling of this new weather.
Why did you have to leave here so quickly?
You could stay here while we play together.
It doesn't want to listen to me, so
I guess I'll have to wait until next time.
Maybe, we'll get lucky and it will snow.
The chance is rare but worth the climb.
For all that feel the way I do,
Just remember that there is always dew.

Skylar Brumfield, Grade 9
Spring Valley High School, WV

Green

Green is the smell of a pine high up in the mountains,
A big green frog stuck on a moist lily pad in a pond.
A slithering snake sliding down a tree
In a humid tropical rain forest.

Green is a farmer slashing down thick grass,
A hunter dressed in camo ready for opening day.
A greedy man laid pondering upon a stack of cash
That most people only dream about achieving in a lifetime.

Is green the color of everlasting life,
Or greed and envy?

Robert Benjamin Smith, Grade 8
Montgomery Central Middle School, TN

Keep It Up Son*

Well son I tell you life for me ain't been no crystal stair
It's had challenges like math and other difficult schoolwork
And having friends that grow up before you
And people close to you dying and being killed in combat
But all the time, I been climbin' on and studying in math
Making new friends and hoping that the war ends soon
So boy don't turn back don't give up and stop studying
Don't stop making new friends and don't stop hoping
That the war ends soon
I'm still climbin'
And life for me ain't been no crystal stair.

Sam Dunda, Grade 7
Meredith-Dunn School, KY
**Inspired by Langston Hughes*

Crying

I see darkness and depression and it feels cold
All I can hear is crying and my heart beat like drums,
It echoes, I look out the window of the funeral home,
It's raining cats and dogs and I cry more
I taste the salt from my tears,
It's like an ocean flooding
I touch her hand and it's an icy feeling
My stomach churns, so I go back to the window
That holds my tears and cries
I feel a cold hand touch my shoulder,
It's my mom she nods and says we are going to the cemetery
The car window is gloomy of rain, we stand there
I lay a blood red rose on her coffin; I look at the other graves,
They are like lost souls of other sad people, they are dead and gone
The tears sting and rush down my face like waterfalls
They lower my great-grandma down,
Down in a deep, dark, and depressing, black hole of fate when they cover her with muddy dirt,
The rain stops and a rainbow appears
And that was the sign that she looks down at us and I love her.

Katie Kelley, Grade 7
Mount Washington Middle School, KY

My 12th Birthday I Will Never Forget

On my 12th birthday, I came home from school and set my huge, heavy backpack down.
As soon as I did the phone rang eagerly.
As I picked the phone up, I read the Caller ID and discovered it was my mom. She told me she was gonna take me somewhere special for my birthday.
"Where are we going?" I queried.
"Where do you want to go?" she replied questioningly.
I told her a few places like Glow Galaxy, Southern Ice, and even the park.
"Well when I get home, we will just drive around." she stated.
When we got in the car and started driving, she asked me a funny question.
"Lexi, what does every teenager need?"
I gave her multiple options including an iPod.
I mean, why not?!
"We will just go to CVS then." she stated.
So as we started driving towards it and parked, but I noticed that we had parked the car kinda far.
It happened to be parked right in front of a Verizon Wireless Store and I knew right away that I was getting a cell phone.
Finally!
We walked into the store, got my phone and the number, installed the service, and walked out with it. And that's my 12th birthday I will NEVER forget.

Alexandria Kennelly, Grade 7
Freedom Middle School, TN

Where I Am From

I am from Lincoln County, West Virginia, where I was raised beside my mamaws and papaws,
I am from Sissonville, West Virginia, where I moved beside my other mamaws and papaws since I was four.
I am from playing with neighbors for many years.
I am from the state of West Virginia, where I am proud to be a hillbilly,
I am from fixing roofs and mowing lawns,
I am from gardening to helping my papaw,
I am from hunting in Putnam County and fishing for trout,
I am from eating water melon with my papaw on the porch and spiting the seeds in the dirt,
I am from spending time with my family and friends.

Joshua Davis, Grade 8
Sissonville Middle School, WV

Stress

Stress is all that comes
To this little house of dread
Stress is all that comes
The day they told me he was dead
I've worked to lift that black cloud away
But I'm caught in its dark trap
And it's here to stay
Rain has fallen from my eyes and thunder from my fists
It doesn't mater what I do the truth will never twist
Stress is all that comes to this little house of dread
Stress is all I see the day they told me he was dead
The single black rose fell from the sky
Suddenly he was cursed to die
Fate took a pull and stole him away
The ending sad curtains fall like a play
Stress is all that comes
To this little house of dread
Stress is all I see
The day they told me he was dead

Melanie Osborne, Grade 7
Ramsey Middle School, KY

Hoping to See You Again

When I go off to war
My wife and my children cry
And I know never to ask why
When I see them it pains me to my core

An "I love you daddy" from my son
Fills my head with doubt
They are the one thing I couldn't live without
For the kids this can't be fun but I'm almost done

For the military I do what I can do
I go off and fight with my gun
And all I can think about is my son
The best I can do is come back to you

Melanah Carter, Grade 7
Ramsey Middle School, KY

Where I Come From

I am from rednecks, country boys, and rebels.
I am from a long line of moonshiners.
I am from hunters and fishers.
I am from crazy and wild family.
I am from sneaking out of the house, and chillin' with my friends.

I am from dirt and gravel roads.
I am from four-wheelin' and dirtbikin'.
I am from muddin' and getting the truck stuck.

I am from friends and family.
From hate and love.
Good times and bad.

Glen Damron, Grade 8
Sissonville Middle School, WV

Snow

Snow swirls around me
Cold air surrounds me
As I stand still
Watching the snowflakes fall gently to the ground.

I gather a handful of winter
And start rolling it around
Making a snow friend
To share my joy

I collect stones
To make the mouth
And two sticks to make arms
And a nose

I frolic in the snow
With my friend
And I never want to go inside.

Katy McNamara, Grade 7
Grey Culbreth Middle School, NC

Through All That I Can

Through all the hatred and soft-spoken lies
I stand as tall as I can
Through all the drama and short cut rolling eyes
I stand as tall as I can
Through all that attempt to tear us apart
I stand as tall as I can
Through all the dirt and pain I've been through
I stand as tall as I can
I CAN stand
I WILL stand
I MUST stand
To rise and forgive all turmoil of humans
I must stand as tall as I can
...to discontinue a false labeling barcode.
I stand as tall as I can
Through all that I can
I MUST STAND!

Charell Vincent, Grade 8
Roanoke Valley Early College, NC

Inside

Sunny on the outside blue on the inside
Nervous and crazy but yet trying to hide
Trying to decide
What's going on in my mind?
Now I am falling behind
In deep sorrow
Not knowing what is coming tomorrow
No matter what they say
Impossible is just an excuse for someone to get their way
Sometimes it gets rough
But I know my heart is tough

Kassey Bishop, Grade 8
Montgomery Central Middle School, TN

Rain

Rain is the liquid life.
Life dances in its presence
And fears its absence.
But people fear its coming,
And in fear they run,
And duck for cover.

Trees love it.
They drink it.
And yell in joy when they see it,
But they hide for,
It can be wicked and destroy.

It snaps trees like tooth picks,
And floods homes.
When mud slides are made,
It sucks lives away
As it flows.
But that is what we have to take,
To live on Earth.

Mason Gardone, Grade 7
J Graham Brown School, KY

The Race

proceed to the finish line
ready to go
anticipation fills the air
nervous, excited
runners get set, go
off, speedy and quick
wind blowing through my hair
blazing, scorching sun
dry mouth
sweat dripping down my face
pushing myself, harder
adrenaline rush
the finish line in sight
almost there
the sound of cheering and shouting
finally…
finished

Madelynne King, Grade 8
Shepherdstown Middle School, WV

That Night

I love to kick; play with my team.
To be the best it is our dream.
We worked so hard all through the fall.
The game was won by those few calls.

We screamed and shouted at those refs.
We were so angry when we left.
It is now starting to get cold.
We start to work towards our new goal.

Shannon Marshall, Grade 9
Spring Valley High School, WV

What's in My Purse!

Keys that are too heavy
Pens out of ink
Receipts that do no good
My little black bonnet hood

Sticky coins in the bottom
Phone ringing off the hook
My book that I don't really read

There are random things
Makeup in the zipper
My wallet full of nothing
A comb

I have my cinnamon and spice lotion
My magic face potion
My iPod and headphones
All of this I call my own

Abbie Holderfield, Grade 7
Meredith-Dunn School, KY

Life

There may be some sadness.
And there may be some loss.
But this is your life,
And you're the boss.

Live life to the fullest.
Try not to cry.
Don't let me catch you,
With a tear in your eye.

Life's not always fair,
And sometimes it's hard.
So scream at the world.
But don't let life catch you off guard.

Ashley Botner, Grade 8
Boyle County Middle School, KY

Halloween

It's a night filled with fright
Candy and treats
Fun and delight
And even more sweets

It's a night filled with new faces
It could be scary
Going to new places
The costumes will vary

It's a night filled with fear
What a scary scene
It's screams that you hear
Because it's Halloween

Katherine Boekhoff, Grade 7
White Station Middle School, TN

The Window

Like teardrops
The rain swirls swiftly down
Down, down
Down the pane of the stained glass window
Curving along the side of a face
A face of a mourner
She weeps for her love that left her
The glass eyes drip their tears
Down, down
Down the window pane
Her deep black dress seems as soft as silk
The cascades ripple into nothingness
Like the tears that she cries
Nothing will compare to her pain
Like comparing earth to the sun
To her there is no better brightness
Than the sweet soft silent light
That lies ahead of her
She is waiting
Living her life in a window of sorrow

Isabella Letson-Ettin, Grade 8
J Graham Brown School, KY

Shadows

Swiftly, quickly
No one must know
Ignore all the sick
Ignore who you know

Run, run
Through all the trees
Fly past the suns,
Swim past the seas,

Don't let it catch you
The dangerous foe
Whatever you do
Just quickly go

It will go faster
Go faster too
Faster, faster
It can't catch up with you.

Maggie Cline, Grade 9
Middle Creek High School, NC

Dogs

They bark and growl,
They yelp and howl,
Big and small,
I love them all.
But one that's far better than the rest.
My Charlie, I love the best!

Bradley Caldwell, Grade 8
Elkton School, TN

A New Year

I am the little New Year, ho, ho!
Here I come tripping over the snow.
Shaking my bells with a merry "din"
So open your doors and let me in!

Presents I bring for each and all
Big folks, little folks, short and tall;
On this day everybody will win
So open your doors and let me in!

Some will have silver and some will have gold,
Some will have new clothes and some will have old;
Some will have brass and some will have tin.
So open your doors and let me in!

Some will have water and some will have milk,
Some will have cotton and some will have silk!
But each from me a present may win —
So open your doors and let me in!

Cash Smith, Grade 8
Signal Mountain Middle High School, TN

The Lower Rebellion

I am the mother, The father, I'm me.
I am the Sister, The Daughter, The son.
I'm the Brother; Sad, the best I can be,
For I'm stuck under the shadows of one.
I'm the writer, the Block, the Poet.
The Artist Unknown. I'm the Hard Worker,
The people I am, I call, You know it.
I call for You, the Son, Ma'am and Sir.
I am You, And We and She, the Teachers
all underpaid, Not the Lawyers am I!
I am those even below, The freaks, the Creatures,
I call so silent, a fear from your lie.
My call is quiet; Invisible tears.
So, so silent. But so loud in your ears.

Cassidy Metzger, Grade 9
Spring Valley High School, WV

Fear

The only thing we have to fear, is fear itself.
— Franklin Roosevelt
Fear is the death of someone you love
The not knowing,
Telling ghost stories at night,
Fear is fires in large cities; it's the sound of that awful siren
That sends a shudder down your spine.
It surrounds and awakens you from sleep.
It's the hushed sounds of blankets
As you toss and turn with the unknown.
Fear is a mind like a foggy morning,
Which leaves you defenseless.
It is a war against yourself: the one you might lose.

Ellen Kanavos, Grade 8
Baylor School, TN

My Life in Black

My life is in black,
I cannot see the sun.
With every word you say to me,
the more monochromatic my mind becomes.

You fill my life with torture and hate,
with every day that passes me,
I become more and more in pain.

I walk by like nothing's wrong,
when deep inside I want to cry.
I can't even hear myself think
with all the words you're yelling at me.

I feel my soul escaping from what
seems to be a fallen me.
When all I ever wanted in life,
was to be a bird, and be free.

Elizabeth G. Shelton, Grade 8
Henderson County North Middle School, KY

So Close Yet So Far

It was the 4th quarter the score was tied
We had the ball and were ready to win
As I waited to play I was nervous
The ball came bouncing down the court ready to score
We scored a couple of points as did the other team
By the time the quarter was over there was overtime
Everyone played their hardest
But we had gone through 2 other overtimes
Everyone played their hardest
I became slow and weak and out of breath the other team the same
But before I knew it we had lost

Jory Dickison, Grade 8
Boyle County Middle School, KY

Winter

A cold snap comes
The trees are bare
Fall has passed
Some are in despair
Summer is missed
People have started to wrap gifts
Lights glow through the night from a Christmas tree
People have house decorating contests
I wonder who will win.
Bells start to jingle and jangle
Children start to make their lists for Santa
Hot chocolate's scent fills the room
Smoke floats out of chimney tops
Carols are sung
Snowflakes timidly fall from the sky
The sound of fire cracking like a whip
Winter is the best

Katie Burkich, Grade 8
Boyle County Middle School, KY

Mom Who

Mom who is as happy as the sky is blue
is good at saying I love you
who looks like me
who is really smart
who wishes to make everyone happy
even if she is not
who likes to know all details
and wishes to be in the sun
who wishes she didn't have to clean but does
who is a strong Christian
who is mainly easy going
Mom who can get annoyed with messes
but is pretty forgiving
who treasures her husband and children
Mom who can always talk
even through a door that is locked
Mom who can get worried quick
if our text doesn't get to her in a zip
Mom who loves me dearly
who will be in my heart forever
Mom who will always be my hero forever and ever

Morgan Albright, Grade 9
Spring Valley High School, WV

The Soldier

He heard the blast before it reached him
The overwhelming pain, the sorrow
for those he leaves behind
As he fell towards the earth
he thought about his life
and why he was here now
fighting in this foreign land
He decided that he was there
because of his undying love
for helping those in need
and those who need assurance and protection
As he took his last and final breaths on this world
he heard his name being called in the distance
Before his eyes closed for the ultimate time
he offered a prayer for his family
and to the one calling his name

Jansen Berryhill, Grade 9
White Station High School, TN

What If...

What if the sun stopped shining?
What if the moon never came up?
What if leaves never grew back?
What if the bees started to slack?
What if it never rained?
And the sky was plain?
What if stars forgot to shine?
What if there were no more fishes in the lakes?
What if Mother Nature took a break?

Hannah Moore, Grade 8
Weddington Middle School, NC

Dreamland Paradise

A dreamland paradise
It is abstracted and different.
Very beautiful all the same though.
I think I have seen this somewhere...
Still as I stare at it, it seems so new.
I think it is still changing.

My eyelids seem to shut, but...
I still see the dreamland paradise.
I will cherish it forever.
This small little dreamland paradise.

I close my eyes again,
And breath in deeply, then I am there.
I can smell the dream dust,
Circulating the air.
The wind blows, causing the flowers to sway.
I touch the colored tree,
And I can feel a magic.
Then I lay there,
Forever in the dreamland paradise.

Breanna Tinsley, Grade 7
Center for Creative Arts, TN

Spotlight

Inside I am looking,
I see the sun coming over the trees,
like a bright diamond,
shining directly at my bedroom window,
I hear the birds' chirping in to the wind,
as it goes on and on,
Chirp! Chirp! Chirp!
I slowly start to smell the spring morning flowers,
As I open my bedroom window,
I could taste their delightfulness,
I could feel the wind bursting through my window,
It felt like a tornado being devastation to a town,
with out my window I'm a prisoner,
locked up in my cell,
but when my window opens,
I'm the spotlight.

Austin Collins, Grade 7
Mount Washington Middle School, KY

Who Am I?

Who am I?
Better question is "What am I?"
I'm not something
you can own or buy at the store.
I'm not something you can grasp in your hands.
I am something
you can hold with your heart.
I am the feeling of joy and pleasure.
I am pure Happiness

Maya, Grade 7
White Station Middle School, TN

Why Did I Go?

How did I get,
The noises in my head,
I know they came with me when I
Returned from Afghanistan.
Why did I go?
I was gone for six months
Without my family,
Out in the field with the grunts.
Why did I go?
I don't know why I'm here.
I got off the plane And I realize
Danger was near.
Why did I go?
I have no clue,
What are we
doing here,
What will I do?
Why did I go?
For so many months,
Oh I was gone for 24 months,
Oh why did I go?

Adam Cischke, Grade 7
Ramsey Middle School, KY

Fall Country

Leaves of orange, red, and brown
Much quieter than any town
Wind blowing through the trees
Lets us feel the cool, autumn breeze

In the morning, as we sit by the fire
We watch the sun get higher and higher
The cold in the air saddens all
The time that I fear is now here
It's time to say goodbye to fall

As winter comes in
My mind goes back to then
Even when the trees grow tall
I will always love and remember the fall

Kalyn Floyd, Grade 9
Roanoke Valley Early College, NC

The Pain

I laugh and smile like nothing's wrong
The truth is I'm hurting
I look to you for guidance and strength
But when you're gone, I have nothing
You may not feel the same
But I pray that your feelings will change
I don't know what I would do without you
So please, please don't go
I need you here with me
The pain…is back.

Paquasha Jones, Grade 9
Roanoke Valley Early College, NC

What Am I?

I am small or tall whatever you consider.
I lift my legs high and keep my head high as I prance.
I am warm and fuzzy but, I think what I want and attempt what I choose.
I am beautiful with my long elegant tail and flowing mane.

Once I go through the gate the lights are on me and the crowd is cheering as I go by.
I think I am the greatest and I can prove that in Freedom Hall.
Freedom Hall is wild when I go by each section the crowd cheers for me
to rack faster than my competitor.

We see who gets more cheers, who is the crowd favorite,
and who they want to win.
Each time we go by they get louder and louder
as we go faster and faster.

I am a wild animal that can be tamed but still I have a mind of my own
that will not be tamed by any human.
I have my good days and my bad days just as everyone else does.
I know when my time to shine is when the crowd cheers I turn on and you better sit back.
So what am I, you may ask?
I am an American Saddlebred! All horse all American.

Sloane Fleig, Grade 8
Hebron Middle School, KY

I See Grandpa

Inside looking out,
I see little snow flakes dancing and laughing
in the cool air as they land on the icy ground.
I hear
The ice being crushed as the vehicles pull in the parking lot,
CrUnCh, CRuNch.
I smell,
The medicine that had been injected in him
Like a bolt of lightning.
I feel a sudden shiver from the snow that
Had melted on the window.
I taste the tears that race each other down my
Cheeks, on my lips.
I fear grandpa will rest too long and I won't have time to say goodnight

Grandpa was gone.

Madison Garbrough, Grade 7
Mount Washington Middle School, KY

I Couldn't Yet Say Goodbye*

Cries heard around the world, I couldn't yet say goodbye
Someone hit the Towers, in the morning hours
Death and horrors all around, until the Towers hit the ground
Tonight my parents will tuck me in, singing a lullaby with a tear in their eye
Yet to understand, I couldn't yet say goodbye

Kaylea Dunham, Grade 7
Norwayne Middle School, NC
**A tribute to 9/11*

Unconscious

Unknown warmth sunk in to the back of your calves
A slight wind gets caught in your hair, this time you promised the moon you'd share it with her,
Sometimes everything seems so lonely, but don't worry, you're very content
All you have brought with you is a never opened suitcase of memories and your own satisfaction,
The only proof of time is how small things are when you look down,
Sometimes, when the horizon is most colorful, a light swarm of slightly salted water will delicately land on your tan skin, as if to keep the balance of pleasantness and the somewhat inconvenient
A glowing light that you usually to refer to as "Sun" will always wake you up, it never apologizes, but you understand
Around the time when you first start yawning, the tiny white spots of brightness appear in the sky; you like to tell them stories about another land, with "clocks" and "cars." A mature voice will sometimes chime in and interrupt them, making sounds of concern and fear, but when you open your mouth to reply, nothing comes out
Someone is calling your name, you heard it, but you aren't listening, this happens very often
You turn to see a mountain of painted wooden slabs all hammered together,
As you get up to go climb it, you fall to the matted grass where you had awoken
The voice comes back again, you are now getting somewhat frustrated and choose to ignore it
Out of a very strong curiosity, you don't give up and decide to crawl up the stairs. You start lightly falling into somewhere new
You landed in to a room where the only familiar thing was your suitcase that you never opened
Something in a white coat looks down at you and makes a familiar noise, the same one that always interrupts your thoughts; another something comes near you with wet but familiar happy eyes
"Do you remember me?"

Gabriele Jones, Grade 8
J. Graham Brown School, KY

No One Would Understand Why

The afternoon sun spotted through the dense forest of tall, majestic trees.
My large rough brown rock covered with moss and the cool murky water dribbling past my bare toes.
Wet sand marked with footprints of the shy animals.

Hundreds of birds chirping their calming melodies.
Creek water rippling over thousands of smooth worn pebbles.
Refreshing silence of the forest without the constant hum of technology.

Fresh forest air dancing on my exposed skin.
Damp fall leaves crushed on the forest floor, revealed by the melting snow.
Sweet blooming wildflowers.

The cool taste of spring wrapped around the musty tarp sheltering me from the world.
Wild strawberries served on broken glass from the creek bed.
The slight mist bouncing off the creek as it rushes smoothly past me.

This place is beautiful, is paradise.
This is my home in the beauty of nature.
No one would understand why.

Kristin Shriver, Grade 9
South Charleston High School, WV

A Special Moment

Me and my lovely Dad spend a great time together every nice hot summer.
We always go to a nice truck stop and we eat their delicious food.
When we are on one of those boring interstate roads my dad lets me drive that big 18 wheeler on that long boring road.
It was not boring to me because I had the wheel and pedal in my control.
Also, he buys me toy trucks every time I go with my Dad.
I'm real glad I'm with him because I don't see him a lot.
So that's my time with my special Dad.

Phillip Jones, Grade 7
Freedom Middle School, TN

Two Dimensional World

In school one day I got awfully bored and decided to take a look, in what seemed to simply be my sister's doodle book.
My sister is an artist you see and she has this book that's red, and on the cover it boldly reads: don't read it you'll end up dead.
I don't really pay attention, although I'm polite and kind, so when I saw the writing here nothing crossed my mind.
I open it and fall in, I fall down and thump! Don't want to do that again, I'll wind up with a bump.
I stand up and look at my hand, thinner, than a knife, then I blink and look around, I'm in a 2 dimension life.
In this 2 dimensional world all homes and buildings are flat. There are no workouts and no gyms because here no one's ever fat.
Kids look like they're in comic strips and balls are hard to bounce. Frisbees, well, they work just great but they barely weigh an ounce.
I'm not sure I want to stay here, it's getting kind of odd but if I tell someone where I've been, they would think my brain was made of sod.
I walk right off the page, that's all I had to do, and right before I knew it I was in my 3-D shoes.
I think I'll stop with pictures and I'll start to write some more.
But don't look inside my poem book, you'll start falling through the floor.

Marie DeGreen, Grade 7
Villa Madonna Academy, KY

The Lonely Boy

Outside looking in I can see tangled, twisted, and twined cords.
I see a poor lonely boy lying stiffened like a rock on a dull bed, full of gloomy puffy clouds.
There sits a poor lonely boy struggling to keep his life.
I could see him strangling to get out of that position that he was sunken in.
The poor lonely boy couldn't be tamed any longer in that hospital bed.
I could hear the poor lonely boy popping off the straps that were keeping him in the exact spot that he didn't want to be.
I could smell all the sicknesses around me, they were crawling on me, trying to find another victim.
I could smell all of the medicine the poor lonely boy had in his system.
I could feel the coldness of the thick glass, every move I would make a path of sweat would follow my hand as I moved it.
I could just taste all of the sickness in the air.
It was breaking through the glass trying to get to the other side where the poor lonely boy was weakening.
Without my window I would have lost the thought of the poor lonely boy on the other side of the glass.

Cheyenne Bratcher, Grade 7
Mount Washington Middle School, KY

Writing Can't Be

You can't just find a poem like a dime on the floor. You can't just pick it up and put in your pocket.

A poem can be anywhere, and everywhere. It can be hiding underneath the stack of books on your shelves that you never bother to pick up. Or beneath the keys on your keyboard.

It could be stuck in between the bricks on your house. It could be hiding in your creaky attic floorboards. It can be hiding between small pieces of a track. Or trapped in your clogged house gutter. Maybe behind a neighbor's tall wooden fence.

Could be at the bottom of my 3rd grade soccer trophy. Or in between the stack of newspapers my parents read every morning. Even in the pocket of your backpack you never look at, or on top of the skyscraper you see every day.

Writing can be hiding anywhere, if you just look closely.

Jack Frierson, Grade 8
Baylor School, TN

Neon Tree

A neon tree stares at me, it's colors; pretty as can be, reminds me of you. It reminds me of you because when I snooze I don't lose the memory of your beauty. You always remind me of your beauty as you stand out of the crowd because everyone stares at you.
You are truly a sight to see and my memories of your are priceless. As my sight is gone I still have you; I am thinking of you.
A neon tree is killing me when it blossoms and they die, I feel hurt inside my neon tree you truly are and that is a neon tree that finally dies without peace.

Kyle Peaugh, Grade 9
Henderson County Sr High School, KY

Beautiful Disasters

The rose among the wretched weeds,
The diamond in the rough,
The grace in raging thunderstorm,
The rest when times are tough.
The slow yet beautiful rebirth,
After a destructive fire,
The small bit of self-control,
When in a fit of desire.
The rainbow in the downpour,
The brightest star in the night,
The breathtaking sunset,
Before the end of all light.
This, my love, is you,
When you hold me in your arms,
And I know it is impossible
For me to come of harm.
For every one disaster,
Has a beauty of its own.
You are that familiar warmth,
When I'm feeling so alone.

Raini Hern, Grade 9
Robert C Byrd High School, WV

If I Had the Chance

If I had
The chance
To start my
Life over I
Would go and
Sit and watch
The sun go down
And stare at
The stars laying
On the beach
Feeling like
I am laying on
Clouds, staring at
The gods, waiting
For my time to run
Out

Colton Jones, Grade 7
Elkton School, TN

Mountain Land

Through the woods
Across the mountains
Along the shore is the river
Running through the rocks
On the sides of the bank
Weaving around the country
With fish and other types
In the river
Going on and on
Always in my heart

Isabel Vazquez, Grade 8
Heritage Middle School, TN

The Joy of My Life

Outside looking in I see my new baby niece! Her beautiful face!
My sister's face stunned with joy. All the doctors and nurses
Surrounding her like a pack of wild wolves
Surrounding their kill. I hear the screams of a newborn baby!
I hear laughter and conversation. The joyful laughs of a new mommy and daddy.
The conversations of my sister and her husband,
Welcoming their new baby to this world!
Prayers to God for a safe delivery of the baby.
I smell the cleanliness of the hospital. The cafeteria food drifting
Up the stairs, and into the hallway. I smell the janitors
Cleaning supplies. I taste the moist sweat on
My lips from worrying about the baby. I feel the cold metal of the door handle.
Moist from the clamminess of my hands. I feel the soft, chubbiness, of a newborn baby!
I see The Best Thing in the World!!
Without this memory holding window I wouldn't been able to see the Joy of My Life be born.
I wouldn't have seen her cute face soft as a duckling's feather,
I wouldn't be as happy as I am now
To see the joy of my life to BE BORN!!

Aly McCawley, Grade 7
Mount Washington Middle School, KY

Warriors of Beijing

IT WAS BATTLE TIME.
The warriors of Beijing were on the front line.
Against the Great Wall of China they looked superior
It was them who had won the epic battles in the past.
They in their royal majestic armor
They who had muscle as burly as bricks
It was they who were going to win
No one doubted them, not even the Emperor
Who in the land of China would question the warrior's authority?
It was they who had stood in the excruciating snow and blizzards
Every extreme condition made the soldiers more vulnerable
They cried a stupendous battle cry that could be heard even in the Himalayas
The warriors held a long spear in their right hand
The left held a circular, gold shield
To the right of the foot soldiers were the horses
For on top of these horses sat the greatest of warriors
These were the men who had years of training for a day like today
And they were going to lead the Army of Beijing to victory!

Nithya Vemula, Grade 7
White Station Middle School, TN

Roller Coaster

As the coaster zooms down the hill
I scream loudly with fear and thrill
How much longer shall this ride last
I'm not quite sure how much time's past

Screaming people near and from far
This ride has been very bizarre
As it nears closer to the end
The joy warms my body within

Braxton Cole, Grade 9
Spring Valley High School, WV

Watermelon

I am in my garden,
In which I can grow.
My center will never harden,
As you already know.

I smell like jam,
And taste like jelly.
I am sweeter than ham,
And I'm good for your belly.

Jared Allen, Grade 8
Elkton School, TN

Balls of Fluff

When you look into the sky,
You might see a little fly.
But if you look even further
Into the heavens,
You will see white, gray, and black
Balls of cotton.

These clouds will move with the wind.
They might look like a bunny,
Or even a turtle.
Clouds will light up another world
In your deep, imaginary mind.

They will fill up with water
Almost every day.
And one day it might even rain.

Don't worry!
They will come back
And form another amazing picture
For you to remember forever.

Lulu Abdun, Grade 8
White Station Middle School, TN

Glow

Light shines
In all directions
I don't want to see
My reflection
It's so covered in sin
So help me
To let this fire burn
And help me
I've got so much to learn
No one can take it away
I am my own worst enemy
I cannot let it stay
It'll eat me
Day by day
Lord, help me
Glow

Mary Daley, Grade 8
North Raleigh Christian Academy, NC

A Glimmer of Hope

Winter creeps along
Like a lion hunting down its prey
Covers everything in its path
Under a cushion of white fluff
The cold hushed breath
Strips the trees bare
Wanders about until its duty is fulfilled
Its curse can only be broken by
Spring's cheerful dance of hope

Sara Jones, Grade 8
White Station Middle School, TN

Changes

Inside looking out,
The green sea of grass waving, the cows waltzing across the field,
Brown fences stretching far and beyond,
But it changes.
Stillness. Nothing. Peace.
Broken houses, miles apart,
Dirt,
Green here and there,
Flowers, shrugging in the harsh climate, cactuses shrieking for water,
But it changes.
It's as hot as the sun. The cars are worms, wiggling through the streets,
Busy people scrambling throughout the city,
Lights shine like stars in the sky,
But it changes.
Mountains graze the sky, rivers rush as fast as a mustang,
Healthy grass stretches like skyscrapers, blue skies go on forever,
But it changes.
Now everything's familiar, the same as we left it,
My house welcomes me joyfully,
Although I will miss the changing scenery,
Home is the best.

Gabriela Almanza, Grade 7
Mount Washington Middle School, KY

Maine

This is a tribute to my best friend Michael.
Michael, you are my best friend.
Even though you live far away, the time I spend with you is the best of all my friends.
Curtis Cove and Sandy Beach are our kingdoms,
which we conquered with little resistance.
The islands there are ours and the seas belong to us.
We become captains of industry with our zoos
and the Agency's most important agents on our missions.
We share the exclusion from the world of peers and their games.
We are men at sea but boys inside
and are still able to have a good time even though it is not permanent
and we will have to go back to the rest of the world where our troubles lie.
We have carefree conversations about whatever we want
in our secret mapped hiding sports.
We could talk all day in our tree house and sing jazz in the cat corner.
Bottom line, we do everything together because we are one person in two bodies.

Joseph A. Marino III, Grade 8
St Agnes School, KY

My Favorite Animal

He is the king of the jungle
The hair on his head, longer hair than anybody's
His roar is so loud when you get closer to him
You feel that your heart will stop
He sleeps in the day so he can relax then he hunts at night,
when he hunts, you cannot feel when he walks; then. . . SNAP, he's caught you.
His eyes are gold and rich, he stares at you, he studies you, what are you going to do?
His ears know where you are, he will find you
And that's why the lion is my favorite animal.

Akram Ibrahim, Grade 7
East Millbrook Magnet Middle School, NC

Headaches

It comes with the rain.
As it starts to patter on the roof.
As the leaves decay.
It's like the pounding of my heart.

It stings like a bee,
As lightning crackles,
Through my head.
As the light of heaven recedes,
And the darkness of the under world
Engulfs me.

The disgusting tangy taste of the medicine
As the pain recedes, and God's light repels the dark
And locks it in the world below.
As I sigh with relief and relax.

And then it starts to return.

Martin Walsh, Grade 7
J Graham Brown School, KY

Strange Places

Writing isn't like anything else,
you can't just walk into a store and buy it.
It's complex and hides in the strangest places,
it can pop out of anywhere;
flowers, beds, chairs, even doors.

Writing hides in the dewdrop on a blade of grass,
or the leaves on a tree.
Writing hides in the American Revolution,
and the Boston tea party.
Writing hides in the sound your pencil makes
as it scratches against your paper.
Writing hides in the sound your recliner makes
as it rocks back and forth,
and in the warm sensation of the fire in the fireplace.
Writing hides in the loud voice of the TV,
and the red feeling of being angry.
Writing hides everywhere.

Melissa Karman, Grade 8
Baylor School, TN

The Feeling of Relief

The feeling of relief
The feeling of excitement
The feeling of love taking over
The feeling of tears running down your face
The feeling of being proud when you see the service ship coming
The feeling of seeing the American flag waving in the air
The feeling of seeing your loved one again
The feeling of your loved one serving our country
The feeling of them coming closer to you
The feeling of holding them in your arms once again
The feeling of them being home and safe
The feeling of relief.

Allisyn Melcher, Grade 8
West Middle School, TN

The Picture

A blue bouncy ball flies through the air.
A shattered picture hits the ground in a million pieces.
Thinking about my punishment I hide it behind the couch.

Another box is packed
And put into a stack.
I hadn't thought about the picture in many months.
But when they move the couch it all comes back to me.
The look on my moms face was like a bipolar happy sad look.

Not angry the picture was broken.
But relieved it was found.

Nathan Harrod, Grade 8
Bondurant Middle School, KY

World of Disney

In the middle of a sunny afternoon
And I was getting on my first plane ever.
It was me and no other girl.
We flew to Florida.
I was as excited as a person with ten cups of coffee.
My mom and I went to all of the parks.
I got an autograph from Frozone.
Chip and Dale were very flirty.
Dale kissed me on my cheek.
When it was the last day I whispered "Bye Dale."
I just sat on the plane sitting as still as a statue thinking
About why that was where dreams come true.

Jasmine McNair, Grade 7
Freedom Middle School, TN

Halloween

Halloween is filled with fright.
Witches and monsters go bump in the night.
Trick or treating is so sweet.
Mountains of candy that monsters eat.
Carving pumpkins is great and fun.
Put lit candles in when you're done.
If you see a black cat, a witch is near.
You'd better fun fast and don't shed a tear.
Boo! Boo! Hope you don't see ghosts.
They are rude and not very good hosts.
All of this fills children with fright.
So until next year, have a creepy night.

Pesleigh Hall, Grade 8
Elkton School, TN

When He Came

We were but a little village,
but then He came,
and we became a thriving town.
Outside of our village was a moat,
hardly big enough for a boat,
but then He came,
and it became a rushing river.
Beside the moat was a hill,
next to the hill a mill,
but then He came,
and they became;
a mill and a mountain!
Near our village was a thicket,
but then He came,
and it became
the largest forest in all the land.
Now our village lay on the edge of a desert,
but then He came,
and it became a massive lake.
And so goes the story of the man who came
to our little village and made us a city.

Jonathan Snoddy, Grade 8
Deerstream Learning Center, NC

Dream

Golden Gates, open
Joy, Peace, Hope,
over fill me,
just as water overflows
from a glass of water.

Sounds like a thousand
angels voices singing
old hymns.

Shhh, the trees
Whispered
To me.
As I walked toward
the Golden Gates
of Heaven.

Rachel Blackwell, Grade 8
Bondurant Middle School, KY

Video Games

I love video games
They are so cool
The Xbox 360
And PS3 rule

They're entertaining
And fun to play
But when I get in trouble
They're taken away

James Shefte, Grade 7
East Millbrook Magnet Middle School, NC

Blind Truth

Everyone is a person
And every person has a story
They sometimes forget
That they are dealing with a fellow human being
Instead they gun down each other with words
We try to meet the false image of perfection
Provided by none other than modern day vampires
The media
A seemingly endless war
Started in one presidents reign
Not yet ended in another
Because of what?
Not even the dead could say
Do they not hear the cries for help?
Our most beautiful, irreplaceable havens are being invaded
Rain forests that stood tall and majestic for hundreds, thousands of years
Reduced to broken stumps and smoldering ashes in a matter of days
The animals driven out of their homes or off the face of the earth
But even though they are blessed with eyes
They choose to remain blind
To the truth they will not see

Lakia Mcleod, Grade 9
Middle Creek High School, NC

Desperate Cries for Hope

So here we go all over again;
Here I am trying to force you to be my friend.
I've said it time and time again that I'll stop trying to please everyone.
But guess I haven't stopped since then.

No more will I cry.
Or even give a sigh.
As far as people they're not worth
The tears that I shed and as much as I hurt.

So here we go all over again.
A promise that I'm going to keep better than then.
Eventually I'll smile, not hurt.
Because as far as people they're not worth
The tears that I shed and as much as I hurt.

Jade Gary, Grade 7
Roanoke Valley Early College, NC

The River

Below the bridge lies my world
Beneath the surface is where my joy lies
Beside the strange creatures is where my curiosity takes over
Above the water are those who's love will never end
Upon the grass holds my favorite memories,
Of my imagination flowing freely
Among all our friends and family is happiness
As we talk, laugh, and enjoy the night
Despite our good time, it has to end
Until tomorrow, my joy, happiness, and peacefulness lies below the bridge.

Hope Jones, Grade 8
Heritage Middle School, TN

The Run

In the race I run alone
There is no sound in the air
Where I stare at the finish line
All my family can do is stand there
I think about it once, with no fear
Then a second time, running along the path waiting
I take a deep breath and get ready for the finishing steps that come
Then I step on it, a perfect spring I'm fine
The race is all that matters here
With the others behind and the time soon to be expired
I'm ready to win with no fear
I look at my competition and they're tired
I go into my thought about to win
Taking a deep breath and looking over once more
I cross, the perfect win begins
I cross with the ribbon; everyone is wild and some in tears
I finally won the championship we take
It's about time I beat everyone after this long year

Keagan Hinkle, Grade 8
Boyle County Middle School, KY

Where I'm From

I am from running barefoot outside,
To the splashing of the pool!
I am from camping under the stars,
and making wishes.
I loved the beach from the day I washed up on the shore.
I danced, giggled, and laughed my way into everyone's hearts.
I am from a quiet family, but I am spontaneous!
From the love of God I was raised.
I am from watching movies and eating sugar.
But most importantly,
I am from Sissonville, West Virginia

Andrea Harmon, Grade 8
Sissonville Middle School, WV

Loneliness Is Great

Sitting near the tall pine tree,
Staring as far as the eye can see.
Prancing around in my field of paper flowers,
Clouds so high, as tall as towers.

Touch the sky, fingers stretched out,
If I don't I might begin to pout.
Kaleidoscope sun of orange and red,
A powerful light that pulls you out of bed.

It feels so good without someone near,
Yapping all day in your ear.
Loneliness is a great thing,
As to all the joy it brings.

So, listen here when I tell you,
I'm through with all the things you do.

Annie McConkey, Grade 7
Center for Creative Arts, TN

The Silver Wall

Trapped in a jungle of boxes
Trying to find his family
He searched throughout the gigantic maze of rooms
But he could not find his way
Every room looked the same

Finally, the boy gazed through the window
Through the window was a moving truck
Finding his father entering the door

He was confused like a fly in a room
The boy was lifted like a bird by his father
But he did not understand
Why brown boxes were everywhere

The aroma of food danced in the air
Scared and hungry like a stray animal
Following the aroma to his mother
He then pondered about his brother

Entering the maze of rooms
He found one with a silver wall
He looked through the silver wall for his brother
But all he could find was

Himself

Deepak Sathyan, Grade 9
White Station High School, TN

Good Morning Stream

The stream flowing smoothly across the mossy brown rocks
My reflection staring back at me
Fish move by me hastily, their scales shimmer in the peaking sun
The cool water glides along my fingertips like the blade of a knife.

The glorious voice of the forest ringing in my ears
The wind seems to sing to me
animals start waking from the midnight slumber
The sound of the peaceful silence

Fresh oxygen rushes over me from the forest around me
Dense moisture lingers overhead
Scent of the super natural
The mist off the flowing water

The sweetness off the honey suckle flowers
The liveliness of the waking forest
The taste of the fresh air
The apple tree

Happy thoughts filled my mind with greatness like I am a kid again
How did God make this wonderful place?
The world is at peace
What would it be like to stay here forever?

Abby Bare, Grade 9
South Charleston High School, WV

River Bank
I sat on the river bank,
With two guys Jack and Frank.
We were skipping rocks
Through the woods scurried a fox.

We were waiting for the fish to bite
Jack was flying a kite.
We reeled in and checked our bait,
Not expecting our great fate.

We cast our line,
Each of our casts were fine.
Jack had a bite,
The fish put up a great fight.

In the end we caught 20 fish,
They made us a great dish.
This day was great
Because of our fate.
Hunter Anderson, Grade 8
Boyle County Middle School, KY

Performance
Light pink satin
against waxed mahogany floor.
The wind caresses my skin
as I leap and begin to soar.

Swirling, Twirling, Whirling,
I smile as I gracefully land.
Leaving a trail behind me
like footprints in the sand.

Swirling, Twirling, Whirling,
I begin my most difficult move.
I spin; light and strong
my ending perfect and smooth.
Sidney Cobb, Grade 8
Bondurant Middle School, KY

My Puppy
My puppy is cute and very sweet
He has tiny little feet
He is white and brown with curly hair
He runs around everywhere
He's very soft and fuzzy too
My puppy is just like me and you
He eats, he sleeps and likes to play
He's into something every day
Our paper towels he likes to shred
He drags his toys into my bed
He's wild and crazy
He can be a pest
But I think my puppy is the very best!
Hal Lemon, Grade 8
Elkton School, TN

PopPop Who
PopPop who is slept-in sheets
Whose head is like a melon
Who is full of laughter and smiles
He smells of Old Spice
Of forests and crisp air
He calls me his ham-bone
He tells me he loves me
PopPop who is the flora of the Earth
Who is hats, V-necks, plaid and corduroy
He is silly songs
Sang just for me
He is long walks
Who is like Christmas time
Always making me happy
PopPop whose love and care wafts over me
Who always seems content with life
PopPop who reminds me of the fall leaves
Whose skin is coarse but loving
When he is gone
My world will never be as bright again
Braden Ferguson, Grade 9
Spring Valley High School, WV

I'm Not Dead
You think I am dead
because all my leaves have fallen
I watch you play in the snow

The snow is my blanket
it keeps me warm at night
You climb on my branches

Cause you think I am dead
but I am not dead
think what you want because

I know I am not all alone in the snow
warm as a fire deep down
under in the snow
Vaughn Derry, Grade 7
East Millbrook Magnet Middle School, NC

I Stand There
I stand there
Warmed by the sun
Blown by the wind
Cooled by the water

I stand there
Burnt by the sun
Pushed by the wind
Healed by the water

I stand by the ocean
Isobel Brunsting Frazer, Grade 7
White Station Middle School, TN

Sports
I like sports
Sports are fun
Even when
Coach makes us run

Soccer balls on the ground
Soccer balls in the air
My friends and I
Run everywhere

I dribble the ball
As I go down the court
The hoop looks so far
I feel so short

My friends and I
We like to win
Sometimes we lose
But will try it again
Haley Garner, Grade 7
Elkton School, TN

Love Games
Love is a game
that fools you;
It smells of sweet flowers
which fumes are deadly,
It tastes bittersweet,
It feels like a miniscule cactus needle
which isn't painful when puncturing
but brings forth pain once inside,
It looks like a serpent
that persuasively coaxes you into its lair,
It sounds like glass shattering
a beautiful piece of art demolished,
That is the very thing that fuels life
but can and will do the very opposite.
Danielle Kang, Grade 8
Leesville Road Middle School, NC

I Wish
I wish for a pair of wings,
So I may be able to fly.
I wish for immortality,
So that I may never die.
I wish for a dozen roses,
So I can tell you how I feel.
I wish I was on a game show,
So I can make a deal.
I wish I could be with you,
Until time has stopped…
I wish I could see you,
So that my heart drops.
RJ Sprouse, Grade 9
Robert C Byrd High School, WV

To My Mom and Dad
I know things don't go
the way that you plan.
You want me to do well,
you want me to be great.
When I doubt myself
you tell me I'm ok.
I love you
because you never doubt me.
I feel as free as the stars
and I know
even when people
are mean to me,
you love me with
all of your hearts.
I love you
with all my heart,
and I will someday
make you proud.
Thank you
for loving me every day.
Stuart
Stuart Green, Grade 8
St Agnes School, KY

Rose Who
Rose, who is sweet as candy
And smells like harsh,
Old people perfume
Who has reflection pool, gray eyes,
Wrinkled skin, and fluffy white hair.
Whose gums are shiny from no more teeth
Who wears old granny sneakers
And walks turtle speed.
Who is an excellent cook
always in the kitchen
Whose thumb is green
always in the garden
Mother nature in the flesh
Who is never too serious
Who is a dog ready for a road trip
Loves walking on the beach
Who is a spring of life
And winds her day down in bed
Reads a book with her bug eyed glasses
Fluffs her marshmallow pillows
And sleeps until the next bright day
Alex Bradley, Grade 9
Spring Valley High School, WV

Life Is a Roller Coaster
Life is a roller coaster
Be prepared to feel the rush
But wear a seat belt
Because it sure is a ride.
Kylee Nelson, Grade 8
Weddington Middle School, NC

School
I try so hard to impress my teacher, but the harder I try the worse it gets.
Reading, oh, how much I hate it.
I read and read every day and it doesn't help me.
When I get to math class I love it.
It's easy and fun,
But when science comes it's even better than social studies.
Oh, how I love science!
It's my writing and reading that kill me in school.
I wish…
I wish…
Oh how I wish that I was good at reading.
This is how God created me
And I love what He has done.
But I need to be good at reading,
I need…
I need…
And need it for school,
Because without it I won't be successful.
That is what I hate about school.
Myles Pace, Grade 8
Weddington Middle School, NC

Meaning of Family
I hear wind howling in the background
I smell cold air and sweet smells
I taste coldness, dryness of the air around me
Family laughing as if they were best friends

The turkey on the dinner table is a gift from above
I'm in the cold, looking into the bright room where my family sat
I see my family, all gathered together
I think to myself
Without my window I would not truly understand the meaning of Family

I sit there, not quite ready to join them
Still trying to understand myself and them
For without them, I would be lost.
Collin Keith, Grade 7
Mount Washington Middle School, KY

The Greatest: Muhammad Ali
He was a great boxer, yes he was,
Pounded every punch, the crowd with applause.
He hurt his opponents with great force,
They would cry in pain, of course.
He was proud of his race, said "Black is beautiful,"
Was arrogant, sometimes in his quotes, dull.
He said he would win every match,
Sometimes he would KO the opponent, and it would not be a fair catch.
His slogan was fly like a butterfly, sting like a bee,
He seemed like a giant, his opponent, a flea.
He was the fasted, the fiercest, certainly not the most humblest,
But the thing to describe him the best,
Is to call him the greatest!
Miguel Vivar, Grade 7
White Station Middle School, TN

Thirty Seconds

My mother's and my eyes
Became glued on to the monitor
Waiting for plane DL6776's status
To be changed to "At Gate"

Our eyes were on fire
And they watered with tears
We were afraid to blink because
We didn't want to miss a second

As the status blinked and changed
Our hearts became a soaring kite
When I saw a dark figure waving
From gate A7,
My heart swelled up like a balloon
Because then I knew that it was he returned from Korea

The thirty seconds he was walking
The thirty seconds he was approaching
Seemed slow as a cloud's movement
But became the happiest moment in my life

Soon, I was in his arms
I couldn't believe that it was he
My dad, my father, my protecting knight.

Gyuri Han, Grade 7
White Station Middle School, TN

Old Allegheny Mountains

The old Allegheny Mountains surround me as I gaze
A wide mountain range, a morning sky filled with haze
I see the Blackwater River gushing deep below
Dark clouds absorb the tree tops with snow

The animals rustling, preparing to leave
The powerful wind whipping, then coming to a breeze
The lonely trees cling together, cracking, prepared to fall
The faint chatter of the river tearing through the mountains

The smell of old dying rhododendron fills my lungs
The sweet sap on the evergreens hardening in the freeze
The smell of purity, die around me

The snow melts as it hits my mouth
The taste of the morning air in the back of my lungs
The bitter coffee warms my lips

The dry air being impaled by the wet, heavy snow
The cold wind stings my nose
The excitement of snow makes my face glow

I am happy and at peace with nature
It is amazing seeing the trees glitter white with snow
I think I better go, before the snow covers the road

Alex Ball, Grade 9
South Charleston High School, WV

These Moments

The feeling of going somewhere new.
The rush of excitement getting on a plane,
Like reuniting with an old friend.
The plane whispers to me,
"Welcome. Have the time of your life."
Whoosh! And up high we go!
The moment I look out the window,
And see the life I've left behind.

It looks so small.

And I long for the new land
I long to walk on the different culture;
My feet swallow up the history and life.
The experience is rich,
Like the expensive milk chocolate we all wish for.
But it has to end,
Eventually.
But it's the moments I wait for.
It's these moments I hope to achieve.
Many times.

Erin Woggon, Grade 7
J Graham Brown School, KY

A Feeling of Contentment

Happiness is a perpetual smile,
Making its rounds to all
It smells like a spring daffodil popping out after the rain,
Excited to show off its new color
It tastes like a warm Krispy Kreme Doughnut,
Slowly melting in your mouth
It feels like rays of the sun warming your back,
On a carefree summer day
It looks like a bluebird splashing up water,
Cleaning her cobalt-tinted feathers
It sounds like the final whistle to a championship,
Proclaiming that your team has won
It walks in your life at any given time,
Happiness can come into your life lifting your spirits,
Giving you an internal smile.

Caroline Smith, Grade 8
Leesville Road Middle School, NC

The Universe

The universe is a beautiful place
Full of wonderful creations.
Large amounts of planets, like the human race.
God made us people, and we made nations.
The universe is full of divine creatures
so we are told, by our preachers.
Every day we learn the new features of this vast space
and that's what we come to expect, without any trace.
So now you know the universe is not a dream,
but the universe is as real as it seems.

Thomas Ferrrera, Grade 7
St Vincent De Paul School, WV

Will Pappas, in Memory

The summer sun beams down on us,
As if the rays were the heavens reaching out,
The trees whisper in the wind,
Blowing the sweet smell of watermelon,
In the moist green grass of the Pappases' backyard,

Sorrow and sympathy fill the air,
As shadows creep up on us,
I wipe away my tears and turn away,
From the melancholy memories,
Of my dear friend Will,

He dreamed of cars and monkeys too,
Of watermelon clouds racing by,
But most of all he dreamed of hope,
And life, and love, and strength of the days to come,

Will became a family member,
On the summer of '08,
Which started quick, but ended slow,
For my brother Will passed away,
On June 19, 2008,
And now he's forever in my heart.

Harry Arcamuzi, Grade 7
White Station Middle School, TN

Night

The Night…Sweet Night. How I love thee
You are dark and luminous
You are a black sea
You are bright and mysterious
You surround me

The Night…Sweet Night. How I love thee
You are my embrace
I feel secure in your arms when you hold me
In my heart you have a place
You are all I see

The Night…Sweet Night. How I love thee
You make one laugh and smile
When your stars wink at me
I can see them for miles
As I sit under thee

The Night…Sweet Night. How I love thee
When your moon is high in the sky
She watches over me
And sings me a lullaby
So the nightmares will flee

Elesia Saunders, Grade 9
Robert C Byrd High School, WV

In a Daze

I was breathing hard
Laying on the tumble track
Dizzy and sick

My legs collapsed out from under me
And I had passed out cold.
Before I was doing backhand springs like there was no tomorrow
I was feeling a little woozy but I thought I'd be okay

Apparently not

Matt ran to get a wet towel
When I put it around my neck it felt as if it had frozen me
I sat in front of a fan feeling so sick and scared

My head was spinning,
My stomach turning,
The burning heat trapped me in a daze.

Alexis Stratton, Grade 8
Bondurant Middle School, KY

Clouds and People

Clouds and people are alike in many ways
We both have those long lasting weeks
Then we finally bust open that one dreary day
Rain or tears may fall down onto the peaks
But one must stay strong for the sun to come out
Not giving anything or anyone any slack
With your glad feelings jumping about
But then suddenly! The tears and rain come back
The feelings of happiness start slowly drifting by
Many things getting in your way making you cry
Jut wanting to stay there being you and just to lie
Makes you just want to soar free and high

Caylyn Mann, Grade 8
West Middle School, TN

I Am

I am full of ambition; hope you may say.
I want the world to see the importance in life.
I wish those around me would open their eyes.
I don't understand the rude words slung around.
I hear crude remarks; words I'll never forget.
I see the effects in others' faces.
I feel the sharp pain and hurt they have received.
I get angry when people make comments and walk on by,
while others stand embarrassed and cry.
I dream about a chance to spread compassion, for you see
I am just a girl trying to make a difference.

Jess Johnson, Grade 8
Grayson County Middle School, KY

Euphoria

A waterfall with colors of silvers and blues,
A weeping willow tree swinging in the breeze,
The thick bed of blue sky covering me like a small child's beloved blanket,
A mother duck with her newborn babies following her every movement.

The trickle of the stream rolling over tiny rocks and pebbles, making the most serene noise,
The frogs croaking a tune of love, calling their mates,
The humming birds as they sing their songs of peace and serenity,
The moss at my feet smash it to the earth as I walk.

The water from the waterfall as it sprinkles my face ever so delicately,
Tropical flowers blooming into unique, special creatures,
The pure effect of one of a kind nature circling around me,
The fresh cut grass like the smell of my hometown.

The afternoon air pouring over quickly, oh too quickly,
The cherries I'm picking from the trees, with a taste so pure and so scrumptious,
The magnificent summer breeze just rolling in.

The cool breeze, like a kiss from a butterfly upon my cheeks,
The overwhelming beauty as it takes my mind to new places, I've never experienced before,
God touching my heart as I am amazed with my surrounding.

About how much I want to share this with so many family and friends,
Being in total peace is what life is all about,
The trees remind me of gentle guardians watching over me, as I am in the state of EUPHORIA.

Zoey Oberst, Grade 9
South Charleston High School, WV

Where I Go

The pond is only awake when I'm asleep.
I say a hello by skipping the first rocks I notice across to the other side.
Splash! It waves back as the water ripples where it skipped.
I can see its heart beating...It's what keeps the minnows swimming.
It's what makes me keep showing up every day, whether it's freezing, scorching, storming, or just perfect weather.

I stick my feet in the gentle water and let the day wash off wiggling my toes.
My worries vanish and the rest of the day is lull.
And I have a quick moment without a care in the world...

Deep breathes in rhythm, followed by a sharp glisten in my eye wishing the next day won't ruin it...
But I can see the future now...almost as if every 24 hours is set to reset but I'm meant to show up here.
I realize this is too good to be true. I remember a year's worth of memories here but all in only a few minutes.
I think of all the possible ways why this is so, but I only have one...I'm dreaming.
I don't want to accept it. I'm missing everything already when it all still sits there in front of me.

I squinched and didn't want to open my eyes back up.
But pushing myself to do such a difficult task,
I open my eyes...I knew it, I was only a dreaming
There's nothing more that I can do but attempt to remember that celestial place.
The pond is only awake when I'm asleep...

Jacob Baunach, Grade 8
J Graham Brown School, KY

I Promise

I promise I won't back down
There's a lot of problems coming around
At times I really want to give in
But to my word...I won't back down

I won't let others make me fall apart
I won't let problems tear me down
I may stumble a bit in this race,
But to my word...I won't back down

I must continue to step along and never fall
I'll need to be watchful for many predators
A prey to others, I'll never be
But to my word...I won't back down

I might become heartbroken and feel defeated
Many of my "friends" may become traitors
But I'll try my best to survive
I promise you, I won't back down

Marziana Morlett, Grade 8
Roanoke Valley Early College, NC

Blue

Blue can be light or dark
A sea of darkness and sadness surround me
Waterfalls cascading over mountains of ice
Pools of sadness cascade into the sea of my brain

Quiet or calm the sky can be happy or sad
Aquamarine is quiet yet so calm like the sky
Dark igloos fill with sadness
The icy blocks of ice built the igloos of sadness

Penguins quickly speed down mountains of ice
Peacocks flounce with light and dark shades of blue
Polar bears jump on sheets of ice and this is why
Blue can be light or dark

Daulton O'Brien, Grade 8
Montgomery Central Middle School, TN

Lonely Soul

Outside looking in I think of childhood memories
That are no more
I see a little boy that I used to be
I hear laughter and feel sadness
Now the room is empty just like my soul
The boy is gone and everything I loved went with him
The walls start to sob in loneliness
The house is no longer fun or great it has become a hollow house
Strangers come in and ruin everything
They start to take over like a virus
I see myself crying in the last gaze of my childhood
I feel so sad as if I'm a ghost, nobody to love or care for
I'm no longer a person but a mere lonely soul

Dustin Satori, Grade 7
Mount Washington Middle School, KY

The Important Place

Inside looking out
In the place called important
Papers, words, sentences sprawled everywhere
Some say it's like jail
Others hear differently
The smell of new text books cloud noses
The holding of rough pencils
The sound of ticking from a clock
Tick...Tick...Tick
The clock taunts me
But it just hangs there unimportant
So much time
In a place so dull
So familiar
Hoping for a ring
But it won't come
I won't get out
Because I'm trapped from the glass

Makaela Phillips, Grade 7
Mount Washington Middle School, KY

Gymnastics

Flipping, flopping tumbling around
swinging, twisting around the bars
all events...
steady and ready to compete
the "Star-spangled Banner" playing
I'm ready attempting to score that perfect 10
knowing all skills are perfect
remember all the idols — Nastia Lukin and Shawn Johnson
I'm standing waiting
my heart racing
the judges salute
I step onto the floor
my music starts suddenly everyone is staring at me
I do twist, jumps and turns
BAM!
I do my finishing pose
perfect!

Elaine Hinkel, Grade 7
East Millbrook Magnet Middle School, NC

Change

Her bones crack and pop as she wakes
Winter is hard on her
Winter leaves her bare
She shivers in the brisk wind
But a change comes

She jumps and dances about
Bursting with colors
Everyone is happy even though they destroy her
The sun shines on her face and she glows
A change a great change for Mother Earth

Milana Hendricks, Grade 9
Weldon High School, NC

Tahorse

Bright and colorful
With it's tiger print and horses body,
It stands still in the jungle as
I look at it.
Four legs I see with paws rough
One large wing that dings and sings.
It soars the sky.
Purrrrrrpurrrrr
As we land on the ground,
Stretching up and down and all around.
All around people scream,
Wow, what a beautiful thing.

Kristen Gray, Grade 8
Weddington Middle School, NC

Seasons

Spring brings flowers
Scented and sweet
Summer brings laughter
And unbearable heat
Autumn brings colors
Red and orange leaves
Winter brings snow
That covers the trees
And as the year
Draws to an end
The seasons start
All over again

Mikaela Billiet, Grade 8
W P Grier Middle School, NC

Grades 4-5-6
Top Ten Winners

List of Top Ten Winners for Grades 4-6; listed alphabetically

Allen Chen, Grade 4
Highlands Elementary School, IL

Alexander Chojnowski, Grade 6
Immaculate Conception Academy, ID

Kallie Fisher, Grade 4
The Mirman School, CA

Yuna Kim, Grade 5
Edwin Rhodes Elementary School, CA

Jewel Mason, Grade 6
Chester E Dye Elementary School, MO

Andrew McInnis, Grade 5
John G Dinkelmeyer Elementary School, NY

Sam Roberts, Grade 6
St Philip Fine Arts School, AB

Alysa Rogers, Grade 5
Foothill Elementary School, CO

Ashley Workman, Grade 6
Southwest Middle School, AR

John Xue, Grade 6
Chapin Middle School, SC

All Top Ten Poems can be read at www.poeticpower.com

Note: The Top Ten poems were finalized through an online voting system. Creative Communication's judges first picked out the top poems. These poems were then posted online. The final step involved thousands of students and teachers who registered as the online judges and voted for the Top Ten poems. We hope you enjoy these selections.

The Beautiful Beach

Silky smooth sand washed against my feet
The book in my hand is my new born baby
The sun is shining and bright like a copper penny
Waves look surprised to see me
Seashells dance on the sand
Crash! The waves collided like two speeding cars
Mean waves start to glare at me
Sand runs screaming away from my feat
People start to scatter away from me
Big waves start to see the sun glow
People start to see the show
Making the waves laugh by doing a dance
Families cheered and said, Hooray, Hooray!
Thanking me all day
Sunrise to sunset, time to say good-bye
I love the beautiful, dancing, screaming water.

Je'Nira McKoy, Grade 4
Bailey Elementary School, NC

Fall

As I walk through nature in fall,
I hear the different sounds of her call.

She is quietly telling me "pitter-patter —
squeaky squeaky," wait that may be the
sounds of a pond nearby and a squirrel
stuffing his cheeks.

When the wind starts to blow the colors start
to fly, red yellow, orange and sometimes
green; beautiful, bright colors in your eye.

When the clouds get ready to leave and
the blue sky comes out;
Then more and more people can enjoy fall as
they move about!

Ashyia Williams, Grade 4
Kinston Charter Academy, NC

University of Tennessee

Tennessee is the best
Of all the colleges east and west.

Tennessee games are a hurricane wave
Where all the fans scream and rave.

Orange and white they proudly wear
Like a ball of fire in the air.

The mascot, Smokey, that they have found
Pumps up the crowd, which makes lots of sound.

When I grow up that is where I will be
On the road to the University of Tennessee!

Molly McKenzie, Grade 5
Evangelical Christian School Ridgelake Campus, TN

Military Child

I am a military child born in Germany
who wonders about the soldiers.
I wonder what happens outside the military base.
I hear the National Anthem outside my house.
I see jets flying over my head.
I want to know what goes on in Iraq.
I am a military child born in Germany
who wonders about the soldiers.

I pretend I am one of the soldiers fighting at war.
I feel glad when my dad comes back from war.
I touch hearts of many soldiers.
I worry about the soldiers at war.
I cry when we move from our house.
I am a military child born in Germany
who wonders about the soldiers.

Xavier Wells, Grade 5
Mcbride Elementary School, KY

Dance

Dance is so cool because you learn and have fun. You can even learn jumps and leaps to the sun.

Jazz, Tap and Ballet are types you can choose. Each one has a different type of shoe.

I like Jazz
It teaches you splits, jumps, and kicks too.

I like Tap
Because I love to hear rhythm of the (tap clap).

Ballet is the most graceful one of all
It teaches you balance and how to stand up tall.

I could never choose just one because all dance is just so FUN!

Anna Katherine Hendricks, Grade 4
Stantonsburg Elementary School, NC

Old Pencil

Hey!
Come get me!
You left me here in 4th grade!
I've been chewed up, stepped on, played with, pulled on,
And I really need a band-aid!
I am sitting on the floor right now,
Looking halfheartedly at the ceiling.
Then back down at the broken pieces of lead,
Which don't look very appealing.
I hope that you come get me quick!
It is a choice that you can pick!
But please, please! Choose right now!
Before I get stepped on.
Owwwwwww!

Daniel Andrussier, Grade 5
Hunter GT Magnet Elementary School, NC

My Brother

I am a loving and caring brother
I wonder when I will next see my brother
I hear my brother laughing
I see my brother smiling I want to see my brother
I am a loving and caring brother

I pretend my brother is always there
I feel my brother's loving hands
I touch my brother's scar
I worry about my brother
I cry when I think of my brother
I am a loving and caring brother

I understand my brother can't see me
I say it's going to be okay
I dream to see my brother soon
I try to see my brother
I hope he comes soon
I am a loving and caring brother

I am...

Brian Sanders, Grade 6
Bernheim Middle School, KY

Fall

Fall is when insects crawl,
And when birds call,
The chill in the air
Makes my grandpa want to sit in his armchair.

The leaves are colorful and crackle under your feet.
The street is orange, red, and brown and so is the town.
The nights are shorter and cooler,
And the stars twinkle and glitter.

The morning dew forms on the grass
And it is as clear as glass.
If you walk in the dew,
And wet your shoe,
People will take pity on you.

Fall is the season for the fair,
But parking is a nightmare!
Fall is a very interesting season,
But that is all
I have to say for fall.

Jackson Cowsert, Grade 5
Cowsert Christian Academy, NC

All the Things in My Drawer

I walked into my room and sat down by my desk,
opened my drawer and looked inside. This is what I saw.
Gray white and funky pencils,
Old math homework from last year,
Game chargers for psp,
My hot wheel cars,
Red, green, blue bookmarks,
Black scissors with skulls on them,
Three in one oil, Axe spray can,
Black and white phone case,
AC/DC pencils,
Blue compass with golden lock on it,
Brain age game,
Red paper airplane,
Money book mark,
Las Vegas playing cards,
Harley Davidson wallet with sliver chain,
Presidents bookmark,
I keep all the things in there because they are
stuff that my dad has gotten me sometimes when he travels to work.
I keep them all there so I know where they are.

Dylan Day, Grade 6
Baylor School, TN

My Bedroom

I walk into my room messy like a jungle
I examine my organized books
Full of information only Einstein knows
My stereo blaring no silence can stay
But it can find its way
Calmness takeover stillness
Waiting for a moment to dash
I smell the aroma of hamburgers
That my mom has prepared
But can't tell what the nasty smell is
My mouth dry as a desert I refresh with water
I snatch my body spray
Yuck!! Some gets into my mouth
Finally, I lay on my soft, silk, and soothing pillow
Thinking of this dramatic day
I relax and reach for my scrapbook
And add on memories of best friends
Friends = good times to end this day
I erase all of the secrets, stories, and rumors
I settle into my sacred room
HAPPINESS

Kelsey Trunnell, Grade 6
College View Middle School, KY

Winter

Cool fog of the frosty night
In the moonlit glow with white color
Snowflakes dance softly in the winter wind,
And Santa's sleigh happily gliding with the clouds.

Hope Wagner, Grade 5
Walton-Verona Middle School, KY

Sports

Sports, sports so fun,
they will bring you happiness until you're done.
They will tire you out,
but I assure you won't pout.

Jacob Epperson, Grade 4
Evangelical Christian School Ridgelake Campus, TN

I Am From

I am from a family who loves to hunt. We own over 70 guns!
I only have 2 so far. . . That's okay because my two sisters have none.

Now. . . about our hunting bows. . . our family owns three.
Millie, my sister, and my mom both have one, and my dad has the third. . .
But my grandfather has over twenty bows. . . now that's a ton!

I am from hunting deer, dove, geese, squirrel, frog, raccoon, turkey, coyote, and groundhog. . .
to always hunting at Fred Kelly's farm of 100 acres.

I am from having times when my dad's missing, but we know he's fishing.
My dad loves to fish when he's not hunting. He has over 20 poles.
I have 5; Millie has 2; Maryn has 1; and my mom has none.

My dad goes crazy over fishing.
My grandfather is the same.
I see where I get my praise for fishing-fame one day!
Who knows. . . I can make a living from fishing for pay!

I am from a mom who never wants to fish
to having two sisters who don't either.
That's okay with me. . .
It means I have more time with my dad
and less time with my annoying little sisters
or from hearing Mom brag about being a better fisher. . . even though she never fishes.

These are the people, places, and things I am from.

Jace Hammons, Grade 5
Burgin Independent School, KY

I Am a Military Brat That Gives My Dad Confidence

I am a military child at Fort Knox, Kentucky
I wonder why we have to watch friends come and go
I hear the weeping of families wishing for their military soldier to come home safely and soon
I see pictures of my dad while he is at war praying for his safety
I want the wars to be over and the world at peace once again
I am a military child at Fort Knox, Kentucky

I pretend the wars are going good so far, but I truly do not know
I feel grateful once my daddy is home and everything is fine
I touch my heart hoping he is O.K.
I worry that we will move once again away from a place I have started to call home
I cry when my daddy has to deploy
I am a military child at Fort Knox, Kentucky

I understand that the soldiers have to deploy and we have to be strong
I say he is my hero that proudly serves our country
I dream that he is safe at home with me and my family
I try to be strong and supportive to my family and others
I hope for all to go well at war
I am a military child at Fort Knox, Kentucky

Lacey Bowen, Grade 5
Walker Intermediate School, KY

Sun

The sun is very torrid, a marvelous thing
Its rays beating down on us giving us a tan
Giving sugar to leaves and light in the sky
Burning our skins, until it turns red

In the summer when school's out we want to play
The sun won't let us, because it's so scorching
On a very blazing day it will give you a stroke
The worms get shriveled up on the sidewalk

The sun shines down in the hot afternoon
Creating a mirage of water tricking us
We try to hide in the shade "oh its so hot"
"I wish it would rain"

The sun is immense, we see it miles away
We could enjoy it, on a freezing day
It makes the moon shine so bright
All the water evaporates when the sun shows itself

Diego Marchena, Grade 5
Love Memorial Elementary School, NC

I Am From

If you guessed right, I am from Kentucky.
I live in Burgin...
where I feel special with my two hair bows.

I am from loving to talk to my friends
to speaking with my teachers,
Mrs. Mays and Mrs. Henson.

I am from loving to play video games
inside with my family,
going outside to play with my dog, Taz,
texting on my cellphone,
and jamming to music on my iPod.

I am from helping my mom, Ina, clean the house.
My mom and I also like to enjoy games on my D.S. Light...
Mario, Cooking Mama, and Nintendo Dogs.

These are the people and things about me that I enjoy.

Marie Rankin, Grade 5
Burgin Independent School, KY

My Dog Bear

Bear runs like a lion when I call his name
Always digging holes in the sand
With surprise he barks at the pine cones that fall on his house
The metal gate invites me into his pen
Playfully I go into his house like an invited guest
The spider webs hang thick like silky string from the roof
With speed Bear creates a dusty storm that sticks to my mouth
Bear is the best dog.

Nicholas Lewis, Grade 4
Bailey Elementary School, NC

Daddy Love — Cancer

You raised me as your own
And now I'm almost grown
I sat and watched you sleep
And now you hold me as I weep

Gracie is looking so much like you now
The words fumble out as I mumble wow
I wear your shirt to bed every night
Hoping to myself the bed bugs don't bite

Even though you're sick and weary
Please don't be bleak and dreary
Hospital beds, IVs, and the bright light
I know it's a tough battle but fight daddy fight

I prepare myself for what's to come
When I'm nervous I sing or hum
If God takes you away from me
I guess then you will finally be free

Jessica Renee Downs, Grade 6
Bernheim Middle School, KY

Friends

Friends are people who you hang out with
You talk to all the time
Sometimes you talk to them a little bit
Most of them are very kind

They make you feel better when you're down
They always tell you the truth
They will try to save you if you drown
They are great like Babe Ruth

Most of them are helpful
They always have your back
I am very grateful
To have friends like that

Through good times and bad times
And the thick and the thin
True friends would put their lives on the line
And stick by you until the end

Isaiah Norman, Grade 6
Snowden School, TN

Mackenzie

Mackenzie is my only cousin but still
The best.
She is only two but still fun.
She lives in Texas but I still love her.
I miss her all the time but I know I'll see her again.
I've only seen her twice in my life.
When she wakes up from her nap she says my name.
I can't wait to see her again more than anything.

Rebekah Killian, Grade 5
Providence Academy, TN

My Friends

My friends are awesome.
They are funny, cool, amazing, nice and smart.
They are the best.
My friends always help me get through things.
They tell me secrets, that I won't tell.
My friends make me laugh and smile.
They always text or call me, and my battery runs dead.
They are very cool, fun, funny, and always awesome.
I hope I never forget them.
I have the best friends ever!

Kayla Dominguez, Grade 5
Paint Lick Elementary School, KY

My Best Friend

My best friend is the sweetest, nicest, person I know.
Her name is Emily.
I couldn't have chosen a better person to be my best friend.
I think she gives really good advice.
She is never mean.
She isn't pushy.
She doesn't like to boss people around.
I think she is really hyper.
She really likes to read.
I think Emily is really, really awesome!

Kaleigh Mosier, Grade 5
Paint Lick Elementary School, KY

Snow

Snow is crystal clear.
Seeing the snow makes me squeal.
How I love hot cocoa in the winter.
Warm and toasty in the house.
Eek! I think I hear a mouse.
Scratching all around the walls.
When I hear Santa coming,
On Christmas Eve night,
From the cookies, he takes a bite,
Merry Christmas to all and to all a good night.

Cameryn Dowdy, Grade 4
Moyock Elementary School, NC

Christmas

I see children playing in the snow.
Carolers going from house to house that I know.
I smell soft, warm cookies being made.
Delicious pumpkin pie being eaten.
I hear bells being rung outside the churches.
The pitter patter of little feet running to the Christmas tree.
I taste snow falling on my tongue as cold as ice.
Hot chocolate burning in my mouth like hot coals burning in a fire.
I feel the presents that Santa left behind,
And the scruffy Christmas tree as I pass by.

Trinity Owens, Grade 5
Providence Academy, TN

Mrs. Fields

M y favorite teacher
R eading teachers are the best
S pecial in her own way

F avorite color is blue
I s not a morning person so don't mess with her in the morning
E arns her pay check
L ikes to teach social studies
D oesn't like strong coffee
S mart

Hannah Gregory, Grade 5
Carver Elementary School, NC

Scarecrow

S cary as he can be
C rows are frightened
A ny animal that sees him will run away
R abbits will not steal carrots
E agles will fly away
C rows will not steal corn
B asically animals will never come back
O ats will not be taken
W ell that is good, but don't you think a scarecrow
can get lonely?

Kiersten Daniel, Grade 4
Centennial Elementary School, TN

Winter

When the snow is falling from the heavens
And children laugh and play in the snow
Tasting the soft white flakes
There is only one thing that means —
It's winter!
When the sweet hot chocolate is poured
And the crackle and smell of fire fills the air
When there is a snow war outside
The kids throwing snowballs like madmen —
I just can't believe it's winter!

Seth Norton, Grade 5
Providence Academy, TN

When I Look in Your Eyes

High Mountains and deep blue skies
None of that is better than when I look in your eyes.
Watching the sunset or the sunrise
None of that is better than when I look in your eyes.
Even if I won a grand prize
I'd trade it all in just to look in your eyes
There is nothing I wouldn't do
Just to be able to look at you.
I've been love struck so many times
But none of that is better than when I look in your eyes.

Jemario Dye, Grade 6
Snowden School, TN

My Older Sister

Mom was cleaning,
I was beaming,
Mom said we were going to have a guest,
And that I was a pest,
I wondered who was coming,
And why Dad was humming

When she walked through the door I was nervous,
I've never had an older sister before, how could she be my sister?

As Mom explained everything to me I felt like my life was a lie,
I thought I was going to die,
Now I wasn't the older sister anymore,
I wanted to walk out the door

After supper, we played with my tea set,
I wondered how awkward it was going to get,
The *Clang!* of our cups, the answer to all of my questions

She is now a friendly face,
And now I don't think she's from space,
We're now like two peas in a pod,
If I see her, I give her a nod

I love my sister, yes, it's true,
And I know she loves me too

Rebecca Wells, Grade 6
Bernheim Middle School, KY

Black

Black is the horrid
smell in your bathroom.
Black is used in
a burning fire.

Black is the burnt
burger under your buns.
Black is a dark
gloomy abyss.

Black is a dark
color.
Black is a color
you can see.

Black can be good.
Black can be bad.
Black can be different emotions
like bad, sad or even mad.

Black can be found at least everywhere.
Black is a rebalance
to people's souls.
Black is even a person like me and how I feel.

Michael Ayers, Grade 6
Bernheim Middle School, KY

Oh! December

Oh! December! December!
How I love December!

In this time of year there are times I hold so dear.

The first one that comes to mind
is my birthday time.
That would be December 18th.

We celebrate with presents and cake
that my mother takes time to bake.

But the real reason I love December
is not my birthday presents and cake,
But the birth of my Savior,
Who died for my sake.

That is the real reason I love December!

Gracie Ward, Grade 4
Evangelical Christian School Ridgelake Campus, TN

Sports

Playing games and winning games are all the same to me,
I practice that shot, I shoot that shot, I score that goal,
Man! I might even get to play in the Super Bowl!
I swim fast, I catch that pass, I'm always in a hurry,
With all the athletic ability, we're going to win, surely!
I dribble that ball, and then rush to get a Gatorade,
I know that with all the work I can't afford to fade,
I hit the ball,
I'm running bases all day,
I scissor kick the soccer ball,
I bike at least 11 miles,
I make a pass and kick a punt,
Playing games and winning games are all the same to me,
I practice that shot, I shoot that shot, and even score a goal,
Sports are my life and always so much fun,
If I keep on working very hard,
I'm bound to become number one!

Grey Tucker, Grade 5
JJ Jones Intermediate School, NC

Horses

Two horses, standing in the snow,
their breath a mist in the cold.

It is quiet as a mouse, perfect as a sunset.
The two animals are strong and peaceful.

They huddle together, begging each other for warmth.
They are wild like party animals.

The horses' tails swish, startling flies.
They canter away, leaving the snow quiet.

Jenna Rochelson, Grade 4
Nature's Way Montessori School, TN

Being Sick

There once was a girl with the chickenpox,
Who wore her polka-dotted, crazy socks;
The disease made her sick,
Kidney stones, not her pick.
She lied, "Being sick, to me, it ROCKS!"

Jordan Mader, Grade 5
Mineral Wells Elementary School, WV

Billy Willy

There once was a mare named Lilly,
Who had a young colt named Billy;
Little Billy had a fright
In the middle of the night,
When he met his twin brother named Willy!

Adriana DuVall, Grade 5
Mineral Wells Elementary School, WV

Beaches

I
Love to walk
Along the beaches
At night time
Because you can see the sunset

Jennifer Vinton, Grade 5
Walton-Verona Middle School, KY

The Horse

There once was a horse from Maine,
Who spoke to his master Cain;
The master was cruel,
And threw all his tools,
While the horse galloped off to Spain.

Megan Melrose, Grade 5
Mineral Wells Elementary School, WV

My New Car

Car
Smoothly glistening
Driving very fast
I watch it for
Excitement

Robert Susewell, Grade 4
E O Young Elementary School, NC

The Horse from Peru

There once was a horse from Peru,
Who spoke to his master named Lou;
His master was well-pleased,
As he fell to his knees,
While his horse galloped off with no shoe!

Jessica Turner, Grade 5
Mineral Wells Elementary School, WV

The Creek Adventure

My dog loves our walks to the creek.
She brightens up when she sees the leash.
She runs as fast as a speeding bullet
To the big red stop sign on the corner.
When we get back down to the creek, she frolics around while I sniff the sweet breeze.
You'd think she would be freezing in the cool mountain stream,
But instead, she pounces on the water like a fox after its prey.
I hear the birds chirping and singing
Until my excited dog comes near.
Splish! Splash! She disturbs the peaceful creek.
She swims around like a playful otter.
The walk seems to take forever,
But I like the sight of the trees and the smell of the breeze.
We stroll over the long bridge.
We hear the cows mooing just beyond the fence.
When it's time to go home,
My dog is pooped.
But after all, it was an awesome walk!

Baxter Wells, Grade 5
Providence Academy, TN

City Walk

I'm ready for my walk through the city
The buildings tower, oh so high
An awesome smell jumps into my nose
The pushcart man yells "Hot dogs for sale!"
My money leaps into the man's hands
My teeth are angry wolves ripping into the hot dog
The hot dog is as delicious as a feast
Cars drive by at top speed and a Mustang shows off its colors
Car exhaust sweeps over me and makes me cough loudly
I step into a store to get a drink
Coca-Cola dive bombs my tongue
I step outside of the store
Closing my eyes, I let the sounds soak into me like water into a super absorbent sponge
Cars roar like lions, and people chatter like chipmunks
I free myself from the cities clutch and leave the middle of the city
Humming like a bee, I go to the edge of the city to find my house
My dog is a long lost friend hugging me
I smile, I feel calm and content

Jared Duncan, Grade 5
Bailey Elementary School, NC

The Doctor's Office

Children waiting with impatience and curiosity
Tears of babies dripping down their faces, frightened and confused
Children coughing and complaining hoping to feel better
The aroma of medicine seeping into my nose
The sweet fresh air among the office
I watch as the doctor puts a spoon full of medicine in my mouth EEEWWW!
I open my lollipop and thrust it into my mouth YUM!
I clutch my mother's hand waiting for my shot
My legs shaking like an earthquake
Now I'm on my way and the door swept me away to go home

Skylar Lanham, Grade 6
College View Middle School, KY

I Am an Awesome Military Brat

I am an awesome military brat.
I wonder what my dad does at work.
I hear gunshots and booming sounds.
I see friends leave.
I want my dad never to deploy.
I am an awesome military brat.

I pretend I am in Iraq with my dad.
I feel happy when my dad's deployment is over.
I touch my heart when I say the Pledge.
I worry if he will get hurt.
I cry when he leaves.
I am an awesome military brat.

I understand what he does.
I say he will be all right.
I dream about him.
I try to hold my tears at school.
I hope the war will end soon.
I am an awesome military brat.

Taylor Veen, Grade 5
Walker Intermediate School, KY

I Am a Military Son

I am protective of my brothers and sisters and I love animals.
I wonder if I will join the military like my dad.
I hear my dad saying that he is going to deploy.
I see different uniforms all the time.
I want to help my dad.
I am protective of my brothers and sisters and I love animals.

I pretend that I am in the military.
I feel sad when I see my dad leave.
I touch my dog when I hear my dad on the phone.
I worry my dad will get shot.
I cry when my dad leaves.
I am protective of my brothers and sisters and I love animals.

I understand my dad has to leave.
I say I will get my dad to stay home nights more.
I dream I am in the Army.
I try to get my dad to stay home.
I hope to have my dad stay home.
I am protective of my brothers and sisters and I love animals.

Steven Hawes, Grade 5
Walker Intermediate School, KY

I Am...

I am happy
I wonder if my parents are moving to New York
I hear teachers yelling
I see students get in trouble
I want to be smart
I am happy

I pretend to be bored
I feel happy
I touch my food
I worry when I don't go to school
I cried when my grandmother died
I am sad

I understand what they say
I say I am smart
I dream to be
I try hard to be smart
I hope to be smart
I am happy

Ryan Torres, Grade 5
Tates Creek Elementary School, KY

I Am

I am loyal and funny.
I wonder if I am a good friend.
I hear people talking about me behind my back.
I see my friendship between you and I.
I want us to be friends forever.
I am loyal and funny.

I pretend that I am mad at you when I'm not.
I feel our string of friendship to make sure it's still there.
I touch you to make sure you will stand behind me if I fall.
I worry that when we fight we may never get over it.
I cry when I think of us never being friends.
I am loyal and funny.

I understand you will always be there for me.
I say you're always gonna be my best friend no matter what.
I dream that me and you will fight and always get over it.
I try to get through the day when you're not there.
I hope me and you will always stay best friends.
I am loyal and funny.

Haley Hodge, Grade 6
Bernheim Middle School, KY

Hope

Hope is what keeps us strong,
Hope helps us find where we belong,
Hope is what shines through the clouds on our darkest days,
Hope is what gleams in our eyes in every gaze,
Hope gives us life, so cheer and chant along

Jacqueline Ashford-Lavy, Grade 5
Hunter GT Magnet Elementary School, NC

Young Boy Named Chris

There once was a young boy named Chris,
Every time he would shoot the ball, he would miss,
The kids passed him the ball,
So hard he would fall!
If he missed the crowd would say, "Boo! Hiss!"

Chris McNeil, Grade 5
Walton-Verona Middle School, KY

I Am

I am creative and miraculous
I wonder what I will be when I am older
I hear warm bread crackling and rising
I see cupcakes and beautiful clothing
I want to design that beautiful clothing and those cupcakes
I am creative and miraculous
I pretend to be Coco Chanel
I feel beautiful sketches
I touch that clothing that used to be beautiful sketches
I worry about what I will be when I am older
I cry when I get hurt
But, I am creative and miraculous

I understand beauty
I say good and bad
I dream about traveling the world
China, Africa even South America
I try to be myself
I hope to be unstoppably creative
Because I am creative and miraculous
That's who I am

Juliana Manson, Grade 5
Duke Middle School, NC

Pain and Love

Your brother or sister has an accident and they didn't die.
Your mother or your father wanted to cry.
You love them as much as you did before,
Even though you feel a little sore.
But you realize they are not the same,
And you feel very ashamed.
Your heart is broken.
You wish the words were spoken.
What do you do
Is up to you!
Love and pain is the same.
Just remember to take the claim.

Jaspreet Bhutani, Grade 5
Duke Middle School, NC

The Fourth of July

The fireworks are banging like guns.
The kids are happily laughing like it's Christmas time.
I can feel the warmth from the fire.
The sparklers are gently tapping me.

I smell the cookies in the oven.
I can smell the smoke of the fireworks.
I like the warm soft cookies.
I like the moist crisp chicken.

The fireworks are flashing.
I see Americans celebrating our independence.
The Fourth of July.

Dylan Cassedy, Grade 5
Providence Academy, TN

Monkeys

I like monkeys, because they're cute
I like monkeys, and maybe you do too!

I like monkeys, on my shirt
I like monkeys, shaped like a dessert.

I like monkeys, on my backpack
I like monkeys, that are named Jack.

I like monkeys, on my earrings
I like monkeys, that bling bling.

I like monkeys, that are on my favorite purse
I like monkeys, dressed like a nurse.

I like monkeys, everywhere I go
I like monkeys, and now you know!

Sharidon Sinks, Grade 4
Centennial Elementary School, TN

About Me

I am from Kentucky.
I am just an ordinary girl.
I have 2 BFF's (Eden and Abigail).
They are just out-of-this-world!

I am from playing basketball
for the Burgin Middle School team.
We shoot the ball from way downtown.
We win, and the other teams leave with frowns.
We really make them look like clowns!

I am also from having a golf cart
and riding it all day...
then going into the house
and drawing away.

That's who, what, and where I am from.

Autumn Ransdell, Grade 5
Burgin Independent School, KY

Another World

If there was another world with life, that would be quite a sight
With organisms and flowers, plus heavy rain showers.

With lots of divine dining
And no children whining.

Even if that world was close,
Of this one I would make the most.
Because my mom would worry,
If I left her tomorrow,
She would be filled with sorrow
Oh yes, my mom would worry.

Evan Scully, Grade 4
Moyock Elementary School, NC

My Pet Clown Fish

Orange and white
Very bright
Not very funny
But cute like a bunny
They swim around in their tank
With an old ship that sank
They have a scuba diver
And submarine with a driver

Benjamin Agapos, Grade 4
Evangelical Christian School Ridgelake Campus, TN

SEC Football

SEC football is number one.
That's because it's so much fun.
The rivalry is so intense.
There's nothing like a good defense.
Auburn Tigers and the Crimson Tide,
They're the best rivalry with so much pride.
The Auburn Tigers is my team,
Playing for Auburn is my dream!

Will Nearn, Grade 5
Evangelical Christian School Ridgelake Campus, TN

Chocolate Bar

I remember the day I was new,
My sugar crystals dancing with joy,
But now week one, wait no it's two,
People throw me back like I'm some old chew toy,
Come on people buy me now,
I have chocolate chunks,
Wait I hear footsteps go boom pow,
No, they put me back again, clunk.

Amelia Zane, Grade 5
Hunter GT Magnet Elementary School, NC

Sunshine

Sunshine is like millions of smiles so bright and so warm.
Crawling through the sky, bringing warmth and happiness.
A lot like friendship. Always there for you.
Like a brother, a sister, mom or a dad.
Like Jesus and God always watching over you.
So far and so big, so friendly and warm, magical and bright.
What could be more helpful than yellow sunshine?

Hunter Clark, Grade 5
Walton-Verona Middle School, KY

I Am a Military Child

I am a military child.
I don't like it when I have to leave my friends.
When I say good-bye, I give them something to remember me.
When I get up early in the morning, I am mad and cranky.
When it is my birthday, my step-dad has to work all day.
I feel sad when I have to move away.
I am a military child.

Arianna Else, Grade 5
Walker Intermediate School, KY

Hunting

The buck walked toward me like a super model
His hooves crunched the falling leaves like a bulldozer
Picking up my gun, gripping it so tight my hands ached
My scope was set, my finger on the trigger
Joy flowed through my heart
The buck heard a sound
He was spooked like I am when I hear sounds in the dark
He ran like a racer to the middle of the field
Boom! The sound of the gun echoed through the air
Climbing down I could feel victory
The deer was waiting for me

Chandler Bryant, Grade 4
Bailey Elementary School, NC

At the Beach

Blue oceans quickly rolling to shore
Creatures, fish, and crabs rushing through the sand
Kids screaming like police sirens
Birds chirping happily along the water's edge
The dead salty fish at the beach as my family goes by
Delicious food tempts my taste buds
Saltwater tastes nasty when huge waves pull me under
Soft sand blows in my eye, blinding
Pointed rocks in the water, stab my foot, like a knife
Crabs, crawl creepy
Excited

Geison Sales, Grade 6
College View Middle School, KY

On My Farm

My apple tree as I sit under it.
A red barn that is as red as an apple.
the wood bees driving into the wood.
The birds singing in the trees like a humming bird.
The pine trees with pine scent.
My tractor exhaust from the exhaust pipe.
The water from the well pipe.
The corn right from the stalk.
The barn doors as I open them.
The tractor steering wheel as it starts to turn on me.
Secure and safe sitting on my house's front porch.

Connor Bennett, Grade 6
College View Middle School, KY

Basketball

Basketball is fun.
You get to play and run.
Players both short and tall,
Dribble and pass the ball.

While you're on the court,
You should be a good sport.
The players run as fast as lightning.
Sometimes their faces can be frightening.

Rachel Webb, Grade 5
Evangelical Christian School Ridgelake Campus, TN

The Go-Kart Racer

My name is Chase Overholt
and I am a go-kart driver.
I race every week
and when I am racing my dad says Go! Go! Go!
you are doing good, good, good
Then all of a sudden, I hear a big Boom! Boom! Boom!
The boy behind me is bumping me
and he wrecks me
and I get mad
and then I hit the wall and then I go home.

Chase Overholt, Grade 4
Tazewell-New Tazewell Primary School, TN

Cupcakes

Ting and crack the yokes fall into the bowl
The powder of the mix is drifting through the air as I pour it
Rumbling sound of the mixer is roaring like a lion about to attack
Heating of the oven is like a feisty fireplace
The oven mitt feels like a warm blanket
Cupcakes are baking in the oven calling me to eat them
The timer dinging
Icing dripping onto my fingers
Pink sprinkles and delicious chocolate in my mouth
Out-of-this-world cupcakes!

Mallory Clagg, Grade 4
Bailey Elementary School, NC

Change the World

Any one person can save the earth,
Do their best, show their worth,
Coral reefs are being destroyed,
Too many troops are being deployed,
If you could change the world, what would you do?
Would you pick up trash from the ocean blue?
Would you find a solution,
To help stop pollution?
The world cries out with a sigh,
"Help me or I'll die."

Chris Toy, Grade 5
Duke Middle School, NC

And I Cry

I cry most nights 'cause my
friends died in the war.

I miss them very much
and wish I could see them
just one more time.

I'll always remember
the day they lost their lives
in the war.

Cassie Brock, Grade 4
Tazewell-New Tazewell Primary School, TN

All About Me

I am from having Rocky, my dog, that plays with his toys…
from dawn to dusk.
Rocky will make you blast out with laughter,
and he has a sense of humor.

I'm from always being outside with my friends after school…
until I am made to go inside where it is dark and cool.

I am from going place-to-place with my BFF's together.
We're always having fun times.
With them, things could not be better!

I am from Nana, who forgets things…
to Dad forgetting too!
I am also from having a younger sister who loves to sing…
to Mom, who is so…so funny with jokes that zing!

I am from singing, drawing, and playing with my friends…
to enjoying shopping for clothes with them.

I am from liking to go over to my friends' houses…
to talk, dance, or play…riding bikes and roaming.

These are the people, places, and things I am from.

Sarah Harmon, Grade 5
Burgin Independent School, KY

Where I Am From

Where I am from, I watch tv…ICarly is my fav.
The episode with the voting of a talent show was a rave!

Where I am from, I go door-to-door selling cookies for a cause…
from time-to-time…for the Girl Scouts…which I love!

Where I am from, I pack my bags for five full days…
for the fun of 4-H camp in the summer's sun rays.

Where I am from, I answer questions back-to-back
for the academic team of Burgin Elementary School.

Where I am from, I kick the ball, run, and skip.
Nothing will change my love of being physically fit.

Where I am from, I play a trumpet and a violin…
for the love of music is still alive within.

Where I am from, I love the shine form Herrington Lake
and the small size of my Burgin School being unique.
My hometown and school shall always be the best place to be.

This is where I am from.
It is what makes me…me!

Heather Bowman, Grade 5
Burgin Independent School, KY

Bees

Bees in the day are a fright
But at night
They are yellow pieces of the sun
They keep flowers alive

They are an awesome sight

Bees in the sky
Go really high
Like a bird
But better

Bees can fly

Bees are making honey
While the sky is so sunny
We eat it up
It is so good

Bees make honey

Bees fly away
On a winter day
So they'll be okay
When the snow comes
Bees are wonderful pieces of nature
Hurray!

Chip Raynor, Grade 5
Hunter GT Magnet Elementary School, NC

A Moment of Despair

Here I am standing
Waiting for you now
And when I see you coming
I see a star shine
Then you come and say
I have missed your love
I tell you that I love you
and believe that you were saved
Now that you've told me
To let you go
I tell you that I love you and
I will always cherish this day
On that day you made me smile
I kept it for a while
And believed that you were saved
That made me feel alright
Now I woke up from that dream
Then cried myself back to sleep
Hoping to see you there
So I'd feel your care
And not feel any despair

Carmen Danley, Grade 6
Snowden School, TN

I Am

I am — kind/funny
I wonder — Am I a good sister?
I hear — Yelling and door slamming
I see — Hitting each other
I want — to stop fighting with my brothers
I am — kind/funny

I pretend — That I hate them
I feel — Sad
I touch — The door when I go to slam it

I worry — That it's never going to stop
I cry — When I and my brothers fight
I am — Kind/funny

I understand — That we're siblings
I say — I hate you
I dream — That we'll stop fighting
I try — To get a long with them
I hope — We get along very soon
I am — Kind/funny

Bethany Mann, Grade 6
Bernheim Middle School, KY

The Silence of Death

All Hail Hitler! We heard out our window.
They knocked on our door
We answered
They took us away
"To where?" I asked
"Silence!"
The silence of death
We arrived
The barbed wired fence
The guard houses
The smokestacks
The songbirds on the chimneys
The silence of death
They took my parents
To the smokestacks
That's them rising now
It's the silence of death
My name is Rueven
And this is my story
It is called
The silence of death

Cameron Sanders, Grade 6
East Mooresville Intermediate School, NC

Life

L ife
I s not to be taken
F or granted
E njoy yours while you still have it.

Morrell Pruitte, Grade 6
White Station Middle School, TN

Over the Hills

Over the hills
And deep in the woods
I saw a bird fly just as it should
And landed just in front of me
That is something I'd like to see
Once again and see the bees
Smell the sweet flowers
Find the little bird
Who I'd like to see
Over the hills I go again
To see that bird
Once again over the hills
And deep in the woods

Sayer Kirk, Grade 4
Burlington Day School, NC

Family

Your eyes are brighter
Than the stars, your
Voice is softer than the
Clouds. We were together,
But now we are apart,
But still we are a family,
Just one of us has gone
Apart. We will make new
Friends and meet more people,
But it will never change
The bond that we all
Have because we are...
FAMILY.

Clayton Greer, Grade 5
Providence Academy, TN

The 60s Dance

The 60s are gone
The people who danced
To the music are gone

The people who saw them
Dance groove and saw their high
Hair are gone too

The 60s are gone
and the people who saw them
are gone.

Peace Out

Samantha Anderson, Grade 5
Cool Spring Elementary School, NC

Colorful Pond

Glistening water
filled with color from trees
soon fade away

Zachary Williamson, Grade 4
Carver Elementary School, NC

The Box
I recently received a big box.
Inside was not a fox.

There was neither a cat nor dog,
Not even a slimy, green frog.

There was not a camel,
But it was a mammal.

Inside was a big, fuzzy llama,
From my pet-sending mama.
John Michael Dickinson, Grade 5
Evangelical Christian School Ridgelake Campus, TN

Veterans
Their eyes have seen the sights of war.
They'll never forget when they put their lives on the line.
They are our veterans.
They will always remember every letter sent,
And every note received.
They fought for our freedom
They know the feeling of misery,
The feeling of pride and respect.
They will never forget when they served
They are our veterans
And will always be.
Hunter Lanterman, Grade 6
Saint Pauls Middle School, NC

The Bear Who Gave Me Care
When I was a little boy, I had a bear named Greg.
I played and watched TV with him.
Now, I wonder if he could teach me how to spell words.
I even pretended to
feed him lunch.
Oh, I loved Greg a lot.
I took Greg on my family trips,
so I could read and talk to him.
Today, I still have it
for special memories "of the
bear who gave me care."
Darin Jones, Grade 6
Woodland Presbyterian School, TN

Seashells
Broken or whole everywhere in the sand
Colorful and not so pretty
Some people make them into necklaces
When they finish gathering them
I like to find them in the water and the sand
When I go to the beach
One time I found a crab shell
And made it into a necklace
Have fun!
Katie Croom, Grade 4
Contentnea-Savannah K-8 School, NC

The Beach
Crashing waves rolling on the deserted shore
Seagulls singing in harmony
Suntan lotion on my face
Rough dry sand sifting through my fingers
Salty sea water in my mouth as I swim
Crowds running towards the water
Screaming and yelling having fun
Fresh air in the wind
Seashells as hard as rock
Sweat drops to my lips
Free and happy to live
Aniah Bland, Grade 4
Bailey Elementary School, NC

My Teachers
My teachers are the very best
Even though they give me tests.

It just will not be the same
Without Mrs. Griffin on that day.

But Mr. Worley is so fun
Especially when the tests are done.

One thing I'll have to remember
I will not have them come next September.
Molly Brown, Grade 5
Evangelical Christian School Ridgelake Campus, TN

Thanksgiving
I love I love Thanksgiving
I love Thanksgiving.
I love fall.
I love turkey and dressing.
I love chicken casserole.

I love sweet potatoes,
I love pies.

I love him,
The day really flies.
Colby Parris, Grade 4
Tazewell-New Tazewell Primary School, TN

State Fair
The beautiful rides light up the sky like lightning
So many games that I cannot even count them all
Children screaming louder than thunder
All the vendors tempting me to play their games
Fresh cotton candy as puffy as a cloud
Hot steamy hot dogs are better than ever
Pigs and cows are running faster than race cars
The music drifts throughout the fair
I feel so happy and excited inside
Logan Edwards, Grade 5
Bailey Elementary School, NC

Soccer
Down by one in the last quarter.
Across the field the ball is coming
from one of my teammates.
In my head a voice is saying (score)
Above the bleachers parents are yelling.
Between me is the goal and the other team
with everything I have, I drive the ball
past all the other players
toward the goal
Into the net score!
Behind we were but not anymore!
Against all odds we've tied the game.
Billy Kratz, Grade 6
Bernheim Middle School, KY

The Eye of an Eagle
Past the river
Near the lakes
In the country
Beyond the zoos
Above the sky
Through the clouds
Beside heaven
Over the dreadful nightmare
Against its evil
Within its heart is golden good
Without a doubt there is no evil
For it is the eye of an eagle
Roby Schank, Grade 6
Bernheim Middle School, KY

Life
Life is like a bomb.
When you make a mistake it goes boooom!
You live it so fast.
It all just zooms.
It's a rock because it's so hard.
Like a nightmare you never wake.
So dark that it scares you to death.
But that's just a risk you have to take.
Dream big so you can succeed.
Work hard so you can achieve.
Don't be scared to face your fears.
God will be with you with many cheers.
Eunise Medina Olvera, Grade 5
Love Memorial Elementary School, NC

Winter
W hite snow falling
I nside my bed snoring
N ests no longer on the trees
T rees have no leaves
E very day drinking hot chocolate
R unning in a snowball fight
Brian Lopez, Grade 5
E O Young Elementary School, NC

Kentucky
I went to Kentucky
Oh my, I am so lucky.
We played Smack the Queen
And rolled in the leaves.
I rolled down a hill.
Then we watched the windmill.
We played go fish
Then we ate a dish.
I played with Sugar and Spice (cats)
And my, it was so nice.
We made some cake
And it was fun to bake.
We ate Mac and Cheese
And I was very pleased.
We ate with Ma and Pa
And that was a ball!
Lucille Maye Hubbard-Wright, Grade 4
Sequoyah Elementary School, TN

Drown Me, Bring Me Back
Drown me in the dark,
Bring me back to light.
I don't understand your ways.

They'll be in the dark,
We'll be in the light.
They don't understand our ways.

We'll be in the dark,
They'll be in the light.
We don't understand their ways

You said we'd always be together, forever.
I say you drown me in the dark.
Bring me back to light,
I don't understand!
Alyssia Locklear, Grade 5
Rex-Rennert Elementary School, NC

Night
When the sun sleeps
The moon wakes
The stars fill the sky
That is night

The sky is black
The sun is gone
The twinkle of stars amazes children
This is night

Nothing lasts forever
The moon and stars leave our view
The sun rises the moon falls
The end of night
Dylan Riggs, Grade 6
White Station Middle School, TN

Thanksgiving
T urkey
H appy
A pple pie
N ice
K eeping warm
S weet
G iving thanks
I nspiring
V ery fun
I ncredible
N ot bad
G etting food
Devon Hernandez, Grade 5
Walton-Verona Middle School, KY

Christmas
Jesus was born.
Oh how great it is!
Sweet smelling food.
Christmas candles burning.
Sparkling, sticking snow.
Christmas music playing.
Children laughing, smiling.
Hot cocoa warms your soul.
Turkey, oh so tasty to your tummy.
Shiny, sparkly presents under the tree.
Cold and wonderful snow.
Christmas!
Cayden Davison, Grade 5
Providence Academy, TN

Something
Something, anything
What do I write?
A poem,
A poem, finish it tonight
A baseball, a dog
Maybe a kite
What's my topic?
I must get it right
Wait, wait
Look what I've done
I've finished my homework
The battle is won!
Andrew Taylor, Grade 5
Duke Middle School, NC

Loneliness
A dark cave, silent
Sad, shy, quiet
Biting nails, crying
A white dove in a flock of ducks
A block of wood, numb
Loneliness
Emma Peercy, Grade 6
College View Middle School, KY

Thanksgiving

I'm thankful for
My family's love
Those here on Earth
And up above.
I'm thankful for
A roof over my head
A warm meal
And a comfy bed.
I'm thankful for
My little pups
And for Vanilla Hoodsie cups.
I'm thankful for
Clothes to wear
And my new blue brush
To do my hair.
I'm thankful for
The pizza maker
The ice cream truck
And the donut baker.
I know there's more you would like to hear
But the turkey's done, so I'll see you next year.

Isabella DeMasi, Grade 4
Moyock Elementary School, NC

A Rainy Day

Drip,
Drip,
Drip,
The rain pours down,
storm clouds take over the sky
the ground starts to grumble
The lightning strikes,
and you hear a big boom!
you wonder,
will it be over soon?
The rain stops.
But is has left it's puddles behind
Next thing you know,
children are outside
with orange, yellow, and green raincoats on,
They splash in puddles,
one,
by one.
The day is done
They all go back to sleep
Hopefully this day won't repeat.

Alasia Burkins, Grade 6
McGee's Crossroads Middle School, NC

Thanksgiving

Thanksgiving is a holiday to say thanks.
Thanksgiving is a time to say thank you Pilgrims and Indians.
It's also a great time to fall into a huge pile of leaves.
Thanksgiving is a wonderful time to fall into autumn.

Jillian Gregory, Grade 4
Stantonsburg Elementary School, NC

My Emotions

My emotions are locked inside me
I don't want them to go away
Floating around the room while people watch

I don't want people to see what I feel
Always judging me
They would laugh if they knew

There are so many reasons I keep them locked in my heart
Sometimes I want to let them out, but I can't
Because I'm afraid to.

Samantha Greenwell, Grade 6
White Station Middle School, TN

Aunt Sonja's House

A newborn soft preemie baby like a soft blanket
Family funny pictures hanging all around on the wall
Newborn baby crying its' lungs out
Motorcycles' loud roaring sound entering the gravel, hard driveway
Strawberry mushy marshmallow Rice Krispies
Vanilla warm sugar air freshener in the wall flower
Cookies, chocolate chips are heavenly as they melt in my mouth
Mini marshmallows melting on mounds of chocolate
The cuddly couch crunching me up into it
The pictures as they say a million words while I look at them,
HAPPY AND EXCITED!

Larisa Sapp, Grade 6
College View Middle School, KY

The Cars

The cars are fast and pretty,
The cars are good and colorful,
The cars have doors,
The cars are shiny black,
The cars have wheels,
The cars are big,
The cars have air bags,
The cars have lights,
The cars have motors,
The cars have names.
I like cars.

Jonathan Paul Collins, Grade 4
Tazewell-New Tazewell Primary School, TN

Christmas

C aring for one another
H oping Santa Claus will come tonight
R ipping wrapping paper covering toys
I ce cold apple cider
S inging carols and reading books
T ouching everybody's hearts with wonderful presents
M erry and jolly are everybody's feelings
A sking each other what they want for Christmas
S aying what could get much more better than Christmas

Carianne Massey, Grade 5
Walton-Verona Middle School, KY

Soccer

Soccer is so much fun.
It's sad when it is done.
The coach sends us out to the field.
We are a strong and mighty shield.
The ball got by.
Because of that guy.
He shoots, he scores.
We go indoors.
I am very sad.
Since today we played so bad.

Aidan Smith, Grade 5
Providence Academy, TN

Chinese Funeral Mask

Tears stick to my cheeks —
trapped by my mask,
Grief pulls at my mouth —
hidden by my mask,
Wilting flowers fill my nose —
floating in and around my mask,
Church bells ring in my ear —
echoing loudly inside my mask,
Farewell words escape me —
then disappear behind my mask.

Shelby Skaufel, Grade 6
College View Middle School, KY

My Name

It is nice, cool, fun, and unique
It is the number 500
It likes playing video games,
Football, and basketball
It loves family, sports and friends
It means all-star,
Champion and professional
It learned from Julius and Waffiyah
By getting love from them
It is the name Zaire Edwards

Zaire Edwards, Grade 5
Southeast Elementary School, NC

The Poison Dart Frog

He's a colorful box of crayons
Hopping like a kangaroo
Eagle-like eye sight
Swims like a fish from a bear
Poison deadly enough to kill 10 people
Darting from tree to tree with strong legs
He invites his prey to dinner
Legs built like steel springs
A tongue like super glue
He's the poison dart frog

Mark Sanders, Grade 4
Bailey Elementary School, NC

The Mistreated Lunchbox

Hey, juice is spilling all inside me
Making me sticky and icky
It's getting your other food soggy,
Please clean me up!

Yesterday you forgot me,
Today you threw me down, what's next?
Will you spin me all around?
Will you leave me on the ground?
Please take care of me!

I remember when you first got me,
I was shiny, clean, and tidy.
You never left me out of sight,
Keeping me close in your arm very tight
Please treat me that way again,
For I am the mistreated lunchbox.

Brooke Shearon, Grade 5
Hunter GT Magnet Elementary School, NC

Let Me Go

You tell me you love me
And really,
We're not meant to be
So just let me go
Stop berating me to talk,
Or are you really that low,
You wouldn't let me free
And live life,
How it's meant to be
So I really just want,
You to set me free
Stop holding me back
Let go of the past
Because you hurt me,
Now you want me back
You got your second chance
It's over now

Grace Miano, Grade 6
East Mooresville Intermediate School, NC

Sorry Dad

I have to say
I did eat the last
Candy bar

I know you were
Going to eat it later
But I couldn't help it

Dad I'm super sorry
I feel horrible but I
Couldn't resist the creamy
Milk chocolate

Sydney McGill, Grade 5
Cool Spring Elementary School, NC

The Time I Won the Game

There I was with 30 seconds left
I thought to myself I got the game
If I get this shot it could lead to fame
I cross everyone over and hit a shot
Now my stomach's really in a knot
The other team shoots the ball
The shot is missed hoping there's no call
My friend gets the rebound
I hope that I am found
Oh no he gets trapped at the free-throw line
He passes it to me this shot is mine
I shoot the ball...2-1...yes, I made it
The game has been won
My coach was so proud
And so was the crowd
What a great time
Now it's finally ok
I hope I make it to the NBA.

Cambron Burke, Grade 6
Bernheim Middle School, KY

Charanda

Morgan I am so
sorry that we
ate at Charanda's
without you.

It is fantastic
and awesome when
we go with the
Patterson's, Craven's
and the Kastor's.

I am so sorry
but it is always
unique when we
have Paco, our
favorite waiter.
But we do miss you
when you're not there!

Madison Deal, Grade 5
Cool Spring Elementary School, NC

Swirly Terror

Heart pumping in fear
Screaming kids jumping around
Touching the cold bars
Holding on tightly
Spinning around and around
Stomach rising to my throat
Want to put my feet on the ground
Body shaking in terror
Hearing the cracking
The ride stopped

Karli Pernell, Grade 4
Bailey Elementary School, NC

I Am

I am loving and kind
I wonder when my brother and I will stop fighting
I hear him call me stupid
I see the hate in his eyes
I want this to come to an end
I am a good sister

I pretend I hate him too
I feel guilty when I say something mean
I touch the tears that fall from my eyes
I worry it will be the same when we get older
I cry when we fight
I am a good sister

I understand when my mom yells "QUIT"
I say I hate him too
I dream that one day we will get along
I try to be nice
I hope he will finally say to me that I am a good sister because…
I am a good sister!

Haley Ogle, Grade 6
Bernheim Middle School, KY

I Am From

I am from Kentucky where I love to have fun
talking to my friends, jamming on my iPod,
Shooting a bow-and-arrow, or fishing with Grandpa.

I am from taking care of my pet dogs and guinea pigs,
Harley, Nicko, Hurley, and Junior…
to running after the dogs when they escape from the house
and playing with the guinea pigs
by watching them scurry under the couch.

I am originally from Louisville, Kentucky,
where I lived in the city…
to moving to Harrodsburg
where I play with my friends and enjoy being silly.

I am from doing all of these fun activities
throughout the year,
and they all make my life burst with cheer!

This is who, what, and where I am from.

Rachel Rath, Grade 5
Burgin Independent School, KY

Christmas

A snowy Christmas sight
with stars so bright
on Christmas night.
Gifts under the tree
got to flee
to open the first gift under the Christmas tree.

Peyton Buckler, Grade 5
Walton-Verona Middle School, KY

Baseball Game

Seats in the stands
The bullpen in the back of the stadium
Dirt and grass spread out and cut nicely
Crowds cheering loudly
The ball hits the first baseman's glove
Fresh hotdogs give the stadium a tasty smell
Chalk decorates the field
My hand stings when I catch a foul ball
Wind blowing making the ball move like a wind vane
Fireworks make the night sky look like broad daylight
I am so excited

Dylan Bottoms, Grade 5
Bailey Elementary School, NC

My Dad

My dad is often in pain
Though he had surgery on his back
He just keeps hurting again and again
I love him so I don't want anything to happen to him
He stayed out of work a couple of days
That's why I worry about him so
My dad says that he is OK
I am still cautious though when around him
My dad is forty-one
He is still very young
I love him very, very much

Gabrielle Faith Stallings, Grade 4
Contentnea-Savannah K-8 School, NC

Not Our Feelings

One side of me is depressed, but the other is happy
I see a part full of smiles, but on their insides they are frowning
I cry on the inside when I am depressed but smile on the outside
Whenever I am happy I eat cake
I am depressed, and everything tastes like burnt popcorn and my mouth becomes as dry as a desert
I am sad but laughing to hide my feelings
Everyone knows their own feelings, but nobody knows everybody's
Nobody shows their own feelings all the time
My own mask

Lauren Johnson, Grade 6
College View Middle School, KY

Spiked Lizard

Alone in the desert with a lizard that's
Lonely and he wants to attack but he is a gentle
Lizard like the sand that lays.
He ran slowly in the hot sun,
And his horns are like knives charging.
He's a small beast
Like the gentle but feisty chinchilla.
He says he has to leave.
He walks into the lonely desert.

Zoe Langtimm, Grade 4
Nature's Way Montessori School, TN

The Love of My Mother
The love of my mother
is so nice and warm,
It's knowing you're protected
from cruelness and cold shoulders,
Her eyes looking at you
is like a hug all day long,
To hear her voice calms your soul
Life without her would be miserable
Appreciation she deserves,
knowing you're safe and productive
once she's fragile and old.
Meredith Sims, Grade 6
Snowden School, TN

The Mouse That Ran
Across the floor
Up the wall
Without a friend
Through the door
Out the hole
Beside the bathroom door
Around the bed
With some cheese
Down the wall
Over the shelf
In a shoe.
Marcus McMahan, Grade 6
Bernheim Middle School, KY

Watch Things Go
Watch leaves fall
Big and small
Watch grass grow
Tall but slow
Watch squirrels climb
To go hide
Watch geese fly
Really high
Watch frogs hop
Don't ever stop
Watch things go!
Madison Hedrick, Grade 4
Moyock Elementary School, NC

Waves and Tides
Tides come in, tides come out
There for evermore
The waves wash up upon the shore
Bringing shells and rocks never seen before
Tides rise and tides fall
Waves make wonder in their hall
Crests of white
Crests of blue
At night they are beautiful too
Finn Tollefsen, Grade 6
White Station Middle School, TN

Purple!
Purple is the beautiful sunset at dawn,
That you see driving down the road at night,
Or out your bedroom window, as you slowly close your eyes and fall asleep,
That's what Purple is.

Purple is a juicy grape,
That when you bite into squeezes out
The most wonderful juice,
That's what Purple is.

Purple is the feel of Kayla O'Neils rug,
So soft and fluffy,
That you could lay on all day long,
That's what Purple is.

Purple is lovely lavender,
The ones that make your senses ring,
It is a very special flower,
That's what Purple is.

Purple is royalty that sits upon the throne,
Its majesty, its enchantment,
And protection
That's what purple is.

Kylie Paden, Grade 6
Bernheim Middle School, KY

I Am From
I love to go down to Herrington Lake to swim and hike on the rocks.
I even have a little place hidden under the dock!

My little place is small and dark.
There's one place to enter and one to go out!
I can always see little fishes swimming about.

I love to sit in my room and read...for hours every day.
I also love to draw, tinker on my laptop, or go outside with Archer, my little brother, and play.

I love to hang out with my BFF's. I have three.
Autumn, Abigail, and Summer C.
We all get along because they're just like me.

I love to play outside in the woods beside my house.
There are plants...from trees to poison ivy...
and animals...from a deer to a mouse.

I love to play fetch in my yard with Belle, my Golden Retriever.
I also enjoy watching Alice, my guinea pig, run around on the floor in my house.
We got Alice when she was a tiny baby, but she is now a young lady.

These are the people, places, and things I am from.
Eden Smith, Grade 5
Burgin Independent School, KY

Pegasus

Regal in the sky,
Beautifully she can fly.
Climbing higher,
But she'll never tire.
Got to be a Pegasus.

Wings spread wide,
and nothing to hide.
An amazing creature,
in every feature.
Got to be a Pegasus.

Untouchable by people,
as she flies by the steeple.
She can't be tamed,
and she can't be claimed.
Got to be a Pegasus.

Katherine Segposyan, Grade 6
Blessed Sacrament School, NC

Ode to My Uncle's Girl Parrot

Oh beautiful white feathers,
Topped with a majestic crown
Beak that looks like sunshine,
But oh what a terrible sound!
The first time I heard it,
I dropped to the ground.
Trying to sleep at night,
Oh she gave me such a fright,
In the middle of the night.
My uncle tried to calm her down,
But she still kept making that awful sound!
I didn't get any sleep all night.
When I awoke my eyes were blurry.
I'm so glad we weren't in a hurry
I love my uncle, I like his house
I wish his birds were quiet as a mouse
I can't wait till I go back and visit.

James Tellefsen, Grade 6
Saint Pauls Middle School, NC

WV Mountaineers

M ind-blowing
O n their way to a championship
U ndefeated
N othing but a team
T errific
A wesome
I ncredible
N ational team
E ducated
E ncouraged
R espect
S cholarships

Patrick Taylor, Grade 5
Mineral Wells Elementary School, WV

I Am

I am curious and kind.
I wonder do I love my sister.
I hear our gripping every night.
I see my tears when I talk to her.
I want a better relationship.
I am curious and kind.

I pretend that she loves me too.
I feel the hatred she has against me.
I touch her shoulder to calm down.
I worry will she ever love me.
I cry when the fight is done.
I am curious and kind.

I understand that we have our fights.
I say that I love her less than I should.
I dream we are best friends.
I try to calm her down towards me.
I hope to be the best sister.
I am curious and kind.

Shelby Hurley, Grade 6
Bernheim Middle School, KY

My Backyard

My dark colored cats by the
House are like
Statues
My beautiful dogs stand
By the barn
Lots of birds singing
Beautifully
Loud
Barking in the backyard
Nice fresh cut grass on
The ground
Fresh corn on the cob
Waiting to be grilled
Fresh clean air all around me
The nasty flying bugs go faster than
A cheetah
Soft fur on cats and dogs
Dumb dogs dig daisies
Daily
HAPPY!

Mikaela Poole, Grade 6
College View Middle School, KY

Turkey Shoot

People shooting their guns
Bullets flying like a bird after its prey
Bang, the bullets hit the targets
Kids screaming and laughing
Aiming for the bull's eye
People claiming their prizes

Erica Cawhern, Grade 4
Bailey Elementary School, NC

Ode to Cheerleading

It's a sport no matter what you say,
Anyone can do it.
But remember it's not as easy as it looks,
It takes a lot of hard work.

It seems as hard as a rock,
But when you win it's amazing.
It's not for everyone,
But it's really a lot of fun.

It's a very active sport,
You can learn a lot.
You have to stay healthy,
That's the life of cheerleading!

Sabrina Traylor, Grade 6
Bernheim Middle School, KY

Bird

Bird
On the tree
Beside the branches
Beneath the sky
About to fly
Up in the sky flying
Down on the grass looking for food
Around a house
Behind a snake
Above the snake onto the telephone poles
Below the snake hissing at the bird
Into noon
Until dark at night in its nest

Heather Crigler, Grade 6
Bernheim Middle School, KY

Sky

The sky is blue and birds fly
Where clouds play and airplanes
Silently go to the sky.

It's where you can always be.
On silent wings where the airplanes
Fly up to the pale blue sky.

Clare Carter, Grade 5
Nature's Way Montessori School, TN

Friend

I have a friend that is fun.
He knows how to make you laugh.
He can get in trouble, sometimes.
He tries to be quiet, but it doesn't work.
I like him the way he is…funny.
Crazy and kind, that is my best friend.
I wouldn't trade him for the world.
My friend Isaac Lyons.

Matthew Green, Grade 5
Paint Lick Elementary School, KY

The Things You Should Care About

One of the biggest things you
Should care about is the Almighty
God.
You should also love
Your great family.
You should enjoy
Having fun friends.
You should be happy
To have protective
Pets.
You should be satisfied
With shelter you have.
You should be content
With your health.
But most of all
You should always care about the Almighty God.

Will Collier, Grade 6
Woodland Presbyterian School, TN

Green

Go green to keep the earth clean.
It's the prettiest color I've ever seen.
Green is the color of the grass.
It is also the color of the trees.
It is my favorite color.
It is my brother's too.
You can find this color in nature,
Or walking on an adventure.
Turtles are varieties of green,
And all the colors in between.
You can use blue and yellow to make the color green.
Everywhere you look from the garden to the trees,
You can always see my favorite color green.
Money is green, you know it comes from trees.
There is so much green, it can always be seen.
That is one reason why my favorite color is green.

Brianna Lainhart, Grade 5
Paint Lick Elementary School, KY

My House

Trees swaying outside my window like hula dancers,
Pink and purple polka dots dance across my bedroom walls,
Voices coming from my television as I watch my favorite show,

Noises in the living room as my dog happily plays,
The sweet aroma of chicken, Mother is cooking,
The stench of rubber as I grab a toy from my dog's mouth,

Water as I brush my teeth after dinner,
Crispy bacon as I chew my breakfast,
A soft soothing sea of blankets I call my bed,
The television remote as I flip through the channels,

Relieved as I lay my head on a pillow that is my lullaby.

Jenna Jones, Grade 6
College View Middle School, KY

I'm Not a Number

At these horrid concentration camps that give me no joy
And where they treat me like a toy
I have to remember something
When they try to tell me that I am nothing, that I am a number
I have to remember something
I have to remember that I am a human being
With a name, not a number
And that I have hope of seeing
I have hope of seeing that I have a future
I have a future of living, and having fun
I have a future that hasn't even begun
I know when I look into a mirror
That I am much nearer
To a future with joy
I have a past to remember,
I am not a number

Taylor Kennedy, Grade 6
East Mooresville Intermediate School, NC

Flying

As I buckle in for my flight across the country,
The rumbling engines push me back into my seat.
I take off from the runway and soar through the marshmallowy
Clouds, and suddenly, the sky becomes crystal clear and
Bright and sunny.
I fly over a huge desert that is dusty and has gigantic
Mountains and deep canyons.
As I look down at the country from 30,000 feet, I see big
Squares that make the ground look like a giant checker board.
From the sky, the lakes look like huge puddles on the ground.
The smaller mountains look like anthills and the trees and cars
Look like little ants.
I know I am almost home because I can see the colorful fall
Mountain colors as we prepare to land.
When we touch down and bounce, the plane comes to a halt,
And I am so glad to be home!

Brock Warwick, Grade 4
Sequoyah Elementary School, TN

Dew

The clear, wet, dew of the night
Gently drifts through the air
To the sweet smelling soft grass.

And, as the dew gently drifts to the ground,
The towering, brilliant sun awakens me.

Then, while the dew stops falling,
I walk outside to feel the cool, wet mist
God sends down from the heavens.

After the mist slowly stops falling,
The sun comes out from behind gray, dark clouds
While the roosters wake up and crow — loud and clear!

Dylan Hester, Grade 4
Love Memorial Elementary School, NC

Life

There is a game called life
But life is not a game
Life is what you make it
So don't make it a shame

There is a cereal called life
But life is not a food
So always use good manners
And don't be rude

Life has some good times
And some bad one's too
But if you stay positive
You'll make it through

So don't complain about life
Just try to smile and laugh
And be very very thankful
For the life that you have

JhaBrelle Hall, Grade 6
Brogden Middle School, NC

My Cousin Trenten

When you were born
I thought you had horns
I just sat there and stared
Come to find out, it was just your hair

We took you home
You were not alone
We all sat there
Wondering about your hair

When you were one
You started to run
I ran with you
Across the whole yard too

Now you're six
There's a lot to fix
I love you anyway
Even when you're far away

Dakota Robinson, Grade 6
Bernheim Middle School, KY

Friends

They always come around
when you are feeling down.
They always have your back
when you are feeling sad.
They are always with you
when you have the blues.
You can count on friends
because they count on you.

Noah Wilson, Grade 6
Woodland Presbyterian School, TN

A Love Ballad

You were Romeo,
I was Juliet,
We loved each other dearly
Right when we met.
I found you at a party
When I was feeling sad
But when you smiled at me,
I was very glad
That day that I met you
I knew that you were mine,
I could tell it just by looking
Into your eyes so divine
A year or two later
You asked me to marry you
So I replied with the answer
Of "I do!"
Soon we married each other
Then we were no longer alone
And soon had six kids
Of our very own.

Rachel Mitchell, Grade 6
Bernheim Middle School, KY

War

A patriotic cause, a signature on paper.
Brutal training, shouts in your ear.
A long trip to the field, terror in your heart.
Running along, the sound of explosions.
A figure in your sights.
A twitch of a finger, a spurt of blood.
One life ended, a candle blown out.
Is this right?

The boom of artillery, the crack of rifles,
Screams of pain, sobs of grief.
The sound of war, the sound of battle.
Is this right?

Never ending, never ceasing.
Anger driven, duty bound.
Whey do we fight?
Why do we kill?
Ask someone else,
Though I doubt they'll know.

Callaway Rogers, Grade 6
White Station Middle School, TN

Forest

Forest
Leaves swaying
Trees growing slowly
Most peaceful place
Amazing

Ruby Doscher, Grade 4
St Thomas More Catholic School, NC

Happy Mask

Happy mask
It feels soft and smooth
on my skin,
Smells like flowers in a
meadow,
When I wear it I'm
relaxed and happy,
Sunshine floods my mind
like it's all I can see and feel,
It tastes like candy in my
mouth,
It sounds like soft music in
my head,
This is my
Happy mask

Jaselyn Gallion, Grade 6
College View Middle School, KY

I Am From...

I am from a chocoholic family
I am from the summer sun
I am from the spring rain
I am from the love of God
I am from a challenging house
I am from a hopeful family
I am from a fashionable family
I am from a gift from Heaven above
I am from beautiful nature
I am from a snowy city
I am from a crazy mother
I am from my birth in Chicago
I am from the most exciting family
I am from the relaxing sun
I am from the most crazy family

Aya Eqal, Grade 5
Tates Creek Elementary School, KY

Ode to Football

Football oh football
The screams the
Cheer
How the appoints
Come on the field is waiting to play
More touchdowns then
Ever before
We play with our hearts
All day long
The steps on the bleachers
On the last second on the board
Of the game
While the winning
Team takes the gold
Ode to football

Brian Schmidt, Grade 6
Bernheim Middle School, KY

Paper Airplanes

I like paper airplanes a lot
Here's a few that really ROCK!
Tri-plane, space fighter, and stealth
You can build them all yourself
But whatever you do
Don't use staples or glue
And don't
Make one that falls ker-plop.

Emerson Taylor, Grade 4
Sequoyah Elementary School, TN

Shrinking Every Day

Every day I get shorter
As your ideas grow,
I shrink
I am the pencil you use every day
Slowly dying
Going
Going
Gone...

Nick Berinson, Grade 5
Hunter GT Magnet Elementary School, NC

The World

Eagles that above us soar
As the mighty lion r-o-a-r-s
Trees and seas that keep us be
Without these things, there wouldn't be me.
Also, the world would be mighty poor
Because they surround the earth's core.
I don't know the reason,
But it all comes and goes by season.

Hannah Rahab Timmons, Grade 5
Love Memorial Elementary School, NC

Fall

Leaves are falling
They are very beautiful
Different colors fall
Red and yellow fall right down
And they make a pretty sound
Everywhere you see the leaves
Raked in piles or spread about
Leaves are falling

Harrison Lee, Grade 5
Hunter GT Magnet Elementary School, NC

Taylor

T aylor is my name.
A lways happy
Y awns frequently
L ooking toward an education
O pen hearted
R eally smart.

Taylor Davis, Grade 6
Saint Pauls Middle School, NC

My Desk

Bobble heads of baseball players that are retired are placed
on the wooden dresser in my room.
Ninja turtle action figures are stationed
in the same position for as long as I can remember.
Series of books I have already examined.
All kinds of cards that I have had for years.
Models of motorcycles that are almost all Harley Davidson.
They're covered in dust which would probably clog up their engine.
All kinds of toy cars that I used to play with, but now I never do.
Lego models I built by hand which really killed a lot of time.
Bunches of pictures of, my family, our pets, and me.
Hats still suspended on the hooks from all over the United States.
Baseballs I used to hit with my dad but now I'm too big.
A school box from kindergarten with about fifty crayons.
I never use it because the crayons are about six years old.
A dusty lamp that I never use because my desk is too full of junk.
Inside the desk are old school books, most are my sister's,
math, English, science, social studies.
Inside the school box are pencils I haven't used in forever.
Last are trophies from baseball, basketball, football, soccer, lacrosse, and some medals.
All of these things are important to me because
they each show a bit of my life and a bit of my personality.

Connor McJunkin, Grade 6
Baylor School, TN

Brianne Bell

Brianne
Tall, sweet, random, funny
Relative of Brian, Joanne, and Aislinn Bell
Resident of Cox's Creek, Kentucky
Who reads Twilight, Evermore, Blue Moon, and Shadowland,
Who likes Kentucky, reading, and music,
Who loves my daddy, little sister, and mommy,
Who fears snakes, spiders, and big words,
Who wishes that everyone was peaceful,
I will be a successful student and a good person,
Who admires Eminem, Stephanie Meyer, and James Patterson,
Who needs more songs on her iPod, more space, and a room to herself,
Who aspires to be a writer or an editor,
Bell

Brianne Bell, Grade 6
Bernheim Middle School, KY

Topsail Island

Sun setting over the water like a ball dropping to the floor
The pier gleaming like lightning
Waves crashing on the shore like thunder
Small children laughing like a comedian making jokes
Sea water running up my nose like a race car
Racing sand going through my fingers as water running out of a sink
Beach balls jumping like kangaroos
Seagulls flapping their wings as fans
Dolphins look like black figures surfing through the waves
I feel calm and peaceful

Abigail Turik, Grade 5
Bailey Elementary School, NC

Ode to Johnny

Oh, dear baby brother, you are the best that you can be. You are so overwhelming with cuteness, I can't stop myself from giggling when I look at you. Even though you are so cute, you are so very strong, and along with that strongness, you are very powerful. You love to be held, and you can stop a heart right in its tracks! You have big yawns when you're sleepy, and you absolutely hate tummy time! You always eat a lot, maybe that's why, dear baby Johnny, you are almost always happy. You just adore bath time, and that is why you smell good every second of the day. Oh, dear baby brother, I'm so happy you were born, and that you are you. And I am so happy that I have someone to share my love with, like Y-O-U!

Amiah Weitzel, Grade 5
West Liberty Elementary School, WV

Daddy

Daddy you're the best from the rest and you're almost always dressed in uniform. I love you with all my heart and from the start you're the one who knew me most. I love to sing and dance like you don't you think we're the best of two. Someday I want to be just like you and do the wonderful things you do. When you go on a trip I miss you so much. There is nothing in the world that can separate the Saunders bunch. When you and I go out to lunch I think of what you do very much, I say to myself I am looking at a man so brave with loving care for me and my family, our country that makes me so proud and so happy to have a wonderful father like that.

Paige Saunders, Grade 5
Moyock Elementary School, NC

My Dog, Maggie and Me

Sat beneath a big oak tree. We were enjoying the summer breeze. When the wind began, blowing the leaves. We ran home and went to bed. But then I hit my head at the door. Then as soon as my mom came outside she said, What did you break this time and I said I did not break anything I just fell down.

Savannah Greenwell, Grade 6
Bernheim Middle School, KY

Ode to Happy

Oh Happy, I love to play with you when you're lonely. I love the way your fur goes left to right.
I love the way you do your tricks for a treat. I think you're the cutest dog when you think you're going for a car ride.
Oh Happy, you're the best cocker spaniel I've ever had, because you're the only one I have ever had.

Mike Harriman, Grade 5
West Liberty Elementary School, WV

Ode to Sara

Sara was a good person
She died on Sunday from brain cancer.
Every day she prayed for her friends and family.
She said she loved her family
And she would look down on them
From the heavens.
She also said I will see
You someday.
Her skin shined brighter than the sun
Her eyes sparkled more than the stars
When she died everyone was sad,
But they knew she was in a better place
She died peacefully
We all knew she died peacefully
God said it was her time to go
And He knew she would be okay
Sara, oh Sara we miss you dearly

Bailey Hobbs, Grade 6
Bernheim Middle School, KY

In the Metal Barn, Beside the Hay, with My Kittens

Two kittens wrestling in the hay like young tiger cubs.
Bright, blazing sunlight shining upon me,
as the day goes by.
Laughing
as my beautiful creatures play.
There is rustling of hay, amongst them.
The natural
Scent of hay rising as I sip my orange juice
Morning dew drops soak upon
the wet grass as I make a bed of it.
Juicy grapes soothing my mouth
as I eat my delightful breakfast.
My delicious orange juice cools as it slowly disappears.
The tips of hay are as prickly as a porcupine back.
The smooth feeling of my kitten's woolen coats.
This is my time to get away from the outside world around me,
when I need to think and relax.

Ashley Morgan, Grade 6
College View Middle School, KY

The Amazing Trip in an Airplane
On a day it did not rain,
I went with a friend in his plane.

We took off and soared very high.
It is amazing to be up in the sky.

My friend taught me how to fly.
I'm telling the truth; it is not a lie.

His camera took a picture of us flying.
Both of us smiled—we were not crying.

When we returned to the ground;
You'll never guess what we found!

The helicopter used by "Action News 5"
They let me sit in it, "Man Alive!"
Jonathan Coplon, Grade 5
Evangelical Christian School Ridgelake Campus, TN

An Ode to Style
Oh, style, how I adore you
You're in every belt and shoe

All your boots, so sleek,
I think some of your sandals look Greek!

With all your ruffles, colors, and dots,
I create an outfit in my thoughts.

You are in every bracelet, necklace, and ring.
I find you in almost everything!

Even your winter coats and hats
Are soft and furry just like my cats!

Every single time I go to the mall
I try on style and have a ball!
Morgan Glass, Grade 5
West Liberty Elementary School, WV

Change
As the world turns, and we ride on the train of our
lives, things tend to change
at each stop, people come and go from us
this we cannot change,
when people leave us, we are in great sorrow, but
new people always fill in the place of the old.
The new people in your life fill you with joy where
you once felt sadness.
As they come to love you and you to love them, all will feel better.
You know that you will be loved and cared for forever.
Let the joy and happiness of those around you
embrace you for the rest of your life.
Dawson Lee, Grade 6
Woodland Presbyterian School, TN

My Favorite Things
I am a ten year-old girl who isn't very tall...
In fact, I'm quite small.

I am from loving ladybugs!
I have three stuffed animal "bugs" that I cuddle with...
to having bed sheets with the title of "The Ladybug Picnic..."
with all kinds of ladybugs and flowers on it.

I am from having an older sister, Clarissa, who is in college...
to having a little sister, Emily, who is six and loves butterflies.
Both are a little funny and crazy at times.

I am from having a couch in front of our TV
to staring at it for hours and hours...
while sometimes glancing outdoors.

I am from a mom who has a king-sized bed
that takes up a lot of space...
to loving the room it has to lay on!

I am from a house with a backyard tree house
that is relaxing and cool.
On a hot day, that is where I will be!

These are the people, places, and things I am from.
Cassie Hunter, Grade 5
Burgin Independent School, KY

Through the Looking Mask
A mask
With shaded dark gray eyes
Speaks to the spirits in the
Sky.
With wretched fangs
So sharp and wild;
He portrays sin with his
Horrid smile.
And softened words come from his mouth —
that stretch for many miles.
When all the wicked ghosts have gone
And time has clocked past noon and dawn
The mask becomes the spirit guide
For people whose dear ones
Have died.
Although so frightening
With a face unlike yours or mine —
The mask spoke so gently;
The mask was kind.
So he left all evil spirits behind
And called dead loved ones to
Our minds.
But what else do I find?
To certain people,
The African Mask is blind.
Tori Garmon, Grade 6
College View Middle School, KY

The Tale of Captain Drake

In the 1570's
In the land of Spain
There was a man
Who caused much pain.

His name was
Captain F. Drake;
He was as wily
And cunning as a snake.

He was a pirate
To all of Spain
But a hero
On the English Main.

To the Spaniards
He was cruel and mean
But in England
He was knighted
By the queen.

Although he left a trail
Of destruction in his wake
He will be remembered
As Sir Francis Drake.

John Haynes, Grade 6
White Station Middle School, TN

A Cookie's Prayer

Please eat me, little Tommy
Please swallow me, I plea
I'm stuck on a boring old plate
Why don't you come see me?

I'm golden brown and yummy
With little chocolate gems
I'm great with a glass of milk
Please dip me from my head.

I know you're a big boy Tommy
But please think I'm sweet
I know you're a big eight year old
But you really need a treat.

Wait, what's that
Who's coming down the stairs?
By golly, it's Tommy
I bet he does care!

Look Tommy's picking me up
He's dipping me in milk
I'm now in his mouth
I'm gone in one big…
Gulp!

Sydney Horwitz, Grade 5
Hunter GT Magnet Elementary School, NC

My Pony

I used to have a Shetland Pony.
I always called him Little Tony.

We played and played together.
No matter what the weather.

Little Tony could run and run
so fast. We thought those days
would always last.

But I grew up and Little Tony
grew old, and now those
memories have turned to gold.

Madison Spencer, Grade 4
Centennial Elementary School, TN

Autumn Leaves

A lways beautiful
U niversal beauty
T aking your breath away
U nbelievable
M ajestic
N ever ending leaf piles

L eaves everywhere
E cstatic
A mazing
V ast trees
E lectrifying
S uperb

Brent Robinson, Grade 6
Woodland Presbyterian School, TN

Football

W ild and wonderful
E xcellent touchdowns
S uper in every way
T otally awesome

V aluable trophies
I nterceptions are great for them
R ough and tough
G reat players
I mmaculate jerseys
N ever bad sportsmanship
I magine always winning
A nticipate

Domonic Shamblin, Grade 5
Mineral Wells Elementary School, WV

The Lonely Tree

Lonely little tree
In middle of desert
Looks so lonesome

Nicholas Abbott, Grade 4
Carver Elementary School, NC

Critters

Butterflies
hovering
Dragonflies
buzzing

Beavers
constructing
Opossums
playing dead

Crocodiles
chomping
Tigers
roaring

Turtles
floating
Frogs
hopping

All sorts of critters doing their stuff.

Jack Martinez, Grade 5
Hunter GT Magnet Elementary School, NC

Love vs Hate

I don't believe in love
I don't believe in hate
I don't love hate
Or hate love
I'm not afraid to die
I just don't want it to hurt
Hate and love are just words
That hide true emotions,
That hide lies beneath welcoming smiles
I'm not crazy
I'm just speaking the truth
That everyone's afraid to hear
And can't handle
Love is a monster
It hides behind it's believers
Hate is a mime
It hides behind silence
I've gone through the tears and lies
I'm done with the gossip, hugs and fights
It's all just a war
Between love and hate

Ari Brooks, Grade 6
McGee's Crossroads Middle School, NC

Friends Together

You are my buddy, a cupcake of life.
We are together, but sometimes with strife.
You're like a kitten, and I'm like the cat,
We are together, and that is that.

Natalie Young, Grade 4
Nature's Way Montessori School, TN

I Am an Army Child

I am an Army child.
I wonder what my dad thinks when he is gone.
I hear tanks all day long.
I see jets shooting along the sky.
I want every rough day to fly by.
I am an Army child.

I understand they are trying to help.
I say that I have to help the team.
I dream that there could just be world peace.
I try to be respectful of them and always think true.
I hope my brother will too.
I am an Army child.

I pretend like I am training when I go to the field.
I feel so good when I hear soldiers come home on the radio.
I touch my heart when they come home.
I worry about my mom when he is gone.
I cry when she cries.
I am an Army child.

Armani Bostic, Grade 5
Walker Intermediate School, KY

Christmas

The ground is white with snow.
The presents are under the tree.
The warm cookies come out of the oven.
The warm hot chocolate is heavenly.
The fireplace is crackling.
The sound of Christmas carols fills the air.
The cool taste of peppermint is pleasant.
The warm sweetness of apple cider is great
The snow on my face feels cold.
The prickly needles of the Christmas tree tickle my fingers. . . .
Ah, Christmas !

Jerica Fore, Grade 5
Providence Academy, TN

My Life as a Boy

I am from Kentucky, a warrior of the wildcats.
My home is peaceful. . .
with my older sister, Sierra, and my mom and dad, too.
I am just a boy who plays soccer and lives in Burgin, Kentucky.

I am from always thinking of soccer and how I always rule.
I play defense, a special part of the game.
I defend the best I can.
I'll keep winning with my team, Heat.
We'll win. . .no matter what.

I am from eating tacos to rice.
I eat 'til I'm too full.
Then I sit and relax away. . .
until I'm better at the end of the day

Tanner McGinnis, Grade 5
Burgin Independent School, KY

Military Brat

I am a military brat and I was born in Texas.
I wonder what it is like at war.
I hear the guns shooting at night.
I see my dad about to leave for his plane at the airport.
I want my dad to return as fast as he can.
I am a military brat.

I pretend to be in the army fighting the other armies.
I feel happy when my dad comes home safe.
I touch my heart and I am proud to be an American.
I worry I will never see my friends again.
I cry when my dad leaves.
I am a military brat.

I understand we have to move every two or three years.
I believe we have to fight for what is right.
I dream I can help my dad when I am older.
I try to make sure I do the right thing.
I hope I can be fast like my dad.
I am a military brat.

Joseph Rodriguez, Grade 5
Walker Intermediate School, KY

My Family

My family is very strong like me
My family is actually very sweet
My family can be a little strict
My family always acts like this
My family is not always boring

When my family has things to do, they're flying and soaring
My family is actually sometimes crazy
They're even sometimes very lazy
Me trying to think about facts of my family
Makes me laugh because I know I have a great family

Andrea McNeil, Grade 5
Southeast Elementary School, NC

Ode to Christmas

Oh, Christmas, you bring so much fun,
from snowy lawns to little fawns.

I enjoy all the fluffy white snow,
and all the snowballs we throw.

The gifts from your parents, grandparents, and Santa.
You might be very cold, but you are so fun it's hard to notice.

When it's time to put up the tree,
You make it feel so very free.

It's hard to see you leave, but
Hopefully you'll come back next
year, I believe.

Lexi Sparks, Grade 5
West Liberty Elementary School, WV

My Dog Mickey

My dog Mickey —
Black and white, Boston Terrier
His fur is as soft as a fluffy pillow,
He wants to play with everyone he sees,

My dog Mickey —
He thinks I'm his older sister,
His playmate, his companion to comfort in bed,

My dog Mickey —
We're both smart,
Energetic, and sometimes lazy,

My dog Mickey —
I learned to understand
what he had been through,
He keeps me company
And cheers me up,

My dog Mickey —
I love him like I love my family,
He will always be mine!

Katie Alexander, Grade 6
Johnson Traditional Middle School, KY

Carrots

My friends have dared me to eat a carrot.
I told them I'd rather them dare me to cook a parrot.
I took the carrot and thought I'd pass out.
In my mind I would cry and say goodbye.
"I don't want to eat this," I said out loud.
They laughed and called me a scaredy cat.
I told them if they kept making fun of me,
I'd let my brother's rat run free!
They coughed and they scoffed until my face turned bright red
And stood there knowing that they were probably dead.
They ran to their van and my face was tan again.
I never heard from them,
But learned from them to never dare a person again.

Holly Huffman, Grade 4
Evangelical Christian School Ridgelake Campus, TN

Smokey Mountains

Tired people walking down the streets like sleepy bears
The bear standing proud like he is a king
Hearing the rush of the water in the stream
The wildlife living their uneventful day like elders
Fresh funnel cakes from the store shouting "Eat me, eat me"
The stuffy mist high in the sky like heaven
Hoarding the crunchy BBQ from the restaurant
Chewing the bright red candied apple from the store
Retrieving a rock that feels like slobber from a stream
Smelling the pollinated flowers from the garden
This is paradise

Ian Alward, Grade 6
College View Middle School, KY

Frog Mask

A colorful green face camouflaging among the trees
as it glimpses
around in the woods

The bright eyes beam into the
light of the day

His magnificent red mouth
smiling to his pals

A wee nose in the middle of his face

Then the free spirits begin dancing around
in the center of the forest

Frog Mask

Autumn Coomes, Grade 6
College View Middle School, KY

Dreams from the Holocaust

At this very moment,
I sit quietly and content,
For the land that I call Thee,
I am not sure what it looks like,
But I believe there will be mountains where I can hike,
and for now I just sit and wait,
As I watch my parents' fate,
No matter how good I am to the soldiers,
They just laugh at me and pound my shoulders,
I am lonely and very bony,
They do not feed me,
I cry and cry just thinking about my friends,
Now my hair has grown back and is long enough to bend,
So I wait for the land,
My land that I call Thee.

Abigail Rose Pepper, Grade 6
Peppertree Home School Academy, NC

Fifth Grade

Fifth grade is a hard grade.
We work all day and sometimes play.
Math, reading, social studies, science,
We study all day.
We get resources to get a break!

Math is harder in fifth grade.
Reading is faster than ever.
Social studies is most awesome.
Science is a great experiment!

We change from class to class,
With every teacher teaching different subjects,
Some teachers are mean, some teachers are nice,
And some teachers are even new!

Mariana Yanez, Grade 5
Rex-Rennert Elementary School, NC

I Am a Military Brat

I am a military brat
I wonder if I'm ever going to stop moving
I hear the song that brings the flag up and down every day
I see a person wearing an Army uniform everywhere I go
I want my dad to stay home during the summer
I am a military brat

I sometimes pretend that my dolls are soldiers
I feel happy when my dad comes home from work
I touch my heart and I am glad to say the Pledge of Allegiance
I worry that the enemy will come to America
I cry when my dad has to go away for a long time
I am a military brat

I understand the Army has to change plans sometimes
I know God has a plan
I dream the Army will stop sending people to war
I try not to worry so much
I hope we will win the war
I am a military brat

Ciara Olmeda, Grade 5
Walker Intermediate School, KY

Miserable Concentration Camp

The wind was blowing,
The lightning was so bright it hurt to look at it.
The thunder was so loud it hurt your ears to be outside.
The storm was brewing and it was very cold.
The cries of children were as loud as a train whistle,
For they were cries of pain and sorrow.
Why, oh why does this concentration camp
Have to be so miserable?
The Nazis were still making us work
Even through the storm.
The rain stung you like bees stinging you
When you mess with them and they get mad.
Why, oh why does this camp
Have to be so hurtful?
I wish we could just get out of here without
Hitler or the guards seeing us.
But, I know from other people attempting
That there is no use in getting out of
This miserable concentration camp.

Megan Robillard, Grade 6
East Mooresville Intermediate School, NC

Flower Flag

"Rambunctious" red roses,
Big blue buttercups,
And wide, white lilies running all around on the grass
Snacking, having a great time;
But when they're done,
They huddle up close and go to sleep,
Thus creating the US Flag!

Dominic Collins, Grade 5
Mineral Wells Elementary School, WV

I Am a Military Child

I am a military child.
I wonder what my dad does when he goes to war.
I hear sounds of a tank and it makes me scared.
I see the flags waving all around.
I want my dad to come home.
I am a military child.

I am so sad.
I pretend that I am playing soccer with him.
I feel alone without my dad.
I touch his picture when I am sad.
I worry that he is going to die.
I cry when I hear on the news that some Soldiers died.
I am sorry for the families of those Soldiers.
I am a military child.

I understand he has to go.
I say to myself he is all right.
I dream that he will come home.
I try to stop crying when I see his face.
I am glad when my dad returns home safe to me.
I am a military child.

Sarah Ghiglieri, Grade 5
Walker Intermediate School, KY

Ode to Broccoli

Oh Broccoli
Why do you taste so bad
Why can't you be something that everyone enjoys
With your leafy taste
Foul smell
I hate you so much
Especially with cheese
When you're cooked
Your odor is so bad everyone stops to take a breath
Oh why did they create you
You just look like a mini tree
I hate you stupid broccoli
And you hate me!

McKenzie Gunter, Grade 6
Bernheim Middle School, KY

My Girl

There is a girl who makes my heart skip a beat.
When we are apart, I can't wait 'til we meet.

When we are together, it's a real treat.
She's so fun and cute and amazingly sweet.

Her blonde hair and brown eyes go great with her smile,
And she dances or prances once in a while.

But before I go, I should tell you more.
She's not a girl, she's my Labrador.

Sam Reynolds, Grade 5
Providence Academy, TN

Smoking

Smoking can harm your brain,
It can cause very great pain.
If you smoke pails and pails,
It will erase important brain cells.
Doctors are trying to find a cure.
Don't smoke — then you'll be safe for sure.
They will teach you in school,
Actually, smoking is NOT very cool.

Alyssa Nicole Sronce, Grade 5
Love Memorial Elementary School, NC

The World of Sports

The world of sports
Has many twists and turns
Also crashes and burns
But the way it's handled
Decides the outcome
So pick yourself back up
And let it all go
Behind you

Malik Dixon, Grade 4
Contentnea-Savannah K-8 School, NC

Bravery

Hero, Fireman
Strong, withstands weathering
Fierce, facing much treachery
Helpful, puts out fires
Saving lives, Facing fears
Giving their best,
Running into burning buildings,
Firemen

Alli Risley, Grade 6
College View Middle School, KY

Sears Tower

The Sears Tower stands strong,
But is not very long
Maybe was a target in 9/11
But still here in 2007
Tallest building in the United States
It also is a workplace.
In Chicago nice and tall
The Sears Tower has it all.

Kendall Hart, Grade 5
Hunter GT Magnet Elementary School, NC

Who I Am

Who I am,
I like to play around,
Go outside, play with my cousin,
Who I am,
I like to play with Legos and get new toys.
I can be lazy, but not all the time.

Jasmine Parson, Grade 5
Harvest Preparatory Academy, NC

I Am an Army Brat

I am an Army brat who was born at Fort Carson, Colorado.
I wonder if I will ever grow up to serve my country like my father.
I hear the sounds of the bugle play throughout the day.
I see shades of green worn by men and women that serve in the Army.
I want my son to serve in the military if I have one.
I am an Army brat who was born at Fort Carson, Colorado.

I pretend to be a teacher.
I feel happy when my dad comes back from Iraq or TDY.
I touch my heart with my right hand when I do the Pledge of Allegiance to the flag.
I worry about my father when he is gone off to war.
I cry about my dad leaving.
I am an Army brat who was born at Fort Carson, Colorado.

I understand that the soldiers make a sacrifice for their families and our country.
I say he is my hero for the sacrifices he makes.
I dream that he and his soldiers come home safely.
I try to be a leader for my friends who make the wrong choices.
I hope that the wars can end soon and all service members will unite with their loved ones.
I am an Army brat who was born at Fort Carson, Colorado.

Takia Murray, Grade 5
Walker Intermediate School, KY

Military Brat

I am a military brat born in South Carolina.
I wonder when the fighting is going to stop.
I hear the sounds of guns on the range.
I see lots of friends leave and new ones come.
I want daddy to never get deployed again.
I am a military brat born in South Carolina.

I pretend I'm a sniper in the jungle.
I feel happy when Daddy comes home every day.
I touch the hand of a soldier and thank him.
I worry that if Daddy gets deployed he might not come back.
I cry when my friends leave.
I am a military brat born in South Carolina.

I understand that when daddy gets deployed he has to stay because that's his job.
I say America is the greatest place in the world.
I dream of the day when there is no more fighting.
I try to always say the Pledge of Allegiance every day.
I hope that all our soldiers come home safely.
I am a military brat born in South Carolina.

Mark Barfield, Grade 5
Walker Intermediate School, KY

Everyone's Best Friend

Everyone needs a companion,
Someone who will stand by your side and will never let you down.
Dogs are always those types of companions.
They always love you no matter what.
If you treat them badly one day then the next day they still want to be your friend.
With the smile on their face and the wag of their tail they always try to make you happy.

Rachel Hale, Grade 6
Woodland Presbyterian School, TN

The World Is Wonderful

The world is great so
they say. Come with me
and I'll show you today.
Everybody says the world
is nice. Come with me
and I'll show you it
twice. The world is pretty
as it lies, from dawn
to dusk as the day dies.

Cole Ross, Grade 4
Centennial Elementary School, TN

Jumping Beans

Kids at the Jumping Beans
Play the games of flip and flop
They run under the bars and on top
Bouncing in the air flip and flop
Fighting and sliding one on top
Eating and drinking with a flip and flop
Amazing fun till they stop
Kids at the Jumping Beans
Play the games of flip and flop

Tyson Royster, Grade 4
E O Young Elementary School, NC

Halloween

H oods galore
A ngels roaming
L umber Jack
L aneka in a funny dress
O ld scary people
W ood chops every where
E vil stuff going around
E astern culture joins in
N asty things happening

Laneka Littlejohn, Grade 5
E O Young Elementary School, NC

Veterans

V ery sad
E every day
T eamwork
E ncouraging
R etaking pain
A mmunition
N ever lose
S oldier

Zack Folden, Grade 6
Temple Hill Elementary School, KY

White Winter

Running in white snow
drinking warm hot chocolate
on shivering night

Tavius Neal, Grade 5
E O Young Elementary School, NC

My Memory Closet

I open the closet door
and stand just outside
of the three foot by three foot closet.
My hand-me-down dress shirts from my mom's friend's son
hang from cheap plastic hangers just over the hideous green carpet.
I reach behind the wall of shirts
pull out my special leather box and open it up.
Inside the box is a lot of foreign money I got from my mom.
Winter clothes, blankets, hats from all over the United States,
baby clothes, and capes for Halloween are tossed in a corner.
Lay on white metal shelves above twenty DS games.
Two snow globes from Monticello and Disney World wait to be shaken.
The last things bring back good memories,
the eleven soccer trophies
I got from eleven seasons of practices
and tournaments.
This memory closet holds so many memories
for me from my two month old baby clothes
to my eleven year old soccer trophies.
I hope I can look back at these things
and remember the stories behind them.

Tristan Benedict, Grade 6
Baylor School, TN

Paris

The beautiful Eiffel Tower glimmering in the dark like snow,
glimmering as crystals in the evening.
I'd like to be a mime strolling through the streets of Paris they have
secrets locked inside of them like a pirate's treasure chest.
The sound of pretty music playing with beautiful dancers dancing at the
sight of the moon.
Accordions playing in the distance like a king's musician playing for his king.
Sniff, sniff, ah the fine aromas in the air as if I am in a candle shop.
French bread, yum yum, the taste of thick butter melting in my mouth.
Yum soft ice cream running down my throat.
The feel of rubber bike handles as I roam down the streets.
I feel the shivering poles of the Eiffel tower.
Great.

Bre Griffith, Grade 6
College View Middle School, KY

Christmas Eve

I gaze at my stuffed animals in the bed, and in my reflection in my bedroom mirror.
I absorb the familiar scent of my room and the leftovers that are on the table downstairs.
I hear my parents whispering as if they were mice keeping secrets to themselves.

I taste toothpaste, which reminds me of peppermints and candy canes.
I feel my stuffed animal named Fiddle, a little dog, and a friend.

I cannot go to bed like a bear who can't hibernate.

For, tomorrow everyone knows what it is, but I know it much differently:
Jesus' birthday.

Aaron Basham, Grade 5
Providence Academy, TN

Christmas

C aring for others
H appy holidays
R andolph is on the way
I cicles on the trees
S anta is coming
T rees left with no leaves
M erry X-mas to you all
A warm fire is burning
S now on ground and everywhere

Leigh Mathews, Grade 4
Carver Elementary School, NC

Christmas

C hrist
H appiness
R eligious
I mportant
S tar
T insel
M erry
A we
S eason

Reed Allbert, Grade 4
Centennial Elementary School, TN

Christmas

C herish
H ope and joy
R eady for the holiday
I s a time for singing and having fun
S ome time for happy and joy
T he brightest time of year
M erry Christmas
A n exciting time of year
S omething special

Madison Ray, Grade 4
Centennial Elementary School, TN

Courageous

Facing gunfire,
Brave, saving others,
running into burning buildings
helping others
unafraid, doing the unusual
hero, fighting for our country

Shawn Stewart, Grade 6
College View Middle School, KY

A Day at the Beach

Waves crashing
Times of fun and laughs
Playing in the waves
Beautiful colors
Summer memories

Elliana Lynch-Daniels, Grade 4
St Thomas More Catholic School, NC

I Am a Military Child

I am a military child that helps my family in any way possible.
I wonder if my father will rejoin the Army.
I hear the phone ring and hope that we don't have to move again.
I see my mother and father stressed out because of their homework.
I want my mother to not to feel the pain in her arm/hand because of surgery.
I am a military child that helps my family in any way possible.

I pretend to be in charge of many people just like mom.
I feel my dad's heart vibrations when I lay my head on his chest.
I touch my mom's cheek as I say good night and that I love her.
I worry we will have to move again.
I cry when I realize I have done something wrong that will hurt my parents.
I am a military child that helps my family in any way possible.

I understand that my parents will not always be there to say "I love you"
I say no matter what happens I will always be there in your heart forever.
I dream that we will one day have world peace.
I try to not worry so much about the fate of my family.
I hope that my family will always be safe.
I am a military child that helps my family in any way possible.

Holly Wilson, Grade 5
Walker Intermediate School, KY

I Am a Military Brat

I am a military brat helping my family not to worry
I wonder if my dad thinks about us while he's gone
I hear the thoughts of my family wondering if he's okay
I see the look on my mom when she doesn't want to go alone
I want him to see the misery we have while he's gone
I am a military brat helping my family not to worry

I pretend that my dad is here telling me to clean my room
I feel the way anyone else would feel when he comes home but I have greater joy
I touch and smell his clothes and imagine him wearing them
I worry that he might be wounded or hurt maybe even on the inside
I cry when we have to move but I know it's for a good reason
I am a military brat helping my family not to worry

I understand that my dad works for the country and for our freedom
I say to myself: 4 more days to go
I dream about what life would be like if he would never go. Would it be bad or good?
I try to think that he would want me to be brave
I hope that the life we have will grow and be better and better while life still goes on
I am a military brat helping my family not to worry

Lily-Dubh Kimball, Grade 5
Walker Intermediate School, KY

Why We Do!

Why do we stand on the front lines when we don't have to?
Why do we defend our country when we don't need to?
Why do we help others in need when somebody else is already helping?
Why do our soldiers defend us?
The reasons we do this?
We're Americans!

Josh Thornton, Grade 6
Woodland Presbyterian School, TN

The Wanderer

Dark as night a creature lurks
Amongst the nighttime shadow
Merciless, an empty soul
Wanders a red painted meadow
Many enter, none come back
All who do have never entered
Stray too far from the path
You'll be trapped at the center
Of a never-ending nightmare

Molly Horan, Grade 5
Duke Middle School, NC

Beauty Is...

B ig blue
E ntering the stadium
A fter the talk
U nder pressure
T rampling the other team
Y ear 2009-2010

I ntention to win
S core to win

Hunter Bailey, Grade 6
Morton Middle School, KY

Christmas

C arols
H oliday
R eindeer
I cicles
S anta
T oys
M istletoe
A ngels
S now

Alex Bowers, Grade 4
JJ Jones Intermediate School, NC

Anne Frank's Journey

My family and I are hiding
The Nazis are knocking down the doors.
We hear them yelling in German
And the sounds of guns reloading.
I'm hoping they won't find us
Even though they know we're here.

Brianna Dennis, Grade 6
East Mooresville Intermediate School, NC

Spring

Spring
Warm and colorful
New, bright, and wet.
Blooming, flowery, budding, and growing.
Spring

Matthew McIntyre, Grade 4
Sequoyah Elementary School, TN

My Lovely Christmas Tree

The beautiful girl sits by my window,
She thinks about all the past holiday memories,
She remembers the time that I opened the DSi,
She remembers the time my sister jumped on her trampoline,
right beneath her feet,
She watches my family just giving an appreciative glance,
She listens to all the happy conversations that we share,
She makes the front window of the house a tree land,
When I walk by, she prickles and tickles me,
Even the cat likes to tease her by trying to take her decorations,
She stands so tall and she is so chubby that she doesn't need anymore Christmas attire,
Little does my family know, but she is my best holiday friend,
I sit beside her and read books about Santa and the reindeer,
I wrap packages and leave them to her care,
And on Christmas day, she is always waiting to share hidden treasures
with just me.
My lovely Christmas tree.

Sydney Clifton, Grade 4
JJ Jones School, NC

After Sunset

The glowing light gleaming from the sky slowly floating down to rest after a long day of ups,
Now After Sunset I am gazing at the ups in life and the downs.

The way God made us unique,
With our own ups and downs,
With our own likes and dislikes.

After Sunset we are all special because,
God made us unique,
With our own ups and downs,
With our own likes and dislikes.

After Sunset,
We are all special in our own ways.

The glowing light gleaming from the sky slowly floating down to rest after a long day of ups,
Now After Sunset I am gazing at the ups in life and the downs.

Haley Clift, Grade 4
St Mary's Episcopal School, TN

The Woods

A white tailed rabbit dashes through the dry leaves on the forest floor
Acorns cropping from the trees like water from a cloud on a rainy day
Blue babbling brooks being beautiful
Birds singing the wonderful spring song
The tiny pond's clear and fresh water speckled with Minnows
The fragrant scent of pine riding the air's waves
Bitter, yet sweet blackberries as their juice runs down my throat
Oak bark, as rough as sandpaper
The crunchy and sweet taste of granola I brought along
The cold, yet relaxing touch of the river as I dip my bare feet in.
Calm

Noah Dickens, Grade 6
College View Middle School, KY

Halloween

There's lots of costumes
To give you a fright on Halloween night.
If you don't want a fight
you better not come out on this creepy night.
If you scared of the dark don't go to the park.
You go to the houses if you get a sudden chill
you better start pacing, monsters are so cool
But if I were you I'd keep it in the sack.
Because it's Halloween night, it's Halloween night
try to stay up all night without one fright.
You can't go home because you're not going without a fright.
It's Halloween night, it's Halloween night.

Madalin Jane Worley, Grade 4
Central Elementary School, NC

My Secret Pond

The sun sets and reflects into the crystal water below,
I could tell that I would never want to go,
When you waves crash against the fractured rock,
It makes me wonder and think a lot.
Why does the moon smile whet it sees your waves?
Or when you blow why do the palm tree sway?
But, I forget when I feel your cool water brush against my skin
And when I hear voices it has to end,
I put on my shoes because someone is to come,
I turn my back and start to run,
As I go I think above and beyond,
All because of you, my secret pond.

Jaclynn Jasso, Grade 6
Saint Pauls Middle School, NC

Storms

Storms deadly and beautiful,
With their dark clouds swirling around,
Lightning flashing, cutting across the sky,
Debris flying, whirling through the air,
Water slamming, rolling into the rocks.
Trees bending, tearing at the wind,
Rain falling, striking at the grass,
Thunder clapping noise across the heavens,
Everything stops,
Dark clouds move away for the light to shine.

Uhlan Larrie, Grade 4
Harvest Preparatory Academy, NC

Dogs

I have a dog that's black and white.
He is fast and lazy.
He is fat.
He follows me wherever I go.
He bites me on the legs and
He plays with me all day long.
He bothers me a lot.
I love my dog a lot.

Matthew Gilbert, Grade 4
Tazewell-New Tazewell Primary School, TN

Soccer

Teammates passing the ball to score
Kids falling as frustrated creatures
Balls hitting the net like big punches
Families cheering for the teams
Mud splattered uniforms
A goalie protecting their nets like it's a ticking bomb
Victory fills the air at the final goal
My team is victorious

David Solana-Luna, Grade 4
Bailey Elementary School, NC

Cupcake

A cupcake is full of delight,
My favorite part is the icing which is white.
I know it's not good for me,
I know it's not right,
If I could just have one bite?
If you don't give it to me I'll put up a fight.
Cupcakes are just so delicious am I right?
I just can't help swallowing the beautiful sight!

Katie Nolen, Grade 5
Love Memorial Elementary School, NC

Robert

Handsome, cool, hard-working
Son of Innea
Loves family, friends and foes
Feels happy, excited, and blessed around his kids
Gives love, understanding and sweetness
Wants to see his kids graduate
Dreams of seeing his kids happy
My father

Alexis Fogg, Grade 4
Bailey Elementary School, NC

What Is Happening

In the morning the moon shone bright.
The rabbit crawled as loud as it could — moo.
All the people fell asleep and walked around town.
The butter flew high in the sky
While dinosaurs roamed the ground.
The dinosaurs ate all that didn't mind,
Which was all that they couldn't find.

Samantha Auman, Grade 4
Montessori Community School, NC

My Dog Chloe

My dog, Chloe, is so hyper,
Hyper like a child who has had too much sugar.
She is black like midnight, without any stars in the sky.
My dog, Chloe, has eyes as blue as the ocean.
Chloe is small like a mouse.
I feel that my dog Chloe is the best dog I have ever had.
My dog Chloe is amazing.

Payton Conley, Grade 5
Paint Lick Elementary School, KY

Basketball

Basketball
With the ball
In my hands,
Against some tall people
Like some towers
Down the court
Into the air I go
Without control I draw a foul
Until I foul all the tall kids out
About to take the lead
Down by two
For a three
Since then we've beat Eastside every time

Austin Smallwood, Grade 6
Bernheim Middle School, KY

I Saw Santa

With a snap at the back
And the toys in the sack
The reindeer are on their way

With Rudolph to lead
As quiet as a mouse
They land on top of my house

With the tapping of a hoof
Santa climbs on the roof
He leaves the present and says
"Merry Christmas Rachel"
And disappears into the darkness.

Rachel Lehkamp, Grade 5
Walton-Verona Middle School, KY

My Favorite Singer

T errific
A wesome
Y outhful
L oving
O utstanding
R espectful

S weet
W ealthy
I ncredible
F ree
T errific, Taylor Swift is Awesome!

Haley McIntire, Grade 5
Mineral Wells Elementary School, WV

Together We Can

Together we can change the world,
Together we can make sparks fly.
Together we can yell "We're Free,"
Together we can make the world shine!

Zac Lee, Grade 5
Bostian Elementary School, NC

Death

When you're dead, what will you do? Where will you go? Will you go up or down?
Those are the questions you may ask.
Death is quiet, peaceful. It does not hurt.
You just lay there and slowly drift into a long sleep that you will never wake out of.
No more dreams no more of anything just darkness, bliss.
Some of you may be scared of death but don't be, everyone dies at one point in a lifetime.
So just lay down and close your eyes, and slowly drift into a long sleep.

Marinille Fager, Grade 6
Elizabeth City Middle School, NC

Boo Bear

Boo Bear is the most important stuffed animal of my childhood.
He is like a brown chestnut roasting on an open fire on Christmas Eve.
He speaks to me like a best friend and cares for me like a mother with a new born.
He was the most important because we are best friends and we still are.
It will never change.
He is big and warm as night.
I've always wanted to share with the world that our stuffed animals are our best friends.

Kenedee Cummings, Grade 6
Woodland Presbyterian School, TN

Christmas

The beautiful sight of the decorated Christmas tree, as beautiful as the snow.
The sweet smell of the Christmas cookies smell like scented candles.
The melody of the Christmas songs, much like magic.
The yummy taste of the eggnog is like nothing else.
The shapes of the tree decorations, some are the same as others.
Christmas is wonderful but, the Bible tells the true meaning of Christmas.

Logan Brown, Grade 5
Providence Academy, TN

Caring Soldiers

That big white house takes them too many places far away from their
family and friends
As their family sits and waits for them to come back home for the holidays
They sit over the years and say to themselves, when can we see you
again?

Mika Ogborn, Grade 5
Temple Hill Elementary School, KY

A Rock

I am as hard as steel but some can crumble to dust with ease.
I am several hundred feet high yet the size of a mouse.
I bathe in water for millions of years.
Some that are skinny are skipped across water but some stay dry forever.
Some are lost in the desert and some live in the deep dark depths of the ocean.

Nathan Griffith, Grade 5
Hunter GT Magnet Elementary School, NC

Pie

Apple, banana cream, and blueberry
Different flavors may vary
Without my delicious pie
I might as well die

Emilie Pray, Grade 5
Walton-Verona Middle School, KY

Shoe

Leather sneakers
Squeaking, annoying, loud
Comfortable, cozy, crinkled, worn
Footwear

Autumn Lockhart, Grade 5
Mineral Wells Elementary School, WV

Home Alone with the Cat

The cat meows, with a soft purr
a gift: just as precious as gold or myrrh
soft and furry
at times like curry
all to say, "I love you"
with a quiet mew.
Sitting on my lap with heat
like a really heavy sheet
no bustling noises
no mad kitty poises
all is perfect without a sound
nothing like a hunting hound
eyes closed, my mind is blank
for you this love
I have to thank

Noah Syverson, Grade 6
Fred J Page Middle School, TN

Touchdown!

Touchdown, touchdown
Run the ball
Touchdown, touchdown
In the fall
Touchdown, touchdown
What a call!
Touchdown, touchdown
There's the kick
Touchdown, touchdown
Is it Michael Vick?
Touchdown, touchdown
Wow he is fast!
Touchdown, touchdown
Football's a blast
Touchdown, touchdown

Isaac Holley, Grade 4
Centennial Elementary School, TN

Christmas Tree

C reamy white ornaments
H olly hanging on the door
R ed and green around the tree
I place the star atop the tree
S tockings stuffed with toys and trinkets
T insel, treats and even more
M ini mountains line the tree
A n awesome sight for sore eyes to see
S t. Nick has done his job again

T ime to open all the presents
R eady the camera
E veryone is excited
E verybody loves this Christmas tree

Gavin Phillips, Grade 5
Moyock Elementary School, NC

In My House

In my house I learned
that pointing is rude,
to always do my homework,
and eat all my food.
In my house I learned
how to do my hair,
to always use my manners,
and what not to wear.
In my house I learned
that I am what I am,
not to copy or mimic,
and not be a ham.
In my house I learned
that family comes first,
to say all my prayers,
and to be a joyful burst.
In my house I learned
a great deal of things
and someday I'll pass it on
to my offspring.

Lydia Jackson, Grade 6
East Oldham Middle School, KY

Same, But Different

My friends come and go,
as I do now and then.
But, where ever I go on post,
I run into them.
My dad comes home tired,
but happy to be with us all.
Then we know it's time for rest,
when we hear the bugle call.
I hear guns and cannons,
and think of the things I fear.
I see soldiers marching and yelling.
It seems kind of weird.
When Dad leaves for a while,
Mom is way too busy.
But when he comes home,
we are no longer dizzy.
Military life is the same, but different.
Some things are old, some new.
Although it is tough, I still have fun,
and you can still be YOU!

Jordan Tyler, Grade 5
Walker Intermediate School, KY

My Parents Are My Own Alarm Clock

My parents are my own alarm clock,
They may not go "beep, beep, beep,"
Or "ring, ring, ring,"
And neither do they vibrate,
Instead they say,
"Get up for school or you'll be late."

William Stiffler, Grade 5
Duke Middle School, NC

My Test

I'm sitting here doing my test,
I'm going to do the very best.
I'll have a good time,
This test is so prime.
Question by question blasting through,
Oh no, oh no, what do I do?
First it's the functions,
What's a conjunction?!

Let's skip that,
So I skipped while I sat.
This page is a curve,
It's all about verbs.
Linking, helping, or action?
Can't I be doing a fraction?
Don't get a 2,
What do I do?

Emily Gay, Grade 5
Hunter GT Magnet Elementary School, NC

The Sound of Music

Laid back relaxed
As the notes flow across the staff

The sound of music

Feeling the vibe of the
Beat makes me want
To move my feet

The sound of music

Makes me feel the need
To jig my legs and bop
My head to the sound
Of the beat

Now that's the sound of music.

Makayla Brown, Grade 6
Johnson Traditional Middle School, KY

Adventure

Over the hills
Beyond the trees
Above the lakes
Underneath the sun
Behind the fern
Among the grass
On the cliffs
Off the river
Beside the birds
Across the forest
Past the bad times
To an adventure of dreams

Jacqueline Goff, Grade 6
Bernheim Middle School, KY

The Blue Jacket

Please, don't leave us behind!
You need me to go through this cold season.
Don't leave me hanging on top of your school seat!
You need me to keep you cozy and warm.

I am the hot cocoa you miss during the cold, snowy weather that you desperately want to drink.
I am the missing firewood to create the fire for warmth.
I am the unfixed heater in the car.
I am the missing blue sky that surrounds the sun
I am the ugly duckling feeling unloved, lonely, and left behind.

Please come and find us.
Wear us over your arms, shoulders, and back because we terribly miss you,

For I am the little baby crying for her mommy.

Jennifer Yu, Grade 5
Hunter GT Magnet Elementary School, NC

I Am an Immigrant

I am an immigrant coming to the new world.
I wonder will I pass the inspection.
I hear a thousand different languages at once.
I see the most people I've ever seen thousands of people ready to go to the new world.
I want to get out of here. The noise the sight it's just too much.
I pretend I am a billionaire in the new world with the best job ever.
I feel nerves. Will I pass the inspection? Will my family pass the inspection? Will my new life be good or bad?
I touch my mother's hand. It gives me hope and comfort.
I worry that I may get separated from my family.
I cry my brother and father have not past the inspection. Now what will I do?
I am an immigrant taking my first steps on the new world.
I under stand that my brother and father were unhealthy which as a result didn't give them permission to the new world.
I say "Mommy will I ever see Daddy and Bubby again." "I don't know" she replied.
I dream that I might see my brother and father again.

Daniel Howard, Grade 5
St Joseph School, KY

I Am an Immigrant

I am an immigrant. I am scared. I don't know anyone around me. All of us are on a boat.
I wonder if anyone will like me in the new land. Will I make friends?
I hear a horn. It's very loud.
I see a statue. It looks like a woman is trying to greet us. We're here.
I want my family. I bet they miss me like I miss them.
I am starving, and alone. What kind of food is this? Whoever heard of "candy?" I don't like it very much.
I pretend I have my friends, my family and a huge feast right beside me.
I feel sad. Who will I talk to? Where will I live? How will I make money?
I'm worried I won't pass. I need to make money so I can be with my mama.
I cry. Something is wrong. What's this white stuff on me?
I am being checked again. What for?
I understand I have a cold.
I say "it's just a cold."
I dream of my mama. She will be here soon. I passed.

Holly Farwell, Grade 5
St Joseph School, KY

I Am

I am kind and patient.
I wonder about technology.
I hear wind breezing.
I see birds.
I want to build a robot.
I am kind and patient.

I pretend I am a scientist.
I feel smart
I touch the sky
I worry about natural disasters
I cry when I get hurt
I am kind and patient
I understand electronics intelligence
I say life is good, no matter what
I dream for the holidays
I try to stay on task in school
I hope for a better planet
I am kind and patient

Ryan Mills, Grade 4
Centennial Elementary School, TN

How I Feel

My heart bangs like
a drum
I see zebra stripe black circles
my brain turns black
I run in my room and cry
I talk to myself

My niece makes me mad
when she acts like a fired
up demon

My mom when she says things
that annoy me

I stay in my room
and calm down
when it's all over I see
dark ink blue all over
I feel relieved and relaxed

Kathryn Richardson, Grade 6
Johnson Traditional Middle School, KY

Life's Lighthouse

Life is like a lighthouse
standing on the bay.
Sometimes life's spotlight's on you
and sometimes it's away.
No matter who that spotlight's on
no matter who is gleaming,
Don't ever let that stop you
from doing your best and beaming.

Noah Clapacs, Grade 5
Duke Middle School, NC

Chocolate Bar

Creamy...delicious
Has an amazing taste;
Observe the masterpiece
Ceasing unhappy thoughts;
Out of this world
Luxurious and great;
An awesome treat that no one hates;
The best is Hershey's and
Everyone should love it!

Banned for people on diets;
Addictive to the weak but...
Required for my dessert.

Brandon Wilhoit, Grade 4
Sequoyah Elementary School, TN

A Swan and Music

A swan is like music
Flowing softly
Gently splashing
Trying to find the perfect tune
Melodious rhythm
Spreading its great wings of imagination
Pleasant sounds
Graceful movement
Peaceful background
Perfect harmony
Majestic posture
An extraordinary wonder
A swan is like music

Nicholas Schwartz, Grade 5
Hunter GT Magnet Elementary School, NC

False Mask

The masks we wear are not true
For we are really blue
Laughter rings in their ears
But behind the mask there are tears
Sometimes cracks appear
And we show some fear
We show some tears
And when we show how we really feel
They make it some big deal
We fix our mask
To what they ask
But we are still blue
For the masks we wear are not true

Hayden Elliott, Grade 6
College View Middle School, KY

The Moon

The moon at the
night goes away in the
morning soft light

Treqwon Alston, Grade 5
E O Young Elementary School, NC

Rainforest

As I walk through the rainforest
The scent of fresh rain fills the air
Monkeys swing from the vines
Beautiful birds singing
Noisy crickets chirping
Smooth banana gooey in my teeth
Rain dripping from the leaves
Chocolate cocoa beans
Juicy pineapples
Moist moss sinking between my toes
I feel relaxed

Jacob Glover, Grade 5
Bailey Elementary School, NC

The Ball Game

Boom! Boom! Pow!
Kick the ball across the ground.
Red team versus white team.
Hear the voices shouting loud.
Go! Run! Block that goal!
Watch the players run around.
Tweet! Tweet! The whistle blows.
In the net the ball was found.
Victory, victory, we win the game.
Do you hear the sound,
Of a soccer game going down.

Katherine Dansereau, Grade 4
Sequoyah Elementary School, TN

The Beach

Ocean waves crashing against the shore
Crabs crawling cautiously
Seagulls squawking spontaneously
Cute little dogs catching Frisbees
The smell of salt water fills my nose
Suntan lotion drifts through the air
My hands in the sand digging a hole
Buckets full of salty water
Sandcastle come alive
Mother calls my name
Time to go

Sierra Thorne, Grade 4
Bailey Elementary School, NC

My BFF

K idding girl
A ctor in awesomeness
S creaming down the house
S ell maker for BFF's
I ntelligent in everything she does
D istinguished on the CATS Test
Y ielding the road for people

G rateful for everything

Maddy Hancock, Grade 5
Walton-Verona Middle School, KY

Koala

Look! Do you see her?
Waving in the breeze?
The pool of gray fur there?

Look! There she is.
Climbing like a caterpillar on a leaf.
She is a canyon of sweetness.

Her black eyes shimmer like the stars
As she slowly eats her dinner of eucalyptus.
She nestles down in her bed of limbs and leaves.

Look! Do you see her?
Waving in the breeze?
The sweet little thing
has gently fallen to sleep.

Zoe Doubrley, Grade 4
Nature's Way Montessori School, TN

Happy Mask

I wear the happy mask with great pride
From the feeling I have deep inside
The happy mask feels soft and smooth
When I touch it, I feel soothed
The happy mask is like a beautiful sunset
But I am really feeling upset from remembering all the bad
Things that have happened to me
The mask I wear tastes like ice cold water running down my throat
It sounds like beautiful birds singing
And the beautiful sound of big church bells ringing
And the most wonderful thing of all
Is the wonderful smell of great fall
The mask is worn for dance ceremonies
With the most beautiful rainbow painting of all
And the calm eyes and the big nose
With the fake, happy mask worn by me

Garrett Helton, Grade 6
College View Middle School, KY

My New Lab Puppy

We are supposed to get a puppy soon,
But I've heard that same old tune.

My dad wants to name him Switch,
That name makes me want to twitch.

I just love the smell of puppy breath in my face,
But I just can't keep up with their pace.

Puppies like to talk,
I would rather walk.

I just can't wait to get a new puppy,
I hope I'm lucky enough to get a new puppy.

Kathleen Parrish, Grade 5
Evangelical Christian School Ridgelake Campus, TN

I Cheer

I cheer and I flip!
I dance and I fly!
I really like flying high!
I soar and tumble!
I hope I don't fumble!
I cradle and basket!
I'm made of elastic!
I extension and stance!
I love to dance!
I elevator and show n go!
I scorpion and bow and arrow!
I herkey and pike!
I cheer every night!!
Extensions, liberties and arches oh wait there's more!
I love to full down, a 360 that's fun!
These are some of the ways I Cheer

Abigail Howell, Grade 5
Harding Academy of Memphis, TN

Big Brother

As I travel through this world at a fast paced track,
I honor my big brother, and that's a fact.
I want someone honest, to walk me through life.
For this specific reason; To teach me to do right.
That one of the things that I admire most.
Even though he's blessed he chooses not to boast.
His fire for God is deeply great,
I wish to be like him to read the word an pray.
He supports me in all and everything that I do;
For I love him very much. As so should you.
And every time he chooses to speak or sing a song,
I love to sit and listen and could do it for eternity long.
His words of wisdom; They are clear and correct,
And also he has a heart that no one could neglect.
I love my dad, my sisters and as well my mother;
But I choose to look up to him, MY BIG BROTHER.

Marilynn Jasso, Grade 6
Saint Pauls Middle School, NC

Baby Bro

ZOOM!!! I went down the road to see my baby brother,
To be held at the house by my kind, loving mother
So I can hold him in my palms
But I have to be calm

When I finally saw him, I thought I won the lottery
I was relaxed and still like pottery
I needed to hold him in my palm
And that, would make me calm

Then he was mine to hold
I know he'll be bold
I finally have him in my palm
And now I can be calm

Bailey Sircy, Grade 6
Bernheim Middle School, KY

Heavenly
Paradise
Awesome, fun
Soothing, relaxing, enjoying
Is fun for everyone
Cooling, amazing, stunning
Beautiful, nice
Beach
Blair Lewis, Grade 6
Musselman Middle School, WV

Leaves/Snow
Leaves
Bright, yellow
Falling, raking, scooping
Crunchy, crackling-pure, soft
Falling, shoveling, melting
Moist, fresh
Snow
Leah Ratliff, Grade 6
Musselman Middle School, WV

Happy
Peace, no troubles
Contented, being active
Glad, smiling wide
Joyful, playing with friends
Running, playing tag
Skipping, happily frolicking
Outside, bright and sunny
Hannah Cox, Grade 6
College View Middle School, KY

Spring and Fall
Spring and Fall.
Spring is full of flowers
Little new green leaves.
Spring and Fall.
Fall has lots of colors
Floating on the breeze.
Spring and Fall.
Lily Parker, Grade 5
Nature's Way Montessori School, TN

Shadows
Darker! Darker!
It's the color of midnight,
through the day they hide away.
But at night like bats they fly.
Deeper and deeper they pull me,
and now I come willingly.
The light comes on and then they are gone.
Jerzi Ignaszak, Grade 5
Walton-Verona Middle School, KY

The Bathtub
As I walk into the yellow bathroom
I slip into my white tiled bathtub
My leg throbs with the soreness as I check out my surroundings
I look at the small yellow rubber duck staring at me,
I see in his face sadness and loneliness from no baths lately,
Right next to him is a Barbie doll slouched,
With a blank expression on her face,
A sponge the length of my hand full of water starts to mildew,
A floating sea turtle twelve inches long swims in delight
Two small black and white plastic killer whales chase their next meal,
Two rubber squeaky seals,
Coward from the killer whales chasing them round and round,
And a scuba diver prepared for his adventure
Why do I have all these things in my bathtub?
Entertainment? Enjoyment? Preparation?
Some of these things I may be too old for,
But when you grow up splashing in the tub
Playing with them almost every night
They're a part of me now,
So they sit there in the white cold tile,
Still waiting
Abbey Vernon, Grade 6
Baylor School, TN

I Am a Military Child
I am an American Boy.
I wonder why they make people go to training far away.
I hear machine guns firing.
I see big planes pass over my house.
I want the war to end so my dad doesn't have to go back to Afghanistan.
I am an American Boy.

I pretend I am shooting bad guys.
I feel happy when my dad comes back from deployment.
I touch a gift from him when he is gone.
I worry his friends and he might get shot.
I cry after he leaves.
I am an American Boy.

I understand that he is protecting us.
I say that they should send more troops.
I dream to be in the military like him.
I try not to talk during the Pledge of Allegiance.
I hope the war would end right now.
I am an American Boy.
Chance Kelly, Grade 5
Walker Intermediate School, KY

Grandfather Clock
Tick tock, tick tock goes the grandfather clock.
I wonder why it can be a grandfather clock when my grandfather's dead.
They should call it old clock.
While his memory fades the clock keeps ticking away.
Why oh why do they call it a grandfather clock?
Eli Schulman, Grade 5
Duke Middle School, NC

Happiness

A girl smiling,
Having fun,
Delighted, shining face,
Clapping hands hitting together,
Tears of joy,
Skipping, a bounce in your step,
Funny,
Someone giggling,
Jumping up and down,
Cheerful,
A glowing face

Heaven Ambs, Grade 6
College View Middle School, KY

Purple

It is my favorite color.
Purple is the color of grapes.
Purple is the color of plums.
My nails are always purple.
My pencil is a bright purple.
My dark purple blanket.
It is the best color.
You can mix blue and red to make purple.
I love the smell of purple flowers.
It is the color of my shirt.
I love the color purple.

Morgan Whitt, Grade 5
Paint Lick Elementary School, KY

Together We Can

Together we can get along
We'll work together like the words of a song
If we work together it won't take long
To make our school united and strong

When someone is bullied it hurts us all
If we work together bullying will fall
Respect each other in the hall
Together we'll stand proud and tall

Because together we can!

Collin Wilson, Grade 5
Bostian Elementary School, NC

Hannah

Eyes as blue as the sky
Wavy hair like falling yellow leaves
Fingernails painted like artwork
Jewelry sparkling like diamonds
Her heart sweeter than cotton candy
Her mind works like a fairy tale
She makes me feel safe and protected
Loves everyone like a mother hen
My special friend

Bianca Bailey, Grade 4
Bailey Elementary School, NC

Gone

Loving, kind, sweet, cool, talking still in memories
But we can't see him

We used to walk, talk, laugh, play and do piggyback rides
He was there all my life.

Sweet, fun stores to go to on the weekends
Why can't he come back to see me graduate or see my 13th birthday cake?

I have fun with the memories that we shared
He's gone forever but I think we're still together

He's too far away to touch but he's there so much
Loving, kind, sweet are some of the words

To describe the times but he's gone forever and always
Gone

Carmen Webster, Grade 6
Woodland Presbyterian School, TN

Being Special

Some people say that when you have a nickname,
that you are special.
Our family believes in being special.
There's Daddy bird, Momma bird, and of course me Baby bird.
Our dog Miley is really special.
We call her Bug, Boo Bug, Miley Bug, and Teaty.
She answers to all of them because she knows she is special.

Then there is our Beagle Graham.
He is just Graham the Beagle
who opens the fridge with his paw and drags food out.
He also likes to open the pantry door and get into the garbage.
When we come home we find food all over the house.
Momma bird yells, "I can't believe you did this and I can't believe you did that!"
Graham is a busy beagle and is always getting into trouble.
Maybe one day Graham will get his own special nickname,
But I doubt it!

Caroline Carpenter, Grade 4
Evangelical Christian School Ridgelake Campus, TN

Lost and Found

I walk this world and look with shame on others that mark my name.
I sometimes wonder who am I and why am I here.
Is it to love others or pretend not to care.
I am determined to reach my goals that are quickly slipping away from me.
I am determined to complete any type of challenge thrown in front of me.
I am a believer, I am not lost, but found!
I think it's time for me to wear the crown.
Life is a challenge, and will not be handed down to you.
Gas prices will go up and store item prices will go down.
Through it all, I will not be lost, but found!

Kayla Davis, Grade 6
Weldon Middle School, NC

I Am From

I am from playing video games on HOT summer days
to playing with my dogs, Max and Elly.

I am from being on the Internet looking at games on Gamefly.com
to looking at wrestlers' status on wwe.com
and seeing how well they are doing in the matches.

I am from getting good grades in school
so I can move to the next grade and not get in trouble.

I am from playing on the iPhone until the battery runs down,
and Mom can't check her e-mails...
to playing football outside with my friends.
We throw it in the end zone to score,
and we return kickoffs for a touchdown.

I am from building with my Lego Halo set
to having a small war with toys when I am done building it.
The good guys always win!

That is what I am from!

Billy Chamberlain, Grade 5
Burgin Independent School, KY

I Just Hate When You Blame Me for Things I Didn't Do!

I just hate that you blame for things I didn't do!

What, but I didn't do it!
It makes me want
to yell and scream
you make my body
hot and sweaty
It feels like
sitting in hot lava
It makes me want to throw
things
so all I see is
blood red with
pitch black
I go take a nap
in my dream all I see
is light sky blue
with pinkish purple
I just hate when you
blame me for things
I didn't do!

Laniyah Marshall, Grade 6
Johnson Traditional Middle School, KY

My Dog Ate My Homework

My dog ate my homework it was not right
My dog ate my homework I put up a fight
My dog ate my homework he didn't have to bite
My dog ate my homework I was grounded for a night

Garet Talbott, Grade 5
Walton-Verona Middle School, KY

Masai Giraffe

You have brown horns that are unique amongst mammals
Each made of solid bony core called ossicone
Spots with jigged edges
(no two patterns on you are alike to any other giraffe)
And a long prehensile tongue
You are usually silent
but possess a range of vocalizations
if you see a person
sitting under a tree you snort
You eat willow, bamboo, sugar
maple, elm, hackberry, tulip
poplar an a couple other
varieties of trees that are found on the zoo grounds
You also eat lots of grain
and very small amounts of carrots, sweet potatoes,
and romaine lettuce
You live in southern Kenya and Tanzania
You are my favorite animal because
you usually seep standing up,
Have the longest tail of any land animal
(which can be up to 8 feet long).

John Downing, Grade 5
W R McNeill Elementary School, KY

Monkey

At the zoo
Above a tree hanging
Across from the seals
Along the cage walking
Around many exhibits
Beside its mother
From Africa
Under the sun
Without bananas on the ground
Up in the air a monkey leaps
From tree to tree
Before the storm
Through the zoo
On to great adventures
Throughout the path
Upon a habitat
Beneath the tree during a down pour
Aboard the wind without shelter
Until help I found
Beyond the ground she lays
In a place of doom the little monkey cries for help

Lauren Welch, Grade 6
Bernheim Middle School, KY

Scary Stories

Not far east of the coal mine there lies
A haunted house where men close their eyes.
The house that was once chromed in gold
Is now rusty, dusty, old and cold.

Seth MacAdams, Grade 5
Walton-Verona Middle School, KY

Sweet Joshua

You were only in our lives a short time
but what a difference you made.
Of all the life lessons you taught us
we learned not to be afraid.

We think about you every day
and know that you are here.
Sometimes we see you standing there
and down falls our tears.

Now you are with our Lord
singing with the angels in the sky.
Playing your guitar every day
singing the sweet by and by.

Standing at your grave one day
a rainbow did appear.
I felt your arm around my neck
and knew that you were near.

Sometimes I often think
that you are so far away.
But in our hearts, Sweet Joshua,
you will always stay.

Mary Morgan Adams, Grade 4
Centennial Elementary School, TN

Funnel Cakes

Warm, twisted, and curved
This is how a funnel cake feels
Sweet, and soft
This is how a funnel cake tastes
Crumbly and crunchy
This is how a funnel cake sounds
White, brown, and powdery
This is how a funnel cake looks
Delicious, calming, and comforting
This is how a funnel cake smells

David LaPasha, Grade 5
Hunter GT Magnet Elementary School, NC

Love Is Not Dark

Darkness is evil.
It has no light.
Some say there is.
Some say there is not.
But I believe there is a light.
The light is love.
Love is not a hurt or harm.
It is like a guard.
It helps you in time of need.
With love you are as strong as iron,
As beautiful as the flowers that bloom.
Trust in love.

Tylik Green, Grade 4
Southeast Elementary School, NC

My Little Brother

My brother is 9 years old,
I'm 11 years old.
We like to ride our bikes down the road,
I try to go faster than him,
He tries to go faster than me.
He hates it when I'm on the computer,
He always wants to get on.
Were like cats and dogs,
But sometimes calm as a pond.
I like how he plays with our little sister,
He likes it when I share with him.
I hate it when he doesn't
Clean up after himself.
I think he will always
Ask me for the computer.
I will always want him to
Ride bikes with me.

Michaela Fox, Grade 6
Johnson Traditional Middle School, KY

Heaven

Seeing the clouds open to you
Also see the light beckoning, too.

Open arms to welcome you in,
God will forgive you for your sins.

Angels singing hallelujah,
Do you want to go to heaven?

Seeing your family once again
Worshipping God when you come in.

Getting your wings, starting to fly
Flying with the stars in the sky.

You'll never see blackness again
Light will always be within.

Annashaye Stiles, Grade 5
Moyock Elementary School, NC

Fall

I lay outside on a very cold day,
leaves falling from the sky.
Slowly, slowly leaving their friends scared
to death wondering what will happen next.
The leaves all crumpled up and dry,
laying under the pretty blue sky.
The wind blowing in my face,
the birds chirping pretty songs.
Birds flying high in the sky,
chasing friends by and by.
Even though I am not flying with them,
my friends too will soon be passing by.

Tyler London, Grade 4
Edmonton Elementary School, KY

Will the Earth End?

Will we live to see the earth end?
Or will we die before then?
Will we live to see the sun rise again?
Or will we live our life with sin?

Will we live to see our graduation?
Or will we live past our imagination?
Will we have great fascination?
Or will we live our life of assignation?

Will we live to see the earth end?
Or will we die before then?
Will we live to see the sun rise again?
Or will we live our life of sin?

Riccquel Lofton, Grade 6
Snowden School, TN

Hunting

The guns ready to go
My hope is killing a doe
My dream is killing a giant eight point buck
I hope I have that luck.
We get to the stand
My heart is beating like a band
There in the field he stands
The giant 8 point that I had planned.
I put up my gun
Shoot and he is stunned
We are out of the tree
I have to go see the deer for me.
I am feeling great
As I hold the 8!

Jackson Taylor, Grade 4
Bailey Elementary School, NC

Destination Imagination

DI is so much fun.
Don't stop reading it's not done.
Imagination is the key
To the solution as you see.
There is much creativity
In this activity.
This must sound like a perk,
It involves much teamwork.
Trust, faith, so much more,
Have them all and you will soar.
The reason why DI rocks
You get to think outside the box.
But of course friendship is involved.
That's the biggest problem that is solved.

Will Schneider, Grade 6
Woodland Presbyterian School, TN

The Ocean

The ocean is so beautiful coming
in and out, crushing on the
seashore, throwing shells about.

When it is time to leave, the
ocean gives one last crash as we
all trudge back.

Devin Brader-Araje, Grade 4
Montessori Community School, NC

Friends

Unique, remarkable
Unforgettable, loving
Caring, faithful, joyful
Forgiving, grateful, dependable
Enthusiastic, inspirable, truthful
Successful, strong, extraordinary
Friends

Selena Ventura, Grade 5
Rex-Rennert Elementary School, NC

Gladness

A kid getting a puppy
Surprised, crying like a baby
Cheerful as a clown
Laughing like a toddler
Running like a squirrel
Shouting for joy
Prayers, giving thanks

Courtney Scalf, Grade 6
College View Middle School, KY

Bumble Bee

One, two, three
Bumble bee
Flitting, flying
Making honey
One, two, three
Bumble bee
One, two — OUCH!

Ingrid Trost, Grade 5
Duke Middle School, NC

Hatchet

H ard work in the wilderness
A ction to make a bow and arrow
T ime to survive in the wilderness
C arrying wood to the fire
H ard to survive in the wilderness
E nergy to survive in the wilderness
T o be a survivor means not giving up

Tyler Cotton, Grade 6
Temple Hill Elementary School, KY

Memory Desk

I walk into my blue room
And there my brand new desk sits by the window with memories.
Near my Dell green laptop sits sparkly broken and unbroken headbands
And smooth black hair bows, that I borrowed from a friend.
A long red bead necklace, from sprit week, the best school week.
Sharpened yellow pencils on my college ruled notebook paper,
By my flat blue calculator.
Small thin flash cards sit by colorful used crayons
And different colored markers.
My small multicolored slinky sits by the blue Blue Cross pencil sharpener.
Colorful pieces of bead art ironed into a flower
By my pink and purple Nintendo D.S. light.
Books full of pages for school,
White notebooks,
And colored dividers for my binders.
My thick long white eraser lays at the end of my desk.
My red North Face jacket that I got from Hayden
Sits on my chair waiting to be used.
My brand new wooden desk is full of friends and family memories
That I will keep forever.

Alison Anderson, Grade 6
Baylor School, TN

I Am a Military Child

I am a military child that was born in California and can speak two languages.
I wonder what I will be when I grow up if I will be like my dad or not.
I hear Soldiers training close to my house.
I see my dad leave the house in his uniform everyday.
I want my dad to stay home because I don't want him to die.
I am a military child that was born in California and can speak two languages.

I pretend that I like to go shopping for new clothes.
I feel happy when my dad comes home from his army work.
I touch my dad's picture every day when he is at war.
I worry my dad will not come back from war.
I cried when my dad went to Iraq for the first and second time.
I am a military child that was born in California and can speak two languages.

I understand that Soldiers need to protect our country and us by doing to work.
I say my daddy is my hero because he protects us.
I dream that my dad will be here and not in war.
I try to appreciate the Soldiers because they protect us.
I hope for the war to end soon.
I am a military child that was born in California and can speak two languages.

Ixua Guillen, Grade 5
Walker Intermediate School, KY

Ode to Softball

Oh, softball, the way it makes me grin,
as I place my glove under my chin.
My arm moves very fast.
Soon the ball flies past.
My favorite words to hear all year are strike one, strike two, strike three, you're out.
The coaches shout, "Line up ladies!" while the opposing team whines and pouts.

Marissa Garlitz, Grade 5
West Liberty Elementary School, WV

Seasons

Winter, winter, I feel the cold.
The snow freezes me head to toe.
I wish I did go inside,
For some tea I think I might.

Spring, spring, fertilizer fills the air.
As cool wind blows through my hair.
I need some water to shower my flowers,
As lilies bloom in the sunlit valleys.

Summer, summer, kids' laughter fills the air.
They're screaming loud.
Water balloons flying high.
When kids get in their bathing suits.
I know it's time for summer.

Autumn, autumn, leaves fall.
Watch them twirl and whirl.
Like tiny ballerinas in the sky.
Watch them till they bow goodbye.

Dorothy Shytles, Grade 4
Moyock Elementary School, NC

Candy! Candy! Candy!

On Halloween there's candy almost everywhere you look.
Children screaming — More! More! More!
Knock! Knock! Knock!
And then "oh no!" you exclaim,
There is more,
Banging and clanging on my very own door!
What shall I do?
I'm out of candy you see.
So then I give them almost anything.
First kid gets my favorite snow-globe,
The next one gets a digital clock!
Third one gets a slice of fruitcake,
Next one gets a dirty old sock!
"We want candy" the kids then replied,
"Well I don't have any, I'm sorry" I said with a huge sigh,
"Get her!" one kid screamed,
So then I started to run.
I was never seen again after that day,
All because of a little,
Halloween fun!

Marlee Walls, Grade 5
Moyock Elementary School, NC

Birds

Oh Birds that sit on my gate.
I love you so.
Oh Bird I love you very much please don't leave me.
You sit on my gate every day.
Oh Bird please don't leave my gate.

Casey Hicks, Grade 5
Walton-Verona Middle School, KY

Changing the World, One Word at a Time

Together we can **T**riumph
Together we can **O**btain
Together we can **G**ive
Together we can **E**mbrace
Together we can **T**each
Together we can **H**eal
Together we can **E**nrich
Together we can **R**ise

Together we can **W**in
Together we can **E**ducate

Together we can **C**hange
Together we can **A**chieve
Together we can **N**ever Stop

Emma Milem, Grade 5
Bostian Elementary School, NC

I Am an Immigrant

I am an immigrant.
I wonder if I will ever see my family again.
I hear the wind flowing in the air.
I see a statue that people call the Statue of Liberty.
I want my dream to come true that my family can be here too.
I am frightened of death.
I pretend to fit in with the other immigrants.
I feel sad and lonely.
I touch and feel rugged t-shirts.
I worry I might not pass and be sent back to my country.
I cry to my elf when will I get off the ship and see my family.
I am scared that the food is spoiled.
I understand that my family could not come.
I say I see a wonderful land.
I dream of freedom for my family and me.

Isabella Palmer, Grade 5
St Joseph School, KY

My Sister

My sister is as sweet as honey,
She is both unselfish and kind.
She will always be my sister no matter where she goes.
Sometimes she is my hero,
And does everything with me.
She tries to visit often,
And is always happy looking.
She makes me happy and always will.
Her love weighs a ton.
Even though she has school,
She always makes time for me,
Comes home on weekends and
Takes worthwhile walks me.
She plays games and is a good sport
Is my very loving sister.

Sarah Carroll, Grade 5
Providence Academy, TN

I Am

I am a dog lover
I wonder if I will ever get a dog
I hear dogs bark in my dreams
I see dogs in my dreams
I want a dog
I am a dog lover

I pretend I have a dog
I feel good when I see a dog
I touch the dog
I worry about dogs in the pound
I cry about dogs in the pound
I am a dog lover

I understand I won't get a dog
I say I will get a dog someday
I dream I had a dog
I try to convince my parents to let me get a dog
I hope I will get a dog someday
I am a dog lover

Ben Westlund, Grade 5
Duke Middle School, NC

A Great Granddaughter

I am a great granddaughter
I wonder who made the world
I hear my great grandma talking to me
I see her smiling down at me
I want to see her one last time
I am a great granddaughter

I pretend I am happy
I feel very confident in myself
I touch the wings of my angel
I worry my great grandma might not always be there for me
I cry when I think of her
I am a great granddaughter

I understand I can't always get what I want
I say it's still worth trying
I dream to succeed in most things
I try to talk to her
I hope to make a difference in the world
I am a great granddaughter

Christiana Martinez, Grade 6
Bernheim Middle School, KY

Cold Days

It is turning cold because I see the leaves falling.
It is turning cold because I see people wearing coats.
It is turning cold because I see people outside less.
It is turning cold because I see frost on the ground.
It is turning cold because it is snowing.
It is turning cold because it is winter.

Kaleb Kight, Grade 4
Moyock Elementary School, NC

Education

St. Pauls Middle school is a wonderful place,
From class to class I do race!
Science, reading, history and math,
It's a day full of joy smiles and laughs!
I love math with Ms. Wells as my teacher,
I get so happy every day that I see her!
Assignments are completed and homework is due,
Every day in Math we learn something new!
In science class, Mrs. Edwards and I work as a team,
You would not believe everything that you see!
She has lots of science things in one section
While every day something is added to her collection!
In art Ms. Baker draws lots of things,
Using a marker or paint for painting!
Every day we use one or the other,
I love each day is full of color!
Mr. Weller teaches me language arts and spelling,
I cannot wait to get there every morning!
To have fun this year is my wish,
And to see all sorts of beautiful fish!

Brisma V. Morales, Grade 6
Saint Pauls Middle School, NC

Ode to Disney World

Oh, Disney World,
you are so fun in your hot summer sun.

You make me sweaty, but that is okay
because your breeze makes me feel okay.

You're so cool, and I get to
See lots of neat things too.

You have lots of rides
That are really fun.

My favorite ride is the
Tower of Terror.

Some people say I'm crazy for riding that ride,
But that is okay because I like it anyway.

The one thing I love the most is that I get to
spend time with my cousins, and that is what I love about you.

Megan Ennis, Grade 5
West Liberty Elementary School, WV

The Boy Who Left

The boy who left never said good-bye
The boy who left never had his first cry
The boy who left never said the word LOVE
The boy who left never said Mama or Dada
But that boy who left had a name, his name was Nycere
Nycere, Nycere, Nycere I love you my dear Nycere

Nikki Brantley, Grade 6
Spring Lake Middle School, NC

Bananas

Smash in your mouth
Makes you want to run south
Yellow like the sun
Sounds like a lot of fun

They grow on trees
Swing in the breeze
Falls on the ground
In a big mound

We sell them to the store
They always want more
They taste real sweet
They are good treats

Looks like smiles
That go on for miles
It's good with pancakes
Makes me want to do the banana shake

Andrew Fiedler, Grade 6
Bernheim Middle School, KY

Crush

I wish I knew your face
I'm always in a race
To get out of class
In the hall we always pass

You don't know I'm alive
Even though I strive
To get you to notice me
You don't know how great it could be

Tall and cute
I wish you wouldn't be so mute
Tell me your name
And I'll do the same

I'm crazy 'bout you
And that super cute hair-do
This is truly a rush
But it's not my first crush

Kaitlyn Mitchell, Grade 6
Bernheim Middle School, KY

Baseball

B ases
A rticles about it
S unshine
E asy to play
B ats
A lot of running
L ove for the game
L ots of fun

Cameron Young, Grade 4
Centennial Elementary School, TN

Leaving Home

I will miss the dark green forest
The rolling hills
The fresh, white clouds

I will miss the friends I had
The school I knew
My neighborhood

I will miss the church I loved
My family
The scenery

I will see new scenery
I will join new churches
I will visit my family

I will get new neighbors
Attend new schools
Make new friends

But the things they won't take away are
The dark, green forest
The rolling hills
The fresh, white clouds
My home

Addison Furst, Grade 6
Woodland Presbyterian School, TN

Granny Coleman

I remember your voice
I see a sweet face
I dream I could see you again
Granny I miss you

I know I see your face in the stars
Your cheeks like a rose
On a dark day you die
I see my family crying

You are wearing a bright shirt and
bright pants like flowers
The weather is cold like an ice cube
Inside I smell death in the air
I could hear sobbing

My dry wet face
I love you lots
I miss you like my dead dog
I am wondering if you are happy

I love you like the stars in the sky
I hope I see you again someday
Sadness, sadness, sadness,
Granny Coleman

Samantha Gardner, Grade 6
Bernheim Middle School, KY

Soccer!

With 5 more minutes on the clock
Our lungs gasping for air
chewing our nails
Screaming in excitement
He lines his feet and...
He kicks the ball!
It slips
It slides
All of my family with fingers crossed
The ball in the air!
Waiting,
And then
Then
GOAL!!!
1 to 0
Everybody stands and cheers!

Araceli Mora, Grade 6
McGee's Crossroads Middle School, NC

Nature's Masterpiece

The vibrant colors
of the leaves
are quickly dashing
through the trees.
With reds as red
as a human heart,
the leaves are truly
a work of art.
Now the leaves
are starting to go,
and the brilliant colors
no longer show.
Even though autumn
will soon end,
it will surely come back
around again.

Marie Lawson, Grade 6
Our Lady of Grace Elementary School, NC

Friendship

Friendship is a strong thing.
It is as strong as the wind,
and as delicate as a daisy.

Friendship can be easy to see
or it can be hard to see.

Friendship is a rock
with a big heart.

Friendship is as great
as the galaxy
and as mysterious
as the universe.

Tejes Gaertner, Grade 4
Nature's Way Montessori School, TN

Happy

A bee finding honey
Glad as a cat with a ball
Joyful, running, screaming
Laughing at everything
Joking like hillbillies
Jumping up and down like a rabbit
Blissful, enjoying

Blake Westerfield, Grade 6
College View Middle School, KY

Soldier

S oldier
O perations
L ead
D ominant
I ndependence
E ncouraging
R emember

Joseph Hagerty, Grade 6
Temple Hill Elementary School, KY

The Woman

There once was a woman named Brady,
Who was a very nice lady;
While feeling quite lazy,
She almost went crazy,
'Til she met her old friend Sadie.

Emily Cook, Grade 5
Mineral Wells Elementary School, WV

Flowers

Every time I walk past a flower
I always have a big smile on my face.
Flowers are so bright.
They also give me light.
That's why I love the flowers all around me.

Blair Ashleigh Williams, Grade 5
Walton-Verona Middle School, KY

The Horse

There once was a horse from Peru,
Who spoke to his master with a "Boo!"
The master fell dead,
Right there by his bed,
And the horse galloped off to the zoo.

Jayce Knopp, Grade 5
Mineral Wells Elementary School, WV

Horse from Japan

There once was a horse from Japan,
Who worked for his master named Dan;
The master was pleased,
And fell to his knees,
Saying, "Don't go to Russia with Jan!"

Alissa Walcutt, Grade 5
Mineral Wells Elementary School, WV

I Am a Military Brat

I am a military child who's lived in two different states.
I wonder if I or my brother will serve in the military.
I hear gunshots and I think of my father in the field.
I see movers packing up other people's houses and wonder if we are moving.
I want to move closer to home, but will settle for the next best thing.
I am a military child who's lived in two different states.

I pretend to be the one in the military.
I feel happy and safe when my father comes home.
I touch my father just to know what a hero feels like.
I worry sometimes about my father.
I cry when my father leaves for deployments.
I am a military child who's lived in two different states.

I understand we need soldiers to defend our homes.
I say we need more people like my father.
I dream that our military is the strongest.
I try to be a strong American like my father.
I hope other countries can get along with America.
I am a military child who's lived in two different states.

Kylee Eidell, Grade 5
Walker Intermediate School, KY

Home

Glances at my brother tell me he's working hard on his reading homework
I have sighted Mama Dora watering her petunias during the hottest part of the day
(I bet those flowers are grateful)
The volume of my dogs' yelping increases as they beg me to give
them their freedom from the kennel
I sense the presence of my grandfather bush hogging the field on
his big, green tractor
The delicious aroma of corn, mashed potatoes, peas, green beans,
and rolls my mom has been laboring over
The scent of wet dog as Reese runs through the sprinkler,
flinging mud to Nashville
Spitting out water as my brother squirts his water gun at me
like there's no tomorrow
Ignoring the wind as I run through fields with my trusty canine
Clutching bacon treats as my dogs sit, rollover, beg, anything to
receive one of those delicious treats
Feeling the lock as I imprison my dogs once again
Overjoyed to know my dogs are content, homework is complete,
and relaxation is near.

Kenzie Tomes, Grade 6
College View Middle School, KY

A Stormy Day

Breathtaking raindrops pounding on my bedroom window
Dogs howling at the rain like the wind outside
Plants getting blown out of the ground like Hurricane Katrina all over again
Each boom of thunder is like a beat of a drum
The sight of lightning is like a bright camera flash
My brother wimping under the bed like an unpleased baby
I feel depressed and sad

Mitchell Smith, Grade 5
Bailey Elementary School, NC

I Am an Immigrant

I am an immigrant waiting in line watching others passing and failing the inspection.
I wonder what group I am going to fit into and if my family will pass.
I hear people around me speaking different languages I don't understand. I hear people crying because of their family's separation.
I see families with smiles and families who are sad. I also see a large tall statue that I believe is called the Statue of Liberty.
I want to know what the people are saying and if they are talking about me or my family.
I am very scared because I am getting closer to the front of the line. I really hope I will pass with my family.
I pretend that I have already passed and am on my way.
I feel very nervous, but also a little excited.
I touch my Dad's hand and ask him if he thinks we will pass.
I worry that we will be separated.
I cry because I want to get this over with.
I am next in line.
I understand why I am scared.
I say please help me pass.
I dream of being in the United States with my family.

Delaney Kuhlman, Grade 5
St Joseph School, KY

I Am an Immigrant

I am an immigrant just arriving at a large building people around me are calling Ellis Island
I wonder why we are at this large building when my mother takes my hand and drags me off of the ship
I hear a lot of voices and languages I don't speak
I want to go into the New World so bad
I am wondering why we have to take all these tests
I pretend like I can do anything
I feel happy to be off the ship but scared I won't pass the tests
I touch the freezing cold bench before I sit down
I worry that everyone besides me will pass and go into the New World
I cry because my mom looks so scared
I am wondering how my family feels
I understand that I might not pass and that scares me
I say to my mother what is going to happen to me she does not know
I dream that everything will be okay with me and my family and that we will go into the New World
but for right now I am at Ellis Island

Emily Johnson, Grade 5
St Joseph School, KY

I Am an Immigrant

I'm so scared what if the food I get might give me food poisoning and I don't make it to the next day.
I wonder how many languages are going through my head.
I hear babies crying, people talking about there spoiled food, and 20 different languages.
I see people making nasty faces at there food, my family having a worried look on their face, and people crying.
I want my food to be good, my family not to be worried, and my clothes not to be wet.
I'm having a terrible time on this ship all crammed and wet.
I pretend I'm eating the best food in the world.
I feel crammed and worried.
I touch my sister's hand and ask if it's going to be all right?
I worry I won't pass the exam.
I cry because half my family isn't here.
I'm trying to make my family happy.
I understand why they're worried.
I say no matter what happens I love you.
I am an American.

Macey Heck, Grade 5
St Joseph School, KY

The Pickle

There once was a big green pickle,
That cost just a penny and a nickel;
Said Mama Cucumber,
"I'll sleep and I'll slumber."
While you find someone you can tickle!

Logan Estep, Grade 5
Mineral Wells Elementary School, WV

A Girl Named Ish

There once was a girl named Ish,
Who went to the river to fish;
She caught one, one day,
Then threw it away,
So that day she got her first wish.

Ariel Francis, Grade 5
Mineral Wells Elementary School, WV

A Boy

There once was a boy with lots of toys.
He never shared with other boys.
So he was put in time out.
Then he decided to pout.
He always made a lot of noise.

Jadyn Hollis, Grade 4
Centennial Elementary School, TN

Horse with No Shoe

There once was a horse with no shoe,
Who cried to his master, "Boo-hoo!"
The master was dead,
When he fell on his head,
So the horse galloped off to the zoo!

Tyler Keeney, Grade 5
Mineral Wells Elementary School, WV

A Boy Named Joe

There once was a boy named Joe
Who stubbed his wee tiny toe
He jumped all around
With a mighty big frown
And went to the doctor you know

AJ Welch, Grade 4
Centennial Elementary School, TN

Mr. Mod

There once was nice man named Mod,
Who really was strange and quite odd;
He had a bad day,
And sat down by the bay,
He got eaten by a giant cod!

Hannah Meadows, Grade 5
Mineral Wells Elementary School, WV

Unwanted Everything

I walk into my baby blue room and look at the tall night stand in front
That is holding all of the pieces of my life.
I dedicate myself fully to all of these objects . . .
So this is to the lizard that crawls across my dreams at night,
To my iPod that makes me happy when I am sad,
To my dog's old blue collar that helps me remember her on trips,
To my earphones that plug me into my feelings,
To my journal,
To my school papers I got 100 percent on in fifth grade,
To the books from preschool that help me remember all of my teachers,
To the Baylor honor code that helps to keep me noble-spirited,
To my first pop art painting that reminds me I can do anything,
To my dog's old Halloween costume of a witch that always makes me laugh.
Why do I keep these?
These items are all pieces of me and I'm not letting myself go.
These objects represent many things I have ever said . . .
Like when I said I wanted an iPod,
Or when I went to Wendy's and got my green lizard,
Or when I saw the store blue sky and went in to get my journal.
Thank you my treasures
For bringing back all of my memories of everything I have ever done
Or said, or heard every day of every week.

Mattie Sienknecht, Grade 6
Baylor School, TN

The Game Winning Shot

Three seconds left on the clock,
We were in-bounding the ball at mid-court,
I was wide open and said pass me the rock,
then I pump-faked the shot and drove to the lane,
Hoping for a foul I spun and put up the lay up,
It bounced off the backboard and rolled around the rim,
Next it went in and the ref blew the whistle,
I immediately went to the free throw line while he bounced me the ball,
I dribbled a few times and spun the ball and shot,
Everybody was watching as it hit nothing but the net,
My teammates stormed on to the court,
They lifted me up while everybody cheered!
And that is my game winning shot!

Clay Taylor, Grade 5
JJ Jones Intermediate School, NC

My Heart Is Talking

My heart's wailing to the moon.
The silent moon
In outer space
Giving light, making eclipses too!
Making darkness
Making light
The sun giving light to the moon
My heart's silently talking to the earth, no longer wailing to the moon.

Earth
Where I wish to stay.

Chandler Wise, Grade 6
Hobgood Elementary School, TN

The First Star I Saw Tonight

The sun's going down and I'm getting sleepy.
My eyes start to hurt and I'm getting weepy.
My mom says I should go to bed, but I disagree,
I want to look up at the sky above me.
As I look out the window,
I see a star peeping at me,
Which makes me so happy.
As I say my prayers for the first star, I see,
I plopped in my bed and fell fast asleep!

Sarah Morrison, Grade 5
Paint Lick Elementary School, KY

Memories

Painful memories —
In a way they'll break your heart.
Of all the things to remember,
They are an important part.
Painful memories come back to me sometimes,
When I think of them I'll say
Good-bye to them —
Just for now,
And then I'll run away.

Molly Aslin, Grade 6
Woodland Presbyterian School, TN

Flowers

Flowers, flowers, flowers, oh how
I love flowers.
Tall flowers,
Small flowers,
Long flowers,
Short flowers,
Don't matter what kind
I love them so.

Naomi Nicole Goodie, Grade 4
Tazewell-New Tazewell Primary School, TN

My Dog

My dog is cute and white.
My dog is so white that she looks like vanilla ice cream.
She looks like a cloud when we play outside.
The reason she is so cute,
She loves to wear her dress and play with balls.
Another thing that makes her cute,
She hates strangers.
This makes her very protective of me.

Brianna Wilmot, Grade 5
Paint Lick Elementary School, KY

Bethany

Bethany is my big sister,
I love her very much.
She cheers me up when I am sad.
When I need help, I know who to call!

Alexandria Grimes, Grade 4
Stantonsburg Elementary School, NC

Ode to Owls

Owls fly high in the sky till they reach the starry night
Owls fly free like bees flying around
Owls hunt and caught their prey like wolves in the dark night
Owls fly to the east to hibernate for the winter
Owls stay still in the tallest trees in the dark and scary night
Owls scare birds like ghosts scare people
Owls sleep during the sunny day
Owls awake in the dark night
Owls eat rats and mouse like snakes
Owls are guards at night
Owls are the wise creatures
Owls are courage
Owls are nice if you're nice

Andrea Rosario, Grade 6
Bernheim Middle School, KY

Rivka*

My name is Rivka
and I am a Jew.
I am stuck in Auschwitz
My new name is J356145.
J for Jew.
3 for the number of cows I had.
5 for my family members dead.
6 for my age.
1 for me the only one left.
4 and 5 for the year 1945.
My name is Rivka and I am a Jew
and I was the last Jew out.

Rebecca Walker, Grade 6
East Mooresville Intermediate School, NC
**Inspired by "The Devil's Arithmetic" by Jane Yolen*

Bebe the Blanket

I have something important to me.
She's as special as can be.
My Great Aunt Bonnie gave me this.
Ever since, I've been full of bliss.
She is pink like a rose,
and sweet and plump as Santa's nose.
She's as soft as a bunny,
but to me valuable as money.
She soothes me when I'm sad,
and gives me happiness and makes me glad.
She is always oh so fine.
I'm more than happy that she's mine.

Olivia Forsythe, Grade 6
Woodland Presbyterian School, TN

Mud

Messy, slippery
Oozing, wet, brown
Squishy, squashy, slimy, gritty
Dirt

Levi Hoce, Grade 5
Mineral Wells Elementary School, WV

The Cow

There once was a black and white cow,
Who never did "moo" but said, "meow."
The vet picked a daisy
For the cow that was crazy
"You need help, and you need it right now!"

Caitlin Moore, Grade 5
Mineral Wells Elementary School, WV

Tin Can Man

There once was a strange little man,
Who lived in an old vegetable can;
He stayed right at home,
In his house of chrome,
But never cooked with a pan.

Courtney Vincent, Grade 5
Mineral Wells Elementary School, WV

Hello Kitty

Hello Kitty is so pretty
So is Mrs. Hello Kitty.
I told Hello Kitty hello
And she said her favorite
Color is yellow!

Rahjay Lewis, Grade 4
Centennial Elementary School, TN

Softball

Softball.
So fun!
Hitting balls everywhere,
Never can see them.
Awesome!

Erin Beighle, Grade 5
Walton-Verona Middle School, KY

Fall

Forest
Leaves falling down
A beautiful wonderful painting
Cool

Chan Ng Cashin, Grade 4
St Thomas More Catholic School, NC

Autumn

Wafting the crisp breeze
And hearing the crunchy leaves
Falling down from trees

Hannah Lewis, Grade 6
Musselman Middle School, WV

Thunderstorm

Thunder snaps, boom
Lightning cracks the hard concrete
Rain falls heavily

Nicoria Williams, Grade 5
E O Young Elementary School, NC

Shelf On My Dresser

There are many things on my peach colored dresser
A wallet made of black smooth leather
My memory box that I will look at when I am old, my shot glass from Europe
Old wadded up pieces of paper never to be touched again
My orange bible of the Psalms, my old earphones, broken
The tennis ball I hit back and forth with my grandfather
A sharpie, marsh colored, my dark green flashlight
A twenty dollar bill not to be touched until Christmas
The mouse pad my fifth grade teacher made, mall Tycoon 3
A pocket knife with my initials engraved
My alligator knife made of alligator jaw bone, fake handcuffs
My plastic toy gun, an old gameboy advanced
An air hockey puck in the shape of an octagon
Harry Potter Tapes, the Hobbit on CD
An old fad, a bakugon little toy ball that transforms into a monster
Old clam shells filled with bacteria
A picture of my parents on Easter, a small night light
I keep these things because I don't bother to clean that shelf
I won't clean this until my parents make me
Most of these things do not mean anything to me
But a few of them like the shot glass mean a lot to me

Jordan Kelley, Grade 6
Baylor School, TN

Milwaukee, Wisconsin

Houses lined perfectly with bushes in my uncle's neighborhood
All the houses, built up tall, like skyscrapers
Uncle Scott's job as assistant coach of Marquette basketball team
We emerge from the lounges of the building as we hear:
The loud bah-bouncing of the basketball in the gym
The squealing sound of shoes scraping the waxed floor
Sounds swarm around my head like the buzzing of bees
Our siblings await in their house as we approach the porch
There is a flowing aroma of baby lotion that fragrances my skin
Warm vanilla sugar wallflowers fill my nose to make me feel at home
Sweet sautéed spinach and salty sea salmon water my mouth
Sour lemonade swims down my throat, and I pucker
I twirl varied sizes of cheese wheels in the cheese factory
Cold golden doorknobs, entering the fabulous mall with everything
So excited to reenter the snowy, beautiful place
My sanctuary, filled with amazing family and friends

Macey Higdon, Grade 6
College View Middle School, KY

The State Fair

The smells, sights, and tastes of the fair fill my senses like water flowing in a bucket
Awesomely colored rides are calling to me
Air from the spinning rides are calling to me
Rock music drifts loudly through the air
Hotdogs and fries are delightful like a warm hug
Greenhouses smell like perfume
Sharp darts flying and balloons popping
The lights go down like a setting sun
The people drift away like the summer breeze

Lizeth Estrada, Grade 4
Bailey Elementary School, NC

I Am the Daughter of Two Soldiers

I am the daughter of two soldiers.
I wonder what my parents are thinking about the war.
I hear the missing sounds of them when they are gone.
I see their faces every day.
I want them to stay so bad but they can't.
I am a daughter of two soldiers.

I pretend like I'm my mom or dad fighting at war.
I say I won't cry, but I always do.
I feel terrible when they leave and can't make me laugh.
I touch their hearts so they know I love them.
I worry what will happen to them when they leave.
I cry every day they are gone.
I am a daughter of two soldiers.

I understand why they leave.
I say I will be all right, but I lie.
I dream it will all be over quickly.
I try to fight crying and being sad.
I hope they will always be all right.
I am the daughter of two soldiers.

Victoria Hyde, Grade 5
Walker Intermediate School, KY

I Am

I am a loving sister
I wonder if my brother loves me
I hear my brother cry when I am mean to him
I see tears run down his face
I want to tell him I love him
I am a loving sister

I pretend I'm not mean to him
I feel like I'm a worthless sister
I touch his hurt heart
I worry if he is okay
I cry when he cries
I am a loving sister

I understand what he feels like
I say I'm sorry...sometimes
I dream one day he knows I truly love him
I try not to be mean to him but it is so hard
I hope we become a loving family...eventually
I am a loving sister

Morgan Gravel, Grade 6
Bernheim Middle School, KY

Everest

High above the treetops,
round the mountain we go,
hikers up early,
majestic with its snow,
up and down the hikers go.

Claire Waddell, Grade 4
Evangelical Christian School Ridgelake Campus, TN

Honor of My Grandpa

I love my grandpa,
He's the best.
I went to see him every day when he was here.
He loved his family.
He loved his church.
He loved to go fishing.
He loved to hunt coons.
But most of all he loved ME!!!
He had cancer in his liver,
And while he was sick
he had to stay home
but, he had his family by his side
And when he died he had a smile on his face,
because he knew he would see us again.
Now he's gone,
but not forgotten,
I'll always love and remember my grandpa.
He's in a better place
forever and always
I hope he has the best in Heaven.

Brianna Townsend, Grade 6
Saint Pauls Middle School, NC

I Am

I am caring and hardworking
I wonder how old I will be when I die
I hear my sister laughing
I see people smiling at me
I want peace in the world
I am caring and hardworking

I pretend to pitch in the World Series game 7
I feel lucky for everything that I have
I touch a baseball, the thing I love
I worry that the world will end
I cry when I lose a loved one
I am caring and hardworking

I understand that I will not live forever
I say that a record is meant to be broken
I dream to be Major League Baseball player
I try to give 105% every time I do something
I hope that my dreams will come true
I am caring and hardworking

Ethan Moore, Grade 6
Bernheim Middle School, KY

Thanksgiving

On Thanksgiving we give thanks
On Thanksgiving we don't do pranks
Pilgrims and Native Americans came together
And now since then it's celebrate forever
At the table there will be pumpkin pie
I wonder which pumpkin had to die.

Anthony Jarvis, Grade 5
North Wilkesboro Elementary School, NC

Basketball

B all bouncing on the court
A ll players having fun
S o many kids
K ids having fun
E verybody playing
T alking and shooting
B all going in the hole
A ll players having fun
L urking on the court
L eaning on each other

Megan N. Herbol, Grade 5
Walton-Verona Middle School, KY

Oops!

Hey Mom
I accidentally
challenged Robbie
to a game of baseball.

We were ready but when I pitched
he missed and shattered the window hence
the word OOPS!

Sorry.

Johnathan Canoy, Grade 5
Cool Spring Elementary School, NC

Moonlight

M oonlight
O pen to all
O n the twinkling sky
N ot dark but light
L it by all who seek
I nvisible at day, seeable at night
G rabbing all eyes
H oly shine
T o all a good night

Terese Chando, Grade 5
Hunter GT Magnet Elementary School, NC

Hurt

A person getting punched,
broken hearted
sad, lonely
quiet as a mouse,
sickness,
upset,
afraid of everything,
stressed,
victim, of a bully

Lesley Hooks, Grade 6
College View Middle School, KY

The Turkey That Doesn't Get Eaten

Gobble, gobble what should I do
Thanksgiving is almost here.
I'd be gobbled up before I have a tear.

There may be something, but what should it be?
Going skinny will work
because something is better then nothing.

I know what to do I will make my own weights and skates.
I'm going for some biking, I never would be typing.

I'm really skinny now, but what would people think of me.
too skinny or thick, a disgrace or grace, an ugly monster, what they
will think, I don't know?

A car is pulling up, now what to do,
I'm scared, stepping out are 2
tall men then they say eeeeeewwwwww.

The eeeeeewwwwww is what I loved to hear then I have a tear and a cheer.
I survived this year but next year boohoo.

Keelan Hartmann, Grade 4
Moyock Elementary School, NC

Together We Can
Bills vs Steelers

Together we can win this football game
Steeler's quarterback sacked on the fifty yard line
and twenty five more seconds in the game
the score is fourteen twenty-one Bills
the quarterback threw a gain of twenty-five
yards and still on his feet FUMBLE!
We've got fifteen more seconds of the game
and seventy five more yards to go for the Bills
INTERCEPTION five more seconds in the game he is on his feet running
TOUCHDOWN Steelers the score is
Twenty, twenty-one Bills
It looks like they are going for two
The two point conversion is success
And it's the end of the game the score is twenty-two
Twenty-one Steelers
Together we could win this

Max Steele, Grade 5
Bostian Elementary School, NC

Days in Chicago

The gigantic, old, legendary Wrigley Field is in the near distance
The tall, towering Sears Tower is right in front of me
Families are laughing, joking around and having fun while they roam the "windy city"
The wind is really raging and rustling, through the whole city; everyone is trying to keep their hair from messing up
You can smell the aroma of delicious pizza from miles away
Chocolate pop tarts in my mouth. They are melting in my mouth like ice
The bags in my hand after I finish shopping
Excited

Maddie Connor, Grade 6
College View Middle School, KY

Night

Now the night has fallen
Now the day is done
Now the stars are coming out
One by one by one
Soon millions of stars
Are twinkling in the sky
The night has just come
No need to say goodbye
To the stars, stars, stars
And the milk-white moon
The dawn is coming now
The day will be here soon
And throughout the words I have written
The whole night has gone by
And ever since I went to bed
I have stared up at the sky.

Greta Abbey, Grade 5
Montessori Community School, NC

Burning Fire

My life is walking in a wire
Why won't something change
I'm going crazy
Nothing is going to rearrange,
I need someone to help me
All I want is to be out of this cage
With a life that is free
So please, please, come with me
Down this winding road
Please, please, come with me
Life can be demanding,
But we'll keep on standing,
Staying strong together,
Growing old together,
Watching the world go by.
Burning fire.

Joey Uzarski, Grade 5
Duke Middle School, NC

Veterans

Oh it's such an honor
to hear their great tales.
Soldier after soldier,
risking their lives,
to see our red, white and blue flag
wave proudly in the sky.
How bomb after bomb was fired
as you see our flag standing free.
now it's time to say thanks,
with a hardy wave
we salute you as we say thanks.
So now you know veterans,
are not just here for one day
no, but our veterans are here to stay.

Hannah Stephens, Grade 6
Saint Pauls Middle School, NC

My Aztec Face

"Sit!" what a serious tone
"Wait!" no smile on the priest
today, my tribe is all about a mask
my mask
my Aztec mask
gods and religion are everything
my owl face
my religious face
so today I'm the offering
with my mask I go
a meal for the gods

Hattie Phillips, Grade 6
College View Middle School, KY

The Cobra Bite

If the cobra snake thinks you're bait,
You'll experience a terrible fate.
Imagine feeling that severe pain!
It just might drive you insane.
You'll have a sad look in your eye
Because you know you might die.
When you discover that you're all right,
You'll shake off the terrifying fright
And start celebrating with great delight.
After all, you've survived a cobra bite!

Mark Hiestand, Grade 4
Sequoyah Elementary School, TN

Winter Is...

Winter is very white
With long and cold nights
With lights in the sky,
The heat of the summer will die,
Winter is very cold,
With snow lining the roads,
Winter is very bright,
With twinkling Christmas lights
Winter is a joyous delight,
Watching the starry night.

Emma Cavagnaro, Grade 6
Woodland Presbyterian School, TN

The House

There is a place
I call home
It is not made of brick or stone
It smells so sweet
Sometimes I eat
My door, my bed, my seat
Can you guess where I live
No more hints I shall give
My house is made of gingerbread
Now my poem has been read

Joy Diehl, Grade 5
Mt. Juliet Elementary School, TN

Together We Can

T eam work makes the dream work
O ptimism
G reat things
E xcitedly we can do great things
T hrilling things
H appily
E asily, if we do it together
R eally cool things

W e can reach our goal together
E very goal we make we will reach it

C an do great things
A wesome
N ever give up

Riley Johnson, Grade 4
Bostian Elementary School, NC

When Life Gives

When life gives you
A whole plate of cookies
Take them and run

When life gives you
Teddy Bears
Go have some fun

When life gives you
A mine
You'd think of all the gems

When life gives you
A handful of friends
You take care of them

Katrin Anne Flores, Grade 5
SCAPA at Bluegrass, KY

How Can You Change the World?

You can change the world
Reduce...Reuse...Recycle to
Change the world
Turn off the lights to
Change the world
Do as much as you can to
Change the world
How can you change the world?
Believe
Try
Help
Change the world
Help your community to
Change the world
You know you can

Maya Saterson, Grade 5
Duke Middle School, NC

My First Day

I remember all the smiling faces,
More kids than I could count,
I hoped that they would like me here,
Or at least treat me like I am there,

I knew it would be different,
I hoped it would be good,
A wide variety of people to choose from,
I tried my best to pick the right ones,

STOMPs loud as elephants,
And chit chat down the hall,
Whispers through the classroom,
Facial expressions changed to doom,

Now I have been here for a while,
I have millions of friends,
Though not everything is perfect,
There is so many good things it is terrific!

Hope Streble, Grade 6
Bernheim Middle School, KY

We Used to Be

I always picture you and me
Forever we use to be
We did everything together
But with someone else you rather

As you take your turn
I start to burn
When I think about you
Only it was us two

I started to realize
I began to despise
One day I thought you would be my wife
Now I want you out of my life

You came back to me
You just can't see
Your time is out
You better run about

Nicholas Yates, Grade 6
Bernheim Middle School, KY

Summer Fun

Everyone running and shouting
Jump roping in the hot sun
Some are having lemonade
What a wonderful summer fun
it is on a hot summer day
The sun is very bright
What a wonderland of
Summer fun

Asia Battle, Grade 4
Stantonsburg Elementary School, NC

Missing Them

They look at you,
But don't move.
You cry,
They stare,
Unblinking,
Unmoving,
No warmth.
You know what has happened.

You long for them for weeks or months,
But know they aren't coming back.
You sit,
You think
You believe,
Nothing good is ever going to happen.

You long for their presence,
For their fun,
For their happiness,
You long for them.

Ava Pacchiana, Grade 5
Duke Middle School, NC

A Forest for My Own

The forest I own is a perfect place
A place with no trash and no filth
With trees and leaves and bumble bees
A perfect place you see
The forest I own is a perfect place
A place with no chaos no fighting
A perfect place
With ponds and bays
A perfect place you could say
The forest I own is a perfect place
But in the morning
Your face will magically morph
From sleepy to fresh
But in a split second
The forest disappears
And then I wake up
See the walls around me
Stare into lights
And decide
To make my dreams my reality

Enoch Kuan, Grade 5
Duke Middle School, NC

Taylor

T aylor is awesome!
A sk her if she likes me!
Y o! She's pretty!
L OL she's funny!
O MG her performance was cool!
R ock on Taylor Swift!

Seth Overton, Grade 4
Centennial Elementary School, TN

Brussels Sprouts

Stop throwing us, we are not dodge balls
We are Brussels Sprouts, you know that's all
Don't squish us, that's not cool
Even though we are on the floor at school
We are not your enemies
We are nice friends as you see

Remember we're not soccer balls
So don't kick us down the halls
If you like the color green
We are the greenest things ever seen

We are not your dog's chewing toy
We are full of yummy joy
Eat me, eat me, if you please
then we will stop talking to you, as you see

Kylen Williams-Harden, Grade 5
Hunter GT Magnet Elementary School, NC

Midfielder

Luis, you're in!
Chasing the ball,
Running to charge,
Watching from the corner of my eye,
Swinging my foot in his direction,
Disappointing that he gets away!
Sprinting next to him to the goalie,
Charging ahead so I can block the shot,
Stopping the shot by locking my ankle,
Juggling the ball back up the field,
Clearing the path for the forwards,
Thinking about where the best aim will be,
Kicking the ball at just the right place,
Twirl! the ball dances to THE man,
Swoosh, our forward makes a point!
My job as Midfielder has been a success!

Luis Osorno, Grade 4
JJ Jones Intermediate School, NC

Lighting Up the Night Sky

Lighting up the night sky
right now it sounds like fun.
All of the stars and moon
are out but there's no sun.

Lying down under everything
there it is a full moon.
I see all of the grasshoppers
and the dish ran away with the spoon.

Now I did all of these things
lying down under pretty stuff.
And hearing a lot of insects
I think I've had enough!

Maddy Brewer, Grade 5
Petersburg Elementary School, WV

Baseball

Blake's my name, baseball is the game.
I like to hear the crowd ripple when I get a triple.
I really enjoy my coach and my team,
But those umpires sure can be mean.
Every time he starts to shout,
I hope he says, "Safe" instead of "Out."
That's why baseball is my game.

Blake Foster, Grade 5
Paint Lick Elementary School, KY

Math

Math to me is like trying to find my way out of a maze
Giving me hints and clues like word problems
Numbers flowing through my head
Figuring out what x equals in Algebra
Shapes and size are all around me
Spying to see if fractions can be made equivalent
I feel intelligent and equated

Marco Solana, Grade 5
Bailey Elementary School, NC

Family

Family is very important
never
take it for granted
You will miss them a lot
later in life
even if you will see them another time or place
Family is very important

Olivia Roberts, Grade 6
Woodland Presbyterian School, TN

The Silent Class

We all stare at the teacher
she looks at us
she asks us "why so quiet?"
We still just stare
We listen to her talk
We doze on and off
Then all of a sudden
she is called out of the room
she leaves
we look
we watch
we stare
Then…
BOOM!
We all start talking
we jibber-jabber
we yell
we scream
Then an awkward silence
she walks back in
and the cycle repeats.

TaNia Thompson, Grade 6
McGee's Crossroads Middle School, NC

So Much Depends Upon*

Family to help
you

To love you
forever

And cherish
you

So much depends upon

Friends to be
there

To help you
understand

Help you feel
better

So much depends upon

Soldiers to fight
slavery

To be for
freedom

Haley Tesseneer, Grade 6
Bernheim Middle School, KY
**Patterned after William Carlos Williams*

Old Friends

I remember when
We played in
The club house
And when we
Got hit by
The tree and
Our bikes got
Stolen in the
Bike park and
When I won
The game of
Cops and robbers
I stole all
Of the money
And when we went
To the movies
With our girls
And then got
In trouble they
Were the best
But now you
Left so goodbye.

Nicholas Curtis, Grade 6
Bernheim Middle School, KY

BMX

BMX biking is so much fun.
It makes your heart race,
It makes your heart run.
You fly over tabletops,
And really big jumps,
And go so fast,
You pump through humps!
When you crash and down you fall,
You say you don't hurt at all.
The truth is that you really do,
Just give it a minute, or give it a few.
All the pain you really start feeling,
Makes you wish you would really start healing.
In BMX racing, there is no room for fear,
Especially when the finish line is near.

Noah Davis, Grade 5
Providence Academy, TN

Ode To My PS-3

Ode to my PS3!
It relates to me
Without it, where would I be?
Oh how I love thee
When I win, it makes me feel flashy

When trying to win, its a challenge
Therefore, the room has to be in silence
Making room to play outside gives it a balance

Ode to my PS-3!
How it relates to me
This game is my claim to fame
For every point earned is a valuable lesson learned

James Williams, Grade 4
Weldon Elementary School, NC

The USA

Red, white, and blue,
The colors of our flag stand out proud and true.
There are white stars on a blue field with red and white stripes.
They remind me of the veterans,
Who risked their lives
So the people of the USA
Could live in peace and be free.
They are the heroes
That represent you and me.
They stood together as one.
And they kept fighting till they were done.
They have fallen and lost their lives in wars
We pray for each one of them,
Now that their souls live forever more.

Jovan Lowery, Grade 6
Saint Pauls Middle School, NC

The Beach

At the beach it's always an adventure
The wind blowing my hair like swaying palm trees
Kids laughing and playing like busy buzzing bumblebees
Waves crashing the shore like a summer storm
Swimming sea creatures floating gracefully in the water like angels
Boats moving swiftly across the water
People lying on the beach like statues getting a tan
Seagulls singing in harmony
Swimming in the water like fish
Bitter salty water in my mouth as I gasp for air
Sunset looking like the northern lights
Stars twinkling like diamonds in the night
As I walk from the beach
I feel adventurous

Jada Dunn, Grade 4
Bailey Elementary School, NC

Granny Dear

Dearest Granny we loved you so,
But then came the day when you passed away
Leaving us wishing you were still here.
Oh Great-Granny we miss you dear,
More and more as each day grows near.
Granny dear we know you are near,
High in the sky with wings held proudly,
And a halo on your head,
Thinking of us down here,
On little Earth,
Which you look at so simply,
As you watch us with care.
And we will see you when our day comes,
As an angelic angel.

Riley Patterson, Grade 6
Coopertown Middle School, TN

Seasons

Spring is the season of colors and flowers.
And many short and drizzly showers.
In spring there is spring break;
No falling leaves, so you don't have to rake.

In May, good smells are in the air
Flowers, flowers everywhere.
When spring ends, let's have some fun.
Come out, come out Mr. Sun.

After summer, that's not all.
Leaves are changing; here comes Fall!
Winter snow is on the way.
All the seasons are here to stay.

Kate Perkins, Grade 5
Evangelical Christian School Ridgelake Campus, TN

Baby Cousin

Down the dark hallway
Into the warm room
In the tiny crib
With a tear down her cheek
Underneath the bed was the bear
Upon her bed I put it,
Except she kept on crying
Toward the chest I walked
Down I looked,
To find her blankie
After setting it on her bed,
Along her face, there was no binky
Without a thought, I grab it off the table,
Before sitting in the rocking chair,
Down went little Maggie's eyes, she was fast asleep.

Baylee Thorne, Grade 6
Bernheim Middle School, KY

Christmas Time

Look at those Christmas trees
and those people filled with glee.
The red and green lights
that are like Rudolph's nose at night.
While Santa climbs down your chimney
you're in bed listening to a melody.
You wake from a dream
but all it did seem.
St. Nick had gone,
across the roof he went along.
His reindeer were leading,
but as he was leaving, my heart started beating.
I dashed into the den
where the presents did lay,
for I was happy and opened them without delay.

Kyle Friedlander, Grade 5
Moyock Elementary School, NC

Braces

My job is very arduous
That means it's very hard
I'm here to make sure your teeth are real straight
But that seems real bizarre
I'm on your teeth for three whole years
But please don't cry and shed your tears
I remember when you first got me
The dentist said you need me
The only thing I heard was you shrieking
They gave you laughing gas
That sure made the time pass
When they were done you looked in the mirror
But when you saw me all you did was shiver
Although I'm on your teeth for three whole years
When you're thirteen you'll be the envy of your peers

Pamela Reid, Grade 5
Hunter GT Magnet Elementary School, NC

I Am

I am funny and kind
I wonder why I don't have a guitar
I hear a composer playing
I see a composer
I want a guitar
I am funny and kind

I pretend to be a composer
I feel like a composer
I touch a guitar
I worry about who I am going to be when I grow up
I cry because of a love song
I am funny and kind

I understand the life of a composer
I say what is nice
I dream to be a composer
I try very hard (sometimes)
I hope I grow up to be like my brother
I am funny and kind

Jason Miller, Grade 4
Centennial Elementary School, TN

Ode to Boys

Boys try to get girls by being a jerk
If only they knew it didn't work.
They act sweet, just like a bunny
They call you nicknames like boo bear, boo, and honey.
They try to show off but get hurt instead
"Mom! I need the meds!"
Some try to cuddle with you
But if you were in trouble, you would too.
Boys act dumb, just to get a laugh
But, they never want to take a bath.
One boy can be a girl's life
Just one breakup can stab like a knife
They don't pay attention all the time
They'll do something dumb just for a dime.
They're not all that bad if they try,
Sometimes, they just have to lie,
To get away from a girl's anger
If only they knew the danger.
Some are mean, selfish, rude
That'll never be my kinda dude.

Ida Dewhirst, Grade 6
Bernheim Middle School, KY

What If?

What if on Halloween I break my leg?
What if I get no candy?
What if I break my arm?
What if I break my neck?
Halloween is still going to be awesome, though.

Cali Wilcoxen, Grade 5
Mineral Wells Elementary School, WV

Sandwiches and Cookies

sandwiches
tasty, healthy
good, delicious, best
I love them both
unhealthful, yummy, burnt
chocolatey, oatmeal
cookies

Katy Greer, Grade 4
Centennial Elementary School, TN

Necklace

Necklace
larger, wider
wraps, attaches, constricts
clasp, diamonds, metals, chains
clips, squeezes, glistens
smaller, thinner
Bracelet

Avery Gunn, Grade 4
Centennial Elementary School, TN

It Just Won't Fit

Sometimes your clothes just don't fit.
Your pants are too short
for you to bend or to sit.
Your sleeves are too long
and your hats are too tight.
Why is it some mornings your clothes?
Don't fit right!

Amber Reid, Grade 5
E O Young Elementary School, NC

October

O ctober is here
C andy a galore
T rick or treat
O h so much candy
B est costumes in town
E aster gone past
R esting after a long night

Kelijah Edgerton, Grade 5
E O Young Elementary School, NC

Teacher

T eaches incredible things
E asy lessons for most subjects
A wesome personality
C aring for students
H elps students learn
E asy to please
R eading teachers are the best

Ke'moni Champion, Grade 5
Carver Elementary School, NC

My Bureau

Collecting dust in my tan rectangular room
Lay all sorts of things that I use for fun.
From things that I had when I was young that's broken,
To items that are new.
These are the amazing and cool things about me.
On my bureau lays my bishop hat that I made for a costume,
Under that is huge bucket of change that I collect for air hockey games.
Behind that is a black clock that is always eight minutes off.
Off to the right I have a coconut with no milk in it
That I found when I was in Florida.
Next I have a dead tarantula that my mom got in Peru for me
It's in a glass case.
Near that I have three soccer trophies for first place that I won.
I have my phone that I always forget to turn off.
Then I have my favorite thing of all
My piggy bank that's an elephant that I had forever.
Just one more interesting item of me,
Just above the tarantula,
Lays a stingray egg just waiting to be born.
These are the interesting and amazing items of me.
Those items that amaze me.

Murphy McMahon, Grade 6
Baylor School, TN

Fort Walton Beach Florida

The Pretty Beach,
Soft sand goes over my tan feet and through my toes
Cold aqua blue ocean makes some of the sand moist as it goes over the sand
Little kids running and screaming with joy, as they disappear in a crowd of people
The loud ocean goes "Whoosh" as it goes over people's feet and over the sand
Oily Tanning Oil on my tan body as I lay out in the sun on the beach
Hot delicious food being eaten on a blanket for a picnic
Standing up and walking toward the ocean to wade in
A wave comes at me
I taste the salt water in my mouth
Stand up and run out quickly
Grab my soft towel, and walk up to the condo
Amazing and happy as I walk off the beach.

Jada Head, Grade 6
College View Middle School, KY

Ayla

Blue, fun, smart, crazy!
Relative to Danny and Christina Lang
Resident to Lebanon Junction

Who reads *Diary of the Wimpy Kid*, *Goose Bumps*, and *Scary Stores to Tell in the Dark*!
Who likes basketball, the wii, and animals!
Who loves the basketball team Kentucky, and volleyball!
Who fears clowns, snakes, and tornados!
Who wishes I was rich and had a big house.
Who admires mom and dad!!!
Who needs more shoes and clothes oh and some more cd's!
Lang!

Ayla Lang, Grade 6
Bernheim Middle School, KY

I Am a Military Child

I am a military child who was born in Milwaukee, Wisconsin and has lived in 5 different states so far.
I wonder why military soldiers don't always have weekends off.
I hear the fish tank's filter.
I see planes flying over our neighborhood.
I want war to end.
I am a military child who was born in Milwaukee, Wisconsin and has lived in 5 different states so far.

I pretend my dad is by my side.
I feel safe when my family is around.
I touch my heart and feel happy.
I worry that my dad might die in war.
I cry when someone in my family gets hurt.
I am a military child who was born in Milwaukee, Wisconsin and has lived in 5 different states so far.

I understand that soldiers have to fight in war.
I say that our country should have world peace soon.
I dream our country comes together.
I try to respect our country.
I hope not a lot of soldiers die during the war.
I am a military child who was born in Milwaukee, Wisconsin and has lived in 5 different states so far.

Tabetha Schultz, Grade 5
Walker Intermediate School, KY

Alaska

Excited and talkative people gathering in the ship
Like little lions leaping through a field
Icy and harsh dark blue waters colliding against the Serenade of the Seas
Just as thunder crashes in the still night sky right before a storm
The soft melody of elevator music is playing peaceful, praising music
As if I were standing in front of forty flamingos flapping their wings softly in my ears
Loud footsteps of room servers walking past our door are like many timpani drums keeping to the beat
Boom! Boom! Boom!
The smooth and salty Pacific Ocean air filling my nose like a dentist filling a tooth
The Windjammer's aroma of seafood and sandwiches YUMM!
Cheesy ham sandwiches with a side of fries melt in my mouth with warm and fresh flavor
The sweet and pulpy orange juice runs down my parched throat
Like a raindrop in the Sahara Desert
The railing of the stairs, as I go down to the formal party, is a
Smooth, winding, pristine wood
Elegant doorknobs slowly turning as I wander from room to room
Like a cat prowls through the night
Joyful and amazed in this wonderful place
And only at the end does my happiness fade

Morgan Marksberry, Grade 6
College View Middle School, KY

Winter

W onderful noises in the air and the white snowing ground that makes me smile everywhere.
I can't wait to go outside and play in the cold white snowy ground and feel the coldness in the air.
N ever felt the way I do in the grassless ground and all the dew.
T ell all my friends to come over and play with me and you, and run through all that dew.
E very day I go out but that one day I do I say, "I will miss you and see you next year."
R eally fun to play with you but its your time to go and start a new season even if I don't want you to.

Kali Clark, Grade 5
Woodlawn Elementary School, TN

Football Is Such an Exciting Sport!

Football is such an exciting sport!
You have to be willing to run and take a hit,
If you make a score, that's really great,
On defense, you have to be fierce and even a little wild,
On offense, drop back since you are the quarterback,
On special teams, kick the ball so high,
That it seems like it will touch the sky,
On the sideline, sit on the bench,
While the offense is playing, don't talk to the defense,
1 point for an extra point, 2 for a safety,
3 points for a field goal, and 6 for a touchdown,
When you finally step to the line of scrimmage,
Your legs are shaking, your heart is pounding,
You finally will get a chance to become a hero,
You drop back for a pass, throw the football,
For a TOUCHDOWN!
The sounds from the crowd are like a lion roaring!
Football is such an exciting sport!

Brock Heck, Grade 4
JJ Jones Intermediate School, NC

I Am

I am a loving, caring person
I wonder when the life will end
I hear birds singing in the meadows
I see tropical birds flying above head
I want to be a good mother
I am a loving, caring person

I pretend I am a famous person
I feel sad when I think of Jamie
I cry when I think of Jamie
I am a loving, caring person

I understand life is hard so give it all you have
I say live your life to the fullest
I dream I was dating Dustin Smith
I try to do my best on every test
I hope I become famous and rich
I am a loving, caring person

Brandi Hawkins, Grade 6
Bernheim Middle School, KY

Two Faces

Inside I wear two masks.
One that's happy and one that's angry.
Anger smells repulsive, tastes bitter.
Happiness smells scrumptious, tastes luscious and sweet.
Anger is loud like a herd of wild elephants.
Happiness is quiet like a mouse.
Anger is rough like tree bark
Happiness is smooth like satin.
Happiness is the one I wear every day
When I wear it, it shows I am happy

Rebecca Hamlet, Grade 6
College View Middle School, KY

My Life

I am from fashion and riches
I am from cats and dogs
I am from fighting and characteristics
I am from TV and studying
I am from presents under the tree and flowers in a vase

I am from decorations outside and hair styling
I am from music and karate
I am from church and singing
I am from snowboarding and coloring
I am from designing and organizing

I am from showering and mud puddles
I am from sledding in the snow and picnicking
I am from wrapping and smashing
I am from screaming and peacefulness
I am from energetic and snoring

Destiny Warren, Grade 5
Tates Creek Elementary School, KY

Chicago

Extremely bright yellow lights making the city light up
Tons of people walking up and down the sidewalk

Loud sirens flying through the streets
Panic!
Blazing music playing beside the massively tall buildings is WOW!

The crystal clear ocean washing away sand from a busy beach
Strong perfume covering the city with different samples

Delicious five star meals melting on my taste buds
Pale sand grinding in between my teeth as the wind blows

The massive rides wait for people to board
Pretty purses and perfume I'm going to buy with my dad's money

Excited

McKenzie Smith, Grade 6
College View Middle School, KY

Kwele Mask

The air is stale, death is in the air
The air feels heavy like bricks on my back
It tastes thick and creamy
The mask rests on the woman's face
From a beloved family that cherished her
For tonight, her spirit will find peace in heaven
The people that love her will always remember her
The mask will lie there forever like a statue
The mask guides her spirit to God
The heart shaped mask rests perfectly on her face
As the people dance and sing,
The mask awaits its destiny

Katye Knight, Grade 6
College View Middle School, KY

Santa Claus

Santa Claus, Santa Claus
Oh, fat and round Santa Claus.
He lives at the North Pole,
With the reindeer and the elves.

His favorite thing to do,
Would be to eat and drink.
His favorite food is cookies,
And his favorite drink is milk.

He is very jolly and with every step,
His laughter echoes through the halls.
I guess you could say,
I hear him from dusk to dawn.

HO! HO! HO!

Sarah McClellan, Grade 4
Moyock Elementary School, NC

The Falling Star

About to fall
Above my head
Across the ground
Before it's dead
Beside my feet
Beneath my body
Upon the wind
Throughout the rocks
Toward the water
Down the docks
Until the wind, finally stops
Over and over
Without any life
Behind the sky
Past the clouds
Till it is gone forever

Savannah Mills, Grade 6
Bernheim Middle School, KY

Cheer Up!

No one likes
A person who is sad
So cheer up, be positive
Then everyone will be glad!

A way to stop
From wearing a frown
Is to enjoy what you do
And turn the frown upside down

Always believe
In what you do
Never think you're the worst
There's a lot of greatness in you!

Cameron McNeil, Grade 5
Hunter GT Magnet Elementary School, NC

At the Bat

The score is eleven to seven.
The balls keep going up to heaven.
The ball is faster than a ship.
He hits it up with a rip.
The ball is faster than a rocket.
I can't believe the outfielder caught it.
The batter ties his lace.
And everybody's on base.
He hits a line drive.
We almost scored five.
He almost hits it out of the dome.
He is trying to bring me home.
I think we'll score,
And the crowd starts to roar.
The batter slides to the plate.
The umpire yells "Safe!"
I can't believe we won the game.
Some players made it to the Hall of Fame.

John Weaver III, Grade 5
Providence Academy, TN

Man's Best Friend

Of everyone I've ever known
You've never let me down
We've shared a lot of memories
You're the best friend that I've found.

We like to run and play all day.
You like to sleep in my bed.
Although a bath is not your thing,
You like for me to rub your head.

We share a unique language,
That only we can know.
My heart has a special place for you.
My dog, I love you so!
Thanks for sharing your life with me
Our bond will never end.
Some say you're just a dog,
But truly you're man's best friend.

Sarah Abbott, Grade 5
Lake City Elementary School, TN

Fall Is Coming

Fall is coming
Trees get scared because
Fall is coming to take all your leaves!
People put on your coats
So you will not freeze
The temperature may be 60 degrees
But the wind is so strong
It will blow you away!
You'll know if Fall is coming
So get ready!

Kiara King, Grade 6
Kinston Charter Academy, NC

Wishing Star

When you need a wish
Just call for a wishing star
And wish like it's no tomorrow

You could wish for health
No homework for a week or two
Or just to stay up late at night
Wish like it's no tomorrow

Wish for your birthday to come quicker
Christmas every day
Parties
Wish like it's no tomorrow

Wish to live the cool life; to be famous
Be in magazines or riding in limousines
Wish like it's no tomorrow

WISH, WISH, AND WISH
To be the best person you can be
Wish like it's no tomorrow

Caleb Taylor, Grade 4
Weldon Elementary School, NC

Angry

boom, boom
darkness is all I see
my brain turns icy white

it's too quiet
SMASH
there goes my
new mirror
SCREAMING of agony
is all you hear
for hours

my eyelids drop
I'm very exhausted
as I lay down
my brain turns
pink rose petals
the rain goes
to a light drizzle
as I lay my head
down for a long nap

Alesha Simpson, Grade 6
Johnson Traditional Middle School, KY

Reindeer

Reindeer, reindeer click on the roof
They click on the roof with every hoof
I give them all food for free
And in return they bring Santa to me

Lillie Herbstreit, Grade 5
Walton-Verona Middle School, KY

I Just Want to Say Mom

I ate all
the chocolate
from the
safe box
that is in
your room

and which
you were probably
going to be rude
and save it for
yourself!

Please forgive me
They were so delicious
and chocolately rich

Sarah Horn, Grade 5
Cool Spring Elementary School, NC

Road Game

Across the field
Beneath the roof
Between the fans
Upon the mound
On the rubber
Down on the grass
Toward the ball
Throughout the game
Underneath the dugout
Toward the same positions
Till the 9th inning
Off the field
Aboard the bus
Except the fans
Into the bed
Until tomorrow.

Cameron Campbell, Grade 6
Bernheim Middle School, KY

By the Way

That macadamia nut
shell you found on
the floor was the
one I had eaten

My eyes were
lured to the
nut that you
saved for dad

I hated every
single bite of
that succulent
delicious nut

Owen Stegall, Grade 5
Cool Spring Elementary School, NC

Otters

The otter is a playful monkey.
His fur is as soft as cotton, and
As white as snow.

He swims through the calm
Waters like a magnificent lion
Stalks his prey.

His whiskers are fibers of old
Ropes, his eyes are as black
And as deep as a coal mine.

Beck Hamstead, Grade 4
Nature's Way Montessori School, TN

Soldiers

They protect our home
And help wherever they go
They don't get afraid
They help us stay safe
Our soldiers always save the day

Our soldiers will always be there
And we will never despair
Forever we will be free
In this wonderful country
And never will we ask for mercy

Michael Tsikerdanos, Grade 5
Hunter GT Magnet Elementary School, NC

Freedom

I'm free as flowers
In the summer breeze.
Free as leaves falling
Off a tree.
Free as an eagle
Soaring though the sky.
Freedom is my choice
So I'm taking it for a ride.
Even though I have responsibilities too.
Freedom is Freedom
No matter how much I do.

Michiko Hill, Grade 6
Saint Pauls Middle School, NC

Christmas

C aring for everybody
H o ho ho you hear Santa
R eindeer clacking on the roof
I cicles are freezing on roof
S urprise to get new stuff
T errific to have Christmas
M arvelous to open presents
A wesome to be with family
S anta will be coming

Logan Dunn, Grade 5
Walton-Verona Middle School, KY

Native American Mask

BOOM! BANG! CLAP!
The men in the masks walk out
Chanting chants
Rattling their rattled loud
The hopeful faces all around
Praying that sickness
And injury are all done
The fire is burning
Reflecting in mask eyes
The smell of smoke and medicine
Here comes the miracle
Loud chants, evil spirits get scared
Men dance their hearts out
In hopes of all healing and cures
They shout their last chants
The ceremony is coming to and end
Injured legs can move about
Bad coughs are no more
The mask has done its job
Smiles spread across all faces

Chelsea Sams, Grade 6
College View Middle School, KY

I Am

I am smart and fun.
I wonder how Dovenn can be so funny.
I hear unicorns cry.
I see mickey mouse.
I want a pet cat.
I am smart and fun.

I pretend I'm a princess.
I feel unicorn horns,
I touch my imaginary friend.
I worry about my brothers
I cry when I'm hurting.
I am smart and fun.

I understand my parents.
I say the truth.
I dream of you.
I try hard.
I hop you feel better
I am smart and fun

Jasmine Atchison, Grade 4
Centennial Elementary School, TN

Scares

S omething in the shadows
C an sense your movement
A cting like it is not there
R eaching out and grabbing you
E ntering your house at night
S caring you to death

Dustin Stainback, Grade 5
E O Young Elementary School, NC

I Am From

I am from jumping high with my friends on our dirt bikes
to hitting tree branches as we jump.
I am also from competing in relay races in my uncle's yard.

I am from tackling people in football games and being tackled...
to having my adrenaline go up...I go crazy and tackle a lot!
I am also from making it to a league championship game...
and losing to our opponent.

I am from dunking balls over my friends on my basketball goal
in my driveway...
to making 3's and winning our friendly competitions.

I am from playing the game "Pickle" with my friends
to being the thrower...then becoming the pelted opponent.
I always dodge about 50 pellets because I jump!
If the thrower aims low, I get hit, and it surprises me!

I am form riding the Beast roller coaster in 2010
at King's Island Park
to getting hungry and eating cotton candy.

I am from trying to skate at Finley's Fun Center
but end up falling...
to winning game tickets by jumping on the inflatable trampolines.

These are the people, places, and things I am from.

Hunter Preston, Grade 5
Burgin Independent School, KY

I Am From

I am from playing middle school basketball
for Burgin Independent School...
shooting the ball up and bouncing it down.
I enjoy playing basketball.
Every time I leave the court, I never have a frown.

I am from hanging with my "homies,"
Michael and Micah,
playing Xbox 360 or exercising in the sun...
getting so sweaty, but still having fun!

I am from loving school so much
that I feel like I'm going to puke.
But not too much...
I still want a basketball scholarship to Duke!

I am from rooting for the Duke Bluedevils' basketball team
to booing the Kentucky Wildcats...
from hoping UK falls to last
while Duke wins the NCAA Championship...what a blast!

My name is Jason Alexander, Jr.
These are the people, places, and things I am from.

Jason Alexander Jr., Grade 5
Burgin Independent School, KY

Christmas

I run down the hall on Christmas morning.
I look in my parents' room.
My dad is still snoring.

I wake my parents up.
We go to the living room.
Under the tree is a little gray pup.

I decide to name him Scruffy.
Scruffy is very playful.
He is also very fluffy.

My parents tell me that Christmas is about love.
The dove is a symbol of love.
So when I think of love, I think of a dove.

That morning was so much fun.
We had a great time.
Then out came the sun.

Will Taylor, Grade 6
Woodland Presbyterian School, TN

Big Bear

Some might think that Big Bear is an ordinary bear
Like most bears he is brown with a whole lot of hair
If you met a bear at Yellowstone you surely wouldn't take him home
But this one is different
He's from a store
But he could barely fit through the door
Unlike any bears you have known
Big Bear doesn't have any bones
He is soft as a spider's web made of silk
But he has fur that was not built
He has no shoes or clothes to wear
But have you ever seen clothes on a bear?
His eyes are dark as black as night
But they give him perfect eye sight
He's nice, he's friendly and he does not bite
And he watches over me through the night
He is not made anymore
He is very rare
So there is no other animal like Big Bear.

Joseph Threlkeld, Grade 6
Woodland Presbyterian School, TN

The Signs of Autumn

The forests burn as if set aflame,
fiery red and yellow.
Golden fall sunshine dappling the leaf-littered forest floor.
The harvest moon is an orange orb,
hung low in the late night sky.
Ebony darkness covers the fall landscape like a black shroud.
The crisp autumn wind sweeps across the brittle yellowed grass,
and we know that fall has come at last.

Madison Matthews, Grade 6
Mills Park Middle School, NC

My Mind State

I'm stuck
In my nightmare
Because of the crimes
I did
It's dark and
lonely.
I wish I didn't
do the things
I have done.
I have to run and
hide from the things
I have done.
Don't do the things I did.
I hope you rest in
peace.

Corbin Dillon Pedigo, Grade 5
Temple Hill Elementary School, KY

Anything Goes

A gentle breeze
wind through the trees
blows

A waterfall
a rushing stream
flows

A wise old man
an ancient word
knows

Because in this world
anything and everything
goes

Phoebe Anderson, Grade 6
Woodland Presbyterian School, TN

Butterfly

I see its wings flutter.
I glance at its body as it moves.
It flies into the sky like a long lost bird.

I see it twitch a bit
As I see it flutter so high
Like a long-lost memory
That I still have today.

But, as I see it fly so high,
Its beauty in the sky,
It makes me start to wonder
In a place that I wander…

Why is it here with me!

Kaley Pearson, Grade 4
Love Memorial Elementary School, NC

Guinea Pigs

Guinea pigs, Guinea pigs
I love 'em a lot!
They're fun and exciting
And joyful and smart!

They're round and they graze
They like lettuce and carrots
Apples and fruit
They eat better than parrots!

They jump and run like kangaroos,
And have lots of fun.
They say "Goodnight"
And hug you, too!

They squeak at you when they're hungry,
Like it or not.
They're sweet and cute
And I love 'em a lot!

Ethan Cook, Grade 5
Providence Academy, TN

Pizza

Pizza, mmmmm, yummy pizza,
I could eat pizza,
For the rest of my life.
Take away french fries,
Take away steak.
Take away fish,
Take away cake.
But as long as I have pizza,
I will be set for life.

Pizza, mmmmm, yummy pizza,
Pizza is so saucy,
And so cheesy,
And the crust is oh, so soft.

BUT I'M WARNING YOU!!
Pizza will hook you like a fish,
But you always get reeled into its boat.

Christopher Slaughter, Grade 6
Johnson Traditional Middle School, KY

The Camps

T he only goal
H elp yourself
E xtreme caution at all times

C ounting the days and waiting for
A dolf Hitler to lose power
M y life is on the line
P lease get me out of here
S ave me

Jakob Schall, Grade 6
East Mooresville Intermediate School, NC

Poor Margret

I stare at four walls white as snow
And think of how I just don't know
About the girl named Margret Fleet
Who everyone thinks she's so sweet.
Her life is such a mystery.
She's had such a sad history.
And if you're nice enough to listen
She'll tell you 'bout her mom Kristen.
Her mom died when Margret was five
And her dad just did not survive.
She's now just left all alone.
And all she does is moans and groans.
She's now in a car
But not going far
There's a "CRASH"
Then a "BOOM"
And a "SCREECH"
Last a "VROOM"
Now Margret Fleet
The oh so sweet
Has died just like her mother.

Isabella Xavier, Grade 5
Duke Middle School, NC

Ode to Imagination

Oh imagination,
How very vast you are.

Where is it? You should know,
It's really not that far.

I really enjoy the ample
Amount of fun you give,
Here are some examples:

As a deer shot by Robin Hood,
Hits the cold hard dirt,

And mermaids splash, dive and flirt,
And little sprites tug at your hair,

And knights walk into dragons' lairs,

I enjoy imagination,
as much as jumping on the bed.
What's going on in your head?

Maguire Glass, Grade 5
West Liberty Elementary School, WV

My Star

Oh star, my star,
You're always there for me
Oh star, my star,
You're the best star that'll ever be.

Bonnie Walton, Grade 5
Walton-Verona Middle School, KY

I Am Tough

I am tough and a hard hitter
I wonder if I can run the ball
I hear breathing
I see the crowd yelling
I want to win the game
I am a raider.

I pretend I score touchdowns
I feel sweat rolling down my face
I touch people's hands at the end of a game
I worry if we are about to lose
I cry when we lose sometimes
I am a warrior.

I understand if we lose sometimes
I say, "We are raiders"
I dream I am a quarterback
I try to get tackles
I hope I won't miss a tackle
I am a proud raider.

DreViyon Terry, Grade 5
Tates Creek Elementary School, KY

The Camps

During the hard times,
When I tried to survive.
The Holocaust was not,
the key to our lives.
Lack of food,
a raggedy dress,
I tried and tried
but what came was stress.
We were forced to work,
and slept every night,
thinking about
a way to fight.
Hitler was,
the leader of all.
We tried to survive,
but then came a fall.
We were taken to the showers,
but then we discovered,
these were gas ovens
and we were all smothered.

December Loudermilk, Grade 6
East Mooresville Intermediate School, NC

Who Are You Veterans

Who are you veterans?
The hero of our lives
The thing that makes this
Country free
Without you there is
No place to go in this world.

Mary Altstatt, Grade 5
Temple Hill Elementary School, KY

Hiding Behind a Mask

Hiding behind a mask,
Hiding true feelings,
Riding down rocky, dirt, roads,
Hearing loud, untuned, music,
But, the mask shows a smooth highway,
With a beautiful lullaby,
Always looking joyful on the outside,
Yet, screaming and crying on the inside,
It tastes like sour lemons,
In front of people it's sweet lemonade,
Mismatched looks is how it is,
It smells like rotten tomatoes,
Everyone thinks it smells like daffodils,
Hiding true feelings every day,
Mismatched looks everywhere,
Always hiding behind the mask.

Bailee Jones, Grade 6
College View Middle School, KY

Lambie

A dirty cream
Color and an inch thick strip of
Pink silk ribbon on
The bottom.
24 inches and the head
is a head
of a lamb
and the bottom
is a small blanket.
Lambie
Has a pink heart
With my
Name on it. She was
Given to me by my mom
And dad
Lambie is so amazing!

Bailey Barringer, Grade 6
Woodland Presbyterian School, TN

Who Knows?

Who knows
How many stars
Are in the roof of the sky?
How many fishes
In the deep seas?
How many people
In the whole wide world?
Who knows
Where every evening
The Sun flees to?
Where the moon lights up?
Where dawn starts?
Where the endless horizon ends,
Who knows? Who knows?

Brianna Andrigo, Grade 6
Mount View Middle School, WV

I Am a Dragon

I am a dragon
A bright blue dragon
I fly to the east, and
I fly to the west
I eat a deer or two.

I am a dragon
I burn trees with
My fiery breath.

I am a dragon
A strong dragon
I destroy knights
Who try to slay me.

I am a dragon
A bright blue dragon
I fly to the east, and
I fly to the west
I eat a deer or two.

Jack Nolan, Grade 5
Hunter GT Magnet Elementary School, NC

Spring

Spring
Flowers blooming
Bees buzzing
Spring

Plants growing
Rainy days coming
Spring

Sun shining
Spring break coming
Spring

Makes you want to
Laugh and sing
Spring

Winter is over
Summer is coming
Spring

Kyra Corrigan, Grade 5
Providence Academy, TN

Winter Is Here

Snow flakes falling all over town
Every body rushing all around
there is an icy chill in the air
telling winter is really here
so grab your sled and let's go
Hooray happy cheer!!!

Karman Sandhu, Grade 4
Tewksbury Elementary School, NC

The Walk

I feel an endless breeze.
I walk, my feet hurting.
But it doesn't slow me down.

I feel an endless breeze.
A silent dance in the sky
A hopeful dream that makes me cry
But it doesn't slow me down.

I feel an endless breeze.
The wind carries me fast
Not much longer I have to go
Cause nothing slows me down.

I feel an endless breeze.
I am the wind. I am the breeze
And the dance in the sky. Yes,
I am the dream that makes you cry.

And nothing, no, nothing can slow me down.

Addy Bonovich, Grade 5
Nature's Way Montessori School, TN

I Am

I am the girl who hung the moon.
I wonder who my little brother will become.
I hear him laughing.
I see him playing in the fall leaves.
I want him to be a good person.
I am the girl who hung the moon.

I pretend he won't get older.
I feel his arms around my neck when he hugs me.
I touch his soft wind burned cheeks.
I worry about his future and who he'll become.
I cry when I get mad at him for no reason at all.
I am the girl who hung the moon.

I understand he's growing up fast.
I say I love him more than anything.
I dream he will be successful in life.
I try to help him when he lets me.
I hope I am being a good sister.
I am the girl who hung the moon.

Rachel Hasty, Grade 6
Bernheim Middle School, KY

Reading a Book

Reading a book is like going on vacation.
Visiting places while your imagination takes off!
The shape of words curling
on the page.
Reading is an amazing thing!

Ella Lightner, Grade 5
Walton-Verona Middle School, KY

Take Me by the Hand!

Take me by the hand
And show me a new land,
The land of the free,
The land of the brave...
Take me by the hand
And make me understand
The love and care you stand for,
Take me by the hand
And show me the valleys and hills across the land...
Show me the glory of this land...!

Chasity McClay, Grade 6
Saint Pauls Middle School, NC

Picky Eater

Being picky is terrible because people don't understand,
I only like certain foods that I can count on two hands.
I take my lunch to school just about every day
My mom knows how to fix my lunch just the right way.
I tried a fried pickle once because they said it was good to eat
But the taste of plain pasta and rice just really can't be beat.
When I go to a friend's house, I want to be polite
Even though it usually means I'm going to starve all night.
But I'll keep trying foods in all different ways
Hoping that my taste buds will get bigger every day.

Cooper Whitt, Grade 4
Sequoyah Elementary School, TN

Life

Life is confusing, but in all things, life is not fair.
We must go on in life as we live in harmony.
Harmony is the way we live in peace.
Some things aren't fair in life, but we try to get along.
But sometimes we can't succeed in this goal.
Maybe a nice person died and you loved them,
And you can't ever see them again.
You try to let it go, but you just can't and for a good reason.
Just remember that's the way of life,
You've just got to live with it.

Carter White, Grade 6
Woodland Presbyterian School, TN

My First Dog

At age five I got my best friend.
He was a dog named Gus.
Gus was the perfect dog, sweet, kind, athletic, and fun.
But around Easter, Gus died of cancer.
I was depressed that my best friend had died.
But a year later I got a new dog!
She was named Eleanor.
She is nice but hyper, she is athletic and funny.
But I still really miss Gus and I know he misses me, too.
I love my dog Gus.

Jeb Brady, Grade 6
Woodland Presbyterian School, TN

I Am

I am silly and athletic
I wonder if there's gold at the end of the rainbow
I hear a unicorn cry
I see a star on a horse
I want to be a coach
I am silly and athletic

I pretend I'm a teacher
I feel cold blooded
I touch a unicorn's belly
I worry about nothing there possibly is
I cry about a sick feeling
I am silly and athletic

I understand moments in time
I say bless the Lord for amazing things
I dream about crazy things
I try to do my best everywhere
I hope I'll have my favorite best friend forever
I am silly and athletic

Ashlee Shockley, Grade 4
Centennial Elementary School, TN

I Am a Military Child

I am a beautiful light-skin girl.
I wonder if my dad will be ok when he deploys to Afghanistan.
I hear bombs going off at night while I sleep.
I see families moving without their dads.
I want my dad to come home safely with lots of presents.
I am a beautiful light-skin girl.

I pretend to be strong for my little sisters.
I feel if we play the lottery and win my dad can get out of the war.
I touch his face so I can remember how he feels.
I worry about my mom being without my dad for so long.
I cry when my dad calls only to talk for a minute.
I am a beautiful light-skin girl.

I understand they have to fight for our country.
I say I don't want them to go.
I dream that one day the war will be over.
I try not to cry when I think of him.
I hope I can be strong for him and me.
I am a beautiful light-skin girl.

Aaliyah Leach, Grade 5
Walker Intermediate School, KY

Jewel

J oyful and fun loving
E veryday I play with you, even though I don't want to
W ith me, you also are fun, say you love me, and look up to me
E ven though you're only 4 you want to be just like me
L ove you Jewel and I will always love you too

Hailey Chipman, Grade 5
Walton-Verona Middle School, KY

The Rainbow

The thing I want to say today
Is about something I see in May
It always occurs after it rains
When water touches the sun's rays
You always need a combination of two
Like the drip drop of rain and the sunlight too

It's formed of many colors
That you see everywhere you go
But there are many others that you don't know

If you have guessed what I am thinking
Please do not go
The thing I am thinking now
Is a great rainbow

Dinah Gorodezky, Grade 5
Hunter GT Magnet Elementary School, NC

I Am From

I am from America
I am from eating fried chicken
I am from going to school every day
I am from my nice, amazing mother
I am from Love
I am from God the Father
I am from eating sweet potatoes with my family
I am from buying clothes at the mall
I am from writing my thoughts with a pencil on paper
I am from Lexington, Kentucky
I am from my beautiful, loving grandmother
I am from my wonderful teacher, Ms. Jackson
I am from playing outside in the snow with my friends
I am from dancing on stage
I am from an amazing family

Alexis Moody, Grade 5
Tates Creek Elementary School, KY

I Am From

I am from the color red and PSP games.
I am from a nice mother that gives me lots of hugs.
I am from pizza and chicken.
I am from going to the park and sunny days.
I am from playing with my friends.
I am from vacations to Chicago with my family.
I am from the sound of birds singing and the wind blowing.
I am from playing with my dog.
I am from playing on the computer.
I am from making pancakes.
I am from playing on the snow and making snowmen.
I am from taking care of my dog and giving him a bath.
I am from riding a bike.
I am from reading books.
I am from riding a horse and walking beside it.

Ramiro Juarez, Grade 5
Tates Creek Elementary School, KY

Basketball

Orange balls bounce high
Steady beat on the floor form a rhythm
Players rushing and crashing
Fear of opponents in the air
My heart beating so loud I hear it outside my body
The round ball in my hands is released
Swish! The ball goes in the net
The whistle blares out the end of the game
My team picks me up
The cold, golden trophy in my hand
The shock of proud flows through me

Brooke Bryant, Grade 5
Bailey Elementary School, NC

My Trip to Washington D.C.

I watch the President wave at the people
My parents and I think of what we might see
The traffic sounds as loud as a freight train
Washington has more buildings than spiders have eggs
I wanted to see everything in our nation's capital
The business suits walk quickly through the streets
The Lincoln Memorial was grand and inspiring
The White House whiter than a dove's feathers
Giant flags flew like jet fighters in the air
Aquariums, museums, and shops made my visit
I feel excited and content

Moses Ward, Grade 4
Bailey Elementary School, NC

Christmas Time

Christmas time is here
Get ready to cheer

Close your eyes tight
And remember that Santa's been flying all night

Presents under the tree
Fill you with glee

Families are near
Memories are here

Diamond Jordan, Grade 5
Tates Creek Elementary School, KY

Spring

Spring is my favorite season,
Not too frigid and not too hot.
Do you need another reason?
It's when all the flowers bloom
Why it's not treason.
It's better than summer and fall
Especially winter, it's freezing.
Spring's the perfect season to play basketball
Hanging with friends, not wanting it to change seasons.

Kaitlyn Wilder, Grade 5
Walton-Verona Middle School, KY

The New Born Colt

It dances
Like rain,
The muscles flying freely,
Beneath the fine skin.
Fragile joints, miracle of perfection.
In the steady awareness,
Of the pride of being alive.
The foal lifts with grace, the pointed white hooves.
Between the foal and it's mother,
Is a beautiful love.
It moves with her almost as one.
In no way bound,
While every upright, shining hair,
Dances with joy.
As it welcomes itself,
To the unborn world.

Gwyneth Graham, Grade 5
Duke Middle School, NC

Ode to Daddy

I miss you
I hope ya miss me too
I remember the days when you called me daddy's girl
It's over now because you're dead and gone
I didn't know you very long
I know I have to move on
But I wish I knew you longer
I can remember the day when you went away
If only you could stay
Mom said I could see you still
I wonder why I guess I didn't want you to die
One day I saw you in a dream
I felt like I was gonna scream
I loved you all my life
I know I didn't know you but
I know I owe

Tia Nandram, Grade 6
Bernheim Middle School, KY

Roller Coaster

R eady or not, here we come
O pen the gate, we cannot wait
L aughing out loud, we are ready to go
L ooking ahead, where will we go
E nergy building, we climb, climb, climb
R oaring sound as we are tossed all around...

C lose your eyes really tight
O ver so fast...
A wesome memories last forever
S lowly walking after the ride
T hrilled to be back on solid ground
E ntertainment you will never forget
R e-energized, so happy

Aiden Lamb, Grade 4
Sequoyah Elementary School, TN

Secrets

Secrets are everywhere,
Secrets get passed on,
Secrets can make someone feel alone,
Some secrets are passed around every day;
Secrets can seem to the listener very small,
Secrets can be blabbered and told to all,
Some secrets can last forever,
Some secrets can make others more clever;
Secrets can be important,
Secrets can be in a family, maybe even about your aunt!
Some secrets can be bad!
And when these secrets are told, it can make you mad!
Secrets can live in your head,
Secrets may be dreamed about while you are in bed,
Those kind of secrets stay with you in the night,
And you worry about them until the morning light;
Where ever secrets are found,
You quickly realize,
They can be told to others round and round!

Hannah Chilton, Grade 4
JJ Jones Intermediate School, NC

Nature

So many parts of nature,
Trees, flowers, grass, and plants,
All dance to the music of the wind,
Bees, butterflies, ants, and bugs,
buzz about their busy days,
Lions, tigers, bears, snakes, and crocodiles too,
if given a chance will swallow you!
Gentle animals like lambs, bunnies, and birds
are innocent as a newborn baby,
Nature brings us great pets, too!
cats, dogs, hamsters, and frogs,
Cactus, Joshua trees, Brittle bushes,
These plants probably have heat strokes,
Pigs, horses, cows, chickens and goats,
all go around and tell secrets on the farm,
Bright sunshine, white rain, foggy morning,
setting the moods of every day,
Nature provides many joys of all living things!

Maya Hicks, Grade 5
JJ Jones Intermediate School, NC

Holocaust

H is for Hitler who tried to rule,
O is for Others that were not Jews,
L is for Loaded work that made them pout,
O is for Odd Orders yelled about,
C is for Camps where they were kept,
A is for Austria where the Jews slept,
U is for Until the Nazis did come,
S is for Salvation from what Hitler had done,
T is for Their Tattooed Numbers.

Hannah Carlson, Grade 6
East Mooresville Intermediate School, NC

World Series

Best of seven who will win?
I shall see at the end.
My team is up to bat.
Down by one, we'll get it back.
Buster Posey hit a home run.
Now for sure my team has won.
I love to watch them play.
Maybe that could be me someday.

Chad Cothran, Grade 4
Evangelical Christian School Ridgelake Campus, TN

People

We are people
Isn't it great.
We are fat, skinny, short, tall
And we are black, brown or white.

But we are still people no matter how we look or talk.
So be grateful for how you look.
God made you and you are special to Him.

Nathan Webb, Grade 4
Evangelical Christian School Ridgelake Campus, TN

My Great Grandma

My great grandma was nice and sweet to everyone.
She was 97 years old when she passed away.
Before she passed away she had 10 children,
And they all lived near here if she needed them.
We used to celebrate Christmas, Easter, and
Thanksgiving with her.

We all will be with her some day in heaven.

Alex Baker, Grade 4
Stantonsburg Elementary School, NC

Winner

When you cross the finish line
You know it's your moment to shine
And when you think about the golden medal
You just want to step on the pedal
And when you see the cash
You just want to jump into the money stash
And all of this is just thanks to one thing, winning

Johnny Garcia, Grade 6
McGee's Crossroads Middle School, NC

Ode to Cousin

I used to hold you in my arms
And pat you on your head and call you a loving boy.
Now I look back on those days and cry
And call you a loving boy in the sky I say I miss you.
But God is lucky to have you.
It's been 5 years since then and I still call you a loving boy
In the sky

Dixie Hadley, Grade 6
Bernheim Middle School, KY

Four Seasons

Snow is falling,
the ground is white
the big oak tree has no leaves in sight
the flowers come and bloom
creatures awake at noon
the heat wave strikes
kids hit the pool
the leaves start falling
it's getting cool
the snow is back
you feel the chill
don't worry
spring is coming
it's just over the hill

Erin Sherrill, Grade 5
Cool Spring Elementary School, NC

Ode to Sabrina Owen

We're exactly alike,
And we're very best friends.
I can tell you anything
Until my life ends.

We like the same things,
Such as music and money.
You never get mad at me
And you call me your buddy.

Sabrina, you're awesome.
We're cheer sisters at heart.
Nothing could ever
Tear us apart.

Caity Brown, Grade 6
Bernheim Middle School, KY

Under My Bed!

I think there is something under my bed
It might be big, round and red

Oh how I dread
To look under my bed!

Could it be skinny or fat?
Oh dear it might be a rat!

Oh how I dread
To look under my bed

I think I'll look...
BOO! It said.

Kayla Reep, Grade 5
Love Memorial Elementary School, NC

Splish Splash

Splish Splash Splish Splash
Goes the water in the pond,
Me and my brothers jump into the pond
Splish Splash Splish Splash

Splish Splash Splish Splash
Goes the catfish on the line
Like a whale at the surface of the ocean
Splish Splash Splish Splash

Splish Splash Splish Splash
The catfish talking in a nasal voice
Let go of me you rotten chicken
Splish Splash Splish Splash

Splish Splash Splish Splash
The turtle is faster than a cheetah
Swimming in a pond
Splish Splash Splish Splash

James Raley, Grade 6
Bernheim Middle School, KY

My Mom

My mom is the best
She is so sweet
And a whole lot rest
And she wants everything to be clean

She and I are just alike
She reads a lot of books,
And just like me,
She loves to cook

She is very busy
But fits in time for me
She is very nice
But she really hates bees

I love my mom
Nothing about her I hate
And I wrote this poem
Because she really is great!

Jessica Buxton, Grade 6
Bernheim Middle School, KY

Turned On

Jill turned on her electric iPod,
Bill turned on his electric guitar,
John turned on his boom box,
Mia turned on her DVD,
Mom turned on her radio,
Dad turned on the TV,
I turned on my laptop —
Hey! Who turned off all the lights?

Eric Horlbeck, Grade 5
Duke Middle School, NC

Max, My Dog!

Max my dog —
Black and white as snow
Eyes, brown as mud
Small sized mutt
Loves everybody and loves to run!

Max thinks of me as his tongue post,
And his MOTHER!

We both love to run, but
He stays home when I'm at school!

I've learned how to
Take care of a living
Thing on my own.
My life is different
With Max because
I'm never lonely!

Lindsay Czmowski, Grade 6
Johnson Traditional Middle School, KY

Baby Brothers

I love my brothers
But they are just aggravating
We barely get along
They want me to do everything for them

I love them
They love me
We are like BFF's
But not the girly way

I am way
More bubbly and prettier
Than them
They are just boyish
And weird

I think of us like a running
Faucet that never stops

Nataia Jones, Grade 6
KY

Witches

Flying on their broomsticks
Creeping all around
Scaring all the people
That happen to be in town
With all their potions
And magic spells too
A witch is so evil
You better watch her woo
Remember if you ever see a witch
Don't let her trick-or-treat with you

Anna Katherine Anderson, Grade 4
Sequoyah Elementary School, TN

The Holocaust

You hear the cries of death
As people whisper under their breath
Secrets to stay alive
So they may thrive
And when the Nazis take you away
You must always remember to stay
Hopeful

Emily Killian, Grade 6
East Mooresville Intermediate School, NC

Deer Hunting

H ealthy
U ndercover
N ationwide
T alent
I cy, but relaxing
N ature
G etting the bucks!

Ronnie Drake, Grade 5
Mineral Wells Elementary School, WV

Black Cat

In the fall it's Halloween;
I see a black cat racing around my hat;
I tell the cat you better get back;
In the race it scratches my face;
I'm in so much pain,
All thanks to the black cat
On Halloween.

Shawna Edwards, Grade 4
Edmonton Elementary School, KY

Swish!

Basketball
Awesome, fun
Shooting, dribbling, passing
Making a three pointer
Running, stealing, guarding
Exciting, sweaty
Sport

Brett Linton, Grade 6
Musselman Middle School, WV

Playmates

Kids
Playful, happy
Running, jumping, skipping
Playing on the playground
Laughing, twirling, climbing
Funny, active
Children.

Kaitlyn Busey, Grade 6
Musselman Middle School, WV

I Am From

I am from a mom and dad who are always there for me...
To feed me, to take care of me, and to help me when I get hurt or sick.

I am from a family that likes to go on vacation...
To places such as Boston, Florida, and more.

I am from going to the local county fair...
To being a Kentucky Wildcat fan in the U.S.A.
I am also from horseback riding at Delima Stables.

I am from a HUGE family
With ten cousins, ten aunts, and ten uncles
Who I love the most.

I have three best friends: Eden, Autumn, and Laney.
I have known them forever.
It feels like we are all sisters.

My name is Abigail, and I am from Kentucky.

Abigail Shepherd, Grade 5
Burgin Independent School, KY

Up on My Dresser

On my wooden dresser, I see
Socks random with no match
Snow globe that is barely an inch tall
A lot of gum and chocolate from Halloween,
Marbles striped and colored, Old coins I have found
A polar bear that is hard, not soft
Paper with writing covering it
Erasers of all shape, size and color
Old toys I have gotten for Christmas
Trophies from gymnastics meets
Bouncy balls I won from some pizza place
Batteries that have died
Two boxes full of little metal pieces all the way to the top
Stop watches that doesn't work, half the harry potter series
Recorders from my brother and sister, Playing cards for poker
Soccer ball Piggy bank with nothing in it
Nutcrackers my grandma gave me
All this is up on my dresser, and I see it every night.
All of this stuff is there because it all reminds me of other times in life.

Sumner Smith, Grade 6
Baylor School, TN

Baseball

The umpire is calling strikes so fast like he wants the game over
Outfielders are diving on the green grass like chasing a dog
Fans cheer so loud like the world is coming to an end
A batter hits the ball making it soar in the outfield like an eagle
Hot dusty air choking us like a boa constrictor
Hot dogs, cracker jacks, sunflower seeds, frosty Gatorade filling the stadium
The bat is shaking like an earthquake
Feeling confident as I walk up to bat

Zachary Perry, Grade 5
Bailey Elementary School, NC

It's All About Me

Madison
Friendly, sweet, silly, and smart
Daughter of Adrian and Andrew
Who loves shopping, God, School and Fashion
Who feels happy, sad, and mad
And who is afraid of spiders, snakes, and bad grades
Who's earned honor roll every year
Who hopes to go to fashion week
Resident of Memphis, TN
Ramsey

Madison Ramsey, Grade 6
Snowden Middle School, TN

The Holocaust

The Holocaust so dark and dreary
Full of pain and misery
A time of happiness?
Not in the least!
Hitler such an evil man
Ordered the killing of the Jewish race
"Into the ghettos!" he said
Found out he was Jewish too!
Now the Holocaust is a thing of the past
But it is burned into the minds of those who survived.

Brad Lowe, Grade 6
East Mooresville Intermediate School, NC

I Am...

I am a bird just waiting to fly
To leap out and soar out of the nest
And
I am an ant scavenging for food
Or little grains of sand to build my own pyramid
And
I am a mouse scurrying and hiding
Running from the dangers above...

No matter what I am, I am something

Alex Harris, Grade 5
Hunter GT Magnet Elementary School, NC

My Favorite Place: Washington State

The green trees roll past me as I ride past them.
Crystal clear water feels good down my throat as I swallow.
Coyote's howl talks to me and does do not let me go to sleep.
The rivers flow so softly I could hardly hear the sound of them.
Pine tree aroma fills the house as my dad brings in the tree.
Grandma's pie feels hot and fiery as I try not to spit it out.
Fresh fish tastes like the ocean as I grab my fork for the next bite.
Sharp, stubbly, spiny pine needles prickle my finger as I touch them.
Brown leaves are like soldiers crushed under my feet.
Happiness gets me going better than going to Holiday World.

Calli Whitmore, Grade 6
College View Middle School, KY

The Love of My Life

The love of my life is my nephew
He is the fruit to my loop I don't want to fly the coop
The other half of my heart I love him to death
If he would die, a quarter of my heart would break apart
I don't know what I would do without him
It would be so sad the sky would be cloudy
My life would be stormy, just like the sky
I don't know if I could live without him
I would feel like I could die
I would cry and cry without a single tear in my eye

Paula Mason, Grade 4
Contentnea-Savannah K-8 School, NC

Moms

Moms will be there for you when everybody is gone.
She will hug and kiss you, and she doesn't care who's there.
She will get mad at you because she loves you and
Wants you to do your best in everything.
She will never lie to you, but if she has to she will
Because she doesn't want to hurt your feelings.
She will make your cuts and scratches feel better.
She will cheer you on at your game.
Do you know how I know?
I have a mommy like that too.

Brianna Brooks, Grade 4
Southeast Elementary School, NC

Imagination

Having an imagination is so fun,
that your mind will grow the size of the sun.
You start on a topic, then use your brain,
then you'll start a game.
You think and you think and you think,
then you winkity, winkity, wink.
Then what you see, oh what you see,
is your imagination at work!
You'll have tons and tons of fun,
and your world will never be undone!

Alexa Norberg, Grade 5
Walton-Verona Middle School, KY

I Am From...

I am from Manhattan, Kansas
I am from cool winters and hot summers
I am from a historical place
I am from big towns with small amounts of people
I am from the country
I am from small stores and big houses
I am from a place with big gardens and big front lawns
I am from a place with big cars and small trucks
I am from a lot of snow
I am from a lot of rain

Eli Fox, Grade 5
Tates Creek Elementary School, KY

Me in Africa
Coffee bean shaped eyes looking at me
with tiny little slots I can barely see

The fire in his eyes show his true age
the task he is about to do will make him brave

A nose as long as the Eiffel Tower
the three poles in the back show its power

He now puts the mask on to become a man
as the tribe leader places the mask in his hands

The mask's ears hear all around
hearing the beat as the drum pounds

He puts his crown up on top
the challenges he will face will never stop
Alyssa Bickett, Grade 6
College View Middle School, KY

Slippers
You forgot me!
Don't leave me here alone, come back and put me on
Bring me with you, I'm under your bed

Your warm little toes are like a family of rabbits
Waiting to crawl into their safe warm burrow
In a windy winter storm

Without you I'm like an empty plate
Wishing it was filled with warm, yummy food

Oh I wish you'd put me on, and just run outside and play.
I love the way it feels when you run and plant me
Into the soft, moist soil

So please, come back, and put me on.
Erin Timmerberg, Grade 5
Hunter GT Magnet Elementary School, NC

Cole
I have a little dog named Cole,
Through the tall grass he likes to roll.
He has curly black hair,
He thinks he's the size of a bear.
He is clever in ways but others he's not.
When he barks at the horses, towards him they trot.
Cole is very small,
But his mighty spirit makes him stand tall.
Every night he crawls with me in bed,
And wakes me with a lick on the head.
I am happiest with Cole by my side,
Our love will never divide.
He is my best friend.
Tyler Maddox, Grade 5
Paint Lick Elementary School, KY

I Admire...
I really admire my loving Daddy,
Ever since I can remember
he has called me Maddy.
He is funny, crazy, happy,
and all of the above,
but when you're down and sad,
he gives you lots of love.

He works very hard,
day by day,
but when he gets home it is time to play.
But he is my Daddy,
so I got to love him,
and I wrote this poem because I was just thinking of him.
I'm his only little girl,
as happy as can be,
and I will always know
that he will always love me!
Madison Rumppe, Grade 6
Saint Pauls Middle School, NC

The Great Life
The great life,
Is what I have.
With plenty of fun, and laughs.
I have a great mom,
She loves me so.
Her love is so big,
It can't be told.
I feel like number one,
With the love I get is like a ton.
I have friends,
That will be there until the end,
Again, and again.
My life is great,
So I think you should appreciate.
I thank God for the food, shelter, and many others.
The great life,
Is what is inside.
With great pride.
Dijuan McNair, Grade 6
Saint Pauls Middle School, NC

This Old Door
Look at this door that I have been trying to ignore.
It has cobwebs on the sides and cracks in the middle,
and there are holes everywhere that are not little.
I have been trying to ignore this door for years,
and I have been begging to remove it with tears.
The doorknob isn't painted,
and some people who came over almost fainted!
I have lived with this door for nine years,
and I will live with it for nine more.
It's so hard to ignore this door.
Lydia Heinz, Grade 4
Sequoyah Elementary School, TN

The Test
Tick Tock
The clock is
Ticking
Not much time
Till time's
UP
Thinking I can do it
I start the test
In front of
ME
My hand shaking
My brain working
No matter how
ARDUOUS it is
I have to work
Through it
Tick Tock
The clock is still
Ticking
Time's up
Gigi Cloney, Grade 5
Hunter GT Magnet Elementary School, NC

Basketball
Basketball
Aboard the Bruin Nation
Against any other team
Before you say anything
Through everything keep friends
Along with enemies
Underneath the basket
Toward the ball,
Off the floor, get up!
Past is what you're thinking
From and into the future
By changing your mistakes
Since you've been through a lot.
Behind you, don't worry
Below your heart it pounds
Like "I can't catch up!"
Within you can do anything
With a lot of friends by your side.

Basketball
Natalie Stopher, Grade 6
Bernheim Middle School, KY

Giving Lives
The veterans give their lives for us
To protect our country
Some people do not make it and some do
Without them we would be dead
They love everyone and you know it
We love you veterans.
Kristen Thomas, Grade 5
Temple Hill Elementary School, KY

Summer School
Why am I in summer school?
But not chillin' in the pool
In school I have to walk
Than rather being able to talk

Next I have a math quiz
Instead of having soda with fizz
I must know about the season of fall
Than rather throwing a baseball

In science, I observe a rock
But not fishing at the dock
I still have a spelling test
Than rather getting some rest

In art, I have this clay
But not in football callin' a play
I'd rather be in school in August
Summer break is an important must
Woody Raynor, Grade 5
Hunter GT Magnet Elementary School, NC

Love Ballad
Love the word of the devil
starts out so good
but then turns evil
Love, no good for you, love

It's going so great but then to follow
the heartbreak that
leaves your heart feeling hollow
Love, no good for you, love

But then comes that girl
the one you'll always cherish
the center of your world
Love, no good for you, love

Your love will never be
because inside you know
she'll always be in love with me
Love, no good for you, love
Ryan McKnight, Grade 6
Bernheim Middle School, KY

Play Time
If I jump so high could I
Really, really touch the sky
As I look out to see just how
Pretty everything would be all the
Yellows, purples, reds, blues and greens
All the cool lakes and beautiful streams.
As I slowly drift from the sky
Playtime is fun for you and I.
Cierra Vaughn, Grade 4
Centennial Elementary School, TN

I Am
I am a dead 10 year old boy
I wonder why my dad had to die
I hear people shooting
I see blood everywhere
I want to stop this madness
I am a dead 10 year old boy
I pretend I am alive
I feel like nothing
I touch thin air
I worry about my people
I cry when I think of my dad
I am a dead 10 year old boy
I understand death
I say God help me
I dream of my dad
I hope I come back some day
I am a dead 10 year old boy
Jacob Jefffries, Grade 5
Duke Middle School, NC

Ode to Skitty
Oh, little kitty Skitty,
You are so very pretty.

Your puffy perfect fur,
And your sweet and silent purr.

You meow at the sun,
And you always make things fun.

Sometimes you hide from me,
Up in some large tree.

You do not like my brother.
But you really like my mother.

Itty, bitty, Skitty,
You're my one and only kitty.
Laken Waddell, Grade 5
West Liberty Elementary School, WV

Christmas
Christmas is holly there's a reason
to be jolly. Molly says "oh
sant golly!" Presents are cool.
I hope I get a coat made
out of wool. Christmas is fun.
I wish I could play in the
sun. Christmas trees are tall
but my grandma's is small.
I love to play out in the
snow, but make sure it is
low. The Christmas lights are bright
but Santa sees the sights fright.
Shelby Lee, Grade 4
Centennial Elementary School, TN

My Stepbrother Donye

He's my first stepbrother,
He likes sports like me.
He likes basketball and football.
His favorite basketball team is Oklahoma City Thunder.
His favorite football team is Panthers.
We have lots of things in common.
We have the same basketball team.
We have the same football team.
And they're our favorites.
He's my favorite and only stepbrother.

Aniaz Glenn, Grade 4
Harvest Preparatory Academy, NC

Birds

Birds are different colors and sizes
Birds have feathers
Birds eat worms and insects
Birds lay eggs in nests
Birds tweet songs
Birds are fast
Birds can fly up and down
Birds fight for food
Birds are cardinals, blue jays, crows, and so on.

Jaziah King, Grade 4
Contentnea-Savannah K-8 School, NC

The Forest

Big green trees as big as hotels
Birds flapping their wings
Hearing myself sing
Mist of the water falling on my head like I was swimming
Bark on the tree as rough as a man's face
Sticks that look like swords
Apples hanging from trees as big as gourds
Animals running from their predators like playing tag
Feeling like a winner as I explore the forest

Jeffrey Alvarado, Grade 5
Bailey Elementary School, NC

Christmas, Christmas Please Come

C hristmas cookies baking in the oven
H ouses with smoke coming out of the chimney
R eindeer landing silently on the roof top
I n the living room, the decorated tree stands
S nowflakes gently falling from the winter sky
T oo many cookies for Santa
M ary watching over us while waiting for Jesus to be born
A ny more presents for me?
S kiers skiing down the pure white mountain

Alyson Poore, Grade 5
Walton-Verona Middle School, KY

The Jaguar

The jaguar is the stealthiest creature around
There is no doubt around town
So why can we track them down?
Why is their population going down?
Why are we killing them?
Who wants to be cruel and kill them?
It's not so stylish to be cruel!
Why we are killers, I don't know because it's not cool.
All I know is that we should stop everything.
The primitives were better; they didn't stuff a poor thing!
They didn't kill for fun!
They had a good style, they didn't use a gun.
They were not vile, it's hard to relate.
We should go back to using slate.

Jackson Kennedy, Grade 5
Duke Middle School, NC

Best Ben

On a Mother's Day I got a new best friend.
At first I hated him like a cat hates fleas.
I thought he would chew up my stuff.
I didn't even want him in my room.
It wasn't like that for long though.
Then I loved him like a shepherd loves his sheep.
I thought he was the best in the world.
I even let him sleep in my bed with me.
I love him like a mouse loves cheese.
Now my adorable angel is gone.
I miss my dead doggy.
But I know he's safe now.
This cute, cuddly, comforting companion's name was Ben.
Sweet dreams forever my precious Ben.

Kaycie Way, Grade 5
Providence Academy, TN

Holocaust

The hand raises high above our heads,
a sign of control and a bottomless heart.
A sign of victory for them, and loss for us.
Still, labor rings in our ears.
Hope, starve…death.
And yet, for some reason, we can get up from our
stale beds, a sensational surprise that we keep going.
When we dream of a take off from their sight,
they will laugh and shoot our legs.
Blood pours and terror fills the air.
Laughs of evil and cries of sorrow.
Sometimes, getting up and wondering
is a second option.

Yurika Chisholm, Grade 6
East Mooresville Intermediate School, NC

Beach

Beaches are blue and wide seas
Every summer you see the bright sun
All the time you go you see the smooth sand
You can see all the people having fun
It has pretty white seashells

Myriam Hernandez, Grade 4
Contentnea-Savannah K-8 School, NC

On My Tree

Strings of cold, stale, popcorn
Beautiful flashing, colorful lights
Mother's sweet, old angel on top
Gorgeous, old ornaments
Yummy, flavorful candy canes

Emily De Lisle, Grade 5
Walton-Verona Middle School, KY

The Kangaroo

There once was a big kangaroo,
That lived in the Columbus Zoo;
She used to say ouch,
To the joey in her pouch,
Now her baby is all grown up, too!

Katie Harper, Grade 5
Mineral Wells Elementary School, WV

Cat

Cat
Sneaky, shy
Creeping, sleeping, meowing
Soft, cuddly, beautiful, furry
Pet

Tamika Parker, Grade 5
Mineral Wells Elementary School, WV

Kye's Dilemma

There once was a young boy named Kye
Who accidentally dropped his mom's pie
Its flavor was cherry
With a hint of blueberry
Then he knew he was going to die

Austin McNeil, Grade 5
Hunter GT Magnet Elementary School, NC

Poems

P assionate
O pen-minded
E xtra great
M ysterious
S ensational

N'kya Seward, Grade 5
E O Young Elementary School, NC

The Storm That's Coming

The sky turns to dusk and the clouds dominate the sky
The thunder does a drum roll and finishes with an explosion
The lightning is darting and I am the target
This is when I'm frustrated
You're mean! You're mean! I'm telling! I'm telling!
Waaah! Mommy she hit me!
The sun disappears and its pitch black
The stars hide in fear
This is when I'm frustrated
Be quiet! Be quiet!
Sit up straight! Sit up straight!
No! No! No! No! No!
The wind does the hula-hoop and the twister starts to emerge
The houses get demolished everything is damaged
Then the waves cover the city like a dome protecting it
But instead the waves crash down on the town like a person stomping an ant
The ocean washes away what's left
This is when I'm frustrated
The storm eases slowly
The sun shines its brightness
The birds sing a beautiful melody then I realize that the storm was me

Jaylah Bailey, Grade 6
Johnson Traditional Middle School, KY

Native American Wedding

The slow smell of smoke in the air,
The drumbeats in the young Indian couples' eardrums,
The priest wearing the ceremonial Wakiutl mask,
With red rings around the nose,
a white ring circles the mask,
Like a wedding ring,
The setting for an Indian wedding,
The day Big Hawk is supposed to marry Little Feather,
The campfire is more like a bonfire now,
The smoke's getting heavier,
The drums and singing are getting louder,
All the people put on their Wakiutl mask,
This is the sign that they're married now,
They kiss and start living their new life wearing their Wakiutl masks.

Cade Wampler, Grade 6
College View Middle School, KY

My First Ride

The continuous sound going all around brings fear and nervousness to me,
But as I go along,
The fright is gone, and it's only the water and me.
I get faster and faster by the second,
The only thing I can hear is the motor roaring and yelling
The wind pulls the water up towards me,
And with that, my hair just slaps me in the face
The water is very divine,
And I might say,
That I picked the perfect day,
To go on my first ride!

Haley Clift, Grade 4
St Mary's Episcopal School, TN

Isabella Grace

In memory of Isabella Grace Lasley.
Outside at the funeral was as light like a light bulb shining.
Tears are that of a bang as they hit the floor.
I wish I could see her smile it would be the sun on a rainy day.

I was as sad as a lonely puppy.
Sad sad sad was I.
She was crazy silent.

Her eyes were brightly closed as she lays there dead.
I could hear the joyful tears.
I could feel the dry wetness on my face.
As she lay there lively dead.
I could hear the soft loud music.

Lexi Lasley, Grade 6
Bernheim Middle School, KY

The Game

Before the game I watch *The Boys Of Fall*,
Then I go out, and give it my all.
The field is green, and the lines are chalked in white,
The air is cool, as day turns to night.
Butterflies race in my belly as game time is near,
Losing the game is all that I fear.
Tackle after tackle I try as hard as I can,
When I run the ball, I'm like a wild man.
I will not stop until I get to the goal line,
When I score, I will feel just fine.
As I near that white line, it's the cheers from the crowd I hear,
Some are from those so close and so dear.
This feeling inside me, so wild you cannot tame,
For this felling is my love for the game.

Steven Browning, Grade 5
Paint Lick Elementary School, KY

Just Stay

I feel a pain flowing through me.
Questions go around in my mind.
"Are you going to leave? Are you going to stay?"
I think about it, and then I start to pray.

When I see you, I start to think.
"Will you take me for granted and just leave?"
Just stay, I'll overcome my fears.
I will not be afraid that you will leave if I blink.

I finally realize that you start to notice.
It's me, Just stay. I love you, can't you see.
I have a deep compassion for you.
I ask, "Do you love me, too, Just stay."

Shellie Locklear, Grade 5
Rex-Rennert Elementary School, NC

Benjamin

I'm Benjamin Gibbons, yes that's my name,
My favorite color is blue.

I'm 4 foot 11, with dark, brown hair,
And my eyes are blue too.

I'm 11 years old,
Born on October 15th, in 1999.

I love cantaloupe,
And grape juice, fresh from the vine.

I love to read, and love to draw,
And I love to laugh too.

I'm part Irish and German, part Romanian,
Part French, I'm American and a Jew.

So that's a little you should know about me,
With one more thing to say.

I wrote this by hand, no parents, no help,
And that's all I have for today.

Benjamin Gibbons, Grade 5
Nature's Way Montessori School, TN

My Aquarium

My aquarium is so cool.
I wish I could bring it to school.

I have a lion fish named Chicken Joe.
And his trigger fish friend is named Flo.

Chicken Joe and I thought the damsel fish were great.
Not as friends but as something we ate.

He hangs out upside down.
And always looks like he has a frown.

He eats big chunks of food.
When he's in a good mood.

My fish hang out in the corner each day
It doesn't look like they want to play.

I like to watch them eat
When I'm in bed, not on my feet.

That's why I think my aquarium is so cool.
Maybe you should come see it after school!

Will Eggleston, Grade 4
Sequoyah Elementary School, TN

Why Me?

These smelly stubs with five "toes"
Which I am forced to warm
I have fuzzy glory but I must use it for these stink bombs
Every day I am pulled over this grotesque mass of blubber

As if that's not bad enough
I am forced into a "shoe"
Where smell lingers a long long time
This is too much to endure

I have attempted a daring rescue
Into something called a "hamper"
But once again I have found myself in
A twisting turning mania
It squirts soap and water
And spins so quickly
Then I am taken into a "dryer"
It is so hot in there as I spin around
I am getting dehydrated

Finally someone takes me out
Where I start this painful process over
Again.

Avani Saraswatula, Grade 5
Hunter GT Magnet Elementary School, NC

Soldiers

WAR, WAR, WAR.
That's all I hear
It is pointless for soldiers to go off,
Throwing their lives away
When they land,
on the cold, dark despair of a hole,
with no one to pull them up when they are down.
Family and loved ones hearts are ripped apart,
when they receive the dark letter of sadness.
While the soldiers ashes are being blown away,
in the fog of the battle field.
And the soldier thinks back
before this terror happened.

Shaquay Davis, Grade 6
Saint Pauls Middle School, NC

The Beach

Palm trees waving at me
The hot sand making me dance crazily
Coconut milk refreshing my mind
Waves pulling me forward like tug-of-war
Fresh salt water making me stay
Frisbees flying like a seagull soaring over the ocean
Suntan lotion covering my body
Seagulls plunging into the water and surfacing with a scaly fish
Dogs running into the water leaping for the tennis ball
I feel relaxed and free at the beach

Joshua Eatmon, Grade 5
Bailey Elementary School, NC

The Worst Thanksgiving

I was walking to the table,
But I tripped over a cable,
The turkey went flying,
And my grandma started crying.
The potatoes were all lumpy,
Which made grandpop very grumpy.
The green bean casserole
Was as black as charcoal
So we fed it to the dog
Who ate it like a hog.
Then he got sick
And we all had to witness it.
My cousins started fighting
There was hair pulling and biting.
The men were watching the game on TV
While the ladies were working in the kitchen — naturally.
The pie was then served
Which everyone deserved.
When we were finished with pie
Everyone said good-bye.

Chloe Neunsinger, Grade 5
Hunter GT Magnet Elementary School, NC

Winter Is Here

Winter has come to bring you joy
Little white angels falling from the sky
Dusting the ground
Bringing joy and happiness
Having snowball fights
Building giant snowmen
Tasting the hot chocolate warm on your tongue
Feeling the fire on your back
Snuggling under your covers
Waiting for tomorrow to bring a smile to your face
Giving you pleasure all through the night

Megan Gubbs, Grade 5
Moyock Elementary School, NC

World War II My Great Grandpa Luther Wheet*

My great grandpa in World War II,
The most terrifying war in history.

He was brave to fight in it.
He did it for his country.

He saved lives.
He helped his friends.

He went through a lot with his friends.
And then he saved his friend, but lost his life.

Memories can't blow away in time.
Memories can never leave your mind!

Sidney Wheet, Grade 4
Tazewell-New Tazewell Primary School, TN
**In memory of Sergeant Greg Wheet. R.I.P. Soldier.*

Ode to Pets

Woof, meow, a tweet too,
Pets are always there for you.
Gulp, squeak, nah, bark,
Just never trust a shark.
You can tell them all your secrets.
They will never tell.
Not to mice, rabbits, and crickets,
Or skunks that really smell.
If you don't agree with me,
Just come to my house and you will see.
There are dogs, cats, birds, and fish
You wish you could have one, yes you wish.
Woof, meow, and a tweet.
Gulp, nah, and a squeak.

Alexis Harris, Grade 6
Bernheim Middle School, KY

Fear

Barnabus Browning
Was scared of drowning
So he would never swim
Or get in a boat
Or take a bath
Or cross a moat
He just sat day and night
With his door shut tight
And the windows nailed down
Shaking with fear
That a wave might appear
And cried so many tears
That they filled up the room
And he drowned

Nakei'Briana Simmons, Grade 4
Southeast Elementary School, NC

Changed

I have lived my life many, many years.
Living in rage.
Living in fear.
Living with many, many tears.
Anger through most of my years.
Now a light is shining, the dawn is ahead.
I have found you Jesus.
There is no more dread.
I feel joy.
I feel love.
I have a mighty, mighty friendship above.
Thank you for the ones I love.
Thank you for my peers above.
Thank you for what you have done.

Tristen Crumley, Grade 4
Centennial Elementary School, TN

Forest

Oaks stand like giants,
Willows whip with the breezes,
Redwoods loom like the
Towers of the forest. It
Is a cathedral of trees.

In fall, a patchwork
In spring, verdant and growing
In summer, at the
Peak of life, and at winter
Waiting to begin again.

Ciaran Allen-Guy, Grade 6
White Station Middle School, TN

The Wonder Fair

W inning games
O ne rides up and down
N ew games every time
D own town fun
E ntertaining kids
R eady for more fun next year

F un place to be in
A way from home
I n another town
R are only once a year

Chase Parrish, Grade 4
E O Young Elementary School, NC

Twin Towers

T all
W ill never be forgotten
I n an instant they were gone
N orth tower

T errorist leader
O sama bin Laden
W orld Trade Center
E vacuation
R emembered
S outh tower

Chase Crook, Grade 5
Hunter GT Magnet Elementary School, NC

Like

Like is my favorite word,
I say it all the time.
I say it when I ride my bike,
I say it when I take a bite.

Like is my favorite word,
I say it when I bake a cake,
I say it when I make a shake,
It makes my dad quake.

Curry Allen Shazier, Grade 5
Walton-Verona Middle School, KY

I Am Myself

I am a daddy's girl and love animals.
I wonder why there are clouds?
I hear turtles barking.
I see a unicorn.
I want a new horse.
I am a daddy's girl and love animals.

I pretend I have a real horse.
I feel good about animals.
I touch a blue bear.
I worry about my dog getting to cold.
I cry when my horses get hurt.
I am a daddy's girl and love animals.

I understand when animals are sad.
I say that I believe in Santa.
I dream about my animals.
I try my best at sports.
I hope my dog has fun in 4-H.
I am a daddy's girl and love animals.

Clayre McCallister, Grade 4
Centennial Elementary School, TN

I Am

I am nice and pretty
I wonder if she is all right
I hear a scream
I see a flashlight flickering
I want to have a classmate over
I am nice and pretty

I pretend to be a model
I feel amazing
I touch the sky
I worry about failing
I cry when my nanna died
I am nice and pretty

I understand about math
I say that Mrs. Lori is nice and fun
I dream about Christmas
I try to be good at school and home
I hope I get good grades in reading
I am nice and pretty

Arianna Ewings, Grade 4
Centennial Elementary School, TN

Sweet Treats

I walked down Main Street
With a bag of treats
When I see a street
I think of sweets
I have such a problem with treats
I need to put down the bag of sweets.

Sarah Kimble, Grade 4
Centennial Elementary School, TN

The Race

I had run the race,
At a fast pace.
I was glad to be done,
And I had won!
My parents were proud,
And so was the crowd.
But then I quit,
I said, "This is it!"
I was as mad as a bear,
That my sisters didn't care.
But, one sister cared a bunch;
She gave me her own lunch.

James Zilinsky, Grade 5
Evangelical Christian School Ridgelake Campus, TN

Gray Walls

Staring at the four monotonous gray walls that surround me
It finally soaks in that there is no getting out
People falling and for what reason — I don't know
They are evil and cruel
With hearts of steel
They kill off loved ones
Chuckling at the misery of others
So there I sit
Praying I live another day
To my dismay, I have no idea what lies ahead
I just hope the tables turn

Emily Turner, Grade 6
East Mooresville Intermediate School, NC

Hunting

We went out hunting for deer,
Hoping a bear wouldn't appear.

We sat what at felt like hours,
We thought we had to go back to the tower.

We were freezing and awfully cold,
We thought this hunting was getting old.

We loaded our ammo,
We zipped up our camo and soon we were headed home.

Zachary Bowen, Grade 4
Centennial Elementary School, TN

I Like Cats

Roses are red, violets are blue
I like cats. Do you?
I think cats are cute and fuzzy.
I don't care what color they are.
I like cats eyes. Do you?
Blue or green or brown
I don't care what color. Do you?
I like cats. Do you?

MaKenzie Kay Koger, Grade 4
Tazewell-New Tazewell Primary School, TN

Ding

I love the beautiful sound that I make
It is better than a piece of cake
I am heard a lot around Christmas
And without me it will be an amiss holiday
Ding
And the cow jumped over the moon
With me dangling on its neck
I got back at noon
To hear my brother ring
Ding
Kids zoom up the steps
Making me swing and sway like a gentle breeze
I am like a tether ball
All alone swinging
Back and forth, back and forth
Ding
I am a dangling star on a string,
Falling to the ground is getting sucked into
A black hole and hitting the ground
Is when I am in it
Ding

Mark Christopher Murphy, Grade 5
Hunter GT Magnet Elementary School, NC

My Dream

I see myself in my dream,
sailing over a top of a hill.
Dirt flying everywhere as the
tires land.
I put one foot down, as
I make a sharp turn.
Then I see the mini bumps.
My nerves are getting to
me. I say to myself, "Oh my, oh my,
am I going to make it to the
finish line?"
I push the throttle to speed
up.
Then suddenly, I lose control
on a patch of lose dirt.
I slide off the track and crashed.
"Do I give up?" I asked myself.
"No!" I said aloud. I got myself
up and got back on the track.
I continued racing towards the finish line.
Then I woke up.

Stephen Hodi, Grade 4
Centennial Elementary School, TN

A Little Rose

A rose is a beautiful butterfly.
So gentle, tender and yet still so soft.
But when winter comes, BOOM!
Bye bye little rose.

Chandra Lynn Miller, Grade 4
Tazewell-New Tazewell Primary School, TN

School

Where do I fit?
All my friends from last year
have change, my world is different,
rearrange, lopsided, fractured.

Where do I sit?
Nothing is clear.
This will probably
be a jigsaw year

Chalon Dew, Grade 5
Stantonsburg Elementary School, NC

My Dad

My dad is funny
He loves to have money
My dad plays the bass
He loves to play music
He has lots of friends
He has a lot of talents
He has a lot of instruments
He has lots of family
I love my dad, and he loves me too

Sadie Grace Horton, Grade 4
Contentnea-Savannah K-8 School, NC

My Best Friend

My best friend is caring, loving, and sweet,
I can always count on her.
She is smart and careful,
She is fun to hang out with.
I think she is funny and awesome,
It's sad when she's absent.
Words to describe her are joyful, tall, sweet,
She is creative, smart, funny, and cool too.
My best friend is Kaleigh Mosier

Emily Miller, Grade 5
Paint Lick Elementary School, KY

Excitement

Parade, laughing and partying
Chatterbox, talking nonstop
Pogo stick, hopping around
Yelling, shouting constantly
Dancing, dancing excitedly
Blabbing about it, telling everyone
Carnival, riding scary rides

Toshja'Nae Williams, Grade 6
College View Middle School, KY

Sick Day

I was absent, I was sick
Fifteen popsicles did the trick
My head was hot, my hands were clammy
Coughing a mouthful, it was a whammy.

Shelby Chitwood, Grade 5
Lake City Elementary School, TN

The Beach

Crashing waves upon the shore like lightning in a summer thunderstorm
Children building enormous castles made of sand
People laughing as they are surfing through the rolling waves
The whistle of the excited life guards was saying that it was ready to help someone
Sand is like water pressing through my toes
The waves were calling my name
As I was swimming excitement pulsated through my body
I feel free

Hannah Davis, Grade 4
Bailey Elementary School, NC

Soccer

Big white nets sit on a blanket of green
Girls and boys wait for the chance to score
With the screech of the whistle they begin to run like a tiger after a meal
Acting like warriors in a vicious fight
Kicking legs are like clanking swords
Yelling with joy with every goal
High fives as the day ends
I feel like a pro

Gerardo Salas, Grade 4
Bailey Elementary School, NC

Blank Canvas

The world is my blank canvas
Hopes dreams and memories become colors gaspingly beautiful
As the white bumpy surface meets my color filled brush, worlds collide
My canvas fills with colors even unheard of
Thick creamy yellow to thin watery violet
Sunset clementine to an ocean blue
All life's colors stroked onto my beautiful, lively canvas.

Tara Murray, Grade 5
Hunter GT Magnet Elementary School, NC

The Deadly Places

I hear stories of deadly places
In which are the ghastly faces,
Of the Jews emaciated
By the Nazi's hated,
And their Officials highly rated,
And the mothers who give their last embraces,
But I'm safe right here because these deadly places are being liberated.

Michael Whitfield, Grade 6
East Mooresville Intermediate School, NC

Bye Bye

Daddy I love you even though you're gone,
Daddy I love you, but you chose to go home!
I try like you say for me to do even when momma's not strong.
I try because you said to try even when I'm sad and alone...
But all those good memories is all I ever had.
No goodbye I was too young for momma to even let me say goodbye.
Though it's bye bye the thought still makes me sad and bring drips from my eyes. Bye bye...

Harmonie Braswell, Grade 5
Fairview Elementary School, NC

Florida Gators Stadium "The Swamp"

Orange and blue Nike jerseys as the Gators line up for the beginning kickoff
The football flying fast through the air, a missile
Loud shouts of excitement as the Florida Gators ease down the field play-by-play
Plays being shouted from coach-to-coach on the sidelines
The fresh scent of grilled hamburgers being placed in aluminum foil ready to sell
Fresh cut green grass from a John Deer, a grass eating machine, before the game
Delicious cheeseburgers with pickle, mustard, and ketchup, along with golden French fries with ketchup
Greasy, sugary, golden funnel cake on a white paper plate
Warm Styrofoam cup containing bark colored hot chocolate as hot as lava
Ice cold Dr. Pepper in my freezing hands as I'm observing the game
My adrenaline begins to rush as the Florida Gators score a touchdown off a pass play

Braxton Hurley, Grade 6
College View Middle School, KY

About Me

Tall, talkative, friendly and funny
Relative to Amanda (mom). Dustin (dad). Kylor (little brother)
Resident of Lebanon Junction
Who reads *Go Dog Go*, *Green Eggs and Ham*,
Diary of the Wimpy Kid, and *Just Another Hero*
Who likes to color, to draw, and hangout with friends and family
Who fears heights, clowns, and getting embarrassed
Who wishes for non one to die, to meet Sponge Bob Square Pants, and to wish you were just born with a smart brain
Who admires her best friends, her cousins, and mom and dad
Who needs TV, a basketball, and the internet
Who aspires to be a doctor, a person that helps people that can't help themselves.

Emalee Close, Grade 6
Bernheim Middle School, KY

The Smoky Mountains

Black bears going through full dumpsters looking for an easy dinner
Sparkling go-carts zipping through the wind, trying to pass anyone who lies ahead of them
Laughing kids scream as they get squirted with water from the water boats
Dazzling water crashes over beautiful brown boulders as people try to navigate through the white water
The aroma of warm syrup rushes through my nose as it pours over my pancakes
Fresh air fills my nose as the fog lifts in the morning
Homemade ham and pomegranate melts in my mouth as it is soon gone
Soft arms of the rocking chair whisper relax
GREAT

Jay Newcom, Grade 6
College View Middle School, KY

Ode to My Neighbor

You are my neighbor and I know it's true, you're like my brother but as sweet as my shoe. I can't complain about the things that you do because I don't know what my life would be like if I didn't have you.

We like to play outside when we can, but we like it much better with more than two instead. We like to play with water balloons, but we like to play hide-and-seek too. There is one thing that is mostly true; there is no one just as quick as you.

You are my neighbor and I know it's true, but you're much more to me than what people say about you. I know we fight but that's just what we do. People might say you're too good to be true. But that is just one reason why I love you!

Emily Henson, Grade 6
Bernheim Middle School, KY

Growing Up

Once you were little
Soon you could be a teenager
Or you might be driving
But parents don't worry
They are still the same
They're just growing up
You might go to college
And you won't see your parents as much
You'll graduate
And your parents are very proud
You'll turn 22
Maybe you have a place of your own
And before you know it
You'll be married
Maybe a couple of years later you will have a child
And now it's your turn to be the parent
You'll watch them grow up
Just like your parents watched you
They'll go through all of the above
And life continues on like this
Forever

Ruthie Ivy, Grade 6
Woodland Presbyterian School, TN

Walton Verona Middle School

What is under the rood of Walton Verona Middle School:
Tall children
Dropped pencils
Lab computers
Open doors
Fifth grade teachers
Total entries
Project makers
Boys painting
Children laughing
Gossip girls
Girls with twirls
Total games
Happy teachers
Students walking
Students writing
Teachers assigning work
Smiling students
Slamming lockers
Basketballs
Wonderful teachers

Sadie Pulliam, Grade 5
Walton-Verona Middle School, KY

Birthdays

Everybody has birthdays and each one is nice,
Each one is very fun indeed,
Some have games and others do not,
Every one has a different spice!

Nicholas Lonce, Grade 5
Moyock Elementary School, NC

My Dog

My dog, Cocoa, is really sweet
She is not sometimes very neat
She runs and plays in my backyard
To not love her is very hard

Her brown eyes sparkle like fireworks
I call her name, up her ears will perk
Her fur is brown, with one white spot
Her stubby tail, it wags a lot

When it's storming, Cocoa will hurry
Into the garage, she will scurry
During the day, she lays down to rest
I pet her and she likes that the best

It seems she smiles at me a million times
Then into my arms Cocoa cuddly climbs
At the end of the day, it's hard to say bye
Her big, brown eyes look like they're going to cry

Leah Brewer, Grade 5
Providence Academy, TN

Little Bro Mo

You came from a land so far, far away,
To get there one must travel for days,
Even so God found a way,
For us to get you little bro Mo.

We worked and prayed for years and years,
And when we got you, we were close to tears,
In fact, not getting you was one of our fears,
Yes, my little bro Mo.

You used to live in a concrete room,
As if something had sealed your doom,
But alas! We were to get you soon,
Yes, little bro Mo.

Then across the sea we came,
Flying to China in a plane,
And since then we gave you a new name,
Fun, little bro Mo.

Clara Reynolds, Grade 5
Providence Academy, TN

At Night

When the moon comes out at night
bat and owl take flight;
flying low, flying high, flying up in the sky.
When the sun has gone to bed
snake pokes out his head;
creeping fast, creeping slow, snake knows where to go.
Look around this night
for animals that creep and spy.

Aunalisa Deloris Rose Dodds, Grade 4
Tazewell-New Tazewell Primary School, TN

The Beach

Seagulls flying like falling leaves
Waves are pounding like boulders
Loud sounds erupt from playing children
Salty sea water calls me from a mile away
Beautiful seashells you can touch
Rough sand on the ground
Splashing through the water
So happy to be at the beach

Tatiana Ridley, Grade 4
Bailey Elementary School, NC

Springtime

Flowers are blooming
and the sunshine is here.
I smell the flowers
when they are near.
Bees are buzzing
all around.
Better watch your step
on the ground.

Austin Slate, Grade 4
Stantonsburg Elementary School, NC

What Am I?

By day I'm a sleep,
By night I'm alert,
I'm as fast as lightning,
Some people think I'm frightening,
You freeze when you look at me,
I blend in so greatly,
Only my spots you can see,
Who am I?

Sydni Barnes, Grade 6
Snowden Middle School, TN

Excitement

Entertainment,
Enjoyable, funny
Cool, fun
Jumping, clapping, laughing
Moving, enthusiastic
Alert, delighted
All fired up

DeAshia Archie, Grade 6
College View Middle School, KY

Loving Relatives

Family
Caring, big
Busy, working, playing
Likes spending time together
Laughing, playing, cooking
Loving, providing
People

Makenna Casto, Grade 6
Musselman Middle School, WV

My Desk

My scattered desk, brown hardy wood, holds a decade of treasures.
Foreign currency from all our trips out of the United States.
Rocks from my inherited collection including gems like topaz.
An elegant little jade dolphin from my grandfather.
An old and rugged little black Swiss army knife.
My red medic alert bracelet that I always forget to wear.
A 2005 Riverbend poster that fell off my wall, assembled Lego rocket ship.
A green plastic battery operated fan for camping,
usually used for cooling me down during the summer.
Old pictures of me in my childhood, most of which I do not like.
A pair of two whittled, wooden, drumsticks that look dangerous.
A white mini, flat, soccer ball that I might have used when I was little.
Dad's nasty green, plastic, duck call that looked
like it had been used way too much.
My preread books of interest like Harry Potter and Kingdom Keepers.
A deck of unused playing cards I bring into play on trips.
My dead iron man wrist watch I wear when I go running.
My tub of used freestyle blood test strips that I need to unload.
Some of these things mean so much to me that I treasure them
wish to hand them down later in life, but
others I am just too lazy to dispose of.

Charlie Weeks, Grade 6
Baylor School, TN

I Am an Immigrant

I am an immigrant. I have just arrived to a new country.
I wonder if I am going to pass inspection. If I do I hope my family does too.
I hear voices all around me. I can't understand what they are saying.
I see a beautiful, large statue that people around me are calling "The Statue of Liberty."
I want to be held by my mother, and I want to be with my family.
I am going to try to work my hardest to earn money for food, clothes, and shelter.
I pretend that I can get whatever I want, and that I have a huge house to live in.
I feel so scared, nervous, and weird all at the same time.
I touch foods that I have never seen before in my life.
I worry that my family will die of starvation.
I cry every night because I am cold and hungry.
I am going to try to get a job and earn money.
I understand that we are poor and can't afford stuff that we need.
I say to my mother and father that someday we'll be rich, but they just laugh.
I dream that some day I will understand this new world that people call "America."

Hannah Tucker, Grade 5
St Joseph School, KY

My Papaw's Farm

My papaw working on the tractor like he's walking on water,
Horses grazing in the field, as they talk to the bees,
Tired farm cats purring as I rub their bellies,
Red and green tractors starting to plow,
Yellow, pink, and orange flowers being planted for a new year,
Dust and dirt fly as I run through the field,
Fried chicken fresh from the oven is heaven. Fresh corn from the field tastes so good,
The horse's hair after a cool wash feels soft,
Newborn kittens after they are born meow.
Happy.

Madison Smith, Grade 6
College View Middle School, KY

Cat

Cat
meows, hisses,
growls, claws, climbs
scratches, fangs
Siamese

Grace Tidwell, Grade 4
Centennial Elementary School, TN

A Berry

There once was a big red berry,
It tasted a lot like a cherry;
Then it blew away,
For it wasn't there to stay,
And no one was bright and merry.

Madison Sayre, Grade 5
Mineral Wells Elementary School, WV

Dog

dog
playful, tired
barks, excited, happy
tricks, food
boxer

Kaylee Triplett, Grade 4
Centennial Elementary School, TN

Flowers

Flowers
Tall, beautiful
Swinging, dying, growing
Love the summer wind
Sunflower

Savannah James, Grade 4
Centennial Elementary School, TN

Trees

T all and majestic
R eally heavy to carry
E very day we see them
E very home has stuff made from trees
S easons change them

Robert Gregory, Grade 4
Carver Elementary School, NC

My Cats

Cats
Playful, hungry
Sleeping, loving, energetic
They sleep with me
Kittens

Emily Schreckengost, Grade 5
Mineral Wells Elementary School, WV

I Am a Military Child

I am a Military child and I am special because I help and support everyone.
I am a Military child and I wonder if my dad will be okay.
I am a Military child and I hear the sounds of men and tanks.
I am a Military child and I see my dad leaving for work.
I am a Military child and I want my dad to return from Iraq.
I am a Military child and I am special because I help and support everyone.

I am a Military child and I pretend I am helping my dad.
I am a Military child and am happy when I see my dad.
I am a Military child and I touch my heart because I am happy.
I am a Military child and I worry something might happen at war.
I am a Military child and I cry because my dad is leaving.
I am a Military child and I am special because I help and support everyone.

I am a Military child and understand why he is in the Army.
I am a Military child and say I believe in you.
I am a Military child and dream that he will get out of the Army.
I am a Military child and I hope the world will come together in peace.
I am a Military child and I am special because I help and support everyone.

Selena Reyes, Grade 5
Walker Intermediate School, KY

I Am a Military Brat

I am a military brat that was born in Colorado and lives in Kentucky.
I wonder if dad wants to go to Iraq.
I hear the sound of the tanks.
I want my dad not to go to Iraq.
I am a military brat that was born in Colorado and lives in Kentucky.

I pretend I am at Iraq with my dad.
I feel happy when my dad is here.
I touch my heart to be home with my family.
I worry about my dad getting hurt.
I cry when my dad leaves.
I am a military brat that was born in Colorado and lives in Kentucky.

I understand that my dad has to leave.
I say that people should not have to go to Iraq.
I dream that my dad does not have to go to Iraq anymore.
I try to make my dad proud.
I hope that Iraq and America will just be friends.
I am a military brat that was born in Colorado and lives in Kentucky.

Ciarah Keen, Grade 5
Walker Intermediate School, KY

What If?

What if I don't get anything?
What if Christmas skips over me?
What if I have no presents or candy in my stocking hanging by the Christmas tree?
What if Santa thinks I'm mean?
What if Santa hates me?
What if he puts coal in my stocking? (Santa, please don't do that!)
What if I leave some cookies and milk on my table, will you like me?
Come on Santa, don't you see…

Cassidy Patterson, Grade 5
Mineral Wells Elementary School, WV

My Dog

My dog has black on his ears,
My dog loves cats and kittens,
My dog loves to play with a Frisbee,
My dog has a red collar with spikes,
My dog likes to give me high five,
My dog is very smart.
He can walk on his hind legs for five minutes,
That is my dog, and his name is Corbin.

Brooklyn Felty, Grade 5
Paint Lick Elementary School, KY

Dogs

Dogs are tall, and dogs are small,
Dogs are fat, and dogs are thin.
I don't know when dogs are not adorable,
Dogs are kind, and dogs are sweet.
Dogs love it when you give them treats.
Dogs are loving, dogs are caring,
Dogs are always sharing how much they love you.
You should always love them too.

Brook Webb, Grade 5
Paint Lick Elementary School, KY

Softball

I love it when I hit the ball.
I love to play softball.
I like it when we get your team out.
Then my team will scream and shout.
Even when we lose, which is rarely ever,
We go to Burger House! Yum!...We're so clever!!!
We know we will win the next game,
And if we don't my coach says, it's a shame!

Skylar Molen, Grade 5
Paint Lick Elementary School, KY

World War II

World War II was a horrible thing
It was so sad nobody would sing
Our troops would fight and help end the war
But after all of the fighting, the troops were sore
Always remember, because of those troops we're very blessed
Several men were killed and they are the rest
And when you hear "We live in a free country"
Remember those who died for you and me

Eyan Bowers, Grade 6
East Mooresville Intermediate School, NC

Hurt

Mad, feeling guilty
Sad, blue inside
Crying, tears running down my face
Yelling, screaming loudly
Wounded, deep inside
Pain, hurting like a cut down tree

Christian I. Jones, Grade 6
College View Middle School, KY

Christmas Jingles

The bells are ringing; the snow is falling.
Santa Claus is flying through the sky; saying ho ho ho.
It is time for Christmas night.
Families are gathering; for the celebration.
A blizzard happened on Christmas night;
The freezing snow falls on Christmas night.
Everyone at home having the time of their life;
Then when everyone's asleep Santa Claus comes.

William Zwick, Grade 5
Walton-Verona Middle School, KY

Autumn

Colorful trees sway back and forth
Insects welcome me to pray
Crunch, crunch as I step upon the leaves
Birds sing in harmony as professionals
Niagara Falls seems to appear at my house
Leaves are like flashing lights catching my attention
Wind sways saying hello to the morning sun
I feel welcomed and peaceful inside

Heather Poythress, Grade 5
Bailey Elementary School, NC

The Fall Leaves

I'm the only tree in the field,
And now my friends, the leaves are leaving me,
They are so forbidding,
It's depressing watching them crumble,
Losing their color,
My branches are bare,
I'm so dull without my friends,
I guess I will just grow some new ones

Sophie Clayton-Luce, Grade 5
Hunter GT Magnet Elementary School, NC

A Laugh and a Smile

You can't put me in a box and give me as a special present
You can't buy me in a store, I can't be seen
I'm easy to share it takes a laugh and a smile
Hold on to me forever cause you'll need me all the time
Whenever you feel blue just count on me to pull you through
You can't buy me, you can't see me but you'll always know I'm there
Just a little bit of happiness so easy to find
Just a laugh and a smile away

Allison Pittman, Grade 5
Hunter GT Magnet Elementary School, NC

Family

F orever there
A lways helpful
M akes life fun
I love family time
Laughing everywhere
" **Y**ay," everyone's here

Colton Acuff, Grade 5
Walton-Verona Middle School, KY

Dog

On top of the couch
The dog lies down
Almost as if he lived there.
He puts his chin
Between his paws,
And yawns,
Like he was screaming;
He hears his name,
And comes,
Because now
He knows,
He shall go to sleep.

Dalton Shaub, Grade 6
Sunset Middle School, TN

Dasia Briggs

D aisy
A ctive
S miles
I ndependent
A wesome

B rave
R eader
I ce skater
G reat
G reeter
S leepy

Dasia Briggs, Grade 4
Southeast Elementary School, NC

Christmas

Christmas
Huge, giant, Christmas trees.
Great bright lights.
Yummy, chocolate cookies.
Striped candy canes.
Ringing jingle bells.
The crinkle of the wrapping paper.
The delicious hot chocolate.
Walnut dressing as sweet as sugar.
The smooth, squeaky presents.
A Christmas tree as prickly as a porcupine.
Christmas.

Abby Smith, Grade 5
Providence Academy, TN

Recess

I
love to Run
during recess
on the basketball court
because it feels good
to have the wind in my face.

Taylor Haines, Grade 5
Walton-Verona Middle School, KY

Where I'm From

I am from afternoon swims,
From splashing and diving deep.
I am from endless games of hide and seek.
(Sneaking slowly, ducking behind bushes and trees)
From bouncing from stone to slippery stone and jumping narrow creeks.
I'm from bruises and cuts at the skating rink,
From my mom's lush flower gardens,
I am from my brother's Lego forts.
From my dad's challenging math problems,
Which pushed me to believe I could do anything.
I am from messy paint splatters decorating my apron,
From the wacky pictures drawn along the wall,
From the sharp, but pleasing, aroma of spices coming from the kitchen.
I am from the old, ceramic pottery I used to paint,
that reminds me of happy memories that will stay with me forever.
I am from making coffee for my dad,
carefully mixing sugar and coffee powder.
From delicious honey sticks at the farmers market,
with a scrumptious, tangy taste.
I am from a family of people who are loving and caring,
who make sure I do my best and support me when I do.

Savarni Sanka, Grade 6
Ligon Middle School, NC

My Room

Small TV glares on the channel of *Monk* as I lay on my bed and watch
New white as snow fan gleams as it spins and spins and makes me dizzy
Raging red radio booms out of its old speakers
I can hear the dog barking his head off next door
A fresh aroma of body spray rushes up my nose
Hershey's chocolate is hidden in a stash in my closet that you could smell far away
Good chicken that I eat for dinner sits on my desk
Warm milk I drink for a late night snack, a relaxer to calm me to sleep
Grabbing my black remote to turn off the TV
Gripping my pencil, that has a mind of its own, to finish my last math problem.
Relaxed

Tyler Boling, Grade 6
College View Middle School, KY

Riding in the Car

traffic lights blinking red faster than a mile a minute
baby cows next to their momma cow swimming in a pond
the wind blowing in our faces trying to get fresh air
my family talking about our plans for when we arrive
the truck in front of us coughing up polluted smoke
the stinky cow patties smell as bad as rotten eggs as we pass by
the red Gatorade that I bought from the gas station we passed
Ritz crackers my mom packed for us
pencil I used to beat my brother at tic-tac-toe
the button that makes the window go up and down
my super silly sick stomach is such a pain from being in the car so long

Marie McClary, Grade 6
College View Middle School, KY

I Am

I am a kind and loving dog owner
I wonder what my dog is doing when I am not at home
I hear my dog barking when I leave her alone
I see her pulling me on my scooter
I want to be with my dog Bella
I am a kind and loving dog owner

I pretend she is with me even at school
I feel her soft black and white fur rubbing up against me
I touch Bella's soft ears as she lays on me
I worry that she will be stolen when I am not at home
I cry when I think of her dying
I am a kind and loving dog owner

I understand that one day we will both part from each other
I say live your life like to the fullest
I dream of becoming a vet one day with Bella on my side
I try to do my best at school so I don't have
homework and can play with Bella
I hope Bella and I can be buds forever
I am a kind a loving dog owner

Kahla Nutt, Grade 6
Bernheim Middle School, KY

Wonder

As we think of many things, will our thoughts head yonder?
As the clock will tick
will our thoughts click
or will our thoughts forever wander?
As we think of ideas, they will sometimes blunder.
Our ideas may fall
but the best thoughts of all
are those of excitement and wonder.
Wherever our thoughts will make us go,
our wandering minds will continue to grow,
we will always have new ideas to show,
and our minds will forever ponder.

Chase West, Grade 6
Woodland Presbyterian School, TN

Tractors

Tractors tall, powerful,
loud, and noisy,

Tractors orange,
green, red, blue, and tan,

Tractors,
strong and with big wheels.

Tractors digging, pulling, lifting,
pushing, carrying.

I love tractors.

Isaac Jones, Grade 4
Tazewell-New Tazewell Primary School, TN

Love My Dog

Even though you are kind of mean,
You are the best friend I've found so far.
We've been friends since the day we met.
I will always love you.

You were just two months old when my eyes first saw you.
I know you get in trouble sometimes,
But you are still my little Merle
And I love you.

I like you more and more each day I have you.
Deep down in my heart I store my love for you.
I give you some every time I see you, and it will never run out.
I love you.

I don't know what I would do if I didn't have you.
You are my Merle and
I would never give you away to anyone
I will always love you!

McKenzie Braden, Grade 5
Lake City Elementary School, TN

I Am From

I am from...being born on a farm
in Harrodsburg, Kentucky...
to moving to Burgin, Kentucky, when I was four.

I am from...being an only child
to becoming the middle child of a family
with two older stepbrothers, Ty and Hayden,
a younger stepsister, Elly, and a half-brother, Wyatt...who is three!

I am from...flipping and turning in the air
at the YMCA
to cheering for the Mercer Titans' football team
at Anderson Dean Park.

I am from...hanging out with my friends,
Marie and Shelby,
to playing with my baby bro, Wyatt.

This is what I am from.

Kaitlyn Davies, Grade 5
Burgin Independent School, KY

My Dog's Favorite Game

It's like a blizzard blew through
Fluffy white shreds all over my floor
Covering my socks that are brand new
Making it hard to open the door
My little dog Clover has lots of toys
But they don't seem to satisfy her desires
It's the toilet paper game that she most enjoys
Even though the game usually backfires

Bridget O'Donnell, Grade 5
Duke Middle School, NC

The Touchdown Pass

The quarter back…
Gets the snap
Crowd cheering
Tied game
16 to 16
15 seconds
He drops back
Nervous
He's getting rushed
Drop out of the pocket
Throws at the wide open receiver
They see, they go get him
The ball turning
Spinning caught
He breaks the tackle
He's at the 10, 5, touchdown
The crowd roars
The opponents are still as a pole
The winning team goes
CRAZY

Steven Taylor, Grade 6
McGee's Crossroads Middle School, NC

I Am

I am beautiful
I wonder about the past
I hear people call me China doll
I see people surrounding me
I want to go see what heaven looks like
I am beautiful

I pretend I am people's friend
I feel water when I get in the shower
I touch my bed when I lay down
I worry I might die
I cry when I go to a funeral
I am beautiful

I understand the pain
I say things I should not say
I dream sweet dreams
I try not to let it go
I hope for Haiti
I am beautiful

ReKiyea Lewis, Grade 5
Tates Creek Elementary School, KY

Love

Love is close,
I'll give you my heart,
to be with you,
to love you,
and to care about you,
love never goes away.

Jada Kennett, Grade 5
Walton-Verona Middle School, KY

Home

My home is quiet, lonely, fun
My home is musical, happy
I love my home
At my home I have
Summer, winter, fall, spring

Home
Quiet, lonely, fun
Glad, wonderful
Spectacular

Wes Hines, Grade 5
Hunter GT Magnet Elementary School, NC

Rainforest

Bright green trees
Thick brown tree trunks
Different animals everywhere
Raindrops touch the leaves
Birds flap their wings
Nice fresh air
Beautiful flowers
Wet leaves
Moisture in the air
So calm

Jacqueline Salinas, Grade 5
Bailey Elementary School, NC

Avery

Avery means the world to me.
He loves to run with my dad
And play with Huey, his best friend.
I love to go outside and play rope with him.

I love to watch him run in the yard
And chase lots of birds.
And even once he caught one.
He was as happy as a kid on Halloween.
And that's why I love Avery.

Rachel Killian, Grade 5
Providence Academy, TN

Summer

I smell the salt water in the air.
I see kids splashing in the pool.
I hear the kids laughing.

Summer is a sun wonderland.

I hear dogs barking.
I see the sunflowers pointing at the sun.
I see the cars racing down the road.
I love summer.

Christopher V. Curnell, Grade 5
Nature's Way Montessori School, TN

Memphis Basketball

Memphis basketball is so great,
but Tennessee we mock and hate.
The ecstatic and patriotic fans
sit anxiously waiting in the stands.
As the coach scribbles on his board,
the players dribble down the court.
The day wears on
as the players play on.
During the final seconds on the clock,
the whole stadium starts to rock.
Excitement is in the air
because a game like this is very rare.
The Tigers are up by one
and the other team is almost done.
The buzzer does its thing
and the whole arena starts to scream.

Justin Howerton, Grade 6
Woodland Presbyterian School, TN

I'll Be Okay

Oh, you know I'll be okay,
All through out all my days,
You know I'll be okay.

We are to love each other,
You know we do.
I love you more, you know I do.

Oh, you know I'll be okay,
All through out my days,
You know I'll be okay.

We are to need each other,
You know we do.
You need me more, you know you do.
I promise, I'll be okay.

Toneeya Jones, Grade 5
Rex-Rennert Elementary School, NC

Dogs

Dogs are like dreams,
Always there to talk to.
Dogs are companions,
Always there to bark or be petted.
Dogs are like vacuums,
Always cleaning up the leftovers.
Dogs are hard to be angry at,
Always missing you in your sleep.
Dogs are something to get you out,
Always whining to play fetch.
Dogs are the joy in your life,
Always there for you.
Enjoy it, because,
So will your dog.

Maxwell Bradley, Grade 5
Love Memorial Elementary School, NC

Together We Can

Together we can dream,
as I close my eyes and drift to sleep,
I begin to dream.

Bright lights, big stage,
and the music begins.

With my jazz shoes on my feet,
and my body moving with the beat.

I began to leap and turn across the stage,
with my pointed toes.

As I didn't miss a beat,
the crowd cheered me on,
and the moment was great.
I had stars in my eyes,
and my fame finally came.

The Performing Arts Dance Academy had offered me a scholarship.

Then I heard a loud noise
and I was awoken from my dream.
So when the road is rough
and the day is tough
we can all close our eyes
and dream what our heart desires.

Hannah Jones, Grade 4
Bostian Elementary School, NC

I Am From

I am from gold shoes
I am from science
I am from beauty
I am from coolness.

I am from the fall trees
I am from leaves falling to the ground
I am from the holly and the mistletoe
I am from the Christmas tree with its twinkling lights.

I am from the perfect side of Earth
I am from my mom
I am from Kentucky.

I am from the x's and the o's
The hugs and the kisses.
I am from the hospital
I am from a farm.

I am from fried chicken
I am from life
I am from the poetry of the class
I am from the gold shoes.

Bayleigh Mcmillan, Grade 5
Tates Creek Elementary School, KY

Wolf and Tiger

Fly, fly far away from here
Cry, cry from tear to tear
Like walking through the woods at night
Have you ever seen an elegant faerie's flight?
It's wonderful, beautiful
So unlike me
Trudging through the thick forest
Climbing every tree
Hopping from branch to branch
Swift as the tiger
staring back at me
for I am the wolf
and I have a home
here, looking back at you
Tiger and wolf
natural born enemies
together forever
only to pretend
we're alone

Sarah Berger, Grade 5
J.Y. Joyner Elementary School, NC

My List

I don't want a doll with curly hair.
I don't want a brown stuffed teddy bear.
I don't want a shiny new bike to ride,
or the latest and greatest Barbie doll bride.
You won't find these on my list this year!
I don't want a swing set with monkey bars.
I don't want a telescope to help me find Mars.
I don't want Legos to build a city;
No barking puppies or cuddling kitties.
You won't find these on my list this year!
I don't want a train that whistles and hoots.
I don't want roller skates or cowgirl boots.
I don't want a jump rope or a trampoline;
No Christmas stocking trimmed in red or green.
You won't find these on my list this year!
See my dad's been gone in a faraway place,
Fighting for our freedom and to keep us safe.
I miss him so much and I've been so sad.
All I want for Christmas, Santa, please bring home my Dad.

Shannon Collier, Grade 5
Moyock Elementary School, NC

Upon the Sea

I stand here looking upon the sea
It seems as if it's looking at me
I love to swim, dive, and splash
I hear the thundering waves go "crash"
The beautiful sunset is pink, yellow, and blue
It makes me think that the day is through
I thank God for the wonderful sea
He made it just for you and me.

Benjamin Harris, Grade 5
Providence Academy, TN

Cedar

I loved her so much
I cried and cried
When my mom said she could no longer touch
My own hands
She was a leader
She went to heaven
And we got her ashes
Cedar
My mom put you to sleep
I really wish I could keep you
But you are probably happier
Up there
Above us
In heaven
Because you were old and
And no longer could hold
Yourself together.
I miss you,
Because you were the dog I loved.
Cedar.

Gwen Caudle, Grade 5
Duke Middle School, NC

My Family

I get reminded
A lot of times I forget
I try and try
But my brain can't handle it
It is so much pressure
But the thing that stands out most
Is my family
My family is my heart and soul
They created me
And supported me since the beginning of my time
I love them and I know they love me
We are a happy family
We stick together like glue
In tough situations we work together
They support me in what I choose
We play together
Love each other
We hangout
The most important thing is we are a loving family
I will never forget my family

Noah Chensasky, Grade 6
Woodland Presbyterian School, TN

Sunflower Seeds

Sunflower seeds, they're tasty and pure
There are sweet ones, salty ones, and even chocolate ones.
Now if you want a piece
You have to choose which one you please.
Sunflower seeds come from a flower
They drop to the ground and grow with lots of power.

Ben Pluska, Grade 5
Hunter GT Magnet Elementary School, NC

Katelynn

I am a loving daughter
I wonder what my mom spends her life doing at work
I hear my mother laughing
I see my mom whit a big smile
I want to see my mom now
I am a loving daughter

I pretend she is with me every step of my life
I feel her putting my wet hair up
I touch my broken heart
I worry my mom is safe
I cry about her
I am a loving daughter

I understand this was better for me
I say she is the best
I dream I will live with her forever
I try to make a difference
I hope my mom is okay
I am a loving daughter

Katelynn Coyle, Grade 6
Bernheim Middle School, KY

Mexico

My country is Mexico.
Through my veins flows the blood of Mexico.
I wish to thank Mexican veterans
They risked their lives to let us be Mexico
Instead of being Nueva Espana (New Spain).
I thank them for all they have done for us,
They taught us a good lesson;
Mexican people never give up,
we work hard, never fail,
We keep on moving through life,
and never quit.
Today we are taking our lives a step forward,
We're crossing borders, and getting an education.
Every September 16, we celebrate our Independence.
it is also my birthday, that's why I love Mexico.
If our veterans would of never did this oh my...
We would have never become Mexico, but New Spain.
All thanks to our veterans we're who we are now.
We're are so thankful for what they had done
for our freedom.

Nayeli Estrada Torrecilla, Grade 6
Saint Pauls Middle School, NC

Taylor

T ry to do my best at all times
A chieving my goals, while developing mind
Y earning to learn more each day
L earning all I can in every way
O nly you can determine your success
R emember to be all I can be and do my best

Taylor Evans, Grade 5
Carver Elementary School, NC

Winter

It was very cold out late December
Nobody could control the weather
Wearing red and green sweaters
Mistletoe on every front door
People looking out for the poor

Christmas lights in every front yard
While people are making Christmas cards
Glue, paste, glitter and foil
The stinky, nasty smells of winter projects

Christmas trees are in the house
By the fire, roasting chestnuts

Ornaments shatter and break
As they erode by the air
Gleaming in the light as Santa comes downstairs
To give us toys and a rocking chair

As our Christmas party ends
We will say bye to all our friends
In the dark snowy night.

Frankie Donini, Grade 5
Hunter GT Magnet Elementary School, NC

Princess, My Best Friend

I love my dog Princess
She's so sweet, a small brown cutie-pie
With long soft ears she's so sweet
And loves everyone she meets
I think it's hilarious because
She thinks of me as a giant
Chew toy because she tugs at my shirt and nips at my feet
But in the end she gives me a kiss and I know that she loves me
We both have brown hair but she has brown eyes and I have blue
I love the fact that Princess is always ready to play with me
And she keeps my toes warm at night
She is also very protective to me and I love her very much

Heather Holbert, Grade 6
Johnson Traditional Middle School, KY

Chameleon

The chameleon is clawing the ground.
As he runs like a cheetah on the land,
Jumping from branch to branch,
With splats of yellow as bright as the sun,

Ready to strike at every moment.
You can hear their strike from a mile away.
The chameleon lives in a forest that is as green
As seeing the continents from space.

The chameleon whispers to his friends
As he spies on his prey.

Drake Smith, Grade 4
Nature's Way Montessori School, TN

Hand Sanitizer

Hand sanitizer makes my hands clean,
Hand sanitizer can be clear or green!
Hand sanitizer really stinks,
But with it you don't need sinks!

It kills 99.9% of germs — WOO-HOO!!!
And when you use it you won't get the flu!

You see, hand sanitizer is pretty cool,
You can hook it on your backpack and take it to school!

Splat! It goes onto your hand.
Don't put too much or it won't be grand,
And no one will want to shake your hand!

I think hand sanitizer is pretty great,
And I'll use it 'til I meet my fate!

Merrin Gilmer, Grade 5
Providence Academy, TN

Ghetto Girl

She stands with a dash of hope in her eyes,
a yellow star adorns her chest,
sewn to her dead brother's sweater.
Bored, she gazes intently at a tall cement wall,
the wall that separates her from humanity.
She turns. Her body is numb from the Warsaw winter,
her toes peek out from her shoes, tinged with gray.
Near her lies a body,
his hair frozen in tufts, eyes still gazing at the wall.
She simply steps over his concave abdomen.
Death is the norm.
She continues on to the slaughterhouse,
that twenty people call their home.
There is no food to feed her growing body,
nothing to clothe it but rags.
This is her life.
The life of thousands.

Adriana Lorenzini, Grade 6
R D and Euzelle P Smith Middle School, NC

Father, Can You Hear Me?

Father, can you hear me?
Can you hear my voice today?
Can you hear me when I'm talking?
Can you hear me when I'm walking?
Can you hear me when I dance, clap, and sing?
Can you hear me here?
Can you hear me there?
Can you hear me everywhere?
Can you hear me when I'm praying?
Or even when I'm sleep?
But even though you're gone
Father, can you hear me?

Mackenzie Walker, Grade 6
Snowden School, TN

Socks

Socks, socks, warm, fuzzy socks,
The more, the better, lots, lots, lots.
They're fun to buy, and they warm your feet,
Socks should be the number one treat.

Socks, socks, warm, fuzzy socks,
They protect your feet from sticks, stones, and rocks.
They come in all sizes, short or long.
When you're wearing socks you can't go wrong.

Socks, socks, warm, fuzzy socks,
Some are as soft as the fur of a fox.
Polka dots, designs, and colorful stripes,
Lots of socks, they come in all types.

Socks, socks, warm, fuzzy socks,
They feel great in runs, bikes, or walks.
Socks have colors of all kinds,
Socks will surely blow your mind.

Sofia Murtaugh, Grade 6
White Station Middle School, TN

I Am a Military Child

I am a military child who was born in Colorado Springs.
I wonder how you get in the army.
I hear guns shooting every morning.
I see people moving every month.
I want my dad to stay home.
I am a military child who was born in Colorado Springs.

I pretend to go to the field with my dad.
I feel happy when deployment is over.
I touch my heart and I am proud to be an American.
I worry about my dad having to go back to Iraq.
I am a military child who was born in Colorado Springs.

I understand my dad might not come back from Iraq.
I say I love you mom and dad every night.
I dream about being in the military.
I try to make everybody happy.
I hope for world peace and caring for others.
I am a military child who was born in Colorado Springs.

Jonathan DeMont, Grade 5
Walker Intermediate School, KY

The Aquarium

The door opens to invite me in
Water is everywhere
Sharks, Eels, and Stingrays are swimming around
The odor of fish fills the air
Water splashes against the tanks
We pet the Stingrays
I am in a world of blue
I feel like a fish too

Kedric Anderson, Grade 4
Bailey Elementary School, NC

I Am

I am a loving big sister
I wonder if she knows that I love her
I hear cooing when I talk to her
I see her smile at me
I want her to know I'm there for her
I am a loving big sister

I pretend that I am her big toy
I feel that I'm loved when I'm around her
I touch her baby soft skin
I worry that she'll hate me when she gets older
I am a loving big sister

I understand that we're sisters forever
I say I love her all the time
I dream about getting older with her
I try to play with her after homework
I hope we'll still be close
I am a loving big sister

Brittany Arnold, Grade 6
Bernheim Middle School, KY

Sorry Dad

I was so sorry Dad
It was my entire fault really
I never meant to make you sad
I was being stupid and silly

I know you couldn't have seen it
When I said I hated you
But I really didn't mean it
I promise it wasn't true

I hope you will forgive me
For all the horrible things I've done to you
And I wish that you could see
That I snapped and didn't know what to do

I swear I will always be nice
'Cause once we're together we'll never be apart
From now on no more fights
I'm sorry Dad; I love you with all my heart

Maddie Lange, Grade 6
Bernheim Middle School, KY

Beauty

Beauty is children running around and playing.
Beauty is children learning in school.
Beauty is nature's whisper in your ear.
Beauty is Mother Nature's breath across the nation.
Beauty is people helping out each other.
Beauty is friendships lasting a lifetime,
Beauty is birth.
Beauty is death.

Bryan Saldana, Grade 6
Morton Middle School, KY

Holiday
Christmas
merry, white
caroling, shopping, preparing
gifts, Santa, eggs, bunny
coloring, hunting, rejoicing
happy, bright
Easter
Elle Roth, Grade 4
Centennial Elementary School, TN

De-Cleaners
Slob
Messy, slobby
Not cleaning, not purifying
Disgusting, germy-antiseptic, sanitary
Washing, decontaminating, dusting
Hygienic, unsullied
Germaphobe
Sam Dove, Grade 6
Musselman Middle School, WV

Farming
F un to drive the tractor
A ll of the animals
R eally hard
M y favorite thing is farming
I nternational Harvester
N oisy from the equipment
G ood food after harvested.
Nathaniel Tinch, Grade 5
Walton-Verona Middle School, KY

Elements
Water
Smooth, adaptive
Douse, drench, soak
Soothing, refreshing, light, warming
Burning, lighting, comforting
Red, orange
Fire.
Cameron LeFevre, Grade 6
Musselman Middle School, WV

What If?
What if I can't think of anything?
What if I fail?
What if I can't concentrate?
What if I don't know what to do?
What if I can't answer a question?
Now that I think about it, tests might be
easier than I first thought!
Caroline Affolter, Grade 5
Mineral Wells Elementary School, WV

At the Beach
The wind flowing in my hair
The ocean's sounds deep in my ear
The sand glowing on my feet
My glorious walk on the beach
Brittney Kersey, Grade 4
E O Young Elementary School, NC

Catfish
A catfish I think is kind.
I bet they pay a fine.
A catfish likes to swim.
I think I will name mine Kim.
Kaleb Van Orden, Grade 4
Centennial Elementary School, TN

Christmas
When I wake up
I see presents under my tree
because Santa came to visit me
it was all on Christmas Eve.
Megan Larkins, Grade 4
Centennial Elementary School, TN

Soccer
An organized sport
Fun for the whole family
Always action-packed
Ian McKnight, Grade 5
Mineral Wells Elementary School, WV

Crocodile
A deadly hunter,
A sleek, steady juggernaut
Prey cannot escape.
Joseph Fisher, Grade 5
Hunter GT Magnet Elementary School, NC

Christmas
Giving to others
Presents to the poor and needy
Makes me feel real good
Candra Collins, Grade 5
Mineral Wells Elementary School, WV

Winter
Cold as a freezer
Sweet as a Wendy's Frosty
Sparkles like diamonds
William Railey, Grade 5
Mineral Wells Elementary School, WV

Index